Contents

The sporting life
colour section
following p.80

Yankee cooking (and drinking) colour section
following p.176

CAMBRIDGE

Colour maps
following p.296

Introduction to

Boston

Boston is as close to the Old World as the New World gets, an American city that proudly trades on its colonial past, having served a crucial role in the country's development from a few wayward pilgrims right through to the Revolutionary War. It occasionally takes this a bit too far – what's a faded relic anywhere else becomes a plaque-honoured tourist site here – but none of it detracts from the city's overriding historic charm, nor from its present-day energy.

 The new millennium has seen a major renaissance in Boston. The completion of the seemingly never-ending Big Dig project, the Red Sox triumph in the 2004 and 2007 World Series, the Patriots' repeated Super Bowl victories and the frequent openings of new restaurants, bars, clubs and boutiques have all contributed to the feeling that Boston's future is even stronger than its past.

Despite the occasional wearisome touch, no other city in America gives a better feel for the events and persons behind the nation's birth, all played out in Boston's wealth of emblematic and evocative **colonial-era sights**, conveniently linked by the self-guided walking tour (one of a handful in the city) known as the Freedom Trail. As well, the city's cafés and shops, its attractive public spaces, and the diversity of its neighbourhoods – student hives, ethnic enclaves and stately districts of preserved townhouses – are just as alluring as its historic sites.

Boston is also at the centre of the **American university system**: more than sixty colleges call the area home, including illustrious Harvard and MIT, in the neighbouring city of Cambridge, just across the Charles River. This academic connection has played a key part in the city's long left-leaning political tradition, which has spawned, most famously, the Kennedy family. Steeped in Puritan roots, the districts around Boston Common still exude an almost small-town atmosphere, and, until the past decade or so, were relatively unmarred by chain stores and fast-food joints. Meanwhile, groups of Irish and Italian descent have carved out authentic and often equally unchanged communities in areas like the North End, Charlestown and South Boston.

Today, Boston's relatively small size – both physically and in terms of population (twentieth among US cities) – and its provincial feel actually serve to the city's advantage. Though it has expanded significantly through landfills and annexation since it was settled in 1630, it has never lost its core, which remains a tangle of streets over old cowpaths clustered around **Boston Common** (which was itself originally used as cattle pasture). Delightfully, this centre can really only be explored properly on foot; for even as Boston has evolved from busy port to blighted city to the rejuvenated and prosperous place it is today, it has remained, fundamentally, a city on a human scale.

What to see

The city's epicentre is **Boston Common**, a large public green (and the country's first public park) that orients **Downtown** and is near many of Boston's most historic sights, including the Old State House, the Old Granary Burying Ground and the Old South Meeting House. Little, however, captures the spirit of the city better than nearby **Faneuil Hall**, the so-called "Cradle of Liberty," and the always-animated Quincy Market, adjacent to the hall. Due north, an incomparable sense of Boston's original layout can be found in the compact, seventeenth-century **Blackstone Block**. Boston's **waterfront**, on the edge of Downtown, offers its fair share of diversions, many ideal for travelling families; the action is centred on Long Wharf. Due east of the waterfront lies the rapidly developing **Seaport District**, home to a number of seafood restaurants as well as historic Boston icons like the larger-than-life Hood Milk Bottle (squarely in front of the Children's Museum) and the glossy Institute of Contemporary Art.

The **North End**, modern Boston's Little Italy, occupies the northeast corner of the peninsula, and was cut off from the rest of the city by the old elevated I-93 before the completion of the main section of the Big Dig in 2006. It's home to a few notable relics, such as **Old North Church** and the **Paul Revere House**, and boasts an animated streetlife that's fuelled, in large part, by

▲ Park Street Church

the strong cups of espresso that are proffered in its numerous Italian cafés. Just across Boston Harbor from the North End lies **Charlestown**, the quiet berth of the world's oldest commissioned warship, the USS *Constitution*, as well as the site of the **Bunker Hill Monument**, an obelisk commemorating the famous battle that bolstered American morale in the fight for independence.

North of the Common, vintage gaslights and red-brick Federalist townhouses line the streets of **Beacon Hill**, the city's most exclusive residential neighbourhood; it's anchored by the gold-domed **State House**, designed, along with numerous area houses, by Charles Bulfinch. Charles Street runs south from the hill and separates Boston Common from the **Public Garden**, which marks the eastern edge of **Back Bay**, a similarly well-heeled neighbourhood that features opulent rowhouses alongside modern landmarks such as the **John Hancock Tower**, New England's tallest skyscraper. The neighbourhood also hosts some of the city's best shopping along **Newbury Street**. Additionally, the hip enclave of the **South End**, known for its restaurants and streetlife, as well as the ornate ironwork gracing its well-maintained homes, is also worth a visit.

The Big Dig

In a city whose roads follow the logic of colonial cowpaths, the added confusion wreaked by Boston's "Big Dig" highway reconstruction project – the largest and most expensive in US history – soured the idea of driving here for more than a decade. Thankfully, the final phase, landscaping the space formerly occupied by the unsightly elevated Central Artery (I-93), was completed in 2007. The Big Dig's initial budget of $2.6 billion may have more than quadrupled, but the project – as most Bostonians will tell you – was worth both the cost and the wait. Along with pumping billions of construction dollars into the city, the plan birthed new structures like the Leonard P. Zakim Bunker Hill Bridge (pictured below) and freed up 150 acres of land for park and recreational use, while supplying soil to cap landfills where toxins once seeped into Boston Harbor. Visit ⓦ www.bigdig.com, which has all the history, trivia, artwork and gossip connected with the project; you can learn, among other impressive figures, that during the Dig more earth was moved than during the construction of the Great Pyramids.

The Cape and beyond

If Boston is New England's heart, then Cape Cod is the region's well-tanned arm. For generations, Bostonians have emerged from the city's arctic winters eager to bask in the Cape's three hundred miles of shoreline. While the tone of this 63-mile peninsula varies greatly – from the old-money vibe of Chatham to the raucous good time of gay-friendly Provincetown – its beauty rarely wavers, and your own little piece of paradise is never far. Out on the water, Martha's Vineyard and Nantucket offer enticements of their own, with immaculate beaches complemented by breezy heaths and moors. The Vineyard is the more relaxed of the two islands, known for its endearing gingerbread cottages, vintage carousel (the oldest in the country) and diversity of its residents. Tiny Nantucket gets teased for her hoity-toity attitude ("those pants aren't pink, they're 'Nantucket reds'"), but it's still a bright spot, defined by its storied whaling history and rows of silvery clapboard cottages.

The student domains of **Kenmore Square** and **the Fenway** are found west of Back Bay and the South End: the former is largely overrun with college kids from nearby Boston University; the latter spreads west of Massachusetts Avenue and southwest along Huntington Avenue, and is home to heavyweight local institutions like the **Museum of Fine Arts**, the **Isabella Stewart Gardner Museum** and **Fenway Park**. Below all these neighbourhoods are Boston's vast **southern districts**, home to the **John F. Kennedy Presidential Library and Museum** and the southerly links in Frederick Law Olmsted's series of parks, known as the **Emerald Necklace**; it includes the spectacular **Arnold Arboretum** as well as **Franklin Park**, setting for the Franklin Zoo.

Across the Charles River from Boston is **Cambridge**, synonymous with venerable Harvard University and tech-oriented MIT, but also boasting some of the area's best nightlife and a lively café scene, especially around Harvard Square, which spills over into neighbouring **Somerville** to the north.

The waterfront's Long Wharf doubles as a jumping-off point for escaping the city altogether, on cruises to the idyllic Harbor Islands, or to happening **Provincetown**, Cape Cod's foremost destination; the rest of the Cape is also very much worth a road trip. Further afloat, sun worshippers will want to check out tranquil **Martha's Vineyard** and nostalgic **Nantucket**, two islands known for their fresh seafood and wide swaths of beach. Inland, nearby battle sites in **Lexington** and **Concord** make for easy day-trips, as does a jaunt up the coast to **Salem** and its witch-trials sights, or further on to seafaring towns like **Gloucester** and **Rockport**.

When to go

The city is at its most enjoyable in the **fall** (September to early November), when the weather is cooler and the foliage is ablaze with fiery hues; and in the **spring** (April to mid-May), when the magnolia trees blossom along Commonwealth Avenue and the parks spring back to life. **Summer**, meanwhile, is certainly the most popular time to visit Boston, both for the warmer weather and frequent festivals. However, July and August can be uncomfortably humid, and you'll have to contend with large student-related influxes around graduation (early June) and the beginning of school (around Labor Day, in September).

At the other end of the spectrum, Boston **winters** can be harsh: they tend to run from late November to March, but, thanks to the moderating influence of the Atlantic, mild spells often break the monotony of long cold stretches, and snowfall is lighter than in the interior regions of

▲ Christopher Columbus Park in the fall

9

New England. New Englanders live by a (rather corny) saying: "if you don't like the weather, wait five minutes". In other words, no matter when you visit Boston, be prepared for climate changes in the space of a single day: a December morning snow squall could easily be followed by afternoon sunshine and temperatures in the 50s (Fahrenheit).

Average daily temperatures and monthly rainfall

	Jan	Feb	Mar	Apr	May	Jun	Jul	Aug	Sep	Oct	Nov	Dec
Maximum temperature												
°F	36	39	46	56	67	77	82	80	73	62	52	42
°C	2.2	3.9	7.8	13.3	19.4	25	27.8	26.7	22.8	16.7	11.1	5.6
Minimum temperature												
°F	22	24	31	41	50	59	65	64	57	46	38	28
°C	-5.6	-4.5	-0.6	5	10	15	18.3	17.8	13.9	7.8	3.3	-2.2
Rainfall												
Inch	3.9	3.3	3.9	3.6	3.2	3.2	3.1	3.4	3.5	3.8	4.0	3.7
mm	99.6	83.8	97.8	91.4	82.3	81.8	77.7	85.6	88.1	96.3	101.1	94.7

things not to miss

It's not possible to see everything that Boston has to offer in one trip – and we don't suggest you try. What follows is a selective and subjective taste of the city's highlights, from mouthwatering eateries to engaging cultural sights. They're arranged in five colour-coded categories to help you find the very best things to see, do, and experience. All entries have a page reference to take you straight into the text, where you can find out more.

01 **Boston Public Library** Page **90** • Duck past the signature lions for a glimpse of the building's mural masterpieces – many by art heavyweights Sargent and Abbey – in this barrel-vaulted Boston landmark.

02 Historic burying grounds Pages 43, 45 & 68 •

Memorializing everyone from revolutionary heroes to literary titans, Boston's colonial burying grounds are peaceful spots to contemplate their contributions.

04 Trinity Church Page 90 •

Step inside this 1877 Boston icon and be awed by architect H.H. Richardson's realized vision of "walking into a living painting".

03 Pastries in the North End Page 63 •

Experience the vibrant cafés, bakeries and restaurants of Boston's most authentically Italian neighbourhood.

05 Isabella Stewart Gardner Museum Page 106 •

The exuberant Gardner's stunning collection is housed around a beautiful courtyard in her former mansion.

07 Old North Church Page **67** • The oldest church in Boston, this North End landmark is where the famous lanterns were hung on the night of April 18, 1775, to warn of the advancing British troops.

06 The USS Constitution Page **72** • Navy sailors give tours of "Old Ironsides", the oldest commissioned warship in the world.

08 Cambridge Page **117** • Funky and historic, Boston's laidback sister is known for mixing storied Ivy League culture with diverting museums, cheap eats and unique architecture like that of MIT's Stata Center.

09 **A day in the Public Garden** Page **87** • Take the kids down to Back Bay's idyllic Public Garden for a picnic and a ride on the Swan Boats; you might enjoy it as much as they do.

11 **Boston Athenæum** Page **43** • This venerable private library, endowed with an eye-opening collection of art and books, functions as a scholarly sanctuary in the centre of busy Downtown Boston.

12 **A game at Fenway Park** Page **101** • The country's oldest ballpark is home to the beloved Red Sox and the 37ft-tall "Green Monster".

10 **The houses of Beacon Hill** Page **77** • Be on the lookout for purple-tinted windowpanes, a former status symbol, as you stroll this elegant upper-class enclave.

13 A visit to Provincetown Page **239** • Though out at the tip of Cape Cod, P-town is an easy day-trip from the city, its beaches and streetlife popular with families and gay visitors alike.

15 Walking the Black Heritage Trail Page **80** • The 1.6-mile Black Heritage Trail, beginning at the striking Robert Gould Shaw Memorial, is the country's foremost site devoted to pre-Civil War African-American history.

14 Shopping on Newbury Street Page **88** • Back Bay's swankiest commercial stretch, with everything from colourful boutiques to hip cafés situated in elegant rowhouses.

16 Museum of Fine Arts Page **104** • New England's premier art space features the works of Sargent and Copley, Impressionist painters and one of the world's best collections of art from the ancient world and Asia.

17 **Lilacs at Arnold Arboretum** Page **115** • Jamaica Plain's Arnold Arboretum boasts over three hundred fragrant varieties of lilacs in addition to magnolias, hundred-year-old maples and a particularly striking collection of bonsai trees.

18 **Eating in the South End** Page **96** • Boston's most gay-friendly neighbourhood is also a veritable foodie paradise, and many of the city's best eats are congregated here.

19 **Harvard Museum of Natural History** Page **125** • Rub elbows with meteorites, dinosaur bones, and a one-of-a-kind glass flower collection in this Victorian funhouse of curios.

20 **A concert at Symphony Hall** Page **104** • Home to the Boston Symphony Orchestra – going strong for more than one hundred years – this gilded hall is the perfect place in which to hear classical music.

Basics

Basics

Getting there

Flying is the fastest and often the least expensive option for getting to Boston. Upon arrival, you'll be pleased to find that the Boston airport, Logan International (BOS), is conveniently situated near subways and water taxis that provide fast and efficient city access.

From **overseas**, **seasonal variations** in price are common, with flights generally at their most expensive from May to October; winter (Dec–Feb) is the cheapest time to fly (although we don't necessarily recommend visiting Boston in the dead of winter). For the best ticket prices, book your flight as far in advance as possible and stay for at least a week; additionally, the day you choose for flying can impact on cost – flying in the middle of the week will normally lower the price.

If you're not into flying, **trains** are a good, albeit more leisurely second option for visitors travelling from elsewhere along the East Coast or another major New England city. **Amtrak** has a high-speed service between Washington DC and Boston (which includes New York City), as well as the *Downeaster* line, which runs an inexpensive circuit between Portland, Maine and Boston.

For budget travellers, **Greyhound** and **Peter Pan bus lines** offer the most comprehensive coverage of the region, but customer service (particularly with the former) tends to be lacking; try to book with Greyhound's superior affiliate **Bolt Bus**, or a local bus line like the Plymouth-Brockton bus company.

Driving is obviously another possibility, but can be unpleasant. Beginning a trip by driving to Boston is one thing; once here, it's advised you park your car and leave it for the duration of your stay.

Flights from within the US and Canada

Boston's only airport, **Logan International**, is New England's busiest and has been undergoing an expansion project for the last few years: the international Terminal E opened in 2004, while Delta opened a newly refurbished Terminal A in 2005. In 2009, Logan became the first airport in the country to use an environmentally friendly asphalt to repave a runway.

Fares are lowest in the heavily trafficked Northeast corridor; a round-trip fare **from New York** can cost as little as $90–100, although $120–150 is the more usual price fare; **from Washington DC**, the range is usually $100–150; from Miami $200–250, from **Chicago**, $200–300. The price of flights **from the West Coast** is more likely to fluctuate – round-trip fares from LA, San Francisco or Seattle typically cost $250–400. **From Canada**, be prepared to pay around $300–400 from Toronto and Montréal, and closer to $600–750 from Vancouver.

Flights from the UK and Ireland

Five airlines make the **nonstop** seven-hour flight from **the UK and Ireland** to Boston; most leave early to mid-afternoon and arrive in the late afternoon or evening, though the odd red-eye flight leaves the UK at 8pm and arrives later the same night in Boston. Returning to the UK and Ireland, you're looking at an early morning or early evening departure; the prevailing winds tend to make the trip back modestly shorter than the one over.

British Airways, Continental, Virgin Atlantic and American Airlines fly from London's Heathrow Airport; travellers from elsewhere in the UK will have to connect in London. Aer Lingus and American Airlines operate nonstop services from Ireland.

As there's not a lot of price difference between the major airlines, you'll have to shop around to get the best deals. The standard option, an **advance purchase ticket**, is a non-refundable return ticket that must be purchased 21 days in advance and requires a minimum seven-night stay, up to a maximum of one month; changing departure dates usually incurs a penalty.

Economy **fares from London** purchased 21 days in advance hover around the £400–450 mark. Direct flights **from Dublin** cost around the same, but are pricier (around £800) from Shannon; flights from Shannon with a stopover are also £400–450. There are no direct flights from Cork to Boston; flights with one stopover cost about £600.

Flights from Australia and New Zealand

Flights from **Australia** and **New Zealand** fly to the West Coast before continuing on to Boston, making for a pretty long trip (about fourteen hours to Los Angeles, plus another six from Los Angeles to Boston).

Round-trip **fares** from eastern Australian cities are usually around AUS$1400–1700, while tickets from Perth and Darwin can cost up to AUS$600 more. The best connections

to the West Coast tend to be with United, Delta, V Australia and Qantas.

Flights from South Africa

Flights from **Johannesburg**, **South Africa** to Boston generally have one to two layovers (in Atlanta, New York, London, or Paris), with prices hovering at around $1250 round-trip.

Trains

For those heading to Boston from within the Washington DC and New York shuttle flight radius, **train** travel is a pleasant – but not much less expensive – alternative. **Fares from New York** to Boston (which arrive at Back Bay Station as well as the more central South Station) begin at $128 round-trip, with travel taking between four and five hours; $195 and up gets you a seat on the cushier Acela Express, which offers free wi-fi and saves about thirty minutes off the trip time. **From Washington DC,** the regular train runs

Six steps to a better kind of travel

At Rough Guides we are passionately committed to travel. We feel strongly that only through travelling do we truly come to understand the world we live in and the people we share it with – plus tourism has brought a great deal of **benefit** to developing economies around the world over the last few decades. But the extraordinary growth in tourism has also damaged some places irreparably, and of course **climate change** is exacerbated by most forms of transport, especially flying. This means that now more than ever it's important to **travel thoughtfully** and **responsibly**, with respect for the cultures you're visiting – not only to derive the most benefit from your trip but also to preserve the best bits of the planet for everyone to enjoy. At Rough Guides we feel there are six main areas in which you can make a difference:

• Consider what you're contributing to the **local economy**, and how much the services you use do the same, whether it's through employing local workers and guides or sourcing locally grown produce and local services.

• Consider the **environment** on holiday as well as at home. Water is scarce in many developing destinations, and the biodiversity of local flora and fauna can be adversely affected by tourism. Try to patronize businesses that take account of this.

• Travel with a purpose, not just to tick off experiences. Consider **spending longer** in a place, and getting to know it and its people.

• Give thought to how often you **fly**. Try to avoid short hops by air and more harmful night flights.

• Consider **alternatives to flying**, travelling instead by bus, train, boat and even by bike or on foot where possible.

• Make your trips **"climate neutral"** via a reputable carbon offset scheme. All Rough Guide flights are offset, and every year we donate money to a variety of charities devoted to combating the effects of climate change.

just shy of eight hours (beginning at $180 return) while the express gets you there in six and a half hours (beginning at $304 return).

Although it's possible to haul yourself long-distance **from the West Coast**, the Midwest, or the South the trip is anything but fast – count on three days and up from California – nor is it cost-effective, at around $400 for a round-trip ticket from Los Angeles. The same applies to visitors trying to approach Boston **from Canada** using Via Rail (☎1-888/842-7245, ⓦwww .viarail.ca); you can do so only by connecting with Amtrak in Montréal, and on an indirect itinerary at best. The rail journey can take anywhere from twelve to twenty hours from Toronto and Montréal, and over three days from Vancouver. Fares start at around $250 from Montréal.

On the upside, travellers headed south from elsewhere in New England can easily hop on Amtrak's inexpensive *Downeaster*, which makes stops at various points on its way down from Portland, Maine. Tickets from Portland to Boston's North Station are $24, and the trip takes just under two and a half hours.

Buses

Given how expensive rail travel is in the northeast, getting to Boston by **bus** can be an appealing option, particularly with recent service upgrades such as new, revamped buses and amenities, including free wi-fi. Boston is an especially common stop coming **from New York** or **Washington DC**; barring traffic, one-way trips typically take four and a half hours from New York and ten and a half hours from Washington, with round-trip **fares** costing around $50 and $120, respectively – non-refundable, seven-day advance fares will give you the cheapest rates. The two major northeast carriers, **Greyhound** (☎1-800/231-2222, ⓦwww.greyhound.com) and **Peter Pan** (☎1-800/343-9999, ⓦwww .peterpanbus.com) offer direct routes from Washington DC to Boston; visitors leaving **from New York City** have additional (and better) choices. They're ranked here in descending order (the latter two being adequate): Bolt Bus (☎1-877/BOLTBUS, ⓦwww.boltbus.com), Mega Bus (☎1-877/ GO2MEGA, ⓦus.megabus.com), Fung Wah (☎1-617/345-8000, ⓦwww.fungwahbus .com) and Lucky Star (☎1-888/881-0887, ⓦwww.luckystarbus.com). Fares average about $20–25 one-way (Fung Wah and Lucky Star have fares of $15 one-way) and arrive at South Station in Boston. If you're coming from New York, the worst bus to take is (arguably) Greyhound, with its long boarding lines and poor customer service; if you can, book ahead and get a seat on one of Greyhound's Bolt Bus affiliates instead.

Coming **from Canada**, several daily buses **from Toronto** reach Boston with at least one changeover – usually in Syracuse, New York – contributing to a minimum fourteen-hour ride ($160 return). Direct buses **from Montréal** take around eight hours ($135 round-trip). In both cases, contact Greyhound (☎1-800/661-TRIP, ⓦwww.greyhound.ca).

Driving

There's no way around it: driving in Boston is a nightmare. Signage is inadequate, there's very little parking, drivers are notoriously aggressive and roads are heavily trafficked and confusing.

That said, if you do plan on driving into Boston, two highways provide direct access to the city: **I-90** (the Massachusetts Turnpike, known locally as "The Pike" or "the Masspike"), and **I-93**, known as the Central Artery. The latter cuts north-south through the heart of Boston and provides the most majestic entrance to the city, courtesy of the newly-opened Zakim Bridge; however, don't be surprised if you get stuck in traffic for awhile here, especially if you arrive during **rush hour** (7.30–9am and 4.30–7pm). If you're coming from western Massachusetts, **I-90** is the most direct route to Boston; from points north of the city utilize I-93. Once you reach Boston, Storrow Drive is the main local drag, running alongside the Charles River and providing access to the core of the city.

Airlines

Aer Lingus ⓦwww.aerlingus.com
Air Canada ⓦwww.aircanada.com
Air France ⓦwww.airfrance.com
Air New Zealand ⓦwww.airnewzealand.com
AirTran (American AirTran) US ⓦwww .airtran.com
American Airlines ⓦwww.aa.com

British Airways ⓦ www.britishairways.com
Continental Airlines ⓦ www.continental.com
Cape Air ⓦ www.flycapeair.com
Delta ⓦ www.delta.com
Frontier Airlines ⓦ www.frontierairlines.com
jetBlue ⓦ www.jetblue.com
Qantas Airways ⓦ www.qantas.com
United Airlines ⓦ www.united.com
US Airways ⓦ www.usairways.com
USA 3000 Airlines ⓦ www.usa3000airlines.com
Virgin Atlantic ⓦ www.virgin-atlantic.com

Agents and operators

Airtech US ☏ 212/219-7000, ⓦ www.airtech.com.
Standby seat broker.
ebookers UK ☏ 0871/223 5000, Republic of Ireland
☏ 01/4311 311; ⓦ www.ebookers.com. Low fares
on an extensive selection of scheduled flights and
package deals.
Collette Vacations US ☏ 1-800/340-5158, ⓦ www
.collettevacations.com. Boston figures in various
escorted or independent tour permutations; from the
seven-night "Islands of New England" option, which
includes Boston, Nantucket and Martha's Vineyard (from
$1499), to the "New England Back Roads" tour, which
also covers New England towns like Burlington, Vermont
and Boothbay Harbor, Maine (from $1599); prices
include most meals but exclude airfare/travel to Boston.
Contiki Holidays US ☏ 1-888/CONTIKI, ⓦ www
.contiki.com. Trips for the 18–35-year-old crowd;

the thirteen-day "North by Northeast" tour (from
$1685, airfare not included) takes in Boston and
parts of Cambridge.
IGLTA US ☏ 1-954/630-1637, ⓦ www.iglta.org.
Comprehensive site good at cutting through the clutter
for LGBT destinations, tours and travel agents.
North South Travel UK ☏ 01245/608 291, ⓦ www
.northsouthtravel.co.uk. Friendly, competitive travel
agency, offering discounted fares worldwide. Profits
are used to support projects in the developing world,
especially the promotion of sustainable tourism.
Skylink US ☏ 1-800/247-6659 or 212/573-8980,
Canada ☏ 1-800/759-5465; ⓦ www.skylinkus.com.
Consolidator with multiple offices throughout the US
and Canada.
STA Travel US ☏ 1-800/781-4040, UK
☏ 0871/230 0040, Australia ☏ 134 STA, New
Zealand ☏ 0800/474 400, SA ☏ 0861/781 781;
ⓦ www.statravel.com. Worldwide specialists in
independent travel; also student IDs, travel insurance,
car rental, rail passes and more. Good discounts for
students and under-26s.
Tauck Travel US ☏ 1-800/788-7885, ⓦ www
.tauck.com. Fairly fancy tour operator with three solid
New England tours. They're based out of Connecticut,
giving them New England home-court advantage.
Trailfinders UK ☏ 0845/058 5858, Republic of
Ireland ☏ 01/677 7888, Australia ☏ 1300/780 212;
ⓦ www.trailfinders.com. One of the best agents for
independent travellers.

Arrival

Those flying to Boston will arrive at the city's Logan International Airport, located
on Boston's easternmost peninsula, a landfill sticking far out into Boston Harbor.
From there, you can catch the subway or a water shuttle to Downtown; taking a
taxi is another option. For visitors coming into Boston by bus or train, you'll arrive
at South Station, near the waterfront at Summer Street and Atlantic Avenue; from
there, it's just a short walk or subway ride to Downtown.

By air

Busy **Logan International** – the closest
airport to a major downtown area in the US
– services both domestic and international
flights; it has four terminals, lettered A through
E (there's no D), that are connected by a
series of courtesy buses. You'll find currency

exchanges in terminals A, B and E (daily
10am–5pm), plus information booths, car
rental and ATMs in all four.

After arriving into Logan, the most convenient way downtown is by **subway**. The Airport
T stop is a short ride away on courtesy
bus #11, which you can catch outside on

the arrival level of all four terminals. From there, you can take the Blue Line to State or Government Center **T** stations in the heart of Downtown, and transfer to the Red, Orange and Green lines to reach other points; the ride to Downtown lasts about fifteen minutes ($2). Alternatively, you can take the **SL1 Silver Line** (really a fast bus that poses as subway transit) to South Station, where you can catch the Red Line and continue on into the city ($2), or if the South End is your final destination, transfer at South Station to a Silver Line bus that stops in that neighbourhood. Like bus #11, the Silver Line conveniently makes stops at the arrival level of every airline terminal.

Just as quick, but a lot more fun, are the three **water taxi** companies that whisk visitors across the harbour to numerous points around Boston, including Rowes or Long Wharf near the Blue Line Aquarium **T** station. Water taxis don't run on a set schedule; if there isn't a boat waiting in the harbour, contact them via the checkerboard call box at the Logan Dock (Jan–March daily 7am–7pm; April–Dec Mon–Sat 7am–10pm, Sun 7am–8pm; departure times vary; $10 one-way; ☎617/422-0392; ⓦwww.citywatertaxi.com). From the airport, courtesy bus #66 will take you to the pier.

By comparison, taking a **taxi** is more expensive – from the airport to a Downtown destination costs around $25–35 – but obviously offers the convenience of door-to-door transport.

By bus or train

The main terminus for both **buses** and **trains** to Boston is **South Station**, in the southeast corner of Downtown at Summer Street and Atlantic Avenue. **Amtrak trains** arrive at one end, in a station with an information booth, newsstands, a food court and several ATMs (but no currency exchange); **bus carriers** arrive at the clean and modern terminal next door, from where it's a bit of a trek to reach the subway (the Red Line), which is through

the Amtrak station and down a level. Those with sizable baggage will find the walk particularly awkward, as there are no porters or handcarts. Trains also make a second stop at Boston's **Back Bay Station**, 145 Dartmouth St, on the **T**'s Orange Line. Lastly, Amtrak's *Downeaster* train – which connects Portland, Maine with Boston and points in-between – arrives at **North Station** (on the **T**'s Orange and Green Lines), which is located in the West End near the TDBanknorth Garden.

By car

Driving in Boston can be stressful, and will probably put a damper on your trip if you're a first-time visitor. Boston drivers are notoriously impatient, and the learning curve for navigating the city by car is so steep that ability to do so has become a source of pride and cultural identity for local residents. Boston roads were built on top of colonial cowpaths (and as such are not laid out in any system per se) making them difficult to manoeuvre around. To make matters worse, Boston signage is ridiculously bad. If you are driving into Boston, just be sure to arm yourself beforehand with a good road map and a strong dose of patience.

Two highways provide direct access to the city, **I-90** (on which you can drive from Seattle to Boston without hitting a traffic light) and **I-93**. The latter, which cuts north–south through the heart of the city, was finally put underground in 2006 thanks to the fifteen-year, $15 billion "Big Dig" construction project; the completion of its ten-lane 7.5-mile tunnel made the city less congested and improved the traffic situation in Downtown Boston (it hasn't made the local roads that much more navigable, however). A third highway, **I-95** (also known as Route-128 between Gloucester and Canton) circumnavigates the greater Boston area, affording entry points for its many suburbs (and then continues south all the way to Miami, Florida).

City transport

Much of the pleasure of visiting Boston comes from being in a city built long before cars were invented. Walking around the narrow, winding streets can be a joy; conversely, driving around them can be a nightmare. Be particularly cautious in traffic circles known as "rotaries": when entering, always yield the right of way. If you have a car, consider parking it for the duration of your trip (see p.26) and then get around either by foot or public transit – a system of subway lines, buses and ferries run by the Massachusetts Bay Transportation Authority (MBTA, known as the "**T**"; ☎1-800/392-6100, ⊛www.mbta.com).

The subway (T)

While not the most modern system, Boston's subway is cheap, efficient and charmingly antiquated – its Green Line was America's first underground train, built in the late nineteenth century, and riding it today is akin to riding an underground tram.

Four **subway** lines transect Boston and continue out into some of its neighbouring districts. Each line is colour-coded and passes through Downtown before continuing on to other districts. The **Red Line**, which serves Harvard, is the most frequent, intersecting South Boston and Dorchester to the south and Cambridge to the north. The **Green Line** hits Back Bay, Kenmore Square, the Fenway and Brookline. The **Blue Line** heads into East Boston and is most useful for its stop at Logan Airport. The **Orange Line** traverses the South End and continues down to Roxbury and Jamaica Plain.

All trains travel either **inbound** (towards the quadrant made up of State, Downtown Crossing, Park Street and Government Center stops) or **outbound** (away from the quadrant). If you're confused about whether you're going in or out, the train's terminus is also designated on the train itself; for instance, trains to Harvard from South Station will be on the "Inbound" platform and heading towards "Alewife".

The four lines are supplemented by a bus rapid transit (BRT) route, the **Silver Line**, which runs above ground along Washington Street from Downtown Crossing **T**. More of a fast bus than a subway, the line cuts through the heart of South End. There is also an extended, tunnelled loop connection from the South End to the airport.

Boston has recently installed a new and somewhat confusing system for subway fares. The **standard fare** to board the **T** is $2, payable by the purchase of a "Charlie-Ticket" (presumably named for the Kingston Trio recording of the *MTA Song*, about a man named Charlie who "never returned" from his train ride due to an exorbitant subway exit fare), which can be purchased at any of the ATM-like machines in the stations. However, if you first pick up a free "CharlieCard" (located at most subway stops) from one of the station attendants, then your fare is substantially less – beginning at $1.70 per ride.

Colour scheming

Each of the **T**'s subway lines is coloured after a characteristic of the area it covers. The **Red Line** evokes Harvard's crimson sports jerseys; the **Green Line** refers to the Emerald Necklace (see box, p.103); the **Blue Line** reflects its waterfront proximity; and the **Orange Line** is so named because the street under which it runs, Washington Street, used to be called Orange Street, after King William of Orange. The **Silver Line** is the only exception to the colour scheme: it's coloured for speed – like a silver bullet.

While both cards are reusable, and money can easily be added to either card at any downtown station, the difference between the two is that the CharlieCard has a credit-card thickness and thus a longer lifespan. Note that, rather inconveniently, monthly unlimited CharlieCards are structured in terms of calendar months, and must be purchased before the 15th of the following month (May's unlimited card, for example, would need to be purchased by April 15). If you're planning to use public transit a lot, your easiest and best bet is to buy a **LinkPass** for one ($9) or seven days ($15) of unlimited subway, bus and inner-harbour ferry use.

The biggest drawback to the **T** is the relatively limited hours of operation (daily 5.15am–midnight, Sun from 6am); the midnight closing time means you'll be stuck taking a taxi home after last-call. Free transit maps are available at most stations; there's also a subway map at the back of this book.

Buses

The MBTA manages an impressive 170 **bus** routes both in and around Boston. Though the buses run less frequently than the subway and are a bit harder to navigate, they bear two main advantages: they're cheaper ($1.50 with exact change or CharlieTicket; $1.25 with CharlieCard) and they provide service to many more points. It's a service used, however, primarily by natives who've grown familiar with the byzantine system. If you're transferring from the **T** with your CharlieCard or CharlieTicket, you get a free bus transfer as long as you use it within two hours. The **T**'s LinkPass includes unlimited local bus access with its one or seven days package. Most buses run from 5am to 1am.

Taxis

Given Boston's small scale and the efficiency (at least during the day) of its public transit, **taxis** aren't as necessary or prevalent as in cities like New York or London. If you do find yourself in need, you can sometimes flag one down along the streets of Downtown or Back Bay, though competition gets pretty stiff after 12.30am when the subway has stopped running and bars and clubs begin to close. Really, it's best to just call a cab company directly, or to go to a hotel where cabs cluster.

Chill Out First Class Cab (☏617/212-3763) has 24-hour service and accepts credit cards; Green Cab (☏617/628-0600) and Baní Transportation (☏617/522-4000) run 24 hours but are cash only. Other cab companies include Bay State Taxi (☏617/566-5000) and Town Taxi (☏617/536-5000). In Cambridge, call Yellow Cabs (☏617/547-3000) or PlanetTran; the latter is powered by environmentally-friendly hybrid vehicles (☏1-888/756-8876). As a general rule, rates start at $2.60 and goes up by 40¢ per 1/7th mile.

Ferries

Of all the MBTA transportation options, the Inner Harbor **ferry** is by far the most scenic: $1.70 gets you a ten-minute boat ride with excellent views of Downtown Boston. The boats, covered 100-seaters with exposed upper decks, navigate several waterfront routes by day, though the one most useful to visitors is that connecting Long Wharf with Charlestown, home of the USS *Constitution* (every 30min Mon–Fri 6.30am–8pm, Sat & Sun 10am–6pm).

Another popular harbour route is the **water shuttle** between Logan Airport and Downtown's Long Wharf, a seven-minute trip that makes for a stunning arrival ($10; ☏617/222-6999, ⊕www.harborexpress .com); bus #66 (free) from Logan Airport will get you to the quay.

There are also ferries from Long Wharf to Boston's scenic Harbor Islands (see p.60), the most popular being George's Island (30min) and Spectacle Island (15min). Ferries run May to Oct, and tickets cost $14 (☏617/223-8666, ⊕www.boston islands.com).

Several larger **passenger boats** cruise across the harbour and beyond to reach beach destinations such as Provincetown, at the tip of Cape Cod (see p.240). From May to October, two companies make the ninety-minute trip across Massachusetts Bay. **Boston Harbor Cruises** depart from Long Wharf daily, although the hours fluctuate – check their website for the most-up-to-date times ($79 return; ☏617/227-4321, ⊕www .bostonharborcruises.com; Aquarium **T**). From the west side of the World Trade Center pier, **Bay State Cruises** leaves daily departing at 8am, 1pm and 5.30pm

($79 return; ☎1-877/783-3779, ⌨www .baystatecruisecompany.com, World Trade Center **T**). In summer, these trips are very popular, so book in advance.

The Salem Ferry is another fun jaunt, shuttling passengers from Long Wharf up to Blaney Street in quaint Salem, MA (see p.216). The ride takes just under an hour and costs $24 return (May–Oct only; ☎978/741-0220, ⌨www.salemferry.com)

Commuter rail

The only time you're likely to travel by **rail** in Boston is if you're making a day trip to historical Salem, Revolutionary battlefields in Concord or South Shore spots like Plymouth. All have stations on the MBTA's **commuter rail** (☎617/222-3200 or 1-800/392-6100), a faster, glossier subway than the **T**, with similarly frequent service. Most lines of interest depart from **North Station T**: Salem, Gloucester and Rockport (see p.221) lie on the **Rockport Line** (15min–1hr; one-way $5.25, $7.25 & $7.75 respectively), while Concord is about midway on the **Fitchburg Line** (20min; $6.25 one-way). The exception, Plymouth, is the last stop on the **Plymouth Line** that leaves from **South Station** (55min; $7.75 one-way). Tickets can be bought in advance or aboard the train itself, though doing the latter incurs a service fee of $1.50 to $2, depending on the time of day.

By car

Even if you do better the city's road system (see p.23 for a warning to the contrary), there's still the **parking** to contend with – the price of **parking garages** in Boston is virtually a highway robbery ($25–30 per evening and more overnight). There are metered spots on main streets like Newbury, Boylston and Cambridge, but the chances of finding an empty one on any given evening are slim at best (during the day, it's a bit easier, although still markedly competitive). The parking limit at non-metered spots is two hours, whether posted or not.

Because it's a "9 to 5" type of area, good weekend and weekday night rates can be found **Downtown** and in **the Financial District**. The Garage (☎617/423-1430) at Post Office Square has good weekend deals ($9 per day) and charges $9 for weekday

nights after 4pm (and out before 5am). Center Plaza Garage (☎617/742-7807), at the corner of Cambridge and New Sudbury streets, has spots for $13 (Mon–Fri after 4pm) and $10 (all day Sat & Sun). The Boston Common Garage (☎617/954-2098), literally underneath the Boston Common at 0 Charles Street, has weekday night rates of $11 if you arrive after 4pm and leave by 8am; weekend day rates are also $11. Keep in mind that weekday daytime rates at these are much more expensive, averaging about $8 an hour or $34 for a full day.

In the North End, a great little parking secret can be found at the Parcel 7 garage (☎617/973-6954), at 136 Blackstone St, across from Martignetti's Liquors. The posted rates won't mention it, but if you get your ticket validated at a North End business, the rates are only $1 an hour for the first three hours; after that, prices go way up. You can also **park and ride** at the safe and cheap Alewife **T** stop in Cambridge, located at the intersection of US-2 and Cambridge Park Drive ($7 a day, $8 overnight; ☎1-800/392-6100).

Note that the ubiquitous "Permit Parking Only" signs along residential streets must be obeyed – without the requisite parking sticker, you will be ticketed $40 or towed (expect to pay well over $50 to get your car back). Should you get a ticket, you can try sweet-talking the Office of the Parking Clerk (☎617/635-4410), but it probably won't help.

As with parking, the cost of **renting a car** in Boston can add up; a compact car with unlimited mileage will ring in around $250 a week before insurance. Bear in mind that renting a car at the airport is (unfortunately) usually the most expensive way to go about it, costing about $100 more per week than a car rented locally.

An alternative to traditional car rental is Zipcar, a **car-sharing agency** that has vehicles stationed around eleven major American cities (including Boston, Brookline and Cambridge). Zipcars are rented for $7 an hour, with daily rates of $69 ($79 on the weekend), plus $75 to cover the annual and application fees. Fuel and insurance are included, and when you sign up, you get a "Zipcard" that unlocks any of the many shiny vehicles stationed around town (there are hundreds of Zipcars in Boston alone). It's a good deal if you'll only occasionally need a car, and particularly useful if you might use a Zipcar membership in other cities (☏ 1-866/4ZIPCAR, ⓦ www.zipcar.com).

Car rental agencies

Alamo ☏ 1-800/522-9696, ⓦ www.alamo.com
Avis ☏ 1-800/331-1084, ⓦ www.avis.com
Budget ☏ 1-800/527-0700, ⓦ www.budget rentacar.com
Dollar ☏ 1-800/800-4000, ⓦ www.dollar.com
Enterprise Rent-a-Car ☏ 1-800/325-8007, ⓦ www.enterprise.com
Hertz ☏ 1-800/654-3001, ⓦ www.hertz.com
National ☏ 1-800/227-7368, ⓦ www.national car.com
Thrifty ☏ 1-800/367-2277, ⓦ www.thrifty.com

Biking

Biking runs a close second to walking as the preferred mode of city transportation. It's especially popular along the riverside promenades in Cambridge, though hustling along Downtown streets is quite agreeable by bike as well. The usual precautions – wearing a helmet, carrying a lock and, at night, using bike lights – are advised. The city's outlying areas boast a number of great bike **trails** such as the eleven-mile Minuteman Bikeway, which stretches from Cambridge to Bedford, or the bike-friendly 265-acre Arnold Arboretum in Jamaica Plain.

The best place to **rent a bike** Downtown is at Urban AdvenTours in the North End at 103 Atlantic Ave ($35 for 24hr rental; ☏ 617/670-0637, ⓦ www.urbanadventours .com; Aquarium **T**), they also do fun, low-key bike tours (see p.29). In addition, Community Bicycle Supply, at 496 Tremont St (☏ 617/542-8623, ⓦ www.community bicycle.com; Back Bay **T**), rents bikes for $20 a day, or $25 for 24hr; Back Bay Bicycles, at 366 Commonwealth Ave rents them for $35 a day or $45 for 24hr, cash only (☏ 617/247-2336, ⓦ www.backbaybicycles .com; Hynes **T**). A copy of *Boston's Bike Map* ($5.95) is available at any decent bike store and will help you find all the trails and bike-friendly roads in the area.

Tours

It's hard to avoid Boston's role in Revolutionary American history – it's proclaimed by landmarks and placards virtually everywhere you go. You could spend your entire visit reading each totem yourself, but a far more enjoyable (and informative) way to experience the city's lore is by guided tour. Mind you, the tours listed below aren't just limited to covering colonial-era Americana; you can also sample the city's best Italian salumerias, get romantic in a gondola, or head out of the harbour on a whale watch. There are also two multi-tour passes in the city, which offer discounted packages to several attractions.

Tour companies

On the water

Boston Duck Tours ☏ 617/267-DUCK, ⓦ www .bostonducktours.com. Popular, recommended tours that take to the streets and the Charles River in restored World War II amphibious landing vehicles; kids get to skipper the bus/boat in the water. Tours depart March to November from the Prudential Center (53 Huntington Ave) and the Museum of Science (1 Science Park); shorter night-time tours leave from the New England Aquarium; reservations advised in summer. $31, kids $21.
Codzilla ☏ 617/227-4321, ⓦ www.boston harborcruises.com. If the movie *Animal House* had been set on the water, this unruly boat would probably have been one of the film's main characters.

A self-proclaimed "water coaster", *Codzilla* has a penchant for blaring AC/DC and sports a wicked shark-tooth grin. Expect a cheesy backstory, sea spray and a 40mph diverting joyride. May to late-Sept only. $25.

Gondola di Venezia ☎617/876-2800, ⓦwww .bostongondolas.com. Woo your sweetie with a romantic gondola ride on the Charles. They'll provide the chocolates and accordion player; you complete the look with Champagne and your cara bella. Per couple $100–230.

Liberty Clipper ☎617/742-0333, ⓦwww.liberty fleet.com. This 125ft tall ship takes visitors on exhilarating two-hour sails leaving from Central Wharf (May–Sept; $30). They also do lively Boston Tea Party re-enactment sails ($35).

New England Aquarium Whale Watch ☎617/973-5206, ⓦwww.neaq.org. Guaranteed whale sightings or you get another trip. Late April–Oct, at least one trip per day, with additional tours scheduled in summer. $40.

Super Duck Tours ☎1-877/34DUCKS, ⓦwww.superducktours.com. This young pipsqueak has been stirring up Boston's waters and creating newfound Duck competition. Tours start and end at the Charlestown Navy Yard; it, too, shows off Boston sites as well as its own amphibious prowess. $35.

Bus and trolley tours

Beantown Trolley ☎1-800/343-1328, ☎781/986 6100, ⓦwww.beantowntrolley.com. One of the oldest and most popular history tours, covering everything from waterfront wharfs to Beacon Hill Brahmins, with multiple pick-up and drop-off points around town. A 45min harbour boat tour is included. They also run trips out to Lexington/Concord, Salem and the like. $29.

Boston Super Trolley Tours ☎617/742-1440, ⓦwww.bostonsupertrolleytours.com. A newer fleet of buses with appealing features like double-decker seating, onboard climate control and a free boat cruise (they're affiliated with Super Duck Tours; see above). $36.

Liberty Ride ☎781/862-0500 ext.702, ⓦwww.libertyride.us. Based out of Lexington and Concord, this diverting trolley offers hop-on, hop-off tours covering the area's Revolutionary War and literary history. May–Oct only. $20.

Old Town Trolley Tours ☎617/269-7010, ⓦwww.trolleytours.com. Another hop-on, hop-off trolley tour of Boston, this one on ubiquitous orange-and-green trolleys with thematic routes such as Ghosts and Gravestones and Educational Fieldtrips. $36 (cheaper rates available online).

Walking tours

Boston by Foot ☎617/367-2345, ⓦwww.boston byfoot.org. Informative walking tours (1hr 30min) that focus on the architecture and history of different Boston neighbourhoods such as Beacon Hill, the North End and Victorian Back Bay. Also has "Boston by Little Feet", geared toward the Freedom Trail's smaller pedestrians. $8–15.

Boston National Historical Park's Freedom Trail Tours ☎617/242-5642, ⓦwww.nps.gov/bost. The Boston NPS rangers are amazing – equipped with encyclopedic knowledge, they excel at presenting Boston's history in manageable and entertaining tidbits. Plus their tours are free! Sept–May at least one tour daily at 2pm, more in summer; call for hours and reservations. They also run a great Black Heritage Trail tour (☎617/742-5415).

Movie Tours ☎1-866/668-4345, ⓦwww.boston movietours.net. Get up close and personal with scene locations from Boston-area films such as *Good Will Hunting* and *The Departed*. Walking tour 1.5 hrs; there is also a 2.5hr tour-on-wheels available. $23-37.

MYTOWN ☎617/536-TOWN, ⓦwww.mytowninc .com. MYTOWN, which stands for "Multicultural Youth Tour of What's Now" offers tours with a mission: employ Boston teens, teach them neighbourhood history and presentation skills and "decrease the stereotypes that stigmatize urban neighbourhoods". Tours are youth-led and last 1hr 30min; call for times. $15.

North End Market Tours ☎617/523-6032, ⓦwww.northendmarkettours.com. Award-winning walking and tasting tours of the North End's Italian *salumerias* and the markets of Chinatown. Often booked up, so reserve well in advance. $50–65.

Photowalks ☎617/851-2273, ⓦwww.photowalks .com. Popular walking tours that point out the perfect places to point and shoot. Times vary. $30 each.

Segway Adventures ☎1-866/611-9838, ⓦwww.bostongliders.com. That's right, you can glide around Boston on a segway! Beginning at 75 Commercial St in the North End, tours take in sites such as the Seaport District and the HarborWalk; there's also a Cambridge version. 1hr $60, 2hr $85.

Unofficial Tours ☎617/674-7788, ⓦwww .unofficialtours.com/harvard. Lively tour of the Harvard Campus run by boisterous students easily spotted in their misspelled "Hahvahd" T-shirts. Tours begin by Harvard **T** stop. Suggested donation $10.

Bike tours

Charles River Wheelmen ⓦwww.crw.org. Organizes free weekly cycling events, ranging from "rosy cheeks" rides to hardcore morning fitness workouts.

Urban AdvenTours ☎1-800/979-3370 or 617/670-0637, ⊛www.urbanadventours.com. Popular, leisurely bike tours (2hr 30min) with themes like "City View" and "Funway to Fenway". Tours depart at 10am, 2pm and 6pm ($50) from their North End headquarters at 103 Atlantic Ave; bike rental is also available (see p.27).

Multi-tour passes

Boston CityPass ☎1- 888/330-5008, ⊛www .citypass.com. Tickets to the Museum of Science, New England Aquarium, Skywalk Observatory, Museum of Fine Arts and Harvard Museum of Natural History or the John F Kennedy Presidential Library and Museum. $49 – a fifty percent saving.

Go Boston Card ☎617/742-5950, ⊛www .smartdestinations.com/boston. Unlimited admission to seventy attractions and tours, plus discounts on shopping and dining. One day $50, two day $75, three day $96, five day $135, seven day $165. Discounted prices available online.

The media

Since its auspicious beginning as the birthplace of America's first newspaper (*Publick Occurences*, published in 1690), Boston has continued to hold rank among the country's most media-savvy cities. The left-leaning *Boston Globe*, the city's foremost daily paper, offers toothsome coverage of local, national and international news; their helpful, comprehensive website (ⓦwww.boston.com) provides readers with what is perhaps the best online source for Boston-related information. Visitors will probably notice that Boston is a serious sports town; you can be sure that no matter what's going on worldwide, local sports coverage will feature prominently in the city's dailies.

Whatever your periodical of choice, be sure to browse the offerings at Out of Town News in Harvard Square, an iconic newsstand that's made it all the way to the National Register of Historic Places.

Newspapers and magazines

The city's oldest newspaper, *The Boston Globe* (75¢; ⓦwww.boston.com) remains Boston's best general daily, with an extensive events calendar on Thursdays; its fat Sunday edition ($2) includes substantial sections on art, culture and lifestyle. *The Boston Herald* (75¢; ⓦwww.bostonherald.com) is the *Globe*'s tabloid alternative and is best for getting your gossip and local sports coverage fix. The free and slim daily (Mon–Fri) *Metro* paper (ⓦwww.metro.lu) is available from bins outside **T** stations.

The rest of the city's print media consists primarily of listings-oriented and free weekly papers. To know what's going on, the *Boston Phoenix* (ⓦwww.bostonphoenix .com), available at sidewalk newspaper stands around town, is essential, offering extensive entertainment listings as well as good feature articles. Other freebies like the *Weekly Dig* (ⓦwww.weeklydig.com), *Improper Bostonian* (ⓦwww.improper.com), and the *Phoenix*'s biweekly listings magazine, *Stuff@Night* have good listings of new and note-worthy happenings about town. *Bay Windows* (ⓦwww.baywindows .com), caters to the gay and lesbian population, and is available free at most South End cafés and bars. The *Cambridge Chronicle* (ⓦwww.wickedlocal.com) has news articles and listings about local Cambridge events.

The monthly *Boston Magazine* ($5; ⓦwww .bostonmagazine.com) is a glossy lifestyle publication with good restaurant reviews and an annual "Best of Boston" round-up in August.

TV and radio

Most Boston bars have TVs, and those TVs are usually tuned to sports stations (hey, you gotta watch the game!). Nearly all Boston hotel rooms have cable TV, so you'll be able to catch regular **news** on the four major networks: CBS (channel 4), ABC (channel 5), NBC (channel 7), Fox (channel 25) and CNN, as well as keep abreast of your favourite dramas and sitcoms.

The best **radio stations** are on the FM dial, including WGBH (89.7), which carries National Public Radio (NPR) shows, plus jazz, classical and world music; WBUR (90.9), earnest, leftist talk radio; WJMN (94.5) for new hip-hop and pop songs; WFNX (101.7) for mainstream alternative hits; and WODS (103.3), an oldies station. To get in on Boston's sports fanaticism, tune into WEEI (850AM) for day-long sports talk.

Travel essentials

Costs

Boston ranks among the top five most **expensive** cities in the US to visit. While the high cost of accommodation, food and drink is compensated somewhat by a wealth of inexpensive (and occasionally free) activities, there's no getting around the fact that the first is going to eat up a lot of your budget. Also, most of your major purchases, whether hotel or car rental, will require a credit card imprint, even if you wind up paying the total in cash.

Hotels are, by far, the biggest money-grubbers: expect to fork out somewhere in the $200 range per night just for the privilege of staying in a Boston hotel. The city's B&Bs cost less (around $150 a night) and often have more atmosphere than a chain hotel; long-term accommodation and hostels can take the price down even further.

Food costs are more reasonable – you could get by on $20 a day, if you stay in a hotel with complimentary breakfast, order a bowl of noodles at Faneuil Hall for lunch and eat only at budget restaurants for dinner. That said, scrimping on food costs when Boston has such terrific restaurants seems like a shame.

The best way to stretch your dollar is to book your hotel through a discount agency like Quikbook (Ⓦwww.quikbook .com) or Ⓦwww.hotels.com, and check the Greater Boston Convention and Visitor Bureau website (Ⓦwww.bostonusa.com) for deals. You'll also save on admission prices if you have a **student ID card**, including the International Student Identification Card (ISIC; Ⓦwww.isiccard.com). The ISIC is available through most student travel agencies for $22 for Americans; £9 for UK citizens; AUS$25 for Australians; NZ$25 for New Zealanders; and R100 for South Africans. For the same price, an International Youth Travel Card (IYTC) is available and offers similar discounts to travellers under 26.

Crime and personal safety

Boston is one of the safer American cities, making solo travel, even for women, relatively worry-free. There are, as with anywhere, exceptions; at night-time especially, areas like Dorchester, Roxbury, the Fens, Downtown Crossing and parts of the South End can feel deserted and sketchy – but you're unlikely to find yourself in many of these neighbourhoods after dark, anyway. The **T** is also safe by day and, for the most part, at night; if you stick to the lines that serve the major nightlife areas (especially the Green and Red lines), you're unlikely to have any trouble.

Pickpocketing is not a huge problem, but that doesn't mean it never happens; use common sense and keep an eye on your belongings when at the ATM, on the subway, and paying up at corner stores. If you are robbed, call the police at ☎911. Note that **drugs**, including marijuana, are illegal and you will be fined and possibly sentenced to jail time if caught taking or selling them.

Electricity

As with the rest of the US, electrical outlets in Boston use 110 volts AC. Plugs are standard American two or three-pins.

Entry requirements

Under the **visa waiver scheme**, passport-holders from the UK, Ireland, Australia, New Zealand and most European countries do not require visas for trips to the United States, so long as they stay less than ninety days in the US, and have an onward or return ticket. Instead you simply fill in the visa waiver form handed out on incoming planes. Immigration control takes place at your point of arrival on US soil. As of 2009, there is the additional hassle of the (albeit very straightforward) Electronic System for Travel Authorization form ("ESTA"), which can be filled out online but must be executed at least three days in advance of travel. For more information, head to ⓦwww.cbp.gov/esta. Registration of the form costs $14.

In order to be eligible for the visa-waiver programme, your passport must be **machine-readable**, with a barcode-style number, and be valid for at least six months beyond the period of your stay. All children need to have their own individual passports. Holders of older, unreadable passports may need to obtain new ones or apply for visas prior to travel. For full details, visit ⓦtravel.state.gov or check in with your local consulate prior to your trip.

Canadian citizens, who have not always needed a passport to get into the US, are now required to present a passport when entering the country. Questions may be put to the US embassy at 490 Sussex Drive, Ottawa, ON, K1P 5T1 (☏613/688-5335, ⓦcanada.usembassy.gov).

If you're planning a work- or study-related visit, you will need to get a visa.

A good method for keeping track of your passport information is to email a scanned copy of the first two pages back to yourself and to someone at home before you embark on your travels abroad.

Health

Visitors from Canada, Europe, Australia, New Zealand and South Africa don't require any vaccinations to enter the US, and there aren't any out-of-the-ordinary health concerns to consider when coming to the city.

If you're sick or have been injured, the silver lining (if you could call it that) is that Boston has some of the world's best doctors and hospitals, so once you've made it to the exam room, you'll be in good hands.

For **emergencies** or ambulances, dial ☏**911**. If you have medical or dental problems that don't require an ambulance, most hospitals will have a walk-in **emergency room**; for the nearest hospital, check with your hotel or dial ☏**411**. Should you need to see a **doctor**, the Massachusetts General Physician Referral Service (Mon–Fri 8.30am–5pm; ☏617/726-5800) puts you in touch with physicians at (the excellent) Massachusetts General Hospital; the MGH International Patient Center (55 Fruit St; ☏617/726-2787) is geared toward helping international travellers and offers interpreting services.

Prescriptions can be dispensed at the ubiquitous CVS **drugstore** chain. You can also pick up over-the-counter analgesics here, though international travellers should bear in mind that if you're partial to a particular brand back home, you should bring some with you – you might not find it in the US (this is especially true of codeine-based painkillers, which require a prescription in the US). The CVS store and pharmacy at 587 Boylston St, in Back Bay, is open 24hr (☎617/437-8414; Hynes **T**),

You'll be comforted to know that if you have a serious accident while in New England, emergency services will get to you sooner and charge you later. For walk-in emergencies, the Massachusetts General Hospital, 55 Fruit St (☎617/726-2000, ⓦwww.mgh .harvard.edu; Charles/MGH **T**); Beth Israel Deaconess Medical Center, 330 Brookline Ave (☎617/667-7000, ⓦwww.bidmc.org; Longwood **T**); Tufts Medical Center, 800 Washington St (☎617/636-5000, ⓦwww .tuftsmedicalcenter.org; NE Medical **T**) and Brigham & Women's Hospital, 75 Francis St (☎617/732-5500 or 1-800/BWH-9999, ⓦwww.bwh.partners.org; Longwood or Brigham Circle **T**) all have 24hr emergency rooms. Parents can take their kids to the Children's Hospital, 300 Longwood Ave (☎617/355-6000, ⓦwww.childrenshospital .org; Longwood **T**).

Insurance

In view of the high cost of medical care in the US, all travellers visiting the US from overseas should be sure to buy some form of **travel insurance**. American and Canadian citizens should check that you're not already covered – some homeowners' or renters' policies are valid on vacation, and credit cards such as American Express often include some medical or other insurance, while most Canadians are covered for medical mishaps overseas by their provincial health plans. If you only need trip cancellation/interruption coverage (to supplement your existing plan), this is generally available at about $6 per $100.

Internet access

If you have a suitable laptop, you'll find free **wireless access** is plentiful in Boston. Most hotels have wi-fi, as does the public library, Faneuil Hall Marketplace, the Cambridge-Side Galleria (in Cambridge), numerous local coffee shops (see p.144) and *Starbucks*.

Without a computer, the best way to check your email is to pop into a local university and use one of their free public computers. Harvard's Information Center, in the Holyoke Arcade, at 1350 Massachusetts Ave in Cambridge, has a couple of stations with ten-minute access maximum. The same goes for MIT's Information Center, at 77 Massachusetts Ave (also in Cambridge). Boston's main public library, at 700 Boylston St, has free fifteen-minute internet access on the ground floor of the Johnson building (as well as free wi-fi access throughout). You could also pop by one of the ubiquitous FedEx Office stores; the Government Center location (☎617/973-9000; State **T**) at 2 Center Plaza is open 24hr from Mon–Thurs, as well as Fri until 11pm, Sat 9am–9pm and Sun 9am–midnight, and charges $0.25 per minute for internet use.

Rough Guides travel insurance

Rough Guides has teamed up with WorldNomads.com to offer great **travel insurance** deals. Policies are available to residents of over 150 countries, with cover for a wide range of **adventure sports**, 24hr emergency assistance, high levels of medical and evacuation cover and a stream of **travel safety information**. Roughguides.com users can take advantage of their policies online 24/7, from anywhere in the world – even if you're already travelling. And since plans often change when you're on the road, you can extend your policy and even claim online. Roughguides.com users who buy travel insurance with WorldNomads.com can also leave a positive footprint and donate to a community development project. For more information go to ⓦ**www .roughguides.com/shop**.

Mail

Boston's **postal service** is efficient and has numerous outlets scattered about town. Letters and postcards within the US cost 44¢ and 28¢, respectively, international postcard stamps cost 98¢.

The most **central post office** downtown is at 31 Milk St (Mon–Fri 7.30am–6pm; ☎617/482-1956); Cambridge's central branch is at 770 Massachusetts Ave, in Central Square (Mon–Fri 7.30am–7pm, Sat 7.30am–2pm; ☎617/575-8700). The General Post Office, 25 Dorchester Ave, behind South Station, is open daily from 6am to midnight (☎617/654-5302). You can receive mail at the latter by having it addressed to you c/o General Delivery, 25 Dorchester Ave, Boston MA, 02210. Non-acquired letters are thrown out after thirty days.

Maps

The **maps** in this book, and those given out at Boston tourism kiosks, should satisfy most of your needs; if you want something more comprehensive, best is the rip-proof, waterproof **Rough Guide Map to Boston** ($8.95), a street atlas that pinpoints recommended restaurants, bars, sights and shops along the way. *Where Boston*, a slim complimentary magazine available at most hotels, includes a good map of Boston at the back of every issue. Cyclists might want to pick up *Boston's Bike Map* ($5.95), available at the Globe Corner Bookstore (90 Mt. Auburn St, ☎617/497-6277; Harvard **T**) and online at ⓦwww.massbike.org.

Money

US currency comes in bills of $1, $5, $10, $20, $50 and $100. The dollar is made up of 100 cents, with coins of 1 cent (known as a penny), 5 cents (a nickel), 10 cents (a dime) and 25 cents (a quarter).

Most visitors find that there's no reason to carry large amounts of cash or travellers' cheques to Boston. Automatic teller machines (**ATMs**), which accept most cards issued by domestic and foreign banks, can be found almost everywhere; call your own bank if you're in any doubt. Keep in mind that there's usually a $2 charge (on average) to withdraw money from an ATM that isn't with your home bank.

If you do want to take **travellers' cheques** – which offer the great security of knowing that lost or stolen cheques will be replaced – be sure to get them issued in US dollars. Foreign currency, whether cash or travellers' cheques, can be hard to exchange, so foreign travellers should change some of their money into dollars at home.

For most services, it's taken for granted that you'll be paying with a **credit card**. Hotels and car rental companies routinely require an imprint of your card whether or not you intend to use it to pay.

Banking hours typically run Monday to Friday 9am to 4pm; some banks stay open later on Thursdays and Fridays, and most are open Saturday 9am to noon. Major banks like Sovereign and Bank of America will exchange travellers' cheques and currencies at the standard exchange rate (one or two percent). Outside of banks, you're limited to exchange bureaus in Cambridge, Boston and the airport, which set their own, often higher, commission and rates.

Opening hours and public holidays

The **opening hours** of specific attractions, monuments, memorials, stores and offices are given in the relevant accounts throughout the guide. As a general rule,

Public holidays

The following are public holidays on which banks, post offices and many (although by no means all) shops and attractions will be closed:

New Year's Day Jan 1
Martin Luther King, Jr.'s Birthday Third Mon in Jan
Presidents' Day Third Mon in Feb
Evacuation Day March 17
Patriot's Day Third Mon in April
Memorial Day Last Mon in May
Independence Day July 4
Labor Day First Mon in Sept
Columbus Day Second Mon in Oct
Veterans' Day Nov 11
Thanksgiving Fourth Thurs in Nov
Christmas Day Dec 25

museums close Mondays (the MFA does not, however) and are open Tuesday to Sunday 10am to 5.30pm, though some have extended hours on Thursday and Friday nights and during the summer; a few art galleries stay open until 9pm or so one night a week. Stores are usually open Monday to Saturday 10am to 7pm and Sunday noon to 5pm; some have extended Thursday and Friday night hours. Malls tend to be open Monday to Saturday 10am to 7pm (or later) and Sunday noon to 6pm.

On the national **public holidays** listed in the box above, stores, banks and public and federal offices are liable to be closed all day. The Isabella Stewart Gardner Museum and Institute of Contemporary Art stay open on holiday Mondays – but no others – year round. The traditional summer tourism season, when many attractions have extended opening hours, runs from Memorial Day to Labor Day.

Boston has a huge variety of annual **festivals** and events, many of them historical in scope. For a full calendar, turn to Chapter 19. It's worth noting that during all major festival periods – particularly the Head of the Charles Regatta, the Boston Marathon, Memorial Day and the Fourth of July – it can be very difficult to find accommodation in the city. Book well in advance if you plan to visit Boston at any of these times.

Phones

Boston's **area code** is ☎617; you can reach the city from elsewhere in the US or Canada by dialing ☎1-617 before the seven-digit number; from abroad, dial your country's international access code, then ☎1-617 and the seven-digit number.

Local calls cost 50¢ in coin-operated public phones; when making a local call, compose all ten digits, including the area code. Operator assistance (☎0) and directory information (☎411) are toll-free from public telephones (but not from in-room phones).

Hotels impose huge surcharges, so it's best to use a **phone card** for long-distance calls. In preference to the ones issued by the major phone companies, you'll find it simpler and cheaper to choose from the various pre-paid cards sold in almost all supermarkets and general stores.

Time

Boston is in the East Coast time zone, three hours ahead of West Coast America, five hours behind Britain and Ireland, fourteen to sixteen hours behind East Coast Australia (variations for Daylight Savings Time), sixteen to eighteen hours behind New Zealand (variations for Daylight Savings Time).

Tipping

Wait staff in restaurants expect tips of fifteen to twenty percent, in bars a little less. Hotel porters and bellhops should receive at least $2 per piece of luggage, and housekeeping staff at least $2 per night.

Useful telephone numbers

Area code ☎617
Directory assistance ☎411 or 1-800/555-1212 (for toll-free numbers)
Emergencies ☎911 for fire department, police and ambulance.
Operator ☎0

International calling codes

Calling Boston from abroad international access code + 1 + 617 + seven-digit number.
    To make international calls from the US, dial 011 followed by the country code (note that if you're calling Canada, you simply need to dial a 1, then the area code and number, as though you were making a domestic call):

Australia ☎61	South Africa ☎27
Ireland ☎353	United Kingdom ☎44
New Zealand ☎64	

    For codes not listed here, dial the operator.

Tourist information

The best sources of information for Boston are the *Globe's* Ⓦ www.boston.com and the Greater Boston Convention and Visitors Bureau's (GBCVB) website, Ⓦ www.boston usa.com, which maintains up-to-date information on events about town, a terrific list of special deals, and an online reservation service; agents can also make recommendations and bookings for you (call ☏ 1-888/ SEE BOSTON).

For information once in Boston, stop by the two GBCVB-run **tourism centres**: one is in Boston Common, west of the Park **T** stop, facing Tremont Street (☏617/426-3115), and the other is in the Prudential Center, at 800 Boylston St. Both are open daily from 9am to 5pm. Across from the Old State House, at 15 State St, is a visitor centre maintained by the Boston National Park Service (daily 9am–5pm, ☏617/242-5642); it, too, has plenty of free brochures, plus maps, a bookstore, and bathrooms.

Visitors to **Cambridge** can get all the information they need from the Cambridge Office of Tourism (☏1-800/862-5678, Ⓦ www .cambridge-usa.org), which maintains a well-stocked kiosk in Harvard Square (Mon–Sat 9am–5pm).

Useful websites

Many **websites** contain travel information about Boston. What follows is a short list of both informative and irreverent sites that'll give you the low-down on what's going on around town, local trivia, neighbourhood profiles and other Boston ephemera.

Boston Blogs Ⓦ www.bostonblogs.com. An umbrella site that brings together more than a thousand Boston-area blogs.

Boston Central Ⓦ www.bostoncentral.com. A great resource for all things family, this site includes a kids' shopping directory and a helpful daily events calendar.

Boston Globe Ⓦ www.boston.com. Perhaps the most useful Boston-related website, with extensive events listings, restaurant reviews and (of course) local and national news.

Boston Online Ⓦ www.boston-online.com. General info on the city, including a dictionary of Bostonian English and a guide to public toilets.

Boston Phoenix Ⓦ thephoenix.com. Easily searched site from the city's alternative weekly, with up-to-date arts, music and nightlife listings, restaurant reviews and lots of cool links.

The Bostonian Society Ⓦ www.bostonhistory. org. The official historical society of the city has info on its museum (see p.47) as well as a complete transcript of the Boston Massacre trial.

Link Pink Ⓦ www.linkpink.com. Comprehensive listings of businesses, hotels, shops and services catering to New England's gay and lesbian community.

Massachusetts Office of Travel and Tourism Ⓦ www.massvacation.com. The state-wide tourism bureau is especially useful if you're planning side trips to Cape Cod, Nantucket, or Martha's Vineyard.

Travellers with disabilities

For people with mobility impairments, getting around Boston is possible for the simple reason that the city is relatively flat and curb cuts abound. **Public transportation** can also be used: many MBTA buses and **T** stops are wheelchair-accessible; for detailed information, call ☏617/222-5123, or visit Ⓦ www.mbta.com. In addition, most major **taxi** companies have some vehicles with wheelchair lifts, such as Metro Cab (☏617/ 782-5500).

Very Special Arts (☏617/350-7713; Ⓦ www.vsamass.org) has superior information on the accessibility of museums, sights, movie theatres and other cultural venues in the Boston area. For everything else, contact the **Massachusetts Office on Disability**, a one-stop resource for all accessibility issues whether in Boston or further afield; call ☏617/727-7440 or toll-free on 1-800/ 322-2020.

The City

The City

Downtown Boston

Boston's compact **Downtown** encompasses both the colonial heart and the contemporary core of the city. This assemblage of compressed red-brick buildings tucked in the shadow of modern office towers may seem less glamorous than other American big-city centres, but the sheer concentration of historic sights here more than makes up for whatever's lacking in flash. During the day, there's a constant buzz of commuters and tourists, but come nightfall, the streets thin out considerably.

Boston Common (a king-sized version of the tidy green spaces at the core of innumerable New England villages) is the starting point for the city's popular **Freedom Trail**, a self-guided walking tour that connects an assortment of historic sights by a ribbon of red brick embedded in the pavement. Abutting the Common, several churches and old buildings are worth a peek on your way toward **Washington Street**, where the **Old State House** and **Old South Meeting House** provide high-water marks in pre-Revolution interest, and over at Summer Street, **Downtown Crossing** makes for diverting bargain shopping. Just east, the **Financial District**'s short streets still follow the tangled patterns of colonial-village lanes, though they are now lined with all manner of tall office buildings. A couple of blocks north stands the ever-popular meeting place of **Faneuil Hall Marketplace**.

East of Boston Common, small but energetic **Chinatown** and the nearby **Theater District** are primarily of interest after dark; also in the area is the **Leather District**, a petite enclave typified by brick warehouse spaces and a couple of stylish restaurants. Along the waterfront, scenic wharves jut out into Massachusetts Bay; the most bustling, **Long Wharf**, is the departure point for **whale-watching** excursions and trips to a handful of **islands** that make for relaxing getaways. And finally, across the little finger of water that makes up the Fort Point Channel lies Boston's beloved **Children's Museum** and its modish **Institute of Contemporary Art**.

Though colonial Downtown boasted numerous hills, they've since been smoothed over, and only the name of a particularly pronounced peak – Trimountain – lives on in **Tremont Street**. **King's Chapel**, on Tremont, and the nearby Old State House mark the periphery of Boston's earliest town centre, and the colonies' first church, market, newspaper printers and prison were all clustered here, though they were much closer to the shoreline than the plaques now marking their former sites. **Spring Lane**, a tiny pedestrian passage off Washington Street, recalls the springs that lured the earliest settlers over to the Shawmut Peninsula from Charlestown. The most evocative streets, however, are those whose essential characters have been less diluted over the years – **School Street**, **State Street** and the eighteenth-century enclave known as **Blackstone Block**, near Faneuil Hall.

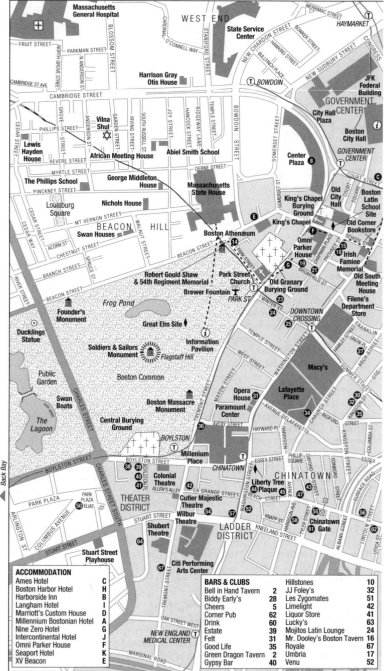

Massachusetts
General Hospital

WEST END

State Service
Center

MERRIMAC STREET

HAYMARKET

FRUIT STREET

PARKMAN STREET

NORTH GROVE STREET

N. ANDERSON ST

BLOSSOM STREET

STANIFORD STREET

CARDINAL O'CONNELL WAY

NEW CHARDON STREET

BOWKER STREET

BULFINCH PLACE

NEW SUDBURY STREET

CONGRESS STREET

Harrison Gray
Otis House

CAMBRIDGE ST AVE

CAMBRIDGE STREET

BOWDOIN

JFK
Federal
Building

GOVERNMENT
CENTER

CEDAR STREET

GROVE STREET

PHILLIPS STREET

ANDERSON ST

GARDEN STREET

IRVING STREET

SOUTH RUSSELL ST

JOY STREET

TEMPLE STREET

HANCOCK STREET

RIDGEWAY LANE

BOWDOIN STREET

SOMERSET STREET

City Hall
Plaza

Boston
City Hall

Vilna
Shul

Lewis
Hayden
House

African Meeting House

Abiel Smith School

GOVERNMENT
CENTER

COURT SQUARE

COURT STREET

Old
City Hall

Boston
Latin
School
Site

REVERE STREET

MYRTLE STREET

DERNE STREET

Center
Plaza 8

The Phillips School

George Middleton
House

King's Chapel
Burying
Ground

Old Corner
Bookstore

PINCKNEY STREET

Nichols House

Massachusetts
State House

King's Chapel

E

SCHOOL STREET

Louisburg
Square

BEACON HILL

MT VERNON STREET

WALNUT STREET

Omni
Parker
House

15
18 Irish
Famine
Memorial

Swan Houses

CEDAR WAY

ACORN ST

CHESTNUT STREET

SPRUCE STREET

Boston Athenæum

14

BEACON STREET

PARK STREET

CHAPMAN PLACE

PROVINCE STREET

19

21

BROMFIELD ST

Old South
Meeting
House

BRANCH STREET

Robert Gould Shaw
& 54th Regiment Memorial

Park Street
Church

G

Old Granary
Burying Ground

Filene's
Department
Store

RIVER STREET

BEACON STREET

Brewer Fountain

PARK ST

WINTER ST

23

FRANKLIN STREET

Founder's
Monument

Frog Pond

Great Elm Site

DOWNTOWN
CROSSING

24

25

HAWLEY ST

SNOW PL

27

ARCH STREET

Ducklings
Statue

Information
Pavilion

TEMPLE STREET

WEST STREET

SUMMER STREET

OTIS STREET

Soldiers & Sailors
Monument

Flagstaff Hill

Macy's

30

32

KINGSTON ST

35

TREMONT STREET

MASON STREET

WASHINGTON STREET

Public
Garden

Boston Common

Opera
House 31

Lafayette
Place

CHAUNCY ST

BEDFORD STREET

KINGSTON STREET

COLUMBIA ST

Swan
Boats

Paramount
Center

34

AVENUE DELAFAYETTE

The
Lagoon

CHARLES STREET

Central Burying
Ground

Boston Massacre
Monument

36

AVERY STREET

HAYWARD PL

HARRISON AVE

PHILLIP
SQUARE

OXFORD STREET

EDINBORO STREET

SURFACE ROAD

BOYLSTON

Millenium
Place

ESSEX STREET

CHINATOWN

KINGSTON STREET

LINCOLN STREET

UTICA STREET

BOYLSTON STREET

BOYLSTON STREET

38 39

41

Colonial
Theatre

Allen's Alley

42

LA GRANGE STREET

Liberty
Tree
Plaque 44

BEACH STREET

43

47

55

56

62

PARK
PLAZA

PARK
PLAZA

ELIAT
ST

50

THEATER
DISTRICT

Cutler Majestic
Theatre 54

Wilbur
Theatre

52

57

KNAPP ST

58

Chinatown
61 Gate

ALBANY STREET

ARLINGTON ST

COLUMBUS AVENUE

STUART STREET

Shubert
Theatre

64

LADDER
DISTRICT

KNEELAND STREET

Stuart Street
Playhouse

Citi Performing
Arts Center

67

TREMONT STREET

NEW ENGLAND
MEDICAL CENTER

OAK STREET WEST

MARGINAL ROAD

Back Bay

South End

40

ACCOMMODATION

Ames Hotel	C
Boston Harbor Hotel	H
Harborside Inn	B
Langham Hotel	I
Marriott's Custom House	D
Millennium Bostonian Hotel	A
Nine Zero Hotel	G
Intercontinental Hotel	J
Omni Parker House	F
Seaport Hotel	K
XV Beacon	E

BARS & CLUBS

Bell in Hand Tavern	2	Hillstones	10
Biddy Early's	28	JJ Foley's	32
Cheers	5	Les Zygomates	51
Corner Pub	62	Limelight	42
Drink	60	Liquor Store	41
Estate	39	Lucky's	63
Felt	31	Mojitos Latin Lounge	24
Good Life	35	Mr. Dooley's Boston Tavern	16
Green Dragon Tavern	2	Royale	67
Gypsy Bar	40	Umbria	17
		Venu	52

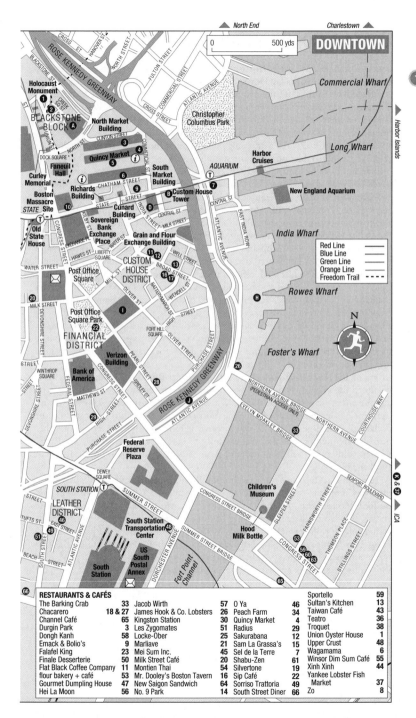

DOWNTOWN

North End   Charlestown

0   500 yds

Holocaust Monument
BLACKSTONE BLOCK
North Market Building
Quincy Market
Faneuil Hall
Curley Memorial
Boston Massacre Site
Richards Building
Cunard Building
Sovereign Bank Exchange Place
South Market Building
Custom House Tower
Grain and Flour Exchange Building
Old State House
Post Office Square
CUSTOM HOUSE DISTRICT
Post Office Square Park
FINANCIAL DISTRICT
Verizon Building
Bank of America
Federal Reserve Plaza
SOUTH STATION
LEATHER DISTRICT
South Station Transportation Center
US South Postal Annex
South Station
Christopher Columbus Park
Harbor Cruises
AQUARIUM
New England Aquarium
Commercial Wharf
Long Wharf
Harbor Islands
India Wharf
Rowes Wharf
Foster's Wharf
Children's Museum
Hood Milk Bottle
Fort Point Channel
ROSE KENNEDY GREENWAY

Red Line
Blue Line
Green Line
Orange Line
Freedom Trail

N

RESTAURANTS & CAFÉS

The Barking Crab	33	Jacob Wirth	57	O Ya	46
Chacarero	18 & 27	James Hook & Co. Lobsters	26	Peach Farm	34
Channel Café	65	Kingston Station	30	Quincy Market	4
Durgin Park	3	Les Zygomates	51	Radius	29
Dongh Kanh	58	Locke-Ober	25	Sakurabana	12
Emack & Bolio's	9	Marliave	21	Sam La Grassa's	15
Falafel King	23	Mei Sum Inc.	45	Sel de la Terre	7
Finale Desserterie	50	Milk Street Café	20	Shabu-Zen	61
Flat Black Coffee Company	11	Montien Thai	54	Silvertone	19
flour bakery + café	53	Mr. Dooley's Boston Tavern	16	Sip Café	22
Gourmet Dumpling House	47	New Saigon Sandwich	64	Sorriso Trattoria	49
Hei La Moon	56	No. 9 Park	14	South Street Diner	66

Sportello	59
Sultan's Kitchen	13
Taiwan Café	43
Teatro	36
Troquet	38
Union Oyster House	1
Upper Crust	48
Wagamama	6
Winsor Dim Sum Café	55
Xinh Xinh	44
Yankee Lobster Fish Market	37
Zo	8

Boston Common and around

Boston's premier open space, **Boston Common**, is a fifty-acre green that effectively separates historic, workaday Downtown from its posh neighbours, the Beacon Hill and Back Bay districts. It's the first thing you'll see emerging from the **Park Street T station**, the central transfer point of America's first subway. While not well manicured like the adjacent **Public Garden** (see p.87), it nonetheless offers plenty of benches and lawn space for taking an enjoyable breather.

Established in 1634 as "a trayning field" used primarily "for the feeding of cattell," as a slate tablet opposite the station recalls, the Common is still primarily utilitarian, used by both pedestrian commuters on their way to Downtown's office towers and tourists seeking the **Boston Visitor Information Pavilion** at 147 Tremont St (daily 9am–5pm; ☎617/426-3115), which is the official starting point of the Freedom Trail. Along the northern side of the Common, the lovely **Beacon Street** runs from the gold-domed State House to Charles Street, opposite the Public Garden (for fuller coverage of Beacon Street, see Chapter 4).

Even before John Winthrop and his fellow Puritan colonists earmarked Boston Common for public use, it served as pasture land for the Reverend William Blackstone, Boston's first white settler. Soon after, it disintegrated into little more than a gallows for pirates, alleged witches and various religious heretics – a commoner by the name of Rachell Whall was once hanged here for stealing a bonnet worth 75¢. Newly elected president George Washington made a much-celebrated appearance on the Common in 1789, as did his aide-de-camp, the Marquis de Lafayette, several years later. Ornate nineteenth-century iron fencing encircled the entire park until World War II, when it was taken down for use as scrap metal; it's now said to grace the bottom of Boston Harbor.

One of the few actual sights here is the **Central Burying Ground**, which has occupied the southeast corner of the Common, near the intersection of Boylston and Tremont streets, since 1754. When Gilbert Stuart, best known for his portraits of George Washington – the most famous of which is replicated on the dollar bill – died penniless, he was interred here in Tomb 61. Among the other notables are members of the largest family to take part in the Boston Tea Party, various soldiers of the Revolutionary Army and Redcoats killed in the Battle of Bunker Hill.

From the Burying Ground it's a short walk to **Flagstaff Hill**, the highest point on the Common, crowned with the granite-pillared Civil War **Soldiers and Sailors Monument**, which is topped by a bronze statue of Lady Liberty and encircled by four plaques displaying scenes of cap-wearing sailors and bayonet-toting infantry. A former repository of colonial gunpowder, the hill overlooks **Frog Pond**, once home to a large number of amphibians and site of the first water pumped into the city. These days, it's a popular kidney-shaped pool, used for wading in summer and ice-skating in winter (there's also an adjacent "Tadpole Playground," perhaps the best one in Downtown Boston). Keep an eye out for the plaque southeast of the pond (before the visitor pavilion) that marks the site of the felled Great Elm; at 22ft in circumference, this regal tree (dubbed Boston's "Oldest Inhabitant") had a spread of 72ft and was thought to be over two hundred years old at the time of its destruction by a gale in 1876. From here, a path east leads to the elegant, two-tiered **Brewer Fountain**, an 1868 bronze replica of one from the Paris Exposition of 1855; the scantily clad gods and goddesses at its base are watched over by cherubs from above. In 2010, after many cascade-less years, the fountain underwent a major scrub-down and restructuring and has now been restored to its burnished, spouting best.

Park Street Church

An oversized version of a typical New England village church, the **Park Street Church** (mid-June to Aug daily 8.30am–3pm, rest of year by appointment; free; ☎617/523-3383, Ⓦwww.parkstreet.org; Park Street **T**) has stood at the northeast corner of Park and Tremont streets, just across from Boston Common, since 1809. Although the building is just a simple mass of bricks and mortar, its ornate 217-foot-tall white telescoping **steeple** is undeniably impressive. To get an idea of the immensity of the building, including the spire, check out the view from tiny Hamilton Place, across Tremont. Ultimately, the structure's reputation rests not on its size but on the scope of events that took place inside: in 1819, the parish sent the country's first missionaries to Hawaii; a decade later, on July 4, 1829, William Lloyd Garrison delivered his first public address calling for the nationwide abolition of slavery (Massachusetts had already scrapped it in 1783); and on July 4, 1831, the classic patriotic song *America* ("My country 'tis of thee...") was first sung to the church rafters.

Park Street itself slopes upward along the edge of Boston Common toward the State House (see p.79). The stretch was once known as **Bulfinch Row**, for its many brick townhouses designed by the architect Charles Bulfinch (see p.79). Today, only one remains, the imposing bay-windowed **Amory-Ticknor House** at no. 9, built in 1804 for George Ticknor, the first publisher of the *Atlantic Monthly*; it's now home to the first-rate restaurant *No.9 Park* (see p.148).

Old Granary Burying Ground

Adjacent to Park Street Church is one of the more tranquil stops on the always-busy Freedom Trail, the **Old Granary Burying Ground** (daily 9am–5pm; free; Park Street **T**), final resting place for numerous leaders of the American Revolution. The entrance, an Egyptian Revival arch, fronts Tremont Street, and it's from the Tremont sidewalk that some of the most famous gravesites can be best appreciated, although, as the rangers will tell you "the stones and the bones may not match up." On the side closest to Park Street Church, a boulder with an attached plaque marks the tomb of revolutionary **James Otis**, known for his articulate tirades against British tyranny. A few tombs down, heading away from the church, rests the remains of **Samuel Adams**, the charismatic patriot whose sideline in beer brewing has kept him a household name. Next to his tomb is the group grave of the five people killed in the **Boston Massacre** of 1770, an event that fuelled anti-Tory feeling in Boston (see p.48). From any angle you can see the stocky **obelisk** at dead centre that marks the grave of Benjamin Franklin's parents.

Somewhat more secure burial vaults and table tombs – semi-submerged sarcophagi – were preferred by wealthier families. **Peter Faneuil**, who gave his money and his name to Boston's most prominent hall, is interred in one of the latter in the left rear corner of the grounds. Midway along the back path is the grave of famed messenger and silversmith **Paul Revere**. Across from Revere, in a red-toned sarcophagus, lies the infamous Salem Witch Trial Judge **Samuel Sewall**; Sewall later apologized for his "condemnation" of "innocent people." Across from the judge's grave on the Park Street Church side, a white pillar marks the resting spot of Declaration of Independence signer **John Hancock**. **Robert Treat Paine**, another signatory, lies along the eastern periphery.

Boston Athenæum

Around the block from the Old Granary Burying Ground, the venerable **Boston Athenæum**, 10 1/2 Beacon St (Mon & Wed 9am–8pm, Tues, Thurs & Fri

The Freedom Trail

Delineated by a 2.5-mile-long red-brick (or paint) stripe in (or on) the pavement, the **Freedom Trail** (ⓦ www.thefreedomtrail.org) stretches from Boston Common to Charlestown, linking sixteen points "significant in their contribution to this country's struggle for freedom." Many of these sites played starring roles in Boston's place in the American Revolution. There's the Revolutionary-era **Old North Church** whose lanterns warned of the British arrival; **Faneuil Hall**, where opposition to the Brits' proposed tea tax was voiced; the **Old South Meeting House**, wherein word came that said tax would be imposed; the **Old State House**, which served as the Boston seat of British government; and the site of the **Boston Massacre**.

Other stops on the Trail, although not associated with the Revolutionary War, are notable for the significant role they played in America's history: the **USS Constitution**, which failed, notably, to sink under British cannon fire, earning her the nickname "Old Ironsides"; **Park Street Church**; and the **Old Corner Bookstore**, a publishing house for American (and some British) writers. You'll also find two instances of British dominion along the trail – the **Bunker Hill Monument**, an obelisk commemorating, ironically, a British victory, albeit in the guise of a moral one for America, and **King's Chapel**, built to serve the King's men stationed in Boston. Finally, you can check out the digs of the gilt-domed **Massachusetts State House** after visiting the gravesites of the Boston luminaries who fought for it; they lie interred in three separate **cemeteries**.

Unfortunately, some of the touches intended to accentuate the attractions' appeal move closer to tarnishing it (for example, the people in period costume stationed outside some of the sights can't help but grate a little). Still, the scope of history that's brought together under the aegis of this humble brick ribbon is quite remarkable. Plus, it remains the easiest way to orient yourself Downtown, especially useful if you'll only be in Boston for a short time, as it does take in many "must-see" sights. You can also pick up a detailed National Park Service **map** at the **Visitor Information Pavilion** (see p.42) in Boston Common, from where the trail begins, or via the friendly **Boston National Park Service** visitor centre at 15 State St. Thrifty visitors take note: most stops on the Trail are either free or inexpensive to enter.

Freedom Trail sights

9am–5.30pm, Sat 9am–4pm; free; ⓣ617/227-0270, ⓦ www.bostonathenaeum .org; Park Street **T**) is one of Boston's most alluring and yet least-visited sights. Established by Boston Brahmins in 1807, this hidden-in-plain-view national landmark stakes its claim as one of the oldest independent research libraries in the country. Best known are its **special collections**, including the original library of King's Chapel – which counts the 1666 edition of Sir Walter Raleigh's *History of the World* among its holdings – as well as books from the private library of George Washington. That said, there is more here than just sober shelves of books. Take, for example, the library's ornate interior and impressive array of **artworks**, including paintings by John Singer Sargent and Gilbert Stuart, which easily rival anything at the Museum of Fine Arts but can be viewed here without the accompanying crowds. In fact, the artistic nucleus of the MFA was spun from the Athenæum's holdings when it opened in 1876; to this day, certain works continue to travel back and forth between the two establishments.

The Athenæum is not exactly welcoming to guests (perhaps explaining its lack of visitors); non-members are confined to the first floor, and everyone has to leave their bags and coats at the front desk – it's all very formal Beacon Hill. Still, if you can handle a bit of scrutiny, it's well worth popping in – sitting in one of its leather armchairs (an experience that's enhanced by knockout views of the Old Granary Burying Ground), you'll feel you've found an oasis of studious refinement in the middle of honk-and-go Downtown Boston. To see the rest of the floors and get a better sense of the collection, join a docent-led art and architecture **tour** (Tues & Thurs 3pm; reservations required; free; ☎617/227-0270 ext.279, ⓦ www.boston athenaeum.org).

King's Chapel Burying Ground and King's Chapel

Boston's oldest cemetery, the atmospheric **King's Chapel Burying Ground**, located at the northeast corner of Beacon and Tremont streets (daily 10am–4pm; free; Park Street **T**), often goes unnoticed by busy pedestrians. Coupled with its accompanying church, however, it's worth a tour despite the din of nearby traffic. There are many beautifully etched gravestones here, with their winged skulls and contemplative seraphim; one of the best examples belongs to an unknown Joseph Tapping near the Tremont Street side. Among the many prominent Bostonians buried here are **John Winthrop**, the first governor of Massachusetts, and **Mary Chilton**, the first Pilgrim to set foot on Plymouth Rock; near the centre of the plot is the tomb of **William Dawes**, the unsung patriot who accompanied Paul Revere on his famous "midnight ride" to Lexington. King's Chapel Burying Ground was one of the favourite Boston haunts of author **Nathaniel Hawthorne**, who visited the grave of a certain Elizabeth Pain, inspiration for the famously adulterous character Hester Prynne in his novel *The Scarlet Letter* (Hawthorne himself is buried in Concord's Sleepy Hollow Cemetery; see p.214).

King's Chapel

The most conspicuous thing about grey, foreboding **King's Chapel**, on the premises of the burying grounds, is its lack of a steeple (there were plans for one, just not enough money). But the belfry does boast the biggest bell ever cast by silversmith Paul Revere (incidentally, it's also the biggest bell in Boston), which you can't help but notice if you happen to pass by at chime time. A wooden chapel was built on this site first, amid some controversy in 1686, when King James II revoked the Massachusetts Bay Colony's charter and installed Sir Edmund Andros as governor, giving him orders to found an Anglican parish – a move that didn't sit too well with Boston's Puritan population – and resulted in the chapel being built illegally, on Puritan land. The present chapel, completed in 1754 by Peter Harrison under instructions to create a church "that would be the equal of any in England," is entered through a pillar-fronted portico added in 1789, when it became the country's first Unitarian Church.

While hardly ostentatious, the elegant Georgian interior, done up with wooden Corinthian columns and lit by chandeliers, provides a marked contrast to the minimalist adornments of Boston's other old churches. It also features America's oldest pulpit, which dates from the late 1600s, and many original pews, including a Governor's Pew along the right wall. The best time to visit is during one of the weekly **chamber music concerts** (Tues 12.15–12.45pm; $3 suggested donation).

Washington Street Shopping District

To a Bostonian, Downtown proper comes in two packages: the **Washington Street Shopping District** (namely the School Street area and Downtown Crossing) and the adjacent Financial District (see p.49). The former, situated east of the King's Chapel Burying Ground, has some of the city's most historic sights – the **Old Corner Bookstore**, **Old South Meeting House** and **Old State House** – but it tends to shut down after business hours, becoming eerily quiet at night. All can be seen in half a day, though you'll need to allow more time if shopping is on your agenda; the stretch around **Downtown Crossing** is full of bargain hunting opportunities.

Narrow and heavily trafficked today, in colonial times **Washington Street** connected the Old State House to the city gates at Boston Neck, an isthmus that joined the Shawmut Peninsula to the mainland, thus ensuring its position as the commercial nerve centre of Boston. The best way to begin exploring the area is via **School Street**, anchored on its northern edge by the dignified **Omni Parker House**, the city's most venerable hotel, which has a rich history: John F. Kennedy announced his congressional candidacy here in 1946; Charles Dickens first read *A Christmas Carol* in its lobby; and Ho Chi Minh and Malcolm X both used to work here, the former in the kitchen and the latter as a busboy. Pop in and order a slice of Boston cream pie (really a layered cake with custard filling and chocolate glaze on top): it was invented here in 1855, and the hotel reportedly still bakes 25 of them a day.

For the rest of its modest length, School Street offers up some of the best in Old Boston charm, beginning with the antique gaslights that flank the severe west wall of King's Chapel. Just beyond is a grand French Second Empire building that served as Boston City Hall from 1865 to 1969; it's near the site of the original location of the **Boston Latin School**, founded in 1635 (a mosaic embedded in the pavement just outside the iron gates marks the exact spot). A depiction of the school's most celebrated dropout, Benjamin Franklin, graces the courtyard (despite good marks, Franklin left school after one year because he didn't want a career in the ministry). Fellow Declaration signer John Hancock was another standout student at this, America's first public school.

The Old Corner Bookstore and around

A few doors down from the old City Hall, where School Street joins Washington, stands the gambrel-roofed, red-brick building that was once the **Old Corner Bookstore** (State Street **T**). In the nineteenth century, Boston's version of London's Fleet Street occupied the stretch of Washington from here to Old South Meeting House, with a convergence of booksellers, newspaper headquarters and publishers; most celebrated among them was Ticknor & Fields, the hottest literary salon Boston ever had. This highly esteemed publishing house was once located in the bookstore itself and handled the likes of Emerson, Longfellow, Hawthorne, Dickens and Thackeray. One of America's oldest literary magazines, *Atlantic Monthly*, was published upstairs here for many years; later, *The Boston Globe* moved in. The space is currently available for lease, although a plaque outside marks its past literary glory; perhaps the next owners will rekindle this site's historic passion for prose.

At the corner of School and Washington streets is the **Irish Famine Memorial** (State Street **T**), commemorating the Irish refugees who immigrated to Boston as a result of the fungal potato crop that claimed one million lives. Its focus is an unsettling pair of statues, one depicting an Irish family holding their hands out for food, the other, a (presumably) Bostonian family that chooses to ignore them.

The Old South Meeting House

Washington Street's big architectural landmark, the **Old South Meeting House**, is one block south of the Old Corner Bookstore, at no. 310 (daily 10am–4pm; $6, kids $1; ⊤617/482-6439, Ⓦwww.oldsouthmeetinghouse .org; State Street **T**). The charming brick church building is recognizable by its tower, a separate but attached structure that tapers into an octagonal spire. An earlier cedarwood structure was replaced in 1729 when the size of the congregation grew, clearing the way for what is now the second-oldest church building in Boston, after Old North Church in the North End (see p.67). Its Congregationalist origins required simplicity inside and out, with no artifice to obstruct closeness to God. This also endowed Old South with a spaciousness that made it a leading venue for anti-imperial rhetoric. The day after the Boston Massacre in 1770, outraged Bostonians assembled here to demand the removal of the troops that were ostensibly guarding the town. Five years later, patriot and doctor Joseph Warren delivered an oration to commemorate the incident; the biggest building in town was so packed that he had to crawl through the window behind the pulpit just to get inside.

More momentously, on the morning of December 16, 1773, nearly five thousand locals met here, awaiting word from Governor Thomas Hutchinson on whether he would permit the withdrawal of three ships in Boston Harbor containing sixty tons of taxed tea. When a message was received that the ships would not be removed, Samuel Adams rose and announced, "This meeting can do no more to save the country!" His simple declaration triggered the **Boston Tea Party** (see box, p.59), perhaps the seminal event leading to the War of Independence.

Before becoming the **museum** it is today, the Meeting House served as a stable, a British riding school and even a bar. One of the things lost in transition was the original high pulpit, which the British tore out during the Revolution and used as firewood; the ornate one currently on view is a replica from 1808. Note the exterior **clock**, installed in 1770, which you can still set your watch by.

Old State House and around

That the graceful three-tiered window tower of the **Old State House** (daily 9am–5pm; $7.50, kids $3; ⊤617/720-1713, Ⓦwww.bostonhistory.org; State Street **T**), at the corner of Washington and State streets, is dwarfed by skyscrapers amplifies, rather than diminishes, its colonial-era dignity.

For years, this red-brick structure, reminiscent of an old Dutch town hall, was the seat of the Massachusetts Bay Colony and consequently the centre of British authority for Massachusetts and Maine; later, it served as Boston's city hall. In 1880, the building was nearly demolished so that State Street traffic might flow more freely, and an unsuccessful bid was made to move it to Chicago in 1880. But while the building's predecessor met its fiery demise in 1711 (owing to a drunken woman's clumsy fire-building skills), the Old State House has remained intact, its fate spared by the **Bostonian Society**, Boston's official historical society and founded specifically to preserve the building.

An impassioned speech in the second-floor Council Chamber by **James Otis**, a Crown appointee who resigned to take up the colonial cause, sparked the quest for independence from Britain fifteen years before it was declared. Otis argued against the Writs of Assistance, which permitted the British to inspect private property at will; legend has it that on certain nights you can still hear him hurling his anti-British barbs, along with the cheers of the crowd he so energized. The **balcony** overlooking State Street is as famous as Otis's speech, for it was from here on July 18, 1776, that the Declaration of Independence was first read publicly in Boston – a copy having just arrived from Philadelphia. That same night, the symbolically British lion and unicorn figures mounted above the balcony were torn down and burned in front of the *Bunch of Grapes* tavern (see p.50); those currently on display are replicas. Just to show there were no hard feelings, Queen Elizabeth II, the first British monarch to set foot in Boston since the Revolution, made a speech from the balcony as part of the American bicentennial activities in 1976.

Today, the site houses a small but comprehensive **museum**: the permanent ground-level exhibit, "Colony to Commonwealth," has a number of well-tailored exhibits chronicling Boston's role in inciting the Revolutionary War. Displays include a bit of tea from Boston's most infamous party; the plaque of royal arms that once hung over Province House, official residence of the colonial governors; the flag that the Sons of Liberty draped from the Liberty Tree to announce their meetings; a dapper jacket belonging to John Hancock; and the most galvanizing image of the Revolutionary period, Paul Revere's propagandistic engraving of the Boston Massacre.

Adjacent to the Old State House, at 15 State Street, lies the downtown **visitor centre** for the Boston National Park Service (daily 9am–5pm; free; ℡617/242-5642, Ⓦwww.nps.gov/bost; State Street **T**), chock full of maps, facts and particularly helpful park rangers; there are also un-crowded toilets.

The Boston Massacre Site

On the Devonshire Street side of the Old State House, a circle of cobblestones embedded in a small traffic island marks the site of the **Boston Massacre** (State Street **T**), the tragic outcome of escalating tensions between Bostonians and the British Redcoats who occupied the city. Riots were an increasingly common occurrence in Boston by the time this deadly one broke out on March 5, 1770. It began when a young wigmaker's apprentice heckled an army officer over a barber's bill. The officer sought refuge in the Custom House (then opposite the Old State House), but when a throng of people gathered at the scene, the mob grew violent, hurling snowballs and rocks at arriving soldiers. When someone threw a club that knocked a Redcoat onto the ice, he rose and fired. Five Bostonians were killed in the ensuing riot – including a young black man named Crispus Attucks, considered the first casualty of the Revolution – resulting in Governor Hutchinson's order to relocate occupying troops to Castle Island in Boston Harbor. Two patriots, John Adams and Josiah Quincy, actually defended the eight soldiers in court; six were acquitted, and the two who were found guilty were branded on their thumbs.

Downtown Crossing

A few blocks south lies a pleasant antidote to those overwhelmed by American history. Pedestrian-friendly **Downtown Crossing**, an outdoor mall area, brims with department stores and smaller shops that cater to bargain hunters of all stripes. Centred on the intersection of Washington and Summer streets, its nucleus for nearly 100 years was, until recently, Filene's Basement, a thrift seeker's delight famous for its legendary "Running of The Brides" event, wherein frenzied brides-to-be feverishly pawed their way to marked-down gowns. Sadly, since 2007 the Basement has been left in the lurch over a botched multi-million dollar property deal, and it's not clear when or if this location will reopen. Although a portion

Views of Downtown

Whether local or from out of town, people can't seem to get enough of Boston's **skyline** – its pastiche of brownstone churches and glass-panelled skyscrapers framing Massachusetts Bay ranks it among the country's finest. No wonder, then, that so many buildings have public (and often free) viewing floors. You can check out Boston from every angle from the *Marriott Custom House* (see p.53), the Prudential Tower (see p.91), the 14th floor observation deck at 470 Atlantic Ave (p.59) and the Bunker Hill Monument (see p.75). The best lay of the land, though, is had from the water; take a walk across the Longfellow Bridge, board the Charlestown ferry (see p.70), visit the Harbor Islands (see p.60), or take a ferry to Provincetown (see p.239) or Salem (see p.216) for a particularly stunning view.

of the corniced facade still stands (as well as its iconic clock), much of the former building is now merely a hole in the ground, and like a jilted bride, the Basement's defunct northern wall is wrapped up in dreary white sheets.

The Financial District

Boston's **Financial District**, a small area east of Washington Street and bounded by the waterfront, hardly conjures the same interest as those of New York and London, but it continues to wield influence in key fields (like mutual funds, invented here in 1925). The area is not entirely devoid of historic interest, though it's generally more manifest in plaques than actual buildings. Like most of America's business districts, it beats to an office hours-only drum, and many of its little eateries and Irish pubs are closed on weekends (some brave new restaurants have begun to make inroads, however).

The mostly immaculate streets follow the same short, winding paths as they did three hundred years ago; only now, thirty- and forty-storey skyscrapers have replaced the wooden houses and churches that used to clutter the area. Still, their names are historically evocative: **High Street**, once known as Cow Lane, used to lead to the summit of the now-vanished eighty-foot-tall Fort Hill. **Arch Street** recalls the decorative arch that graced the Tontine Crescent, a block of stately townhouses designed in 1793 by Charles Bulfinch and unfortunately destroyed by the Great Fire of 1872, which began in the heart of the district. Tucked among the relatively generic skyscrapers are several well-preserved nineteenth-century mercantile masterpieces; or head down to **Franklin Street**, where the curving of the street was designed by Bulfinch to reflect the turn of the Tontine Crescent.

Milk Street and Post Office Square

The most dramatic approach to the Financial District is east from Washington Street via **Milk Street**. A bust of **Benjamin Franklin** surveys the scene from a recessed Gothic niche above the doorway at no. 1; the site marks Franklin's birthplace, though the building itself only dates from 1874.

Further down Milk and just south on Pearl St, the sombre, 22-storey **John W. McCormack Post Office and Court House** is (ironically) no longer the home of either the post office (which has moved to Milk Street) or the courthouse (which has swish new digs out in the Seaport District). Still, the building has left its stamp on the area, most obviously by giving the adjacent **Post Office Square** its name; today, the park's pretty triangular layout and cascading fountains are popular with area professionals (and area visitors, too) during lunch hours. Though it's not officially open to the public, you might try sneaking up to the glass atrium atop the building at **One Post Office Square** for jaw-dropping views of Boston Harbor and Downtown. The city's skyline encompasses the architectural funkiness of the 1980s and a few Art Deco treats, too; the best example of the former is the **First Bank of America** tower at 100 Federal St, to the south, with its bulging midsection, nicknamed the "Pregnant Building."

The prime Art Deco specimen, meanwhile, is nearby at 185 Franklin St – now the **Verizon Building** – a 1947 step-top design. Until 2009, you could check out the fusty nook off the right-hand side of the lobby, which was home to a replica of the Boston attic room where Alexander Graham Bell first transmitted speech sounds over a wire in 1875; the wooden chamber was a meticulously reassembled version of the original that was installed in 1959. Unfortunately, Verizon very recently sold its rights to the building, and in the process dismantled this kooky Boston site; rallying preservationists hope to bring the whole thing back. In the meantime, if you're hankering to pay your respects to the birthplace of the telephone, head to the John F. Kennedy Federal Building at 15 Sudbury St (in Government Center; see below); here, a podium-shaped memorial marks the spot where, on June 2, 1875, Bell made the world's first telephone call (sending text messages to his friends wouldn't follow until much later, however).

Exchange Place, at 53 State St, is a mirrored-glass tower rising from the facade of the old Boston Stock Exchange; the *Bunch of Grapes* tavern, watering hole of choice for many of Boston's Revolutionary rabble-rousers, once stood here. Behind it is tiny **Liberty Square**, once the heart of Tory Boston – the British tax office had its address here, in 1765, and was destroyed by angry colonists – and now mostly of note for its improbable bronze sculpture, called *Aspirations for Liberty*; it's an elegant depiction of rebels rising to hold a (presumably rebellious) baby in honour of the Hungarian anti-Communist uprising of 1956.

Government Center

Tremont Street's major tenant, **Government Center**, lies northwest from Exchange Place along Congress Street. Its sea of towering grey buildings on the former site of Scollay Square – once Boston's most notorious den of porn halls and tattoo parlours – is by far the least interesting section of Downtown Boston. As part of a citywide face-lift, Scollay was razed in the early 1960s, eliminating all traces of its salacious past and, along with it, most of its lively character. Indeed, the only thing that remains from the square's steamier days is the Oriental Tea Company's 227-gallon **Steaming Kettle** advertisement, which has been clouding up the sky across from the Government Center **T** stop since 1873. The area is now overlaid with concrete, thanks to an ambitious plan developed by I.M. Pei, and towered over by two monolithic edifices: **Boston City Hall**, at the east side of the plaza, and the **John F. Kennedy Federal Building**, on the north. One pretty face stands out among the concrete, however: the graceful, curved nineteenth-century **Sears Crescent** building, former publishing house for the abolitionist journal *The Christian Freeman*. Unless the workings of bureaucracy get you going, Government Center is generally just a brief stopover on the walk to Faneuil Hall Marketplace.

Faneuil Hall Marketplace and around

Popular with both tourists and (less so) locals, **Faneuil Hall Marketplace** (Faneuil rhymes with "flannel"), set on a pedestrian zone east of Government Center, is an active public gathering place that's good for a bite to eat and a bit of history (as well as free wi-fi access). Built as a market during colonial times to house the city's growing mercantile industry, it declined during the nineteenth century and, like the area around it, was pretty much defunct until the 1960s, when it was successfully redeveloped as a restaurant and shopping mall.

Faneuil Hall

Much-hyped **Faneuil Hall** (daily 9am–5pm; ☎617/523-1300; State Street **T**) itself doesn't appear particularly majestic from the outside; it's simply a small, four-storey brick building topped with a golden grasshopper weathervane – not the grandiose auditorium one might imagine would have housed the Revolutionary War meetings that earned it its "Cradle of Liberty" sobriquet.

The structure once had an open-air market on its first floor and a space for political meetings on its second, a juxtaposition that inspired local poet Francis Hatch to pen the lines, "Here orators in ages past/Have mounted their attacks/Undaunted by proximity/Of sausage on the racks." Faneuil Hall was where revolutionary firebrands such as Samuel Adams and James Otis whipped up popular support for independence by protesting British tax legislation. The first floor now houses a panoply of tourist **shops**; you'll also find an information desk, a post office and a BOSTIX kiosk. The second floor is more impressive: the auditorium has been preserved to reflect modifications made by Charles Bulfinch in 1805. Its focal point is a showy – and slightly preposterous – canvas depicting an embellished version of "The Great Debate," during which Daniel Webster argued for the concept of the United States as one nation against South Carolina senator Robert Hayne. While the debate was an actual event, the painting contains a number of nineteenth-century luminaries, such as Nathaniel Hawthorne and Alexis de Toqueville, who certainly weren't in attendance – the artist simply thought this would help him sell his painting. More down-to-earth is the story of how Beantown sailors got free passage home from Britain in the War of 1812: captive Boston sailors who escaped to the American consulate were asked what flew atop Faneuil Hall as a weathervane. Those who knew it was a grasshopper were trusted as true Bostonians and given a free ride back; those who didn't were regarded with suspicion.

Dock Square, Blackstone Street and the Holocaust Memorial

Immediately behind Faneuil Hall lies **Dock Square**, so named for its original location directly on Boston's waterfront (carvings in the pavement indicate the shoreline in 1630). The square's centre is dominated by a statue of **Samuel Adams**, interesting mostly for its over-the-top caption: "A statesman, incorruptible and fearless." A dim, narrow corridor known as Scott's Alley heads north of the market to reach Creek Square, where you enter **Blackstone Street**, the eastern edge of a tiny warren of streets bounded to the west by Union Street. Its uneven cobblestone streets and low brick buildings have remained largely untouched since the 1750s; many of them, especially those along Union Street, house restaurants and pubs (like the *Union Oyster House*, which has been serving up seafood since

1826; see p.149). If in the area on a Friday or Saturday afternoon, you'll discover **Haymarket,** perhaps Boston's best-known and certainly its most historic open-air market. Here, energetic produce sellers heckle patrons, and happy shoppers haggle them right back. The crosswalk on Blackstone and Haymarket pays homage to this centuries-old institution with an endearing "sculpture." Made from brass fruit peels and trash shapes pressed into the concrete, it's redolent of the discards that colour the block once Haymarket sellers have wrapped up business for the day.

The corner of Union and North streets marks the location of the former house of **William Dawes,** one of the riders who joined Paul Revere on his midnight ride. Unlike Revere, his house has not been favourably preserved – it's now a *McDonald's* – but you can view a plaque commemorating the site. Just north on Union is the **Curley Memorial Plaza,** a small circle of benches depicting two statues dedicated to James Michael Curley, one of Boston's more enduring twentieth-century political figures. Dubbed the "Rascal King", Curley was four times elected the mayor of Boston, and twice convicted of "official misconduct" while still in office. Just north of here lies a different sort of monument, six tall, hollow, glass pillars erected as a **memorial to victims of the Holocaust.** Built to resemble smokestacks, the columns are etched with six million numbers recalling the tattoos the Nazis gave the Jews and other victims. Steam rises from grates beneath each of the pillars to accentuate their symbolism, an effect that's particularly striking at night.

Quincy Market

The markets just behind Faneuil Hall – three parallel oblong structures and one 1970s concrete mall that house restaurants, shops and office buildings – were built in the early eighteenth century to contain the trade that had quickly outgrown its space in the hall. The centre building, known as **Quincy Market** (Mon–Sat 10am–9pm, Sun noon–6pm; ☎617/523-1300, ⊛www.faneuilhallmarketplace .com; Government Center **T**), holds a super-extended corridor lined with stands selling a variety of takeaway treats – it's the mother of mall food courts – built in 1824 under the direction of Boston's mayor at the time, Josiah Quincy.

Free Boston

With their noticeable lack of an admission fee (some ask for donations), these worthy Boston sights are putting the "free" back into "Freedom Trail":

470 Atlantic Ave observation deck, p.59
Arnold Arboretum, p.114
Athenæum, p.43
Boston Public Library, p.90
Boston Public Garden, p.87
Bunker Hill Monument, p.75
Copp's Hill Burying Ground, p.68
Custom House observation deck, p.53
Faneuil Hall, p.51
Forest Hills cemetery, p.116
Hatch Shell (free concerts), p.83
Institute of Contemporary Art (free 5pm–9pm on Thurs; free for families last Sat of the month), p.59

Mount Auburn cemetery, p.128
Museum of Fine Arts (donation only after 4pm on Wed), p.104
National Park Service (free historical tours), p.48
Old Granary Burying Ground, p.43
Old North Church, p.67
Old South Church, p.89
Sam Adams Brewery tour, p.116
Massachusetts State House, p.79
USS *Constitution* and museum, p.72

To either side of the market are the **North** and **South Markets**, which hold restaurants and popular chain clothing stores. The cobblestone corridors between them host a number of vendor carts offering curios and narrow specializations (one sells only purple objects, another nothing but puppets). You'll also find the usual complement of street musicians, fire-jugglers and mimes, weather permitting. There's not much to distinguish it from any other shopping complex, though there are several good restaurants and a nice concentration of bars (including a replica of the *Cheers* set), which are scarce elsewhere in the Downtown area. Overall, sitting on a bench in the heart of it all on a summer day, eating ice cream while the mobs of locals and tourists mill about, is a quintessential, if slightly absurd, Boston experience.

The Custom House District

The not-quite-triangular wedge of Downtown between State and Broad streets and Surface Road is the unfairly overlooked, rather loosely named, **Custom House District**, dotted with some excellent architectural draws. Chief among them is the **Custom House** itself, built in 1847 and surrounded by 32 huge Doric columns, though the thirty-storey Greek Revival tower was only added in 1915. Not surprisingly, it is no longer the tallest skyscraper in New England (a status it held for 49 years), but it still has plenty of character and terrific views nonetheless; you can check them out from the 360-degree observation deck free of charge (guided tours 2pm daily except Fri; $3 donation; ☎617/310-6300), or even book a room here – it now houses a *Marriott* hotel.

The **Flour and Grain Exchange Building**, a block away at 177 Milk St, is another district landmark. This fortress-like construction recalls the Romanesque-Revival style of prominent local architect H.H. Richardson. Its turreted, conical roof, encircled by a series of pointed dormers, is a bold reminder of the financial stature this district once held. **Broad Street**, which runs perpendicular to Milk Street, was built on filled-in land in 1807 and is still home to several Federal-style mercantile buildings designed by Charles Bulfinch, notably those at numbers 68–70, 72 and 102.

On **State Street**, long a focal point of Boston's maritime prosperity, take a look at the elaborate cast-iron facade of the **Richards Building** at no. 114 (a clipper-ship company's office in the 1850s) and the **Cunard Building** at no. 126, its ornamental anchors recalling Boston's status as the North American terminus of the first trans-atlantic steamship mail service. Trading activity in the nearby harbour brought a thriving banking and insurance industry to the street in the 1850s, along with a collection of rather staid office buildings. A modern exception is the opulent **75 State Street Building**, a medium-sized skyscraper crowned with 3600 square feet of gold leaf and containing a six-storey lobby decked out in marble, mahogany and bronze.

The Theater and Ladder districts

Just south of Boston Common is the slightly seedy **Theater District** – the small area around the intersection of Tremont and Stuart streets. Not surprisingly, you'll have to purchase tickets in order to inspect the grand old interiors of the theatres for which it's named, but it's well worth a quick walk along Tremont Street to admire their facades. At the intersection of Washington and Avery streets,

Banned in Boston

Boston's Puritan founders would be horrified to find that an area called the **Theater District** exists. Their ingrained allergy to fun resulted in theatrical performances actually being outlawed in Boston until 1792, and in 1878 the Watch & Ward Society was formed to organize boycotts against indecent books and plays. Still, the shows went on, and in 1894 vaudeville was born at the lavish (now extinct) B.F. Keith Theater. Burlesque soon followed, prompting the city licensing division in 1905 to deny performances that didn't meet their neo-Puritan codes – thus the phrase "Banned in Boston." In fact, as recently as 1970, a production of *Hair* was banned for a month due to its desecration of the American flag.

Despite this censorship, Boston still managed to become the premier theatre tryout town that it is today: high production costs on Broadway have dictated that hits be sifted from misses early on, and Boston has long been a cost-efficient testing ground. During the 1920s, the heyday of theatre in the city, there were as many as forty playhouses in the Theater District alone. However, the rise of film meant the fall of theatre, and after brief stints as movie halls, many of the grand buildings – most notably the **Paramount**, the **Opera House** (formerly the Savoy) and the **Modern Theatre**, all on lower Washington Street – slid into disrepair and eventual abandonment. The good news is the Opera House has recently undergone a glorious renovation and reopening, and the Paramount, too, was restored in 2010. The Modern appears to be close behind – in 2008, Suffolk University finalized plans to create a theatre and residence hall within this historic space, vacant for nearly two decades.

you'll find the 1928 Beaux Arts **Opera House**, recently renovated after being closed for more than a decade, alongside another rejuvenated gem, the Art Deco **Paramount**, its red and orange light-bulb marquee looking almost garish next to its dainty sister (before its resurrection in 2010, the Paramount's most recent stint – back in 1976 - was as a porno movie house). The **Colonial Theatre** – the oldest continuously-operating theatre in Boston – is just off **Piano Row**, a section of Boylston Street between Charles and Tremont that was the centre of American piano manufacturing and music publishing in the nineteenth and early twentieth centuries. There are still a few piano shops in the area, but the hip restaurants and clubs in the immediate vicinity are of greater interest; many are tucked between Charles and Stuart streets around the mammoth **Massachusetts Transportation Building** and cater to the theatre-going crowd.

South along Tremont is the beautifully ornate and restored **Cutler Majestic Theatre**, and further down the street, the porticoed **Wilbur Theatre** (see p.177), the place to go for (surprisingly) comedy shows; when it opened in 1914, it was the first Boston theatre to have its own guest lounge. Adjacent to the Wilbur, the old **Metropolitan Theatre**, a movie house of palatial proportions, survives as the glittering **Wang Theatre** (now sporting the "Citi Performing Arts Center" corporate moniker) (see p.177), grande dame of the theatre scene. Across the street is the darling **Shubert Theatre** (see p.177), the so-called "Little Princess of the Theater District"; its plush, 1600-seat auditorium is home to the Boston Lyric Opera, as well as some Broadway productions.

The tenor around Washington Street between Essex and Kneeland was pretty seedy from the 1960s to early 80s. Designated an "adult entertainment zone" in the 1960s (when it replaced Scollay Square as the city's red-light district and known, enigmatically, as "the Combat Zone," the latter-day **Ladder District** was home to X-rated theatres and bookshops until trendy restaurants and night-clubs designated it the new "It" spot and pushed the less reputable businesses out.

PR hacks successfully renamed the area after its ladder-like layout (Tremont and Washington form the rails; Winter and Avery streets, the top and bottom rungs), but failed to alter its daylight character, which, despite the addition of a *Ritz-Carlton* at the corner of Tremont and Avery, remains rather dive-y, offering an extension of Downtown Crossing's shops and a handful of bars and restaurants.

One sight of note is the plaque at the intersection of Washington and Boylston streets marking the approximation of where the **Liberty Tree** stood. This oak, planted in 1646, was a favoured meeting point of the Sons of Liberty; as such, the British chopped it down in 1775. If you look up and to the right while standing at the plaque, you'll see where the oak was truly rooted – there is a bas-relief sculpture of a tree implanted in the third floor of the Registry of Motor Vehicles on Washington Street.

Chinatown and the Leather District

Boston's **Chinatown** lies wedged into just a few square blocks between the Financial and Theater districts, but it makes up in activity what it lacks in size. Just lean against a pagoda-topped payphone (yup, they're still here) on the corner of **Beach** and **Tyler streets** – the neighbourhood's two most dynamic thoroughfares – and watch the way life here revolves around the food trade at all hours. By day, merchants barter in Mandarin and Cantonese over the going price of produce; by night, Bostonians arrive in droves to eat in the restaurants. Walk down either street and you'll pass most of the bakeries, eateries and indoor markets, in whose windows you'll see the usual complement of roast ducks hanging from hooks and aquariums filled with future seafood dinners. The area's at its most vibrant during various **festivals** (see Chapter 19), none more so than **Chinese New Year** (late Jan/early Feb), when frequent parades of papier mâché dragons fill the streets and the acrid smell of firecrackers permeates the air. During the **Festival of the August Moon**, held, as you may have guessed, in August, there's a bustling street fair. Check with the Chinese Merchants' Association for more information (T617/350-6303; W www.chinatownmainstreet.org).

The prosperity of Boston's Chinatown has increased dramatically over the last thirty years, and consequently is expanding to the north, now bordering Downtown Crossing and even extending over Surface Road into the Leather District. Despite this growth, the heart of Chinatown still retains a neighbourhood feel, and the atmosphere is best enjoyed by wandering around with no particular destination in mind. There are a few notable landmarks, such as the plaque at the intersection of Tyler and Beach streets marking the site where, in 1761, John Wheatley purchased eight-year old **Phillis Wheatley** to serve as his slave; twelve years later she went on to become the first published African-American woman with "Poems on Various Subjects, Religious and Moral." And of course there's the impressive **Chinatown Gate**, a three-storey, red-and-gilt monolith guarded by four Fu dogs, located at the intersection of Hudson and Beach Streets, a gift from Taiwan in honour of Chinatown's centennial. Adjacent **Tian An Men Park** provides a place to rest, but it's poorly kept and inhabited by aggressive pigeons. Instead, head to the benches at the new Feng Shui-inspired park on Surface Road, just north of the Chinatown Gate (replacing a former Central Artery off-ramp); here, you'll find smooth pebbles, streams and sheaves of leafy bamboo undulating within angular red steel frames. It's an interesting spot that provides a nice backdrop for a *bánh mì* sandwich and other takeaway consumption.

The Leather District

Just east of Chinatown, the six square blocks bounded by Kneeland, Atlantic, Essex and Lincoln streets form the **Leather District**, which takes its name from the nineteenth-century days when the shoe industry was a mainstay of the New England economy, and the leather needed to make the shoes was shipped through warehouses here. Nowadays, the neighbouring Financial District has long since taken over as the economic hub, and Boston's leather industry has pretty much dried up. The distinction between the Financial and Leather districts is actually quite sharp, and most evident where High Street transitions into **South Street**, the Leather District's main drag. Stout brick warehouses replace gleaming modern skyscrapers, and a melange of merchants and gallery owners take over from the suited bankers. Some of the edifices still have their leather warehouse **signs** on them; check out the Boston Hide & Leather Co at 20 East St. Apart from its past, this petite area is known for sleek eateries and a number of galleries, well-situated within the district's warehouse lofts. Nearby **South Station**, Boston's main train and bus terminus, has little to recommend it architecturally.

The Waterfront

Boston's urban renewal programme, sparked by the beginning of the Big Dig in the early 1990s, has resulted in a resurgence of its **Waterfront** area. The tearing down of the John Fitzgerald Expressway (also known as I-93), which, since the 1950s, had separated the Waterfront from the rest of Downtown, has allowed the city to reconnect with the sea through a series of ambitious projects such as the expansion of the New England Aquarium and the conversion of wharf buildings into housing. The most visible change may be the Rose Kennedy Greenway, a thirteen-acre public park beautifying what was once a car-ridden stretch. Highlights of this mile-long ribbon include the Rings Fountain, at Milk Street, which spouts unpredictable bursts of water that kids (and kids at heart) love to

The HarborWalk

The **HarborWalk** officially begins in Dorchester, curving eastwards into the beaches of South Boston and then all the way up to East Boston (a whopping 47 miles in all). Obviously, visitors shouldn't expect to see the whole thing, but it's quite pleasant to walk the portion that meanders through the wharves alongside the Boston waterfront. Start at **Lewis Wharf**, where a gravel path leads to a pretty circular garden. Continue south, passing by **Christopher Columbus Park** and the **Aquarium**. Before arriving at the *Boston Harbor Hotel's* breathtaking vaulted entrance, check out David von Schlegell's *"Untitled Landscape"* on **India Wharf**, two pairs of fifteen foot L-shaped pieces of metal which seem to magnetically compel children (and adults, too) to run between them. Throughout, there are peaceful harbour vistas, complete with sailboats drifting on the water, but the best scenery of the walk is contained between Lewis Wharf and **470 Atlantic Ave**, former site of the Boston Tea Party and current home to a fantastic fourteenth-floor observation deck (daily 10am–5pm; free). For more information, go to the HarborWalk's extensive website at Ⓦwww .bostonharborwalk.com.

run through, and the merry-go-round that pops up in warm weather months between Atlantic Avenue and the Surface Artery Southbound ($3; Ⓦ www.rose kennedygreenway.org).

While the waterfront that's concentrated around **Long Wharf** is more touristy (selling T-shirts, furry lobsters and the like), strolling the atmospheric **HarborWalk** that edges the water affords unbeatable views of Boston, and is a pleasant respite from bustling Faneuil Hall. You'll also find plenty of diversion if you've got little ones in tow at the **New England Aquarium**. Otherwise, you can do some watery exploring on a number of **boat tours**, or escape the city altogether by heading out to the **Harbor Islands**.

Long Wharf and around

Long Wharf has been the waterfront's main drag since its construction in 1710. Not surprisingly, summer is its busiest season, when the wharf is dotted with stands vending ice cream cones and kitschy souvenirs. This is also the main point of departure for Boston Harbor Cruises (Ⓣ 617/227-4321, Ⓦ www .bostonharborcruises.com), which runs **whale-watching** excursions, harbour cruises and ferries to Cape Cod's Provincetown (see p.240). You could also catch a ferry to Salem, MA (see p.216; Ⓣ 978/741-0220, Ⓦ www.salemferry .com). Ferries to the Boston Harbor Islands also leave from Long Wharf; check for schedules at the Harbor Islands kiosk here or at Ⓦ www.bostonislands.com. If you're more interested in an old-school sailing experience, Boston has the good fortune of mooring a beautiful tall ship, the *Schooner Liberty Clipper*, at 67 Long Wharf. This 125-foot long dreamboat offers three trips a day from May to September (2hr; $30, kids $15; Ⓣ 617/742-0333, Ⓦ www.libertyfleet.com; Aquarium **T**).

Situated between Long Wharf and Commercial Wharf, **Christopher Columbus Park** is a pretty green space bisected by a wisteria-laden trellis. This leisurely park also features a rose garden and kid-sized sprinkler fountain, well loved in summer months. In the evening, the park takes on a romantic feel, and you can walk out to the end of Long Wharf for an excellent vantage point on **Boston Harbor**, when even the freighters appear graceful against the moonlit water.

New England Aquarium

Next door to Long Wharf is the waterfront's major draw, the **New England Aquarium** (July & Aug daily 9am–6pm, Fri & Sat till 7pm; Sept–Jun daily 9am–5pm, Sat & Sun till 6pm; $21, kids $13; City Pass accepted; Ⓣ 617/973-5200, Ⓦ www.neaq.org; Aquarium **T**). Especially fun for kids, the indoor aquarium has plenty of fine exhibits, such as the penguins on the bottom floor. In the centre of the aquarium's spiral walkway is an impressive collection of marine life: a three-storey, 200,000-gallon cylindrical tank packed with giant sea turtles, moray eels, sharks, stingrays and a range of other ocean exotica that swim by in unsettling proximity. The aquarium also runs excellent **whale-watching** trips (early April–late Nov; 3–4hr, call for times and specific dates; $40, kids $32; Ⓣ 617/973-5206).

Over the last decade, a multimillion-dollar expansion programme has seen the addition of a West Wing, the Aquarium Medical Center (giving visitors a look at animal care), and a showy **IMAX theatre** that, at more than six storeys high, has the largest screen in New England (daily 9.30am–8pm; $9.95, kids $7.95).

The Fort Point Channel and Seaport District

The rapidly up-and-coming **Fort Point Channel** and **Seaport District** are two spacious, adjoining, harbourside neighbourhoods located across the pedestrian-only Northern Bridge, and the auto-friendly Moakley, Congress and Summer Street bridges from Downtown. The area is full of charming warehouse spaces, and tends toward chic sensibilities, being home to a number of new clothing boutiques, drinking hotspots and art galleries. One of the Seaport District's old-school draws is the range of restaurants near **Fish Pier**, where you can also find a number of **lobster wholesalers**; if you love crustaceans, you'll avoid paying standard market price by braving the aromas at one of these seafood warehouses. Nearby are the affable **Boston Children's Museum**, packed with playful and intelligent children's exhibits, and the pearl in the Seaport District's oyster: the iridescent **Institute of Contemporary Art**, a lustrous space at the forefront of the nation's art scene, and perhaps the most important architectural design to come to Boston in nearly a century. Further in is the **Bank of America Pavilion**, a huge, half-shell amphitheatre that hosts big-name musical acts in the summer, and the **Harpoon Brewery**, a local beer-maker offering spirited weekend tours.

Although the Children's Museum is just a hop from downtown, many of the other sights, particularly those in the Seaport District, are a bit of a hike from the city; this shouldn't preclude a visit, but it may inspire you to take a ride on the Silver Line **T**.

Boston Children's Museum

It's hard to miss the larger-than-life 1930s-era **Hood Milk Bottle** across the Congress Street Bridge from Downtown, one of Boston's best-loved icons and a whimsical prelude to the Children's Museum. Doubling as a food stand, the milk bottle actually serves little dairy produce – most of its trade is in lemonade and hot dogs – though it's estimated that if the bottle was filled with milk, it would hold 58,000 gallons of the stuff.

Behind the bottle, the engaging **Boston Children's Museum**, 308 Congress St (daily 10am–5pm, Fri till 9pm; $12, kids $9, Fri 5–9pm $1; ℡617/426-6500, Ⓦwww.bostonchildrensmuseum.org; South Station **T**), comprises three floors of educational exhibits craftily designed to trick kids into learning about a huge array of topics, from musicology to the engineering of a humongous bubble. In 2007, building renovations expanded the museum's girth, creating more romp room and paving the way for a lovely Nature Walk and deck that opens out onto the Fort Point Channel.

Many exhibits here are also amusing for adults, like the "Japanese House" where you step into an authentic one-hundred-year-old silk merchant's home, or the ball launcher on the first floor, which enables young men and women of steel to propel a tennis ball three storeys up into the air. Before leaving, be sure to check out the Recycle Shop, where industrial leftovers are transformed into appealing craft fodder.

The museum also hosts fun evening events, such as "Movies on the Milk Bottle," where people picnic to films projected onto the bottle's cream-coloured exterior; check the museum's website for a full schedule of goings-on.

The Boston Tea Party

The first major act of rebellion preceding the Revolutionary War, the **Boston Tea Party** was far greater in significance than it was in duration. On December 16, 1773, a longstanding dispute between the British government and its colonial subjects, involving a tea tax, came to a dramatic head. At nightfall, a group of five thousand waited at the Old South Meeting House to hear the governor's pronouncement regarding three ships full of tea moored in Boston Harbor. After receiving word that the governor would not remove the ships, the civil throng converged on Griffin's Wharf. Around one hundred of them, some dressed in Indian garb, boarded the brigs and threw their cargo of tea overboard. The partiers disposed of 342 chests of tea, each weighing 360 pounds – enough to make 24 million cuppas, and worth more than $1 million by today's standards.

While it had the semblance of spontaneity, the event was in fact planned beforehand, and the mob was careful not to damage anything but the offending cargo. In any case, the "party" transformed protest into revolution. The ensuing British sanctions, colloquially referred to as the "Intolerable Acts," along with the colonists' continued resistance, further inflamed the tension between the Crown and its colonies, which eventually exploded at Lexington and Concord several months later (see p.211).

Boston Tea Party Ship

For many years, in the Fort Point Channel alongside the Congress Street Bridge, there was a replica of one of the three notorious ships that launched the **Boston Tea Party**. Unfortunately, the ship and its neighbouring museum (Ⓦwww .bostonteapartyship.com) were closed after the ship was hit by lightning in August 2001; at the time of writing, the museum was set to reopen in 2011. Spirited re-creations of the Tea Party will be held here once it's back on track, but don't be taken in: this is not the site of the actual event, which really took place on what is now dry land, near the intersection of Atlantic and Congress streets. There's a plaque at 470 Atlantic Ave that commemorates the Party with a lively, patriotic poem: "ne'er was mingled such a draught/in palace, hall, or arbor/as freeman brewed and tyrants quaffed/that night in Boston harbor." Bonus: the office building offers jaw-dropping skyline views via its fourteenth-floor **observation deck**, replete with binoculars and benches – simply check in with the security guard in the lobby (daily 10am–5pm; free). There are also clean, 24 hour toilets available.

Institute of Contemporary Art

Looking like a glamorous ice-cube perched above a chilly Boston Harbor, the glimmering facade of the **Institute of Contemporary Art** at 100 Northern Ave (Tues & Wed 10am–5pm, Thurs & Fri 10am–9pm, Sat & Sun 10–5pm, closed Mon; $15, kids free, Thurs 5–9pm free; free for families last Sat of the month; Ⓣ617/478-3100, Ⓦwww.icaboston.org; Courthouse Station **T**), puts on a show before you've even stepped inside.

The museum's permanent collection and gallery space, located on the fourth floor, features works by late twentieth- and twenty-first-century artists, including photography by former Bostonian Nan Goldin, sculptural textiles by Mona Hatoum and figures by Louise Bourgeois. One standout piece is Cornelia Parker's *Hanging Fire*, a beguiling, suspended sculpture comprised of floating charcoal shapes that the artist uncovered at an arson crime site. Ongoing temporary exhibitions, such as a recent display of Philip-Lorca diCorcia photographs (best-known for his surprisingly elegant pole-dancer portraits), are held in the adjacent rooms. Still, visitors may find the collection feels a bit sparse, particularly when you take into account the enormous, gorgeous space designed to house it all together; it's easy to come away with the sense that the best thing on display here is the building itself. Designed by architects Diller Scofidio + Renfro (best known for New York City's High Line park), the museum features a dramatic cantilever shape that extends eighty feet over the water's edge – this extended section functions as the "Founders Gallery," a meditative ledge where, if you look down from the gallery's wall of glass, you'll find yourself standing directly above a jellyfish-laden Boston Harbor.

Elsewhere, the museum houses an innovative theatre space, the glass walls of which (almost like magic) alter their transparency in order to accommodate for lighting; shows here range from modern dance performances to screenings of *The Matrix*. In summer, the expansive front deck plays host to live-music shows and dance nights; check the website for more information. The museum also frequently partners with the Harbor Islands to create very cool contemporary art installation projects amidst the Islands' pristine settings (see below)

Harpoon Brewery

In the outermost reaches of the Seaport District (a 40min walk from South Station) lies the former shipbuilding digs of the **Harpoon Brewery**, the third largest brewery in New England and the site of some fizzy weekend tours (Sat every half hour 11.30am–5pm, Sun hourly noon–3pm; 1hr; $5; free tastings Mon–Fri 4pm, Wed–Fri also 2pm; ⓣ1-888/HARPOON ext. 522, ⓦwww .harpoonbrewery.com; SL2 Silver Line **T** to "306 Northern Ave") Here, you'll coo over the brew's giant silos – said to hold 3800 gallons – and sample crunchy kernels of barley and malt (just don't chew on the pungent pieces of hops). The brewery's aromatic downstairs, where fermentation has taken a firm hold, is Homer Simpson paradise, and the Pavlovian response here ("must, drink, beer!") is killer. Thankfully, the tour's last half-hour is devoted to beer sampling – you can drink all you want (within reason), but just remember to bring along your over-21 ID. Tours are popular and tend to sell out – try to buy tickets early in the day. Take a peek at the website for details on Octoberfest and their other festivals. (For information on the Samuel Adams brewery tour in Jamaica Plain, see p.116).

The Harbor Islands

Extending across Massachusetts Bay from Salem south to Portsmouth, the thirty-four islands that make up the bucolic **Harbor Islands** served as strategic defence points during the American Revolution and Civil War. It took congressional assent to turn them into a national park, in 1996, with the result that six are now easily accessible by ferry from Long Wharf (a seventh, Little Brewster Island, has a ferry that leaves from Fan Pier). Even so, they're still lightly trafficked in comparison to most Boston sights, which makes them ideal getaways from the city centre, especially on a hot summer day, when their **beaches** and **hiking** trails will easily help you forget urban life altogether. Their wartime legacy has left many of the winding pathways and coastal shores dotted with intriguing fortress **ruins** and **lighthouses**, which makes for attractive scenery; the views of Boston from this distance are simply sublime as well.

The Harbor Islands have seen major renovations of late, including faster ferries, contemporary art installations (via a partnership with the ICA), and, most notably, the addition of **Spectacle Island** as an accessible spot. Spectacle has outgrown its murky past (it was formerly a horse rendering plant, then a city dump) to become an environmentally savvy green space. In cleaning up the island, engineers solved two civic headaches at once – disposing of the Big Dig's dirt (3.7 million cubic yards in all) and capping Spectacle's landfill with the project's excavated earth. The island now features a small lifeguarded beach, a snack bar, a green visitor's centre (complete with foul-smelling toilets and an intentional lack of trash cans) and pretty trails heading up its drumlins.

The most popular and best serviced of the islands is still the skimming-stone-shaped **George's Island**, a heavily used defensive outpost during the Civil War era; the remains of **Fort Warren** (April to mid-Oct daily dawn–dusk; free), a mid-nineteenth-century battle station, covers most of the island. Constructed from hand-hewn granite, and mostly used as a prison for captured Confederate soldiers, its musty barracks and extensive fortress walls are on the eerie side, while the parapets offer some stunning Downtown views. You'll get more out of a visit by taking a park-ranger tour (free), where you'll learn the legend of the Lady in Black – a prisoner's wife who was hanged while attempting to break her husband out of jail. Outside the fort, there are shady picnic benches and cobble beaches to explore. The island also hosts performances, be it jazz, children's theatre or a vintage baseball game; check ⓦ www.bostonislands.com for scheduling.

If you're interested in seeing one of the remaining Harbor Islands (outside of the easily accessed Spectacle), it's best to make a full day of it, as island hopping on the shuttle service is a little irregular. The densely wooded and sand-duned **Lovells** is a good bet, as it's home to vibrant tidepools and sand dunes near the remains of Fort Standish, an early-twentieth-century military base. The largest of all, the 134-acre **Peddocks**, is laced with hiking trails connecting the remains of Fort Andrews, a harbour defence used from 1904 to 1945, with a freshwater pond and wildlife sanctuary. Romantic **Bumpkin** was once the site of a children's hospital, whose ruins, along with the casements of an old stone farmhouse, lie along raspberry bush-fringed pathways. More berries grow on **Grape**, an ideal bird-watching spot.

Island bound

A quick fifteen-minute ride connects Long Wharf with central **George's Island** or **Spectacle Island** (May to mid-June & Oct daily on the hour 9am–4pm; late June to Aug Mon–Thurs on the hour 9am–5pm, Fri, Sat & Sun every half hour 9am–6pm; call to confirm times; $14, kids $8; ☏617/223-8666, ⓦ www.bostonislands.com; Aquarium **T**); water taxis ($3) shuttle visitors to the other four islands from these two. Aside from George's and Spectacle, the more remote islands lack a freshwater source, so be sure to bring **bottled water**; you should also consider packing a picnic lunch (best arranged through nearby *Sel de la Terre*; see p.151), though the former two islands offer low-key **snackbars**. You could also forage for **berries** on **Grape** and **Bumpkin** islands. In the interest of preserving island ecology, no pets, bicycles or rollerblades are allowed. You can **camp** for a nominal fee (around $15 a night) on three of the islands (Lovells, Bumpkin and Grape; May to mid-Oct; ☏1-877/422-6762); you'll need to bring your own supplies. In all cases, good walking shoes are required, as most of the pathways consist of dirt roads. The Harbor Islands **information** kiosk, at the foot of Long Wharf, keeps a detailed shuttle **schedule** and stocks excellent **maps**. Visit ⓦ www.bostonislands.com and www.nps.gov/boha for more information.

The most intriguing of the islands is the one furthest out at sea: **Little Brewster Island**. It's home to the 1783 Boston Light, which is both the oldest lighthouse in the country and the only one that still has a Coast Guard-staffed keeper on site. Excellent tours to Little Brewster run from Fan Pier by the National Park Service (late June to mid-Oct Sat 10am; 3hr, bring lunch; $48, kids $40; ☎617/223-8666, Ⓦwww.bostonislands.com; South Station **T**); after meeting the keeper you can traverse the lighthouse's 76 steps (and two ladders) to glimpse its top-notch views. The NPS also runs a new "Three Lighthouse Tour", which pays a visit to Little Brewster and has an accompanying sail past the lights of Long Island and The Graves (late June to mid-Oct Thurs–Sun; $38, kids $19; same details).

2

The North End

H emmed in nearly all around by Boston Harbor, the small, densely populated **North End** is Boston's Little Italy. Here, narrow streets are chock-a-block with Italian bakeries and restaurants and hold some of Boston's most storied sights. And despite the fact that the aboveground highway that once separated the area from downtown has been removed (replaced by the diverting Rose Kennedy Greenway), the area still has a bit of a detached feeling, making it all the more charming.

Here, must-see sights like **Old North Church**, **Copp's Hill Burying Ground** and the **Paul Revere House** can be covered in half a day; just make sure you save time to experience the vibrant cafés, bakeries, *trattorias* and food shops for which the neighbourhood is known. The area's Italian flavour is particularly pronounced during its numerous annual summer **festas** (see Chapter 19), when members of private charity clubs march figurines of their patron saints (usually the same as those of their home towns in Italy) through the streets. The processions, complete with marching bands, stop every few feet to let people pin dollar bills to streamers attached to the effigies.

In addition to the Italian cultural scene, the North End has more recently become known for its sense of style, owing to a number of the city's most put-together clothing and home furnishing boutiques opening their doors here (see Chapter 16). If shopping is your thing, keep an eye out for the tempting stores interspersed throughout the neighbourhood (particularly *Twilight*, p.188, and *Acquire*, p.193).

Some history

In colonial times, the North End was actually a peninsula. Because it was separated from Boston by a tidal creek, a series of short bridges was built to the main part of town. This physical separation bred antagonism, culminating every November 5 in **Pope's Day**, when North Enders and Bostonians on the "other side" paraded effigies of the Pope through their neighbourhoods to a standoff on Boston Common, where the competing groups attempted to capture each other's pontiff. If the North Enders won, they would burn their rival's effigy atop Copp's Hill.

Spiritually, the community was dominated by **Increase Mather**, who ministered at the Old North Congregational Church and whose 1689 "*Memorable Providences, Relating to Witchcraft and Possessions*" probably fuelled the hysteria that led to the Salem Witch Trials (see p.216). But the North End was also the residence of choice for the wealthy merchant class; Massachusetts Bay Colony governors Hutchinson and Phips owned spacious homes here. Following the Revolutionary War, however, many British loyalists fled to Nova Scotia; soon after, the North End became a magnet for free blacks known as the **New Guinea Community**, as well as immigrant groups.

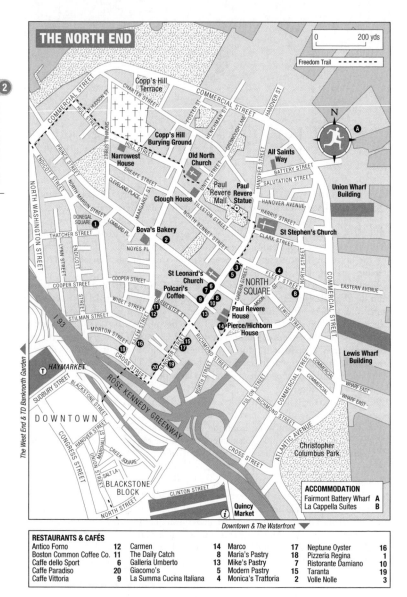

THE NORTH END

Copp's Hill
Terrace

COMMERCIAL STREET

Copp's Hill
Burying Ground

Narrowest
House

Old North
Church

All Saints
Way

Paul
Revere
Mall

Paul
Revere
Statue

Clough House

Union Wharf
Building

St Stephen's Church

Bova's Bakery

St Leonard's
Church

NORTH
SQUARE

Polcari's
Coffee

Paul Revere
House

Pierce/Hichborn
House

Lewis Wharf
Building

HAYMARKET

ROSE KENNEDY GREENWAY

DOWNTOWN

BLACKSTONE
BLOCK

Christopher
Columbus Park

Quincy
Market

ACCOMMODATION
Fairmont Battery Wharf   A
La Cappella Suites   B

Downtown & The Waterfront ▼

RESTAURANTS & CAFÉS							
Antico Forno	12	Carmen	14	Marco	17	Neptune Oyster	16
Boston Common Coffee Co.	11	The Daily Catch	8	Maria's Pastry	18	Pizzeria Regina	1
Caffe dello Sport	6	Galleria Umberto	13	Mike's Pastry	7	Ristorante Damiano	10
Caffe Paradiso	20	Giacomo's	5	Modern Pastry	15	Taranta	19
Caffe Vittoria	9	La Summa Cucina Italiana	4	Monica's Trattoria	2	Volle Nolle	3

The **Irish** were the first immigrants to flock to the area, putting down roots from 1840 on (John F. Fitzgerald, JFK's grandfather and mayor of Boston, was born on Ferry Street in 1863, and the late president's mother, Rose, on nearby Garden Court in 1890). With the onset of the potato famine in 1845, the trickle became a flood – in 1847 alone, some 13,000 new arrivals settled here. Employment opportunities for the Irish were limited, however: "No Irish Need Apply" signs were common, and a decade after their arrival the community began to disperse throughout the Greater Boston area. The Irish were succeeded in the North End by Eastern European Jews, who were in turn edged out by **southern Italians** in the early twentieth century. The Italians have, for the most part, stayed put.

Though **landfill**, which began in the 1820s, temporarily ended the district's physical isolation, it became a place apart once more when the elevated I-93 (or John Fitzgerald Expressway) tore through the city in 1954. But Boston's massive urban regeneration through the Big Dig means that, as with the Waterfront, the North End has again been rejoined with the city, and what was once an unseemly highway is now a pleasant greenway park. In recent years, young professionals have been overtaking the North End's waterfront and are also making inroads into the rehabilitated tenements. Though you can still see laundry dangling from upper-storey windows and grandmothers chattering in Italian, it's feared that the neighbourhood may lose its distinctively Italian character.

Hanover Street

Hanover Street has long been the main connection between the North End and the rest of Boston, and it is along here – and the small streets like Parmenter and Richmond (actually a continuation of each other on either side of Hanover) – that many of the area's *trattorias* and cafés are located. It's also where you'll find a distinctly European flavour: although there are a handful of chain stores in the neighbourhood, the majority of businesses remain refreshingly independent, such as the ever-popular *Mike's Pastry*, at no. 300 (see p.152). The quieter side of the neighbourhood reasserts itself on the short blocks north of the Paul Revere Mall (really a brick-laden park), where, though the restaurants are still filled with diners, the roads are peacefully uncrowded.

Continue north on Hanover to Battery Street for a look at local landmark "All Saints Way", a miniature devotional alleyway squeezed in between nos. 4 and 8. Folksy and sweet, it's decked out with images of saints and watched over by peaceful cherubim.

Paul Revere House and around

The little triangular wedge of cobblestones and gaslights known as **North Square**, one block east of Hanover between Prince and Richmond streets, is one of the most historic and attractive pockets of Boston. Here the eateries recede in deference to the **Paul Revere House**, the oldest residential address downtown, at 19 North Square (mid-April to Oct daily 9.30am–5.15pm; Nov to mid-April daily 9.30–4.15pm, Jan, Feb & March closed Mon; $3.50; ☎617/523-2338, ⓦwww.paulrevere house.org). A North Ender for most of his life, Revere lived here from 1770 to 1800 (except for much of 1775, when he hid out from the British in Watertown). Before being restored to its seventeenth-century appearance in 1908, the small Tudor-style, post-and-beam structure, which dates from about 1680, had served in turn as a grocery store, tenement and cigar factory. It stands on what once was the site of the considerably grander home of Puritan heavyweight Increase Mather (father of Cotton), which burned down in the Great Fire of 1676.

The building is more impressive for its longevity than its appearance, but the third-storey overhang and leaded windows do provide quite a contrast to the red-brick buildings around it. Examples of Revere's self-made silverware upstairs

Paul Revere

It wasn't until decades after his death that **Paul Revere** achieved fame for his nighttime journey to Lexington to warn John Hancock and Sam Adams of the impending British march inland to seize colonial munitions. When he did, it was thanks to a fanciful 1860 poem by Henry Wadsworth Longfellow called *Paul Revere's Ride*. Its opening line, "Listen, my children, and you shall hear/Of the midnight ride of Paul Revere," is perhaps as familiar to New England schoolchildren as the Pledge of Allegiance, but during his lifetime, this jack-of-all-trades was principally known for his abilities as a **silversmith** (with a side business in false teeth) and a **propagandist** for the patriot cause – not so much as a legendary messenger.

Revere's original engraving of the Boston Massacre, on display in the Old State House (see p.47), did much to turn public opinion against the Tories, and he even went so far as to stage an exhibition of more patriotic prints at his North End home on the first anniversary of the incident. During the Revolution, Revere engraved the Massachusetts currency, though a more profitable venture was his post-war bell-and-cannon foundry in Canton, located just south of Boston. After siring a brood of sixteen, he died in 1818 at the age of 83, and rests among his Revolutionary peers in the Old Granary Burying Ground (see p.43).

merit a look, as do the museum's small but evocative rotating exhibits, which illuminate topics such as the mythologizing of Revere's famed horseback ride. The house's new visitor centre is currently under construction; it's hoped to open by 2013 with expanded exhibits, an elevator and (at long last) toilets.

The Pierce/Hichborn House and North Street

A small courtyard, the focus of which is a glass-encased 900-pound bell cast by Revere, separates the Paul Revere House from the **Pierce/Hichborn House** (tours by appointment only; $2; call for times; ☎617/523-2338). A simple Georgian-style residence – and the oldest brick house in Boston – it was built in 1711 by glazier Moses Pierce, and later owned by Paul Revere's shipbuilding cousin, Nathaniel Hichborn, who was considerably wealthier than his more famous relative. Although you won't be dazzled by its interior, the house holds some noteworthy architectural details, including its original staircase and two painted fireplaces, all dating to the early 1700s. Also worth noting are **Baker's Alley**, which runs between the Pierce/Hichborn House and the *Limoncello* restaurant, as well as the vintage brick alleyway just across the street – both prime examples of how narrow the surrounding streets would have been in colonial times.

South from North Square (on which the Revere House and the Pierce/Hichborn House are located), the adjacent **North Street** was somewhat of a red-light district in the early nineteenth century, but today it's merely a pretty residential side street. Its one distinguishing feature, the **oldest sign** in Boston, is affixed to the third floor of the building at the corner of Richmond Street (above *Cirace's* liquor store) – the initials "WTS" refer to Susanna Wadsworth and Timothy Wadsworth, owners of the *Red Lion Inn* that stood here in 1694.

St Stephen's Church and Paul Revere Mall

Further north, at Hanover's intersection with Clark Street, sits the striking, three-storey, recessed-brick arch entrance to **St Stephen's Church**. The church was built on this site in 1714 and replaced by a Charles Bulfinch design in 1804. A fire ravaged the building in 1929, but in 1964 it was restored according to Bulfinch's plan; its interior is a great example of the architect's austere Federal style. A more recent claim to fame is that the funeral for the Kennedy family matriarch, Rose Kennedy, was held in the understated apse, in 1995 (her baptism also took place here, 104 years prior).

Originally called New North Church, St Stephen's received its present-day name in 1862, in order to keep up with the increasingly Catholic population of the North End. Though it seems firmly planted today, the whole building was actually moved back sixteen feet when Hanover Street was widened in 1870.

Just across Hanover, the famous bronze **statue** of Paul Revere astride his borrowed horse marks the edge of the **Paul Revere Mall**, a tree-lined, red-brick park also known as the Prado. This relaxed open space was carved out of a chunk of apartment blocks in 1933 and runs back to tiny **Unity Street** – home of the small 1712 red-brick **Clough House**, at no. 21, a private residence built by the mason who helped lay the brick of nearby Old North Church.

Old North Church

Few places in Boston have as emblematic a quality as the simple yet noble **Old North Church** at 193 Salem St (Jan & Feb Tues–Sun 10am–4pm; daily: March–May 9am–5pm; June–Oct 9am–6pm; Nov & Dec 10am–5pm; free; ☎617/523-6676; Ⓦwww.oldnorth.com), rising unobstructed above the uniform blocks of the surrounding red-brick apartments. Built in 1723, it's the oldest church building in Boston, easily recognized by its gleaming 191-foot **steeple**. The weathervane perched on top is the colonial original, though the steeple itself is a replica – hurricanes toppled both its first, in 1804, and its replacement, in 1954.

It was a pair of lanterns that secured the structure's place in history, though. The church sexton, Robert Newman, is said to have hung both of them inside ("One if by land, two if by 'sea'") on the night of April 18, 1775, to signal the movement of British forces from Boston Common. The signal was intended for colonial militia in Charlestown, just in case Paul Revere was unsuccessful in his crossing of the Charles River. Revere had already learned of the impending British advance and was riding to Lexington by the time the lanterns were in place – he simply needed Newman's help to alert Charlestown in case his mission was thwarted. As it turned out, both Revere and fellow rider William Dawes were detained by British patrols; Dr Samuel Prescott, the evening's third rider (and the one least known to history), is the only one who made it all the way to Concord.

The **interior** of the church is spotlessly white and well lit, thanks to the Palladian windows behind the pulpit. Other details include twelve bricks, set into the vestibule wall, from a prison cell in Boston, England, where an early group of Pilgrims were incarcerated, and the four seventeenth-century cherubim near the organ that were looted from a French vessel. In addition, churchgoers can check their watches by the **clock** at the rear; made in 1726, it's the oldest one still ticking in an American public building. Have a wander, too, among the high box pews: no. 62 belonged to General Thomas Gage, commander-in-chief of the British army in North America, while descendants of Paul Revere still lay claim to no. 54. Beneath your feet, the timber on which the pews rest is supported by 37 basement-level brick crypts; one of the 1,100 bodies encased therein is that of John Pitcairn, the British major killed in the Battle of Bunker Hill. His remains were tagged for Westminster Abbey, but they never made it home to England. The eight bells inside the belfry – open to the public during summer-only **tours** ($8 adults, $5 kids) – were the first cast for the British Empire in North America and have since tolled the death of every US president.

Some of Old North's greatest charms are actually outside the church itself, notably the diminutive **Washington Memorial Garden**, the brick walls of which are bedecked with commemorative plaques honouring past church members, and the inviting **Eighteenth-Century Garden**, its terraces packed with lilies and roses, as well as some curious umbrella-shaped flowers known, appropriately, as archangels.

Copp's Hill Burying Ground and Copp's Hill Terrace

Up Hull Street from Old North Church, **Copp's Hill Burying Ground** (daily dawn–dusk) displays eerily tilting slate tombstones, stunning views and the graves of some significant sons of the North End. The first burial here, on the highest ground in the North End, took place in 1659. Among the 10,000 interred are nearly 1000 men from the "New Guinea Community," a colonial enclave of free blacks at the foot of the hill. One such notable was Prince Hall, who founded the first Black Masons lodge and played an important role in the 1783 act that abolished slavery in Massachusetts. The most famous gravesite here is that of the **Mather family**, just inside the wrought-iron gates on the northern Charter Street side. Increase Mather and his son Cotton – the latter a Salem Witch Trial witness for the prosecution – were big players in Boston's early days of Puritan theocracy, a fact not at all reflected in the rather diminutive, if appropriately plain, brick vault tomb. As for other noteworthy graves, **Robert Newman**, who hung Paul Revere's lanterns in Old North Church, is buried near the western rim of the plot, as is **Edmund Hartt**, the builder of the famous ship the USS *Constitution* ("Old Ironsides"; see p.72).

You'll notice, too, that some gravestones have significant chunks missing – a consequence of British soldiers using them for target practice during the 1775 Siege of Boston. The grave of one Captain Daniel Malcolm bears particularly strong evidence of this: three musketball marks scar his epitaph, which hails him as a "true son of Liberty" and an "Enemy of oppression" (gravestones here are a bit of a jumble; to find Malcolm or to locate other specific names, consult the map at the entranceway). The burying ground suffered further damages in the mid-nineteenth century when a number of gravestones were stolen and (surprisingly enough) used as baking stones, making it a real possibility that you would find someone's epitaph inscribed onto your morning loaf of bread. As you exit the burying ground, keep an eye out for the **narrowest house** in Boston, at 44 Hull St. It really *is* narrow – 10ft wide – but that's about it, as it's a private residence and you can't go in.

The granite **Copp's Hill Terrace**, on Charter Street across from the burial ground's northern side, was the place from which British cannon bombarded Charlestown during the Battle of Bunker Hill. On a winter day in 1919, a 2.3-million-gallon steel storage tank of molasses – used in the production of alcoholic beverages – exploded nearby, creating a syrupy tidal wave 30ft high that engulfed entire buildings and drowned 21 people along with a score of horses. Old North Enders – the kind you'll see playing bocce in the little park at the bottom of the terrace – claim you can still catch a whiff of the stuff on an exceptionally hot day.

Salem and Prince streets

While Old North Church is certainly **Salem Street's** star attraction, the lower blocks to the south between Prince and Cross streets are arguably the North End's most colourful thoroughfare. The actual street – whose name is possibly a bastardization of "Shalom Street," as it was known to the earlier Eastern European Jewish settlers – is so narrow that the red-brick buildings seem to lean into one another, and light traffic makes it a common practice to walk right down the middle of the road. Travelling south, an agreeable onslaught of Italian grocers, aromatic *pasticcerias* and cafés begins rather abruptly at Salem's intersection with Prince Street, starting with *Bova's Bakery* at no. 134 (see p.190). Just a couple of blocks up, the intersection of Salem and Parmenter Streets is the unofficial heart of the North End; locals typically while away the day along the pavement here on folding chairs brought from home. This intersection also finds *Polcari's Coffee* (p.191), a North End landmark and perhaps the planet's best coffee bean and spice vendor. On hot days, a serving of their $1.50 lemon slush – scooped into paper cups from an old barrel at the front door – is a must. The Neapolitan bustle ends at Cross Street; if you continue on, you'll pass the sunbathers and fountain-jumpers of the Rose Kennedy Greenway and then on to the Faneuil Hall Marketplace and Government Center in Downtown.

Serpentine **Prince Street**, a narrow road cutting through the centre of the North End on an east–west axis, is also lined with *salumerias* and restaurants, but tends to be more social. At the corner of Hanover Street and parallel to Prince Street, **St Leonard's Church** was the first Italian-Catholic church in New England when it was founded in 1873. The ornate interior is a marked contrast to Boston's stark Protestant churches, while in front the so-called "Peace Garden" has a hodgepodge design that unfortunately does not inspire tranquillity.

Charlestown

A cross Boston Harbor from the North End, historic Charlestown (fondly called "the Chuck" by residents), is a very pretty, quietly affluent neighbourhood that stands considerably isolated from the city, despite its annexation more than a century ago. Most visitors only make it over this way for the historic frigate, the **USS Constitution** (if at all), which is a shame, because the neighbourhood's narrow, hilly byways, lined with antique gaslights and Colonial- and Federal-style rowhouses, make for pleasant exploration and offer great views of Boston.

There are two main ways to get to **Charlestown**: one is to take the **T** to North Station and walk over the Charlestown Bridge – which affords exhilarating views of both Boston Harbor and the Zakim Bridge. Equally fun, and the better choice on a hot day, is to take the short ferry trip ($1.70) from the waterfront's Long Wharf, which deposits you on the eastern outskirts of Charlestown Navy Yard, where the area's big draw, the USS *Constitution*, is berthed.

Just a few minutes' walk northwest from the Navy Yard, Charlestown's centre, **City Square**, is the point from which most notable streets in the area radiate. Directly north is the neighbourhood's other major sight, the **Bunker Hill Monument**, the northern terminus of the Freedom Trail, which runs across the Charlestown Bridge from the North End. Otherwise, the rest of the district is simply a graceful tree-lined neighbourhood, although it gets a bit dodgier on its outskirts (not a concern if you stick to the USS *Constitution* and the monument). While most people just spend an afternoon here, the area's romantic environs and restaurants, such as the *Navy Yard Bistro and Wine Bar* (see p.153), may tempt visitors back for the evening.

Some history

The earliest **Puritan settlers** had high hopes for developing Charlestown when they arrived in 1629, but an unsuitable water supply pushed them over to the Shawmut Peninsula, which they promptly renamed Boston. Charlestown grew slowly after that, and had to be completely rebuilt after the British burned it down in 1775; almost as many houses were lost in that blaze as had been torched in the entire Revolutionary War.

The mid-1800s witnessed the arrival of the so-called "lace-curtain Irish" (those who were somewhat better off than their East Boston brethren), and the district remains an **Irish** one at heart. The long-time locals, known as "townies," have acquired a reputation for being standoffish, due to such episodes as their resistance to school desegregation in the 1970s, but relations have vastly improved since then. The neighbourhood was once a haven for criminals, too: if a bank was robbed in Boston, the story goes, police would simply wait on the Charlestown

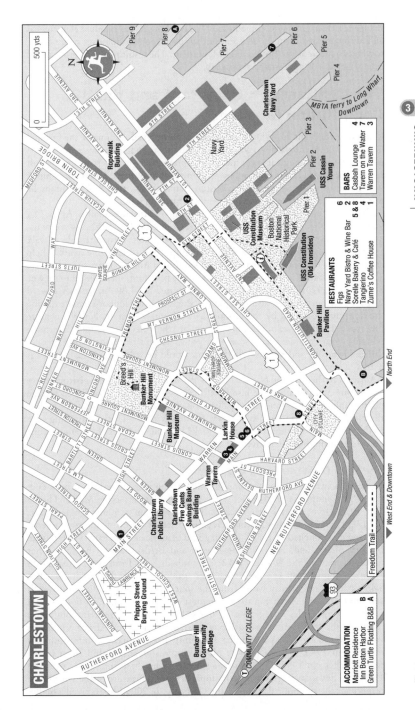

CHARLESTOWN

ACCOMMODATION
Marriott Residence
Inn Boston Harbor   B
Green Turtle Floating B&B   A

RESTAURANTS
Figs   6
Navy Yard Bistro & Wine Bar 2
Sorelle Bakery & Café   5 & 8
Tangierino   5 & 4
Zume's Coffee House   1

BARS
Casbah Lounge   4
Tavern on the Water   7
Warren Tavern   3

▶ West End & Downtown
▶ North End

Freedom Trail ------

500 yds

71

Bridge for their quarry to come home. Today, though, the criminal element has all but disappeared from the area since urban professionals took over many of the rowhouses south of the Bunker Hill Monument. The resulting mood is a tranquil mix of amiable if understated prosperity.

The Charlestown Navy Yard and the USS Constitution Museum

Opened in 1800, the sprawling **Charlestown Navy Yard** was one of the first and busiest US naval shipyards – riveting together an astounding 46 destroyer escorts in 1943 alone – though it owes most of its present-day liveliness to its grandest tenant, the frigate USS *Constitution* at Constitution Wharf. Today, the ship is well cared for by the Navy and the Boston National Historical Park, an umbrella association that preserves nationally significant Boston sights.

It's a good idea to visit the **USS *Constitution* Museum** (daily: April–Oct 9am–6pm; Nov–March 10am–5pm; free; ☎617/426-1812, ⊚www.uss constitutionmuseum.org), located in a substantial granite structure a short walk from the *Constitution*, before you board the ship itself, as its affable exhibits help contextualize the vessel and her unparalleled role in American maritime history. The history of the *Constitution* is covered on the first floor, including the story of how, in the 1920s, US schoolchildren contributed $154,000 in pennies toward its preservation; you can also glimpse the ship's original logbooks and examine the drafting tools used by the *Constitution's* designer. Upstairs is perhaps more fun, with hands-on exhibits putting you in the role of a sailor: determine whether your comrades have scurvy or gout, attempt to balance yourself on a shifting footrope and ponder whether you would be willing to eat a biscuit "as hard as a brick."

Adjacent to the ship, the National Park Service runs a worthy new **visitor centre** (daily 9am–5pm) detailing the history of the Navy Yard. Here, you'll find vintage photographs as well as super-sized pallets of nautical treasures and artefacts, such as the pleasingly named "Warner-Swaysey Twister-Winder." Used for twisting rope in the 1950s, the machine's shape – it looks like one of Madonna's famous cone bras – seems almost provocative.

The USS Constitution ("Old Ironsides")

As tall as a twenty-storey building and 304ft long from bowsprit to back end, the USS *Constitution* (April–Oct Tues–Sun 10am–6pm; Nov–March Thurs–Sun 10am–4pm; free; lower deck only accessible on a 30min guided tour; ☎617/242-5601; ⊚www.history.navy.mil/ussconstitution) is impressive from any angle. Launched in 1797 to safeguard American merchant vessels from Barbary pirates and, later on, the French and British navies, she earned her nickname during the War of 1812; cannonballs fired from the British HMS *Guerrière* bounced off the hull (the "iron" sides were actually hewn from live oak, a particularly sturdy wood from the southeastern US), leading to the first and most dramatic American naval conquest of that war. The *Constitution* went on to win 33 battles – never losing one – before she was retired from active service in the 1830s; stints as flagship with Mediterranean and African squadrons were followed by use as a training ship until her full naval commission was returned in 1940, making her the oldest commissioned warship afloat in the world. When, in 1997, the *Constitution* went on her first unassisted voyage in 116 years, news coverage was international in scale, a measure of the worldwide respect for the symbolic flagship of the US Navy. In 2009, she received a higher honour when she was designated America's "Ship of State", a federal appointment enabling her to function as a legislative site for the signing of maritime treaties and hosting of heads of state.

Though authentic enough in appearance, the *Constitution* has certainly taken its hits (roughly 85 percent of the ship has been reconstructed). Even after extensive renovations, Old Ironsides is still too frail to support sails for extended periods of time, and only makes around six to eight small trips a year (including her annual Fourth of July turnarounds in Boston Harbor). There's often a wait to visit the ship, especially in the summer, and access has been further slowed by increased security checks, but it's nonetheless worth the wait to get a close-up view of the elaborate rigging that can support some three dozen sails totalling almost an acre in area.

After ambling about the main deck, you can scuttle (with a guide) down nearly vertical stairways to the lower deck, where there's an impressive array of cannons, many of them christened with fun fighting names like Raging Eagle or Jumping Billy. All of the ship's 54 cannon are actually replicas, cast in 1928 – when Old Ironsides ceased to be a fighting vessel, its munitions were removed for use in battle-worthy ships – but two functional models face downtown from the bow of the main deck. They still get a daily workout, too, shooting off explosive powder to mark flag-raising and -lowering (8am & dusk, respectively); were they to fire the 24lb balls for which they were originally outfitted, they'd topple the Custom House Tower across the bay in downtown Boston.

The rest of the Navy Yard

Southeast of Old Ironsides lies the arresting hulk of a vessel from a strikingly different era – the powder-grey World War II destroyer **USS Cassin Young** (daily 10am–4pm; free; ☎617/242-5601). While several similar destroyers were made in Charlestown, the *Cassin Young* was built in San Pedro, California, and served primarily in the Atlantic and Mediterranean before eventually being transferred to the National Park Service in Boston for use as a museum ship in 1978. You can rumble around the expansive main deck's depth chargers and tiny infirmary, and attempt your best *Titanic* impression from the bow of the ship (the moment slightly less romantic when you realize you're in the crosshairs of a menacing-looking anti-aircraft gun). The cramped chambers below – the captain's rooms and the ship's barber shop, among them – can be inspected by taking a thirty-minute guided **tour** (11am, 2pm & 3pm; must be over 4ft tall, call to confirm times and arrive 10min early to secure a ticket; free).

At the northern perimeter of the navy yard is the **Ropewalk Building**. From 1837 to the mid-1950s, "ropewalkers" made nearly every single strand of rope used by the US Navy – over 4 million lbs in 1942 alone – in this narrow, quarter-mile-long granite building, the only one of its kind still standing in the country; unfortunately it's not open to the public.

City Square and around

Charlestown's centre is a few minutes' walk northwest of the Navy Yard. At the end of a scenic, harbourfront walk is **City Square**, a small, grassy park that, notably, preserves at its centre the outline of the first public building erected by the Massachusetts Bay Colony, a residence and civic meeting place built for governor John Winthrop in 1629; razed by fire during the battle of Bunker Hill in 1775, its foundation was re-discovered during the Big Dig archeological work of the 1980s. The square is anchored at its northern tip by *Olives*, one of Boston's swankiest restaurants, and the 1913 yellow-brick three-storey Charlestown Municipal Building on its east side.

Main, Devens and Cordis streets

Main Street extends north from the square; at no. 55 you'll find the wooden 1795 house of **Deacon John Larkin**, who lent Paul Revere his horse for his famous ride to Lexington, and never got it back. You can't go inside, so press on to the quaint **Warren Tavern**, at no. 105, a small three-storey wooden structure. Both Larkin's house and the Warren Tavern were built soon after the British burned Charlestown in the Battle of Bunker Hill. The tavern, named for doctor Joseph Warren, personal physician to the Adams family (as in President John Adams) before he was killed in the Battle of Bunker Hill, still functions as a popular watering hole today (see Chapter 12).

West of the tavern, the monumental 1876 **Charlestown Five Cents Savings Bank Building**, at 1 Thompson Square, boasts a steep mansard roof, Victorian Gothic ornamentation and a 1000lb clock; the modest external vault alarm belonging to its original tenants still protrudes from the eastern wall. A good ten minutes' walk further west on Main (to Phipps Street) takes you to the **Phipps Street Burying Ground**, dating from 1630, which has an unusual layout allegedly corresponding to that of Charlestown itself, and quirky epitaphs like that of Prince Bradstreet, memorialized as "an honest man of color." Unfortunately, because it's a Revolutionary War-era burying ground, it's usually locked; call the nice folks at Boston Parks & Recreation (generally Mon–Fri 9am–1.30pm; ☎617/635-7361) a day in advance and they'll open it up for you.

The Battle of Bunker Hill

The Revolutionary War was at its bloodiest on the hot June day in 1775 when British and colonial forces clashed in Charlestown. In the wake of the battles at Lexington and Concord two months before, the British had assumed full control of Boston, while the patriots had the upper hand in the surrounding countryside. The British, under the command of generals Thomas Gage, William Howe and "Gentleman Johnny" Burgoyne, intended to sweep the area clean of "rebellious rascals." Colonials intercepted the plans and moved to fortify **Bunker Hill**, the dominant hill in Charlestown. However, when Colonel William Prescott arrived on the scene, he chose to occupy **Breed's Hill** instead, either due to a mix-up – the two hills were often confused on colonial-era maps – or tactical foresight, based on the proximity of Breed's Hill to the harbour. Whatever the motivation, more than a thousand citizen-soldiers arrived during the night of June 16, 1775, and fortified the hill with a 160ft-long earthen redoubt by morning.

Spotting the Yankee fort, the Redcoats, each carrying 125lbs of food and supplies on their backs, rowed across the harbour to take the rebel-held town. On the patriots' side, Colonel Prescott had issued the celebrated order that his troops not fire "'till you see the whites of their eyes," so as not to waste their limited store of gunpowder. When the enemy's approach was deemed near enough, the patriots opened fire; though vastly outnumbered, they successfully repelled two full-fledged assaults, the even rows of under-prepared and overburdened Redcoats making easy targets. Some British units lost more than ninety percent of their men, and the few officers that survived had to push their troops forward with their swords to make them fight on. By the third British assault, the Redcoats had shed their gear, reinforcements had arrived, and the colonial's supply of gunpowder was dwindling – as were their chances of clinching victory. The rebels continued to fight with stones and musket butts; meanwhile, British cannon fire from Copp's Hill in the North End was turning Charlestown into an inferno. Despite their eventual loss, the patriots were invigorated by their strong showing, and the British, who had lost nearly half of their men in the battle, became convinced that victory over the determined rebels would only be possible with a much larger army.

Retrace your steps to the Warren Tavern and head down crooked **Devens Street** to the south (called Crooked Lane in 1640) and **Cordis Street** to the north, which are packed with historic, private houses, many of which are lovely to look at, though they unfortunately don't offer anything in the way of tours.

Monument Avenue and Winthrop Square

North from Main Street toward the Bunker Hill Monument, the red-brick townhouses along **Monument Avenue** are some of Boston's most exclusive residences, and strolling past the medley of Federal and Revival structures en route to the monument makes for scenic meandering. Nearby along Winthrop Street, **Winthrop Square** (known as the "Training Field" to residents) is Charlestown's unofficial common; the prim rowhouses overlooking it form another upscale enclave. Appropriately enough, considering its proximity to Bunker Hill, the common started out as a military training field; a series of bronze tablets at its northeastern edge list the men killed just up the slope in the Battle of Bunker Hill.

The Bunker Hill Monument

Commemorating the Battle of Bunker Hill is the **Bunker Hill Monument** (daily: July & Aug 9am–5.30pm; rest of year 9am–4.30pm; free; ☎617/242-5641), a grey, dagger-like obelisk visible from just about anywhere in Charlestown, confusingly positioned atop a butte known as Breed's Hill (see box opposite). It was here that the New England militia positioned themselves on the night of June 16, 1775, to wage what was ultimately a losing battle – despite its recasting by US historians as a great moral victory in the fight for independence. The obelisk is notable for being both the country's first monument funded entirely by public donations, and the first to popularize the dagger-like style epitomized by the Washington Monument in DC. The tower is centrally positioned in **Monument Square** and fronted by a strident, sword-bearing statue of Colonel William Prescott, who commanded the colonial troops; inside, 294 steps ascend to the top of the 221ft granite shaft. Hardy climbers will be rewarded with sweeping views of Boston, the harbour, surrounding towns and, to the northwest, the stone spire of the **St Francis de Sales Church**, which stands atop the real Bunker Hill. Afterwards, you can picnic in the grassy park encircling the monument, a favourite local sunbathing spot.

A new three-storey **museum**, housed in the quaint former Charlestown library at the base of the monument (daily: July & Aug 9am–6pm; rest of year 9am–5pm; free) offers appealing exhibits on the battle, the history of Charlestown and some cool ephemera, such as a British drum and two cannonballs from the conflict, and the 1825 competition drawings submitted to determine the monument's design. There is also a hair-raising account of the events of August 11, 1834, when an anti-immigrant mob set fire to Charlestown's Ursuline Convent. Convinced the Irish-American convent was a cover for "horrid crimes," the desecrators went so far as to destroy its altar and mausoleum, pulling the remains of deceased nuns out of their coffins and scattering them about.

4

Beacon Hill and the West End

No visit to Boston would be complete without an afternoon spent strolling around delightful **Beacon Hill**, a dignified stack of red brick rising over the north side of Boston Common. This is the Boston of wealth and privilege, one-time home to numerous historical and literary figures – including John Hancock, John Quincy Adams, Louisa May Alcott, Oliver Wendell Holmes and Nathaniel Hawthorne – and still the address of choice for the city's elite. And, looking around, it's not hard to fathom why. The narrow, hilly byways are edged with brick, lit with **gas lamps** and lined with quaint, nineteenth-century **townhouses**, all part of a historic preservation that prohibits architectural alterations that tamper with the neighbourhood's genteel character.

It was not always this way. In colonial times, Beacon Hill was the most prominent of three peaks, known as the Trimountain, which formed Boston's geological backbone. The sunny south slope was settled by the city's political and economic powers, while the north slope was traditionally closer in spirit to the **West End**, a tumbledown port district populated by maritime tradesmen and sailor's boarding houses; indeed, the north slope was home to so much salacious activity, that outraged Brahmins – Beacon Hill's moneyed elite – termed it "Mount Whoredom."

By the end of the twentieth century, this social divide was largely eradicated. Both sides of the Hill, in fact, have much to offer: on the south slope, there's the grandiose **Massachusetts State House**, residences of past and present luminaries, and attractive boulevards like **Charles Street** and **Beacon Street** (the former is Beacon Hill's main thoroughfare, and full of boutiques, antique shops and cafés; the latter is snugly crowded with prim townhouses). The north slope is home to a wealth of African-American historical sites (owing to the vibrant free black community that lived here in the nineteenth century), as well as the first-rate **Black Heritage Trail** (see box, p.80), a walking tour that explores this community's compelling history, taking in the **African Meeting House** and the stellar **Robert Gould Shaw/54th Regiment Memorial**. Whichever sights you choose to explore, bear in mind that streets here are often uneven, full of cul-de-sacs and at times quite hilly; lovely to see, they're best enjoyed with comfortable shoes and a map.

Beacon Street

Running along the south slope of Beacon Hill above Boston Common, **Beacon Street** was described as Boston's "sunny street for the sifted few" by Oliver Wendell

Holmes in the late-nineteenth century. This lofty character remains today: a row of stately brick townhouses, fronted by ornate iron grillwork, presides regally over the area. The basement level of one of these properties holds what might be the most famous address on the block, **Cheers**, at no. 84 (see p.164), home of the *Bull & Finch* pub. This ultra-touristy bar, whose setting inspired the hit TV series, unabashedly trades on the association and has even added a gift store.

Continuing along, look for **purple panes** in some of the townhouses' windows, especially at nos. 63 and 64; the story behind this odd colouring evinces the street's long association with Boston wealth and privilege. When panes were installed in some of the first Beacon Street mansions, they turned purple upon exposure to the sun, due to an excess of manganese in the glass. At first an irritating accident, they were eventually regarded as the definitive Beacon Hill status symbol due to their prevalence in the windows of Boston's most prestigious homes; some residents have gone so far as to shade their windows purple in imitation.

Prescott House, the Founder's Memorial and Somerset Club

While it lacks the purple-tinted panes, the elegant bowfronted 1808 **Prescott House**, at no. 55 (May–Oct Wed, Thurs & Sat noon–4pm; $5; ☏617/742-3190, Ⓦwww.nscda.org/ma; Park St **T**) is still worthy of a visit. Designed by Asher Benjamin, one of Charles Bulfinch's most prolific understudies, its most distinguished inhabitant was Spanish historian William Hickling Prescott, whose family occupied its five floors from 1845 to 1859. Hung above the pastiche of Federalist and Victorian furniture inside is a photograph of two crossed swords that once belonged to Colonel William Prescott and British Captain John Linzee – the historian and his wife's respective grandfathers. The men fought against each other at Bunker Hill, and the sight of their munitions here inspired William Thackeray, a frequent houseguest, to write his novel, *The Virginians*.

Across the street and just inside the periphery of Boston Common, the **Founder's Memorial** commemorates Boston's first European settler, William Blackstone, a Cambridge-educated loner who moved from England with his entire library to a piece of wilderness he acquired for next to nothing from the Shawmut Indians – the site of present-day Boston. A stone bas-relief depicts the apocryphal moment in 1629 when Blackstone sold most of his acreage to a group of Puritans from Charlestown (and marks the year, 1630, when Boston was founded).

Back on the north side of Beacon Street, no. 45 is one of a trio of **Charles Bulfinch houses** (see box, p.79) commissioned by lawyer and future Boston mayor Harrison Gray Otis over a ten-year period; the four-storey Neoclassical house has been home to the American Meteorological Society since 1958. Just east of here, it's hard to miss the twin-swelled granite building at nos. 42–43, built for Colonel David Sears's family by Alexander Parris of Quincy Market fame (see p.52). Its stern Greek Revival facade has welcomed members of the exclusive **Somerset Club** since 1872, an organization so formal that when a fire broke out in the kitchen in 1945, firemen who arrived were ordered to come in via the cumbersome servants' entrance, a heavy iron-studded portal.

Robert Gould Shaw and the 54th Regiment Memorial

Further up Beacon Street, on the edge of the Common facing the State House, is the majestic **monument** honouring **Robert Gould Shaw** and the **54th Massachusetts Regiment**. The memorial commemorates America's first all-black company to fight in the Civil War, a group led by Shaw, scion of a moneyed Boston Brahmin clan. Isolated from the rest of the Union army, given the worst of the military's resources and saddled with menial or dangerous assignments, the regiment performed its service bravely; most of its members, including Shaw, were killed in a failed attempt

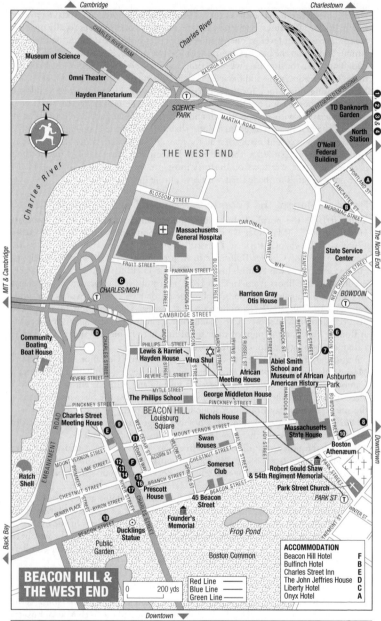

BEACON HILL & THE WEST END

| 0 | 200 yds |

Red Line ———
Blue Line ———
Green Line ———

ACCOMMODATION

Beacon Hill Hotel	F
Bulfinch Hotel	B
Charles Street Inn	E
The John Jeffries House	D
Liberty Hotel	C
Onyx Hotel	A

RESTAURANTS & CAFÉS

75 Chestnut	14	Paramount	12
Beacon Hill Bistro	F	Scampo	C
Caffe Bella Vita	16	Toscano	13
Grotto	6	Upper Crust	15
Lala Rokh	11	Whole Foods	5
Osteria Rustico	2	Zen	10

BARS & CLUBS

21st Amendment	7	Fours	4
Alibi	C	McGann's	1
Bin 26 Enoteca	17	Sevens Ale House	9
Boston Beer Works	3		
Cheers	18		
Emmet's Pub	8		

to take Fort Wagner from the Confederates in 1863. Augustus Saint-Gaudens' outstanding 1897 high-relief bronze sculpture depicts the regiment's farewell march down Beacon Street, with the names of the soldiers who died in action listed on its reverse side (though these were belatedly added in 1982). The wistful angel that presides over the men carries both poppies and laurels, the former a symbol of death, the latter of victory. Robert Lowell won a Pulitzer Prize in 1964 for his poem, *For the Union Dead*, which took its inspiration from the monument; the regiment's story was also depicted in the 1989 film *Glory*, starring Matthew Broderick as Shaw. The monument serves as the starting point of the excellent National Park Ranger-led walking tour of the **Black Heritage Trail** (see box, p.80).

The Massachusetts State House

Across from the memorial rises the large gilt dome of the Charles Bulfinch-designed **Massachusetts State House** (Mon–Fri 10am–4pm, last tour at 3.30pm; free; ☏617/727-3676; ⓦwww.sec.state.ma.us; Park Street **T**), the scale and grandeur of which recall the heady spirit of the then newly independent America in which it was built. Of the current structure, only the central section was part of Bulfinch's original 1795 design; the huge wings jutting out toward the street on either side and the section extending up Bowdoin Street behind the State House were all added much later. An all-star team of Revolution-era luminaries contributed to the original construction: built on land purchased from John Hancock's estate, its cornerstone was laid by Samuel Adams, and the copper for its dome was rolled in Paul Revere's foundry in 1802 (though it was covered over with 23-carat gold leaf in the 1870s). Its front lawn is dotted with statuary honouring favourite sons such as Henry Cabot Lodge and JFK; to the right of the State House is a statue of Civil War General Joseph Hooker, best-known for his alleged procurement of "hookers" for his troops. There is also a statue of Mary Dyer, who became a symbol for religious freedom when she was put to death in 1660 for adhering to her Quaker faith. The statue overlooks a spot on Boston Common where her gallows may have stood (it's believed she was hanged from the Great Elm, see p.42).

The architecture of Charles Bulfinch

America's foremost architect of the late-eighteenth and early nineteenth centuries, **Charles Bulfinch** (1763–1844) developed a distinctive style somewhere between Federal and Classical that remains Boston's most recognizable architectural motif. Mixing Neoclassical training with New England practicality, Bulfinch built residences characterized by their rectilinear brick structure and pillared porticoes; examples remain throughout Beacon Hill, most notably at **87 Mount Vernon St** and **45 Beacon St**. While most of his work was residential, Bulfinch, in fact, made his name with the design of various government buildings, such as the 1805 renovation of **Faneuil Hall** and, more significantly, the **Massachusetts State House**, whose dome influenced the design of state capitols nationwide.

Bulfinch's talents also extended to urban planning. He designed the layout of Boston's **South End**, as well as the now demolished **Tontine Crescent**, a half-ellipse crescent planned around a small park that won Bulfinch praise but ruined him financially; what vestiges remain are found around the Financial District's **Franklin** and **Arch streets**. Bulfinch was also adept at designing massive greystone mercantile warehouses in both Victorian and Federal styles as well as churches – the North End owes **St Stephen's** to Bulfinch. Furthermore, his wide-ranging skill caught the attention of President James Monroe, who in 1818 commissioned Bulfinch to serve as the architect of Washington DC's **US Capitol**.

To check out the interior, head to the visitor's entrance on Beacon Street (easily located via the hilariously huge "General Hooker Entrance" signage behind Hooker's statue). Once through security, make your way up a flight to the second floor, where 40-minute tours start from **Doric Hall** – though you'd do as well to grab a free map and show yourself around. The best section is the sober and impressive **Memorial Hall**, a circular room surrounded by tall columns of Siena marble, displaying transparencies of the original flags carried by Massachusetts soldiers into battle and lit by a vaulted stained-glass window bearing the state seal. On the third floor, a carved wooden fish known as the **Sacred Cod**, which dates to 1783, hangs above the public gallery in the House of Representatives. The politicos take this symbol of maritime prosperity so seriously that when Harvard pranksters stole it in the 1930s, the House didn't reconvene until it was recovered.

Behind the State House, on Bowdoin Street, lies pleasant, flowery **Ashburton Park**, centred on a pillar that is a replica of a 1789 Bulfinch work. The column indicates the hill's original summit, which was sixty feet higher and topped by a 65ft post with the makeshift warning light – constructed from an iron pot filled with combustibles – that gave Beacon Hill its name.

African Meeting House and around

Walk north on sloping Joy Street from Beacon and you'll intersect with tiny **Smith Court**, once the centre of Boston's substantial pre-Civil War black community, and now home to a few crucial stops on Boston's **Black Heritage Trail**.

The **African Meeting House**, at no. 8, is the oldest black church structure in the country (dating to 1806), and in its nineteenth-century heyday served as the spiritual and political centre for Boston's black community. It is also the birthplace of abolitionism: in 1832, William Lloyd Garrison founded The New England Anti-Slavery Society here, the first group of its kind to call for the immediate abolition of slavery, and in 1860 Frederick Douglass gave an anti-slavery speech on

The Black Heritage Trail

In 1783, Massachusetts became the first state to declare slavery illegal, partly in recognition of black participation in the Revolutionary War. Not long after, a large community of free blacks and escaped slaves swiftly sprang up in the North End and Beacon Hill. Very few African-Americans live in either place nowadays, but the **Black Heritage Trail** traces Beacon Hill's key role in local and national black history.

Considered the most important historical site in America devoted to pre-Civil War African-American history and culture, the 1.6-mile loop takes in fourteen historical sights, detailed in a useful **guide** available at the **Museum of African-American History** (as well as the information centres in Boston Common and State Street; see p.42 & p.48). The most fulfilling way to experience the trail is by taking a two-hour National Park Service **walking tour** (Mon–Sat 2pm, June–Aug also 10am & noon; call to reserve; free; ☏617/742-5415, ⊛www.nps.gov/boaf; Park St **T**).

Starting from the **Robert Gould Shaw Memorial** (see p.77), the tour passes **George Middleton House** and the **Phillips School**, which in 1855 became Boston's first racially integrated school. Near the end of the walk, you'll find the **Lewis and Harriet Hayden House** at 66 Phillips St, whose owner, a former escaped slave himself, regularly opened his door to fugitive slaves as part of the Underground Railroad (legend has it he slept with a rifle in his arms in case anyone tried to interfere with his guests). Further east is tiny **Smith Court**, home to the **African Meeting House** and **Abiel Smith School**, both seminal structures in the abolitionist cause.

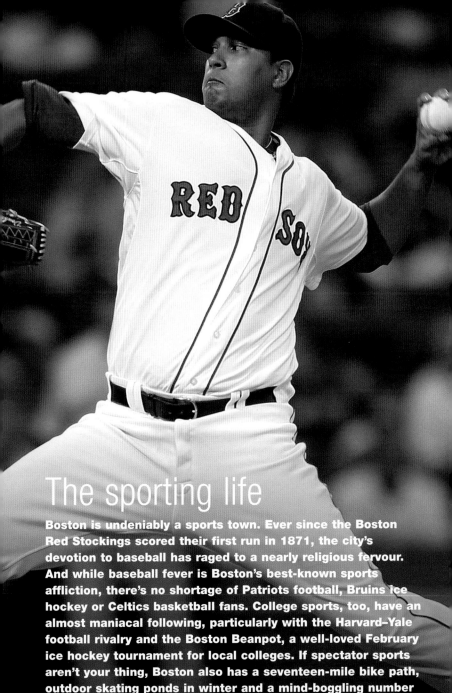

The sporting life

Boston is undeniably a sports town. Ever since the Boston Red Stockings scored their first run in 1871, the city's devotion to baseball has raged to a nearly religious fervour. And while baseball fever is Boston's best-known sports affliction, there's no shortage of Patriots football, Bruins ice hockey or Celtics basketball fans. College sports, too, have an almost maniacal following, particularly with the Harvard–Yale football rivalry and the Boston Beanpot, a well-loved February ice hockey tournament for local colleges. If spectator sports aren't your thing, Boston also has a seventeen-mile bike path, outdoor skating ponds in winter and a mind-boggling number of picnic-worthy public parks.

Title town

You'd be hard-pressed to find a city as fanatical about its sports as Boston. As a result tickets for some of the more popular teams can be difficult, if not impossible, to find at a reasonable price. Love for the Red Sox has only intensified in recent years with World Series wins in 2004 and 2007; tickets for the regular season (which starts in April) sell out fast, but it's possible to score pricey resale tickets. And though they play in a stadium a long drive away, seeing a New England Patriots game live is a rare treat for non season-ticket holders. Their Super Bowl victories in 2002, 2004 and 2005, coupled with the Celtics NBA championship win in 2008, have gone a long way in making locals forget that the Bruins haven't brought home the Stanley Cup since 1972.

All is not lost for crowd seekers, however. If a big game is on, the whole city comes to attention, and it's easy to join in on the fun; even fancy restaurants often have a television or two turned on so their patrons can catch the game. To get in on the action, your best bet is to head toward the

Kevin Garnett, the Boston Celtics ▲

Sign of the Green Monster, Fenway Park ▼

Fenway Park

No team in professional baseball has as distinct a **home-field advantage** as the Boston Red Sox. The oldest Major League ballpark in the country (it dates to 1912), **Fenway Park** is rife with old-school charms like a manually operated scoreboard, its own trademarked colour ("Fens Green") and a whimsically angled playing field known for its crazy caroms. All this is in addition to the legendary 37ft-high **Green Monster** wall in left field, originally built because homeruns were breaking the windows of the adjacent Lansdowne Street businesses.

neighbourhood where the game is playing – Kenmore Square for Red Sox revelry, and the West End for Celtics and Bruins events. Be sure to hit your chosen bar early so you can nab a good seat, then order a local brew and get ready for a wild night spent with an animated crowd.

The race is on

Not all of Boston's biggest sporting events require a ticket. Indeed, two of the city's largest and most loved annual events cost nothing to attend. The iconic Head of the Charles Regatta is the world's largest two-day rowing race, taking place every October and attracting more than 7500 athletes from around the world – not to mention the 300,000 picnicking spectators who angle for views of it from both the Boston and Cambridge sides of the Charles River. Another international attraction, the Boston Marathon is the oldest annual marathon in the world (dating back to 1897), and lures some 20,000 runners to town every April. The 26.2-mile course curves through the suburbs – lined by legions of cheering residents – before culminating on Boylston Street just before The Old South Church. While the events themselves are a sight to be seen, best is the local camaraderie that urges the competitors on from start to finish.

Old-school rivals

Dating from 1875, The Harvard-Yale football game (locally referred to as "The Game") is one of the oldest and most fervent rivalries in college history, bringing as many as 50,000 frenzied fans to its sidelines. In the nineteenth century, the style of the game was closer to that of rugby, and marked by brutal player combat – 1894 saw the most violent skirmish, when seven players were

▲ Head of the Charles Regatta

▼ Boston Marathon

distinction is due less to its architectural character than to its long history of illustrious residents and the sense of elite civic parochialism that has made this Boston's most coveted address. Among those to call the area home were novelist Louisa May Alcott and members of the Vanderbilt family; current residents include former presidential candidate Senator John Kerry, and his wife, ketchup heiress Teresa Heinz.

A jaunt down Mount Vernon Street brings you past some of Beacon Hill's most beautiful buildings. The **Nichols House** (April–Oct Tues–Sat 11am–4pm; Nov–March Thurs–Sat 11am–4pm, tours on the half-hour; $7; ⊤617/227-6993, ⓦwww.nicholshousemuseum.org; Park Street **T**), at no.55, is yet another Bulfinch design, and the only Beacon Hill residence open year-round to the public. Until 1960, it was the home of Rose Standish Nichols, favourite niece of sculptor Augustus Saint-Gaudens (the man behind the **54th Regiment Memorial** on Beacon Street; see p.77); it's now a house museum offering thirty-minute tours. Born in 1872, Miss Rose, as she is known to posterity, had as full a life as her splendid home. A suffragette and pacifist, she helped to found the Women's International League for Peace and Freedom, and made the then-radical decision to eschew the path of marriage and family in favour of single life and a successful career as a landscape gardener. Tours take in her heirlooms, such as striking Asian tapestries, Federal-period furniture and an original self-portrait by John Singleton Copley, in addition to giving visitors perspective on the interior life of opulence led by Beacon Hill's well-heeled elite.

Chestnut and Acorn streets

One block south of Mount Vernon Street (head south on Walnut from the Nichols House), **Chestnut Street** features some of the prettiest facades in Boston, notably with Bulfinch's **Swan Houses**, at nos. 13, 15 and 17, with their recessed arches, Doric columns and even-keeled entranceways, manipulated so that, in defiance of the street's downward slope, each of the three front doors open on the same level plane.

Take Chestnut Street west and you'll arrive at narrow **Acorn Street** (squeezed in between Willow and W. Cedar Streets), which still has its original early nineteenth-century cobblestones. Barely wide enough for a car to pass through, it was originally built as a minor byway to be lined with servants' residences. Locals have always upheld it as the epitome of Beacon Hill quaint; in the 1960s, residents permitted the city to tear up the street to install sewer pipes only after exacting the promise that every cobblestone would be replaced in its original location.

Charles Street

Down the hill from Mount Vernon and Acorn streets, quaint Charles Street provides a pleasant flat respite after the north and south slopes. The commercial centre of Beacon Hill, it's lined with scores of restaurants, antiques shops and hip boutiques. One sight here is the Federal-style **Charles Street Meeting House**, with its set-back, cupolaed roof; it stands on the corner of Mount Vernon and Charles Street. Although it has since been repurposed as an office space and pavement café, the Meeting House was a hotbed of political activity in the nineteenth century.

The Esplanade

Spanning nine miles along the Charles River, the **Esplanade** is another of Boston's well-manicured public spaces, complete with the requisite playgrounds, landscaped hills, lakes and bridges. The nicest stretch runs alongside Beacon Hill and continues into Back Bay, providing a unique, scenic way to appreciate the Hill from a distance. Just below the Longfellow Bridge (which connects to Cambridge, across the river; see

Chapter 9) is the Community Boating Boathouse, the point of departure for sailing, kayaking and windsurfing outings on the Charles (April–Oct Mon–Fri 1pm–sunset, Sat & Sun 9am–sunset; 30-day intro to sailing and kayaking $99, summer programme for kids aged 10–18 only $1; ⓣ617/523-1038, ⓦwww.community-boating.org).

The white half-dome rising from the riverbank along the Esplanade is the **Hatch Shell** (ⓣ617/227-0627, ⓦwww.hatchshell.com; Charles **T**), a public performance space best known for its Fourth of July celebration (see p.206), which features a free concert by the Boston Pops, a pared-down, snappy version of the Boston Symphony Orchestra. Free movies and jazz concerts occur almost nightly in summer; check their website for a schedule of events.

The West End

North of Cambridge Street, the tidy rows of townhouses are replaced by a more urban spread of office buildings and old brick structures, signalling the start of the **West End**. Boston's main port of entry for immigrants in post-Colonial times, this area was populated by a broad mix of ethnic groups as well as transient sailors who brought a rough-and-tumble sex-and-tattoo industry with them. Unfortunately, the West End was razed during 1960s urban renewal, which did much to efface the district's once-lively character.

A vestige of the old West End remains in the small tangle of byways – namely Friend, Portland and Canal Streets – behind the high-rise buildings of Massachusetts General Hospital. Here urban warehouses are interspersed with numerous Irish bars that swell to a fever pitch after Celtics basketball and Bruin hockey games at the nearby **TD Garden**, the slick, corporate-named arena on top of North Station at 150 Causeway St (ⓣ617/624-1000; ⓦwww.tdbanknorthgarden.com). Within the arena's box seats is the affable **Sports Museum** (daily 10am–4pm; hours fluctuate according to events – call to confirm; $10; ⓣ617/624-1235; ⓦwww.sportsmuseum .org; North Station **T**). Here, visitors can glimpse classic Boston sports ephemera, like the lockers of Celtic Larry Bird and Red Sox Ted Williams, as well as the American League Championship banner from when the Red Sox finally beat rival New York Yankees in 2004. There are also old school uniforms and equipment, like a prim woman's basketball uniform from the 1890s, but best of all is the hockey penalty box from the old Boston Garden, which visitors are invited to climb into.

The Harrison Gray Otis House

Back along Cambridge Street at no. 141, the brick **Harrison Gray Otis House** (Wed–Sun 11am–4.30pm, tours every half hour; $8; ⓣ617/227-3956, ⓦwww .historicnewengland.org; Charles **T**), originally built for the wealthy Otis family in 1796 by Bulfinch, sits graciously and incongruously among modern stores and office buildings (another of the family's three houses can be glimpsed on Beacon Street; see p.77). In the 1830s, this building served as a medical facility offering "Champoo Baths" (a sort of old-fashioned aromatherapy treatment) before its later transformation into a boarding house. In 1925, the structure was literally rolled back from the present-day median strip in order to make way for the street. Its first two floors have been carefully restored – from the bright wallpaper right down to the silverware sets – in the often loud hues of the Federal style.

The Museum of Science

Situated on the Charles River Bridge, at the northernmost part of the Esplanade, Boston's stellar **Museum of Science** (July to early Sept daily 9am–7pm, Fri till 9pm; mid-Sept to June daily 9am–5pm, Fri till 9pm; $20, kids $17; CityPass accepted;

T 617/723-2500, W www.mos.org; Science Park **T**) consists of several floors of well-loved interactive exhibits illustrating basic principles of natural and physical science. There's enough here to entertain kids for most of a day, plus fun-loving kid companions will enjoy it, too.

The best exhibit is the **Theater of Electricity** in the Blue Wing, a darkened room full of optical illusions and glowing displays on the presence of electricity in everyday life. Here, the world's largest Van de Graaff generator utilizes 2.5 million volts of electricity and gives daily electricity shows in which simulated lightning bolts flash and crackle. More cerebral is Mathematica, installed in 1961 by design dream-team Charles and Ray Eames. It's fun to alter the course of the sand pendulum and make geometric bubble shapes, but perhaps the coolest part of this exhibit is the chance to experience the design wizardry of these two visual innovators. Throughout the museum, there are great installations, including the cross-section of a 2044-year-old Sequoia tree (born a few years after Julius Caesar), the musical stairs in the Red Wing and "Science in the Park," where kids can let loose and see-saw, race their friends on a lit-up track or try to strong-arm 500lbs of weight.

The museum also houses a five-storey **IMAX theatre** (schedule varies; $9, kids $7; T 617/723-2500, W www.mos.org) and the **Charles Hayden Planetarium**; the latter is undergoing renovations and plans to reopen in 2011 with a 57ft dome, digital surround sound and the latest in HD video. Elsewhere, there's a popular **Butterfly Garden** ($4.50 in addition to museum admission) and **3-D theatre** ($4.50 in addition to museum admission), which screens larger-than-life movies on planets, sharks and bugs; best is the chance to wear those retro-cool 3-D glasses.

Back Bay

M eticulously planned **Back Bay** is Boston at its most cosmopolitan. Beginning at the **Public Garden**, the neighbourhood's elegant, angular, tree-lined streets form a pedestrian-friendly area that looks much as it did in the nineteenth century, right down to the original gas lights and brick sidewalks. Besides the area's café culture, the other main draw here is a trove of exquisite Gilded Age rowhouses; walking around, it seems as if there's no end to the fanciful bay windows and ornamental turrets. Oftentimes, the brownstones get fancier the farther from the garden you go (the order in which they were built), a result of architectural one-upmanship.

Running parallel to the Charles River in neat rows, Back Bay's east–west thoroughfares – **Beacon**, **Marlborough**, **Newbury** and **Boylston streets**, with **Commonwealth Avenue** in between – are transected by eight shorter streets. These latter roads have been so fastidiously laid out that not only are their names in alphabetical order, but trisyllables are deliberately intercut by disyllables: Arlington, Berkeley, Clarendon, Dartmouth, Exeter, Fairfield, Gloucester and Hereford – until Massachusetts Avenue breaks the pattern at the western border of the neighbourhood. The grandest rowhouses are to be found on Beacon Street and Commonwealth Avenue, while Marlborough is perhaps more atmospheric. Boylston and Newbury are the main commercial drags and a shopping excursion on the latter is a must-do Boston experience. In the midst of it all is petite **Copley Square**, surrounded by the area's main sights: **Trinity Church**, the imposing **Boston Public Library** and the city's skyline-defining **John Hancock Tower**.

Some history

The fashioning of Back Bay (as with its neighbour, the South End; see Chapter 6) occurred in response to a shortage of living space in Boston. An increasingly overcrowded Beacon Hill prompted developers to revisit a failed dam project on the Charles River that had made a swamp of much of the area. With visionary architect and urban planner **Arthur Gilman** at the helm of a huge landfill job, the sludge began to be reclaimed in 1857.

Taking his cue from Georges-Eugène Haussmann's new wide boulevards in Paris, Gilman decided on an orderly street pattern extending east to west from the Public Garden, which itself had been sculpted from swampland only two decades before. By 1890, the once-cramped peninsula of old Boston could claim 450 new acres, on which stood a range of churches, townhouses and schools.

Due largely to landmark preservation laws, the exteriors of most buildings remain unaltered, and many retain their old wood ornamentation and Victorian embellishments. All in all, the neighbourhood's authentic charm, as well as the pervasive grace of the bowfronts and wrought-iron terraces, proffers an air of well-heeled serenity that makes Back Bay perfect for an afternoon of store gazing and relaxed exploration.

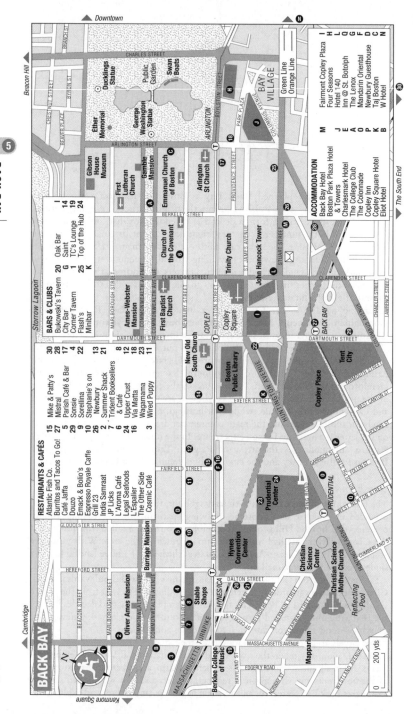

BACK BAY

5

Downtown

Beacon Hill

Cambridge

Kenmore Square

N

200 yds

RESTAURANTS & CAFÉS

Atlantic Fish Co.	30
Burritos and Tacos To Go!	28
Café Jaffa	17
Douzo	5
Emack & Bolio's	4
Espresso Royale Caffe	29
Grill 23	9
India Samraat	10
JP Licks	26
L'Aroma Café	2
Legal Seafoods	7
L'Espalier	6
The Other Side	24
Cosmic Café	16

Mike & Patty's	15
Mistral	27
Parish Café & Bar	5
Sonsie	29
Sorellina	9
Stephanie's on	10
Newbury	26
Summer Shack	2
Trident Booksellers	7
& Café	6
Upper Crust	12
Via Matta	24
Wagamama	23
Wired Puppy	3

BARS & CLUBS

Bukowski's Tavern	20
City Bar	G
Corner Tavern	1
Flash's	25
Minibar	K

Oak Bar	I
Saint	14
TC's Lounge	19
Top of the Hub	24

ACCOMMODATION

Back Bay Hotel	M
Boston Park Plaza Hotel	
& Towers	J
Charlesmark Hotel	E
The College Club	A
The Colonnade	O
Copley Inn	P
Copley Square Hotel	K
Eliot Hotel	B

Fairmont Copley Plaza	I
Four Seasons	H
Hotel 140	L
Inn @ St. Botolph	Q
The Lenox	G
Mandarin Oriental	F
Newbury Guesthouse	D
Taj Boston	C
W Hotel	N

Green Line
Orange Line

The South End

The Public Garden

The value of property in Boston increases the closer its proximity to Back Bay's exquisite **Public Garden**, a 24-acre botanical park founded in 1837 and earmarked for public use since 1859. Of the garden's 125 types of trees – many identified by little black placards – most impressive are the weeping willows that ring the picturesque man-made lagoon. Here you can take a fifteen-minute ride in one of six **Swan Boats** (April to late June daily 10am–4pm; late-June to early Sept daily 10am–5pm; early to mid-Sept Mon–Fri noon–4pm, Sat & Sun 10am–4pm; $2.75; ☎617/522-1966; ⓦwww.swanboats.com), which trace gracious figure-eights in the oversized puddle. The elegant, pedal-powered conveyances, inspired by a scene in Wagner's opera *Lohengrin*, have been around since 1877, long enough to become a Boston institution. The boats carry up to twenty passengers at a time, and in the height of summer there is often a wait to hop on board; instead of waiting, you can get just as good a view of the park from the tiny suspension bridge that spans the lagoon.

The park has another fowl-related draw: a cluster of popular bronze bird sculptures (by the Charles Street entrance) collectively called **Mrs Mallard and Her Eight Ducklings**. The sculptures were installed in 1987 to commemorate Robert McCloskey's 1941 "*Make Way for Ducklings*", a children's tale set in the park (it's unlikely you'll ever pass the sculptures without seeing someone "riding" one of the ducks). Of the many other statues and monuments throughout the park, the oldest and oddest is the 30ft-tall **Good Samaritan** monument along the Arlington Street side; the granite and red-marble column is a tribute to, of all things, the anaesthetic qualities of ether. Controversy as to which of two Boston men invented the wonder drug led Oliver Wendell Holmes to dub it the "Either Monument." Finally, a dignified equestrian statue of **George Washington**, installed in 1869 and the first of the general astride a horse, watches over the garden's Commonwealth Avenue entrance.

Beacon Street and the Gibson House Museum

As a continuation of Beacon Hill's stately main thoroughfare, **Beacon Street** was long the province of blueblood Bostonians. One such building, the Italian Renaissance townhouse at no. 137, holds the remarkable **Gibson House Museum** (Wed–Sun 1–3pm, tours hourly; $9; ☎617/267-6338, ⓦwww.thegibsonhouse.org; Arlington **T**), which preserves the home built for Catherine Hammond Gibson in 1860, twenty years after the death of her well-to-do husband. In the ornate interior, there's a curious host of Victoriana, including a still-functioning dumbwaiter, antique clocks and writing paraphernalia (one of the Gibsons was a noted travel writer). Notable among the various chinoiserie is the stunning gold-embossed "Japanese Leather" wallpaper that covers a good portion of the abode, and a sequined pink velvet cat house or, if you prefer the Gibsons' term, "pet pagoda."

Marlborough Street

Sandwiched between Beacon Street and Commonwealth Avenue, quiet **Marlborough Street** is one of the most prized residential locales in Boston after Beacon Hill's Louisburg Square and the first few blocks of Commonwealth Avenue. Even though the townhouses here tend to be smaller than elsewhere in Back Bay, they display a surprising range of styles when it comes to ornamentation, especially along the blocks between Clarendon and Fairfield streets.

Commonwealth Avenue

The Public Garden leads into the tree-lined parkway of **Commonwealth Avenue**, modelled after the grand boulevards of Paris and Back Bay's showcase street. The 100ft-wide leafy median at its centre forms the first link in Frederick Law Olmsted's so-called **Emerald Necklace**, which begins at Boston Common and extends all the way to Franklin Park in Dorchester. The snazzy *Taj Boston* hotel on Arlington Street forms a fittingly upscale beginning to the promenade, which is peppered with several elegantly placed **statues**; one particularly interesting trio, that of **Abigail Adams, Lucy Stone** and **Phillis Wheatley** is located between Fairfield and Gloucester Streets; there is also a curious statue of abolitionist **William Lloyd Garrison** seated over a book between Dartmouth and Exeter streets. "Comm Ave," as locals irreverently call it, is at its prettiest in early May, when the magnolia and dogwood trees are in full bloom, showering the brownstone steps with their fragrant pink buds.

One set of these steps – the first as you walk along the avenue – belongs to the **Gamble Mansion**, at no. 5. Currently under construction, it's hoped that when the renovations are finished passers-by will once again be able to slip inside for a look at the opulent Louis XV ballroom built expressly for the owner's daughter's coming-out (in the old-fashioned sense) party. You'll have to be content to see the Queen Anne-style **Ames-Webster Mansion**, a few blocks down at 306 Dartmouth St, from the outside. Built in 1882 for railroad tycoon and US congressman Frederick Ames, it features a two-storey conservatory, central tower and imposing chimney. Farther down Comm Ave is the **Burrage Mansion**, at no. 314, a fanciful synthesis of a Vanderbilt-style mansion and the French chateau of *Chenonceaux*; the exterior of this 1899 urban palace is a riot of gargoyles and carved cherubim. Further on, the Beaux Arts chateau at no. 355 is the **Oliver Ames Mansion** (great-grandfather to Frederick), topped by multiple chimneys and dormer windows; its interior now comprises offices and, as such, is not open to the public.

The First Baptist Church of Boston

Rising above the avenue at no. 110 is the landmark belfry of the **First Baptist Church of Boston** (Mon–Fri 11am–3pm; ☎617/267-3148; ⓦwww.firstbaptist churchofboston.org), designed by architect H.H. Richardson in 1872 for a Unitarian congregation, though at bill-paying time only a Baptist group was able to rustle up the necessary funds. The puddingstone exterior is topped off by a 176ft **bell tower**, which is covered by four gorgeous friezes by Frédéric-Auguste Bartholdi of Statue of Liberty fame; a product of his friendship with Richardson that developed at the Ecole des Beaux Arts in Paris. More interesting than what the tableaux depict (baptism, communion, marriage and death) are some of the illustrious stone-etched visages, particularly those of Emerson, Longfellow, Hawthorne and Lincoln. Trumpeting angels protrude from each corner, inspiring its inglorious nickname, "Church of the Holy Bean Blowers."

Richardson's lofty plans for the interior never materialized, again for lack of money, but its high ceiling, exposed timbers and Norman-style rose windows are still worth a peek if you happen by when someone's in the church office.

Newbury and Boylston streets

Take a walk down **Newbury Street** and it's hard to imagine this was once considered one of Back Bay's least fashionable addresses. Thought of as a poor relation to nearby Commonwealth Avenue, Newbury was almost exclusively residential when the earliest buildings were constructed in 1857, and its first retail shop didn't open until 1905. Today the street comprises eight atmospheric blocks of Victorian-era brownstones housing more than three hundred boutiques, art galleries and restaurants, plus chain stores like the Gap and NikeTown. Despite the occasional nod to pretentiousness in some of its swankier spaces, it remains an inviting place to wander around. And not all is shopping: Newbury and neighbouring **Boylston** are home to most of the old schools and churches built in the Back Bay area.

The Emmanuel Church of Boston and Church of the Covenant

On the first block of Newbury Street, sandwiched between fancy hair salons and upscale retail stores, is the **Emmanuel Church of Boston**, an unassuming rural Gothic Revival building. Of greater interest is the full-blown Gothic Revival **Church of the Covenant**, down one block at no. 67. Most passers-by are too intent on window shopping to notice the soaring steeple, so look up before checking out the interior, famous – like the nearby Arlington Street Church – for its Tiffany stained-glass windows, some of which are thirty feet high. The **Gallery NAGA** (Newbury Associated Guild of Artists), in the chapel (Tues–Sat 10am–5pm; ☎617/267-9060, ⊛www.gallerynaga.com), is one of Boston's biggest contemporary art spaces, and stages new exhibits of works by artists from Boston and New England; it's also a nice setting for chamber music performances – the Boston Pro Arte Chamber Orchestra was founded here.

The rest of Newbury Street

Designed as an architect's house, the medieval flight-of-fancy at **109 Newbury Street** is more arresting for its two fortress-like brownstone turrets than the Cole Haan footwear inside. A block down and across the street, **271 Dartmouth**, houses a *Papa Razzi* restaurant, but again the burnt sienna-coloured building with mock battlements hunkered over it steals the show: originally the *Hotel Victoria* in 1886, it looks like a combination Venetian-Moorish castle.

Newbury gets progressively funkier west of Exeter Street, with alternative record stores and two excellent used bookstores catering to a more low-key, student-centred crowd. On the final block, between Hereford Street and Massachusetts Avenue, a span of nineteenth-century **stables** has been converted to commercial space; check out the cavernous Patagonia clothing shop at no. 346 for the best example.

Arlington Street Church

Right on the corner of Boylston and Arlington streets is Back Bay's first building, the squat **Arlington Street Church** (Mon–Fri 10am–5pm, Sun 10am–3pm; ☎617/536-7050, ⊛www.ascboston.org), a minor Italianesque masterpiece designed in 1859 by Arthur Gilman, chief planner of Back Bay; its host of Tiffany stained-glass windows (believed to be the largest assemblage of Tiffany windows unified under one church) were added from 1898 to 1933. A history of progressive rhetoric has also earned it some note: abolitionist minister William Ellery Channing intoned against slavery here just a year before the Civil War erupted, and the church was a favoured venue of peace activists during the Vietnam War; nowadays there's an active gay congregation (the first state-sanctioned same-sex marriage in the United States took place here on May 17, 2004).

The New Old South Church

On the corner of Boylston and Dartmouth streets stands one of Boston's most attractive buildings, the **New Old South Church** (Mon–Fri 9am–5pm; ☎617/536-1970, ⊛www.oldsouth.org). There's actually some logic to the name: the congregation in residence at Downtown's Old South Meeting House outgrew it and decamped here in 1875. The names of former Old South members reads like a who's who of

Boston historical figures: Benjamin Franklin, Phillis Wheatley, Samuel Adams and even Mother Goose all congregated here. You need not be a student of architecture to be won over by the Italian Gothic design, most pronounced in the ornate, 220ft bell tower, its copper-roof lantern, replete with metallic gargoyles in the shape of dragons; the dramatic zebra-striped archways on the Dartmouth Street side are also worth a mention. The church isn't just to be admired from the outside, either: its interior is an alluring assemblage of dark woods set against a rose-coloured backdrop, coupled with fifteenth-century, English-style stained-glass windows. Old South is locally known as the "Church of the Finish Line" due to its location just beyond Boston Marathon's official finish line.

Copley Square and around

Bounded by Boylston, Clarendon, Dartmouth and St James streets, **Copley Square** is the busy centre of Back Bay. Various design schemes have come and gone since the square was first filled in the 1870s; the present one is a remnant from 1984, a square, brick expanse anchored by a fountain on the Boylston Street side.

Trinity Church

The star of Copley Square is **Trinity Church**, 206 Clarendon St (Mon–Fri 11am–5pm, Sat 9am–5pm, Sun 7am–7pm; $5; includes guided tour, call for times; ☎617/536-0944 ⓦwww.trinitychurchboston.org; Copley **T**), for which the original interior design concept was to create the experience of "walking into a living painting." The result is H.H. Richardson's 1877 Romanesque masterpiece, a breathtaking display of polychromatic eye candy fashioned by legendary stained-glass artist John La Farge. The majestic central tower reaches an eye-opening ten storeys, cooly situated between sweeping arches and a glamorous golden chancel. While it's all quite lovely, the church's finest feature is La Farge's aquamarine *Christ in Majesty* triptych, a bold, multi-dimensional stained-glass window. Aim to make your visit when the sun is setting and the stained glass is at its most brilliant, or during one of the **free organ recitals** (Fri 12.15pm).

Boston Public Library

A decidedly secular building anchors the end of Copley Square opposite Trinity Church, in the form of the handsome **Boston Public Library** (Mon–Thurs 9am–9pm, Fri & Sat 9am–5pm; ☎617/536-5400, ⓦwww.bpl.org; Copley **T**). It's the largest public research library in New England and the first one in America to permit the borrowing of books. McKim, Mead, & White, the leading architectural firm of its day, built the Italian Renaissance Revival structure in 1852. The Copley Square facade, with its sloping red tile roof, green copper cresting and huge arched windows, is quite magnificent, while the visibility of the entrance is heightened by the presence of the spiky yet sinuous lanterns overhanging it. The massive inner bronze doors were designed by Daniel Chester French (sculptor of the Lincoln Memorial in Washington DC); inside, a musketeer-like statue of Sir Henry Vane stands guard. This early governor of the Massachusetts Bay Colony believed, or so the inscription relates, that "God, law and parliament" were superior to the king, which apparently didn't do much for his case in 1662, when his freethinking head got the chop.

Beyond the marble grand staircase and signature lions and underneath the coffered ceilings are a series of **murals**, most impressive of which is a diaphanous depiction of the nine Muses. Just to the right is the superlative **Abbey Room**, named for Edwin Abbey's murals depicting the Holy Grail legend, and where

Bostonians once took delivery of their books. Most of these were kept in the imposing **Bates Reading Room**, which, with its 218ft-long sweep, 50ft-high barrel-vaulted ceiling, dark oak panelling and incomparable calm, has awed patrons for more than a hundred years. The library's most remarkable feature is tucked away on the top floor, however, where the darkly lit **Sargent Hall** is covered with more than fifteen astonishing murals painted by John Singer Sargent between 1890 and 1916. Entitled the *Triumph of Religion*, the works are a mastery of detail incorporating appliquéd metal, paper and jewels – most striking in the north end's stunning twin *Pagan Gods* ceiling vaults – and plaster relief, evident in Moses' twin tablets which project from the east wall. Afterwards, you can take a breather in the library's open-air central **courtyard**, modelled after that of the Palazzo della Chancelleria in Rome and centred on a statue of a smiling, nude lady holding a baby in one hand and a bunch of grapes in the other.

John Hancock Tower

At 62 storeys, the **John Hancock Tower**, at 200 Clarendon St, is Boston's signature skyscraper – first loathed, now loved, and taking on startlingly different appearances depending on your vantage point. In Back Bay, the characteristically angular edifice is often barely noticeable, due to deft understatement and wafer-thin design in deference to adjacent Trinity Church and the old brownstones nearby. This modern subtlety in the face of historic landmarks is a signature quality of architect I.M. Pei (of the Louvre Pyramid and Bank of China, Hong Kong fame). From Beacon Hill, the tower appears broad-shouldered and stocky; from the South End, taller than it actually is; from across the Charles River, like a crisp metallic wafer. One of the best views is from the **Harvard Bridge**, which connects the western edge of Back Bay and Massachusetts Avenue with MIT in Cambridge; from there, you'll be able to see clouds reflected in the tower's lofty, fully mirrored coat. With such a seamless facade, you'd never guess that soon after its 1976 construction, dozens of windowpanes popped out, showering Copley Square with glass, due to a design flaw that prompted the replacement of over 10,000 panes.

Today, most of the building is given over to offices, and its sixtieth-floor **observatory**, which afforded some of the most stunning views around, is permanently closed due to security concerns arising after the events of September 11, 2001. (You'll have to head instead to the Prudential Skywalk for deluxe Boston vistas; see below.) Next door is the old Hancock Tower, which cuts a distinguished profile in the skyline with its truncated step-top pyramid roof. It's locally famous for the neon weather beacon on top, which can be decoded with the help of the jingle, "Solid blue, clear view; flashing blue, clouds are due; solid red, rain ahead; flashing red, snow instead" (except in summer when red signifies the cancellation of a Red Sox game). In October of 2004, the beacon flashed blue and red together for the first time to commemorate the Red Sox World Series win: "flashing blue and red, the Curse is dead!"

The Prudential Center

Nothing can cloak the funkiness of the **Prudential Center** ("The Pru"), at 800 Boylston St, just west of Copley Square, its edifice a 52-storey grey intruder to the Back Bay skyline. While it may not be as beautiful as its neighbours, the Pru's iconic outline, which dates to 1964, remains a fond landmark to residents.

Apart from being one of the starting points for a number of Boston tours (see p.27), its chief selling point is its fiftieth-floor **Skywalk** (daily: April–Oct 10am–10pm; Nov–March 10am–8pm; $12; ☎617/859-0648, ⓦwww.prudential center.com; Copley **T**), offering the only 360-degree aerial view of Boston. On a clear day you can make out Cape Cod across the waters of Massachusetts Bay and New Hampshire to the north. If you're hungry (or just thirsty) you can avoid the admission charge by ascending two more floors to the *Top of the Hub* restaurant (see p.165); your bill may well equal the money you just saved, but during most daytime hours it's fairly relaxed, and you can linger over coffee or a drink. Well below, the first-floor **Shops at Prudential Center** is a popular shopping mall, adjoining the hulking mass of the **Hynes Convention Center**.

The Christian Science buildings

People gazing down at Boston from the top of the Prudential Tower are often surprised to see a 224ft-tall Renaissance Revival basilica vying for attention amidst the urban outcroppings lapping at its base. The structure is the central feature of the world headquarters of the **First Church of Christ, Scientist**, 175 Huntington Ave (Mon–Sat 10am–4pm; free; ☏617/450-2000, ⓦchristianscience.com; Symphony **T**), which was founded by Mary Baker Eddy in 1879. With seating for 3000 (and an enormous pipe organ), it dwarfs the earlier Romanesque **Christian Science Mother Church** just behind it, built in 1894 and decked out with spectacular opalescent stained-glass windows. The centre's 670ft-long, red-granite-trimmed **reflecting pool** makes a nice spot for lunchtime lounging, and children are often seen happily running amok in the site's nearby fountains.

The highlights of a visit here, though, are on the ground floor of the **Mary Baker Eddy Library**, in the Christian Science Publishing building at 200 Massachusetts Ave (Tues–Sun 10am–4pm; $6; ☏617/450-7000, ⓦwww.marybakereddylibrary .org; Symphony **T**). The library's original Neoclassical lobby has been transformed into the grandly named Hall of Ideas, home to a wild glass and bronze fountain that appears to cascade with words as well as water; the sayings – a diverse collection of inspiring tidbits – are projected from above for an effect that verges on holographic. Tucked behind the Hall of Ideas is the marvellous **Mapparium**, a curious stained-glass globe whose 30ft diameter can be crossed on a glass bridge. The technicolour hues of the six hundred-plus glass panels, illuminated from behind, reveal the geopolitical reality of the world in 1935, when the globe was constructed, as evidenced by country names such as Siam, Baluchistan and Transjordan. Intended to symbolize the worldwide reach of journalism, the Mapparium has a more immediate payoff: thanks to the spherical glass surface, which absorbs no sound, you can whisper, "What's Tanganyika called today?" at one end of the bridge and someone on the opposite end will hear it clear as a bell – and perhaps proffer the answer (Tanzania).

Bay Village

Back near the Public Garden, one of the oldest sections of Boston, **Bay Village**, bounded by Arlington, Church, Fayette and Stuart streets, functions as a small atmospheric satellite of Back Bay that make for pleasant meandering.

The neighbourhood's overall resemblance to Beacon Hill is no accident; many of the artisans who pieced that district together built houses here throughout the 1820s and 1830s. Like Back Bay, Bay Village was built in 1815 on top of former swampland, its design and construction spearheaded (funnily enough) by a contractor-builder named Ephraim Marsh. A few decades later, water displaced from the filling in of Back Bay threatened to turn the area back into a swamp, but Yankee ingenuity resulted in the lifting of hundreds of houses and shops onto wooden pilings fully eighteen feet above the water level. Backyards were raised only twelve feet, and when the water receded many building owners designed **sunken gardens**. One of the most unusual remnants from the nineteenth century is the

fortress at the intersection of Arlington and Stuart streets at Columbus Avenue. Complete with drawbridge and fake moat, it was built as an armory for the First Corps of Cadets (a private military organization); today it houses Boston's branch of the upscale New York steakhouse *Smith & Wollensky*.

The obvious streets to explore are **Piedmont**, **Winchester** and **Church**, which radiate out from the *Boston Park Plaza Hotel*, anchoring the neighbourhood. Footsteps beyond, lightly trafficked **Melrose and Fayette streets** are also worth inspection: on Melrose you'll find the area's last remaining sunken gardens – tiny, and often gated, private lawns lying just below street level. Bay Village's proximity to the Theater District made it a prime location for **speakeasies** in the 1920s, not to mention a natural spot for actors and impresarios to take up residence; indeed the building at **48–50 Melrose Street** originally housed a movie studio. At 17 Piedmont St, a pavement plaque marks the site of the Cocoanut Grove Fire of 1942, in which 492 people perished in a nightclub because the exit doors were locked. Before leaving the area, be sure to squeeze into *Mike & Patty's* at 12 Church St (see p.154) for a grilled banana sandwich.

6

The South End

The residential **South End**, extending below Back Bay (see Chapter 5) from Massachusetts Avenue to I-93 and the Mass Pike (I-90), has the supreme good fortune of being both quaint and stylish in equal measure. Known for its prominent gay and lesbian population, it's also a foodie hotspot that's given rise to a number of the city's best restaurants, and in addition has generated many seminal art galleries, theatres and standout shopping boutiques.

The neighbourhood's heart is bounded by Tremont Street, Dartmouth Street and Columbus Avenue. This posh enclave boasts a spectacular concentration of Victorian architecture, unmatched anywhere in the US. In fact, the sheer number of such houses earned the South End a **National Landmark District** designation in 1983, making the 500-acre area the largest historical neighbourhood of its kind in the country. The South End is also known for its well-preserved ironwork – a French botanical motif known as Rinceau adorns many of the houses' stairways and windows (see box, p.97). Unsurprisingly, details like these made the area quite popular with upwardly mobile Bostonians (among them a strong gay and lesbian contingent), who began populating the area in the mid-1990s. The upshot has been some of the most happening streetlife in town. The activity is most visible on **Tremont Street** and on pockets of **Washington Street**, a few blocks below the Back Bay **T** (the neighbourhood's only subway stop), although in recent years the area's popularity has enabled the party to spread: voguish restaurants, stores and bars can now be found south of Washington Street ("SoWa") and in the further reaches of the community.

In addition to the Victoriana, the enclave's moneyed townhouses rub elbows with a number of affordable-housing units, namely in the small quadrant below Tremont Street, which is home to a Puerto Rican community, and a patch along Dartmouth Street near Copley Place, where the low-income housing co-op of **Tent City** presides. Parts of surrounding areas, such as Roxbury, are a little rough around the edges, and along the Massachusetts Avenue periphery of the neighbourhood, appropriate caution should be taken at night.

Some history

Like Back Bay, the South End was originally a marshland that now sits on landfill. Though the mud-to-mansion process kicked off in 1834 – predating Back Bay by more than twenty years – the neighbourhood really took shape between 1850 and 1875, when it was laid out according to plans designed by **Charles Bulfinch** some fifty years earlier; its similarity to Beacon Hill, completed just two years prior to development here, is striking, though the South End "look" is more homogeneous and streamlined, dominated by red-brick bowfront townhouses that are modestly taller than their Beacon Hill predecessors. As for green space, quaint slivers like Union Park Square were created to attract wealthy buyers who had progressively been moving to the Boston countryside; the marketing campaign to draw them

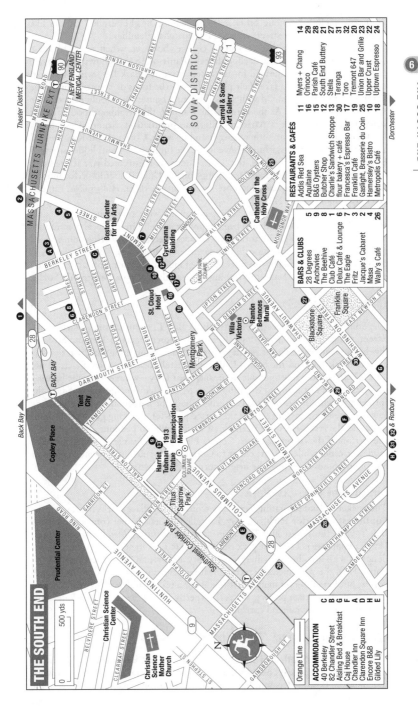

THE SOUTH END

500 yds

Orange Line ▬▬

Theater District ◀

▲ Back Bay

▲ ① ② ③

SOWA DISTRICT

Carroll & Sons Art Gallery

Cathedral of the Holy Cross

Boston Center for the Arts

Cyclorama Building

St. Cloud Hotel

Union Park Square

Ramón Betances Mural

Villa Victoria

Montgomery Park

1913 Emancipation Memorial

Harriet Tubman Statue

Titus Sparrow Park

Blackstone Square

Franklin Square

Tent City

Copley Place

Prudential Center

Christian Science Center

Christian Science Mother Church

Southwest Corridor Park

▶ Dorchester

▶ ③, ⑥, & Roxbury

▶ H, ③, ⑥ & Roxbury

southward included, among other schemes, naming neighbourhood arteries like Appleton and Chandler streets after affluent merchant families.

This development ideology began to change, however, when many of these families experienced financial decline after the **Panic of 1873**. Following the Panic, many of the well-to-do headed for the recently created Back Bay, while waves of immigrants moved in to take their place, shifting the focus of construction in the South End to multi-family dwellings and lodging houses that would be accessible to the working classes. At the turn of the century, the neighbourhood attracted large numbers of the city's **African-American population**; Sammy Davis Jr is a local boy, and Dr Martin Luther King Jr and his wife, Coretta Scott King, rented an apartment at 397 Massachusetts Ave while the future civil rights leader attended Boston University. In the '40s, the South End was an esteemed jazz stronghold, with greats like Billie Holiday, Sarah Vaughan and Duke Ellington performing in the neighbourhood's myriad blue-note venues (one of these, *Wally's Café*, can still be enjoyed today; see p.171).

In the 1970s, as African-American populations were migrating to Roxbury, **Puerto Rican and Dominicans** began moving in and initiated local community housing projects like Villa Victoria. Two decades later, **gentrification** commenced in earnest, leading to, among other things, the opening of several art galleries in the streets south of Washington Street, a geographical concentration latterly going by the name of SoWa (*So*uth of *Wa*shington), recalling Manhattan's trendy SoHo.

Dartmouth Street

The South End's main access point, the Back Bay **T**, opens up onto **Dartmouth Street**, which becomes increasingly upscale the closer it gets to Tremont Street, a few blocks southeast. To the north is Copley Place, a shopping mall that's on the cusp of Back Bay and the South End. Immediately below Copley Place, at no. 130, is Dartmouth's most notable occupant, **Tent City** – a mixed-income housing co-op that owes its name to the 1968 sit-in protest (tents included) staged on the formerly vacant lot by residents concerned about the neighbourhood's dwindling low-income housing. This activism thwarted plans for a parking garage to be built here, and the result is a great example of environmental planning. Built in 1988, the section of the co-op closest to Copley Place blends seamlessly with the mall's modern facade, while the part closer to Columbus Avenue incorporates a series of Victorian houses for which the neighbourhood is known.

Southwest Corridor Park

The pocket of land separating Tent City from Copley Place marks the start of the **Southwest Corridor Park**, a grassy 4.7-mile promenade that connects the Back Bay **T** with the Forest Hill **T** station near the beautiful Arnold Arboretum in Jamaica Plain (see p.114). The park runs parallel to the Orange MBTA line and was designed with low shrubs to increase visibility and give an "open" feeling. Around Forest Hill, the park includes recreational facilities such as tennis and basketball courts, but here it serves mainly as the start of a biking and walking path. Part of another creative urban project, the park expertly covers the tracks of a long-gone nineteenth-century railroad corridor.

Clarendon and Tremont streets

The heart of the South End is at the intersection of **Clarendon** and **Tremont** streets, where an upmarket pseudo-triangle is flanked by some of the most renowned restaurants in Boston (Tremont Street is known as Boston's "Restaurant Row"); the acclaimed *Hamersley's Bistro* (see p.156), at 553 Tremont St, holds fort at the square's southern corner. Smack in the middle lies the domed **Cyclorama Building**, built in 1884 to house an enormous, 360-degree painting of the Battle of Gettysburg (since moved to Gettysburg itself). It was later used as a carousel space, a boxing ring and even the site of the Boston Floral Exchange in 1923; the repurposing continued until 1972, when its current tenants, the **Boston Center for the Arts** (☎617/426-5000, Ⓦwww.bcaonline.org), moved in, providing a home for numerous low-budget theatre troupes and dance companies, and in 2000, two new theatres – the first to be built in Boston in over 75 years (see Chapter 14).

The rest of Tremont Street carries on the high-end restaurant theme set by *Hamersley's*, especially at luxurious eateries like *Aquitaine* and *B & G Oysters* (see p.155). Worth a quick peek en route to gastronomic heaven is the old **St Cloud Hotel**, at 567 Tremont St, a French Second Empire building dating from 1872 that still boasts a facade of white marble and green bay windows; the building now houses private apartments.

Union Park Square

Charming **Union Park Square**, east of Tremont along Union Park Street, is a tiny decorative park which, in typical English fashion, you can walk around but not through – an elegant wrought-iron fence encircles it to make sure you keep off the grass. The oval-shaped park is framed by refined bowfronted rowhouses, representing a pastiche of styles from Italianate to Greek Revival, all of them with larger windows and more elaborate cornice-work than houses on surrounding streets. Keep an eye out for the Frisbee-sized bronze discs embedded in the pavement in front of the homes (and throughout the neighbourhood) – they're remnants of coal-heating days, when the stuff was delivered through the portals and straight into the basement. The best way to see the interior of one of these dignified residences is to take the South End Historical Society's annual October **house tour** (price varies; ☎617/536-4445, Ⓦwww.southendhistoricalsociety.org), when homeowners open their doors to the public.

Washington Street and around

The South End's other major artery (along with Tremont), **Washington Street** intersects with Union Park Street and extends southwest to Roxbury. Intended to resemble a French grand boulevard, it stands out for its generous girth, a quirk that, in recent years, has proven useful for accommodating the Silver Line Ⓣ buses

---

Know your irons

As you walk around the South End, you'll notice a slew of brownstones adorned with curlicued **cast iron** on everything from stairway railings and flower boxes to windowsills and balconies. A distinctive South End feature, the fancy ironwork was, like the area's street-naming convention, intended as a perk to attract upwardly mobile residents back from the suburbs. The arboreal-themed lacing is known as the **Rinceau style** (from the French, and meaning "small branch"), and the neighbourhood boasts around seven variations on the serpentine scroll, ranging from a simple run of acanthus leaves to elaborate arabesques sprouting off from a central rosette. Some of the best can be seen on **West Canton Street** (a few blocks southwest along Tremont Street), where a series of sandstone stairways are trimmed with a wavy version inset with garden roses. Don't let their intricacy fool you, though – by the mid-1850s, technological innovations meant that scrolls such as these were about as easy to stamp out as notebook paper.

that whisk along its right-hand lanes. No. 1400 marks the spot of the pretty 1875 **Cathedral of the Holy Cross**, which in 2002, unfortunately found itself at the centre of the Catholic priest sex abuse scandal. Distinguished by uneven and truncated twin towers – intended as steeples until the parish ran out of money – the vast neo-Gothic interior seats two thousand and boasts some fine stained-glass work, including a multicoloured rose window depicting the Bible's King David.

Another sight nearby is a few blocks southwest, at the corner of West Brookline Street, where **Blackstone Square**, named for Boston's original settler William Blackstone, occupies a city block. Like much in the neighbourhood, it, too, is laid out in English fashion, with diagonal spokes leading to a central fountain. This public space, combined with **Franklin Square** across the street, was once the official entry-point to Boston; nowadays, it's merely an agreeable park used by dogwalkers, bookworms and the like.

Villa Victoria and around

North from Blackstone and Franklin squares, a bronze **plaque** at the corner of Washington and West Dedham streets commemorates the 65th infantry of World War II, a largely Puerto Rican regiment, and along with two large metal "V"s, serves as the unofficial marker of the community's southern frontier.

The real heart of the enclave, though, is two blocks up West Dedham at **Villa Victoria**, a housing project serving 3000 members of the community. This place, like Tent City, was also the result of late-1960s public activism. The buildings, with their purple brick hues and setting around a central square, **Plaza Betances**, suggest a Hispanic influence that sets them apart from the rest of the South End's Victoriana. The main draw here, though, is in the square itself, where the **Ramón Betances Mural** occupies wall space measuring a whopping 45ft long by 14ft high. Created in 1977 by three hundred local teenagers, this colourful mosaic (named after a leader in Puerto Rico's fight for independence from Spain) depicts a hodgepodge of merrily tiled images (including fish, faces, and musical instruments) surrounding a massive sun; a Spanish inscription asserts "let us know how to fight for our honour and our liberty." Meticulously executed and yet unexpected, it may be Boston's best piece of public art.

SoWa Art Galleries and around

Around the intersection of **Harrison Avenue** and **Thayer Street**, near the eastern edge of the South End, a handful of **art galleries** and studios have showrooms in cavernous loft spaces. Wandering around the self-styled **SoWa** district could easily distract you for an hour or so. Certainly, the **Carroll and Sons Art Gallery**, at 450 Harrison Ave (Tues–Sat 10am–6pm; T617/482-2477, Wwww.carrollandsons.net), is worth a peek. Formerly the muse of Bernard Toale, one of Boston's foremost art connoisseurs, it's now run by the Toale gallery's five-year manager, Joseph Carroll, who reopened the space with a new name in 2008. There are a number of other happening spots also gathered at this address, including the artist-owned **Bromfield Art Gallery** (Wed–Sat noon–5pm; T617/451-3605, Wwww.bromfieldartgallery.com) and the **Kingston Gallery** (same hours; T617/423-4133, Wwww.kingstongallery .com). A sort of gallery in its own right, **Bobby from Boston,** a vintage-clothing store distinguished by its beautiful presentation of wares, also holds court in this lot (see p.192). Aim to visit this artsy inlet on **First Fridays** (first Fri of month 5–9pm; Wwww.sowaartistsguild.com), when galleries ply visitors with wine and spaces are abuzz with artists and fans. For a more complete list of galleries, see Chapter 16.

On Sundays from May to October, the **South End Open Market Gallery** (10am–4pm; ☎617/481-2257, ⓦwww.southendopenmarket.com), is held just south of here at 540 Harrison Ave. Fronted by an incredibly vast warehouse edifice, it's run Portobello Market-style, with artists and local food purveyors selling paintings, potted herbs, jars of honey and other crafty ephemera from beneath billowing bright white tents.

Columbus Avenue

Back in the northern section of the South End, **Columbus Avenue** is lined with a number of handsome Victorian houses. At the avenue's intersection with Pembroke Street lies a particularly intriguing spot: a tiny wedge of parkland known, obviously enough, as **Columbus Square**. Anchoring this little green space are two bronze relief sculptures commemorating Boston's role in the Underground Railroad. The 9ft-tall **Harriet Tubman "Step on Board" Memorial**, by Boston sculptor Fern Cunningham, depicts the strident abolitionist leading several weary slaves to safety, while the nearby 1913 **Emancipation Memorial** shows a trio of liberty-seekers that, although thin and barely clothed, bear countenances of stern resolution. More African-American history is found behind the park, along Warren Avenue; the Gothic red-brick **Concord Baptist Church**, at no. 190, welcomed Martin Luther King Jr as a guest minister during his Boston University days.

7

Kenmore Square, the Fenway and west

At the western edge of Back Bay (see Chapter 5), the decorous brownstones and smart shops fade into the more casual **Kenmore Square** and **Fenway** districts. While both areas are somewhat removed from the historical-sights-of-Boston circuit, they're good fun nonetheless, exuding a youthful vibe and, perhaps surprisingly, some of the city's more notable cultural landmarks. The Fenway spreads out beneath Kenmore Square like an elongated kite, taking in a disparate array of sights ranging from hallowed **Fenway Park**, where the Red Sox play ball, to some of Boston's finest high-culture institutions, like **Symphony Hall**, the **Museum of Fine Arts** and the **Isabella Stewart Gardner Museum**. Further west, and more residential, are the communities of **Allston-Brighton** and **Brookline**; the former is home to a young, hip crowd of students, thanks to its proximity to Boston University, the latter boasts the birthplace of JFK. In addition, both neighbourhoods have a number of good eating establishments; Allston-Brighton (or "A-B") in particular has a good bar scene by night.

Kenmore Square and around

Kenmore Square, at the junction of Commonwealth Avenue and Beacon Street, is the unofficial playground for the students of Boston University, as most of its buildings can be found here. Back Bay's Commonwealth Avenue leads right into this lively stretch of youth-oriented bars, record stores and casual restaurants catering to the late-night cravings of local students; as such, the square is considerably more alive when school is in session. Many of the buildings on its north side have been snapped up by BU, such as the bustling six-storey Barnes & Noble bookstore at 660 Beacon St, on top of which is perched the monumental **Citgo Sign**, Kenmore's most noticeable landmark. This sixty-square-foot neon advertisement, a pulsing red-orange triangle that is the oil company's logo, has been a popular symbol of Boston since it was placed here in 1965.

Southwest along Brookline Avenue from the square, you can cross over the Massachusetts Turnpike (via a bridge) to the block-long **Lansdowne Street**, on the northeast side of Fenway Park, a popular stretch of show-your-ID bars and nightclubs (see Chapter 13). There's little point in coming here during daylight hours, though, as most of the action takes place once the sun goes down.

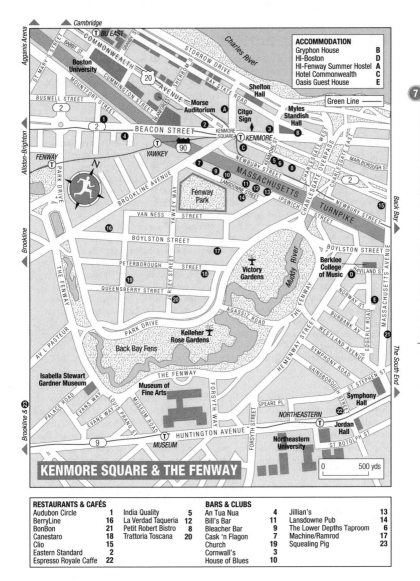

ACCOMMODATION

Gryphon House	B
HI-Boston	D
HI-Fenway Summer Hostel	A
Hotel Commonwealth	C
Oasis Guest House	E

Green Line

KENMORE SQUARE & THE FENWAY

0   500 yds

RESTAURANTS & CAFÉS					
Audubon Circle	1	India Quality	5	An Tua Nua	4
BerryLine	16	La Verdad Taqueria	12	Bill's Bar	11
BonBon	21	Petit Robert Bistro	8	Bleacher Bar	9
Canestaro	18	Trattoria Toscana	20	Cask 'n Flagon	7
Clio	15			Church	19
Eastern Standard	2			Cornwall's	3
Espresso Royale Caffe	22			House of Blues	10

BARS & CLUBS			
Jillian's	13
Lansdowne Pub	14
The Lower Depths Taproom	6
Machine/Ramrod	17
Squealing Pig	23

Fenway Park

Baseball is treated with reverence in Boston, with the **Red Sox** being virtually every Bostonian's – if not every New Englander's – favourite team. It's appropriate, then, that baseball is played here in what is arguably the country's most storied stadium, the unique **Fenway Park**, whose giant 37ft-tall leftfield wall, known as the **Green Monster**, is an enduring symbol of the quirks of early ballparks. Fenway was constructed in 1912 in a tiny, asymmetrical wedge just

The Curse: Reversed!

With the Boston Red Sox having won baseball's coveted World Series titles in both 2004 and 2007, the "curse" that once hung over the team is quickly becoming distant memory. In 1903, the **Boston Pilgrims** (as they were then called) became the first team to represent the American League in baseball's World Series, upsetting the heavily favoured Pittsburgh Pirates to claim the championship; their continued financial success allowed them to build a new stadium, **Fenway Park**, in 1912. During their first year there, Boston won the Series again, and repeated the feat in 1915, 1916 and 1918, led in the latter years by the young pitcher **George Herman "Babe" Ruth**, who also demonstrated an eye-opening penchant for hitting home runs. The team was poised to become a dynasty when its owner, **Harry Frazee**, began a fire sale of the team to finance a Broadway play that was to star his girlfriend. Most of the players went for bargain prices, including Ruth, who was sold to the New York Yankees, which went on to become the most successful professional sports franchise ever, with the Babe at the forefront.

After Ruth's departure, the Red Sox embarked upon a long period in the wilderness, with 86 demoralizing years without a World Series win. This drought began, over the years, to be blamed on the **"Curse of the Bambino"** (aka Babe Ruth) - punishment meted out by the baseball gods for selling off one of the game's greatest players. After coming maddeningly close to the title many times – most notably in 1986, when the Sox were one strike away from clinching the Series before a ground ball rolled through the legs of first baseman **Bill Buckner** – the team finally broke the curse in 2004: after losing the first three games of a best-of-seven series to the Yankees, the Red Sox won four in a row, then went on to sweep the St. Louis Cardinals for the World Series crown. In 2007, the Red Sox began a new tradition of World Series sweeps, beating the Colorado Rockies in four straight games to win their second championship in four years.

off Brookline Avenue, resulting in its famously awkward dimensions, which include an abnormally short rightfield line (302ft) and a fence that doesn't at all approximate the smooth arc of most outfields. That the leftfield wall was built so high makes up for some of the short distances in the park and also gives Red Sox leftfielders a distinct advantage over their counterparts – it takes a good deal of playing time before one gets accustomed to the crazy caroms a ball hit off the wall might take.

In the past, it was rumoured that the Red Sox were planning to move from Fenway, one of the few ballparks from its era that has not been replaced by a more commercially conscious park (indeed, it's the oldest Major League ballpark still in use). Nearly universal nostalgia along with pressure from preservation-minded fans, however, has made such a move highly improbable. Instead, updates like building seats atop the Green Monster in 2003 have been implemented by renowned architect Janet Marie Smith. To sit in these seats yourself, you can take one of the hour-long **tours of the park** (daily hourly, 9am–4pm or up to 3hr before a game; $12, abbreviated in-season tours offer batting-practice access; $20; ☎617/-226-6666, ⓦwww.redsox.com; Kenmore or Fenway **T**), highlights of which include getting up close to the Green Monster, as well as hearing tales about Red Sox greats like Ted Williams, Carl Yastrzemski and Babe Ruth – before he became a Yankee. You'll also glean fun tidbits from Fenway's deep well of lore, such as how the park's scoreboard remains manually operated (its numbers flipped by three guys that rarely ever take a day off) and that, curiously, former owner Tom Yawkey's initials are displayed on the board in a vertical Morse code stripe. More so than touring the park, seeing a game is a must for any baseball fan, and a worthy draw for anyone remotely curious. The season runs from April to October, and tickets can be quite affordable, though difficult to come by: since winning the 2004 and 2007 World Series, Red Sox hysteria has surpassed even its own mind-boggling standards for fan devotion. Check out Chapter 17 for more details on tickets and the team.

The Back Bay Fens

The Fenway's defining element is the snakelike **Back Bay Fens** (daily 7.30am–dusk), which occupies land due east of the stadium, starting where the prim Commonwealth Avenue greenway leaves off. This segment of Frederick Law Olmsted's **Emerald Necklace** was fashioned from marsh and mud in 1879, a fact reflected by frequent vistas of swaying reeds and the name of the waterway that still runs through the park space today – the **Muddy River** – a narrow channel crossed in its northernmost part by an H.H. Richardson-designed medievalesque puddingstone bridge. In the northern portion of the park, local residents maintain small garden plots in the wonderfully jumbled **Victory Gardens**, the oldest community garden in the US. Nearby, below Agassiz Road, the more formally laid out **Kelleher Rose Gardens** boasts colourful hybrid species bearing exotic names like Marmalade Skies, Glowing Peace and Climbing White Iceberg. The area also makes an agreeable backdrop for some of Boston's smaller colleges, such as Simmons and Emmanuel, as well as the Harvard Medical School. Though pretty, the Fens has become a bit unkempt over the years and as such gets a bit dodgy at night – it's best to head onwards before it gets dark.

Frederick Law Olmsted and the Emerald Necklace

The string of urban parks that stretches through Boston's southern districts, known as the **Emerald Necklace**, grew out of a project conceived in the 1870s, when landscape architect **Frederick Law Olmsted** was commissioned to create for Boston a series of urban parks, as he had done in New York and Chicago. A Romantic naturalist in the tradition of Rousseau and Wordsworth, Olmsted conceived of nature as a way to escape the ills wrought by society, and considered his parks a means for city-dwellers to escape the clamour of their everyday life. He converted much of Boston's remaining open space, which was often unappealing marshland, into a sequence of meticulously manicured outdoor spaces beginning with the **Back Bay Fens**, including the **Riverway** along the Boston–Brookline border, and proceeding through **Jamaica Pond** and the **Arnold Arboretum** to Roxbury's **Franklin Park**. While Olmsted's original skein of parks was limited to these, further development linked the Fens, via the Commonwealth Avenue greenway, to the Public Garden and Boston Common, all of which now function as part of the Necklace.

To get a better handle on this pretty piece of parkland jewellery, sign up for a free walking tour with the **Emerald Necklace Conservancy** (☎617/522-2700, Ⓦwww.emeraldnecklace.org). Additionally, Olmsted fans won't want to miss out on the **Frederick Law Olmsted National Historic Site** at 99 Warren St (see p.108).

The Berklee College of Music, Symphony Hall and Jordan Hall

The renowned **Berklee College of Music** makes its home east of the Fens near Back Bay, its campus buildings concentrated mostly on the busy stretch of Massachusetts Avenue south of Boylston Street, an area with several appropriately budget-friendly eateries. In addition to coordinating the BeanTown Jazz Festival every September, there's nearly always something musical going on in the Berklee environs – check @ www.berklee.edu/events for a list of current (and often very inexpensive) performances. Looming a few short blocks south, **Symphony Hall**, home to the **Boston Symphony Orchestra** (see p.175), anchors the corner of Massachusetts and Huntington avenues. The inside of the 1900 McKim, Mead and White design, modelled after the no longer extant Gewandhaus in Leipzig, Germany, resembles an oversized cube, apparently just the right shape to provide the hall with perfect acoustics. **Jordan Hall**, venue for the **New England Conservatory of Music**'s chamber music concerts (see p.175), is a few blocks down on Huntington, at nos. 290–294.

The Museum of Fine Arts

Rather inconveniently located in south Fenway – but well worth the trip – the **Museum of Fine Arts**, at 465 Huntington Ave (daily 10am–4.45pm, Wed–Fri till 9.45pm, Thurs & Fri West Wing and selected galleries only after 5pm; $20, by contribution Wed after 4pm; CityPass accepted; ☎617/267-9300, @ www.mfa .org; Museum **T**), has been New England's premier art space since 1870 and boasts one of the most distinctive art collections in the country.

Recently, the illustrious three-floor granite complex has proven too small for its **extensive collection**, leading to the construction of an all-new, 133,000-square-foot American Wing. This addition, which welcomes 53 new galleries, will make a home for over 5,000 artworks and encapsulate a glass-enclosed courtyard, a state-of-the-art auditorium and a brand-new special exhibitions space. One other projected goal is the improvement of museum "wayfinding" – navigating the labyrinthine corridors and galleries is currently a bewildering experience, even with the museum map in hand. All in all, this is an incredibly exciting time for the MFA, and when the full-scale building opens its doors in 2011, it will surely be a sight to be seen, worth a visit for even the most nonchalant art appreciator.

Trying to see all of the massive collection in one day can be daunting; conveniently, the **entrance fee** entitles you to visit the museum twice in a ten-day period provided you keep the original ticket. Perhaps the easiest way to stay focused is by concentrating on one particular main building: the **West Wing** holds substantial Impressionist art and blockbuster **special exhibits**, while the adjoining **Huntington Building** contains one of the best collections of arts of the ancient world and Asia. The two buildings are joined by interconnecting galleries, which culminate in the Huntington Avenue-side **rotunda**, the second floor of which is a must-see for the outstanding John Singer Sargent **murals** decorating its walls and ceilings.

West Wing

The modern, greystone, I.M. Pei-designed **West Wing** is currently going through a bit of a shake-up due to the installation of the new American Wing, and as such the contemporary American artworks and colonial portraits – both seminal to the museum's collection – you would have previously found here are being shifted over to as-yet unopened galleries. Instead, keep an eye out for the first-floor's **Modern Art** room (largely populated by Europeans such as Matisse, Picasso and Mondrian), where you'll find **Gauguin**'s sumptuous display of existential angst *Where Do We Come From? What Are We? Where Are We Going?* The second-floor **Impressionism** room is another gem, home to crowd-pleasing favourites like Monet's water lilies and Edgar Degas' charming sculpture of a *Little Fourteen-Year-Old Dancer*. This room also depicts a fine selection of **Post-Impressionist** art, including **van Gogh**'s richly hued *Lullaby: Madame Augustine Roulin Rocking a Cradle (La Berceuse)*.

The Koch Gallery

The **Koch Gallery**, which connects the West Wing to the second floor of the Huntington Building's rotunda, ranks among the MFA's more spectacular showings. Designed to resemble a European palace hallway, its wood-inlaid ceilings cap walls hung two-high with dozens of portraits, religious pieces, and landscapes of varying sizes. The doors at the far end put you in the upper Rotunda, under John Singer Sargent's superb murals (see below).

Huntington Avenue Building

Connected to the West Wing by both the Lane and Koch galleries, the 500ft granite-faced **Huntington Avenue Building** was the first MFA structure to open on this site in 1909. Here you'll find the museum's impressive collection of **ancient world** and **Asian** arts.

Ancient world and Musical Instruments galleries

A series of MFA-sponsored digs at Giza have made its **Egyptian collection** not only the standout of the museum's **ancient world** holdings, but also one of the finest and most extensive of its kind in the world. Eight galleries over two floors feature some 40,000 objects, including sculpture, pottery and sarcophagi ranging from prehistoric times to the Roman period. Best among the first-floor findings is the small gallery on **Egyptian Funerary Arts**, with gorgeous blue canopic jars, pristine shrouds and mummies – including one for a baby crocodile that likely served as a well-to-do family's pet.

Across the hall, it's worth popping into the **Musical Instruments** gallery, even if just to glimpse item #12 – one of the world's first saxophones, made by Adolphe Sax himself. This room is also home to a number of gloriously painted pianos.

The Shapiro Rotunda

Between the second-floor Egyptian and Asian galleries is the outstanding **Shapiro Rotunda**, its dome and en-suite colonnade inset with twenty **murals** and fourteen **bas reliefs** by John Singer Sargent, who undertook the commission following his Boston Public Library work (see p.91). Operating under the belief that mural painting – not portraiture – was the key to "artistic immortality," this installation certainly guaranteed the artist a lasting place in the MFA and some controversy to boot: when the ten-year project was completed shortly before Sargent's death in 1925, his Classical theme was falling out of vogue and his efforts were considered the "frivolous works of a failing master." Today, after a 1999 refurbishment that revitalized the works – much of which depict debates between Classical and Roman Art using figures from Greek mythology – it's clear that what many had described as a confused set of subjects (art, theatre, philosophy, mythology and architecture) is actually a brilliant representation of the museum's collections, portrayed through a visual feast of fluid lines and colour schemes.

Asian galleries

South of the rotunda, the **Asian galleries** – though they're among the best of their kind in the world – don't get nearly the attention they deserve, perhaps due to their awkward layout. Best is the magnificent recreation of Japan's oldest surviving **Buddhist temple**, complete with tranquil lighting, tapered wooden columns and coffered ceiling. Seven Buddhas dating to the ninth century recline inside the darkened temple; two of them represent the Buddha of Infinite Illumination. Wandering into its meditative alcove, you'll feel you've stumbled upon a marvellous museum secret.

The **Chinese** section is equally superb, particularly the **Chinese Furniture Gallery**, a dull name for what is in fact a remarkable life-size staging of an upper-class Chinese house. Arranged beneath its pagoda-style roof are ornate examples of sixteenth- and seventeenth-century Chinese furniture, such as handsomely carved teak day beds, lacquered tables inlaid with birds and flowers and household items like the strategy game Wiegi, in which the goal is to surround other players' pieces.

Isabella Stewart Gardner Museum

Less broad in its collection, but more distinctive and idiosyncratic than the MFA, is the neighbouring **Isabella Stewart Gardner Museum**, 280 The Fenway (Tues–Sun 11am–4.45pm; $12, $2 off with an MFA admission receipt (within two days), free admission for those named "Isabella"; CityPass accepted; ☎617/566-1401, Ⓦwww.gardnermuseum.org; Museum **T**). Spirited Boston socialite Gardner (1840–1924) collected and arranged more than 2500 objects in the four-storey Fenway Court building she designed herself – right down to the marbleized paint technique she demonstrated to her workers atop a ladder – making this the

Heist at the Gardner

In the most famous unsolved **art theft** of all time, the Isabella Stewart Gardner Museum was robbed on March 18, 1990. At around 1.30am, as the city's St Patrick's Day celebrations were coming to a close, two men dressed as police officers knocked on the side door of the museum and were allowed to enter by security guards. Within minutes, the guards were overpowered and the men pillaged some $500 million worth of art, including two Rembrandts and a Manet. The empty frames are still on display, an homage to the works and a placeholder for their return. Despite the lure of a $5 million reward and numerous leads that have implicated everyone from the IRA to the Mafia to a notorious art thief, the paintings have yet to be recovered. Adding insult to injury, if the thieves were captured today they possibly wouldn't face prosecution, owing to the Massachusetts statute of limitations on robberies.

country's only major museum that is entirely the creation of a single individual. The fine art collection, including works by Titian, Rembrandt and Whistler, is presented alongside a colourful mix of furniture, textiles and objects culled from around the globe; Gardner's goal was to foster the love of art rather than its study, and she wanted the setting of her pieces to "fire the imagination." Your imagination does get quite a workout: there's art everywhere you look, with most of the objects unlabelled, placed in corners or above doorways, for an effect that is occasionally chaotic, but always striking. Gardner's will stipulated that every piece in the galleries stay put, or else the entire kit and kaboodle was to be shipped to Paris for auction and the proceeds given to Harvard. And therefore it ruffled some feathers when, in 2010, museum officials unveiled an ambitious plan to construct a new glass-and-copper entrance wing for the museum, albeit one that was to be situated a respectful 50ft from the original building. Slated to open in 2012, the addition, whose approval proceedings went all the way to the Massachusetts Supreme Court, will generate a new greenhouse and horticultural classroom, in addition to an information space called "**The Living Room**," dedicated to the Gardner museum's own intriguing history.

The key to getting the most out of a visit is to engage as Ms Gardner wished, speculating on why an artwork is placed where it is, and looking for relationships with surrounding objects. If possible, aim to join the hour-long **tours** (generally Tues–Fri 12.30pm & 2.30pm; free), but get there early as only fifteen people are allowed at a time, and spots are first-come first-served. Alternatively, self-guided audio-tour equipment can be rented for $4.

The first floor

The Gardner is best known for its spectacular central **courtyard** styled after a fifteenth-century Venetian palace; the second-century Roman mosaic of Medusa at its centre is fittingly surrounded by stone-faced statuary and fountains, and brightened up, year round, by flowering plants and trees. However, the museum's greatest success is the **Spanish Cloister** flanking the courtyard, a long, narrow corridor just through the main entrance that perfectly frames **John Singer Sargent**'s ecstatic representation of flamenco dance, *El Jaleo* (meaning "The Ruckus"), and contains fine seventeenth-century Mexican tiles as well as Roman statuary and sarcophagi. A door nearby leads discreetly to the **Monks Garden**, a Mediterranean outdoor space bursting with palms and bougainvillea (currently closed due to the adjacent expansion project).

The floor's final room, the **Macknight**, was Gardner's writing room when she was in residence and frequently doubled as Sargent's guestroom; atop one of the bookshelves is a poignant late-life portrait of his hostess, *Mrs Gardner in White*, which demonstrates the closeness of their friendship.

The second floor

Up one level, a first-rate display of **seventeenth-century Northern European** works was diminished by a 1990 **art heist** in which two Rembrandts and a Vermeer were among thirteen artworks stolen (see box opposite); you can still spot the missing works by their empty frames.

The magnificent **Tapestry Room** is hung with rich mid-sixteenth-century Brussels tapestries; it's a sumptuous backdrop for the weekend chamber orchestra concerts held here from September to May (℡617/566-1401). Extending north from the Tapestry Room, the **Short Gallery** depicts a notable painting of the hostess herself, Anders Zorn's vivacious *Isabella Stewart Gardner in Venice*.

The third floor

Right at the head of the stairs, the third-floor's **Veronese Room** is a stunner, with ornate gold and robin's-egg blue leather coverings embellishing the full length of its walls. The ceiling – which is hung with Paolo Veronese's massive sky-blue canvas *The Coronation of Hebe* – is also showstopping.

Between the stairwell and the **chapel** is the **Gothic Room**, a sombrely decorated chamber whose chief attraction is **John Singer Sargent**'s controversial life-size *Portrait of Isabella Gardner* that prompted the public to rename her "Saint Isabella," thanks to the halo effect of the background. The portrait was considered so "provocative" by Gardner's husband that he asked that it not be displayed until after her death (when it did indeed cause a stir).

Allston-Brighton and Brookline

West of the Fenway lie a few residential areas, accessible on the Green Line, that feel more or less like pleasant extensions of Boston and Cambridge. In fact, **Allston-Brighton**, a triangular community that spreads south from the Charles River down to Beacon Street, was originally conceived as a Cambridge adjunct. Nowadays, it's home to a delightful concentration of ethnic restaurants (centred on the intersection of Harvard and Brighton Aves), a plethora of Jewish delis and bakeries, and innovative shops and bars crammed into a couple of blocks along Harvard Avenue.

Much of the activity in the leafy, affluent town of **Brookline** is focused around **Coolidge Corner**, at Beacon and Harvard streets (hit up *Kupel's*, at 421 Harvard St, for exceptional bagels). Of note in these parts is the **Coolidge Corner Theater**, at 290 Harvard St, a refurbished arthouse cinema with a great selection of film offerings. Another draw is the nearby **John F. Kennedy National Historic Site**, at 83 Beals St (mid-May to late-Oct Wed–Sun 10am–4.30pm; $3; ☎617/566-7937, Ⓦwww.nps.gov/jofi), which preserves the outwardly unremarkable home where JFK was born on May 29, 1917. Inside, a narrated voiceover by the late-president's mother, Rose, adds some spice to the roped-off rooms; another option is the park ranger tours that are given every half an hour. To get to the heart of Brookline, take the Green Line's C branch to Coolidge Corner or D branch to Brookline Village.

Far from being some dusty collection of cars, the **Larz Anderson Auto Museum**, at 15 Newton St (Tues–Sun 10am–4pm; $10; ☎617/522-6547, Ⓦwww.mot.org) is all swank and curve. Housed in the carriage house of a palatial nineteenth-century estate, the museum centres on 21 beautifully preserved antique automobiles, many accompanied by complementing Hollywood gowns. While the museum will mainly be of interest to little ones, the displays *are* charming, and its grounds – with views of the Boston skyline – make for a great post-trip picnic.

Along the suburb's southern fringe is the **Frederick Law Olmsted National Historic Site**, at 99 Warren St (☎617/566-1689 Ⓦwww.nps.gov/frla). Known as Fairsted, this expansive house doubled as Olmsted's family home and office. Almost one million landscape schemes are archived here, ranging from his work on Yosemite Valley to New York's Central Park, and while the surrounding grounds are (unsurprisingly) quite idyllic, the park site is closed for renovations until 2011.

8

The southern districts

The parts of Boston most visitors see – Downtown, Beacon Hill, Back Bay and the North End – only comprise a small portion of the city. To the south of the city centre lies a vast spread of residential neighbourhoods known collectively as the **southern districts**, including largely Irish **South Boston**, historically African-American **Dorchester** and **Roxbury**, and the artsy community of **Jamaica Plain**. Though they do offer a more complete picture of urban life, these areas are unlikely to divert your interest if you're short on time. Nevertheless, JFK-junkies will be rewarded by Dorchester's worthwhile **John F. Kennedy Presidential Library and Museum,** and no one should miss Jamaica Plain's superb **Arnold Arboretum**, with its world-renowned array of lilac and bonsai trees; the two are easily accessible by the **T**, and combine to make a terrific half-day outing (by car).

Once rural areas dotted with the swanky summer homes of Boston's elite, in the late-nineteenth century the southern districts became populated by middle- and working-class families pulled from Downtown. Three-storey rowhouses soon replaced mansions, and the moniker **"streetcar suburbs"** – after the trolley that debuted in 1897 and connected these once remote areas with Downtown – was coined as a catchall for the newly redefined neighbourhoods. Today, the districts retain a vibrant immigrant, blue-collar, young family and student population – all seeking the lower rents and less-harried vibe that accompanies life lived just outside a major city.

South Boston

Across the Fort Point Channel from Downtown and east into Boston Harbor lies **South Boston**, affectionately referred to as "Southie". Originally a peninsula separated from Boston proper by waterways, it was connected by bridge in 1805, and throughout the nineteenth century it grew, augmented by landfills, and in population, thanks to a steady influx of immigrants.

Known for its Irish-American population, South Boston's Celtic heritage is quite evident on the main commercial boulevard, **East and West Broadway**, where seemingly every laundry, convenience store and restaurant has a sign plastered with shamrocks. South Boston also cites the 1997 film *Good Will Hunting* as a claim to fame; in this cinematic paean to the neighbourhood, Southie featured prominently as the cultural backdrop for Will Hunting's path to mathematical truth and personal harmony. In 2006, the neighbourhood again hit the silver screen with Martin Scorsese's *The Departed*. The film's main character, Frank Costello,

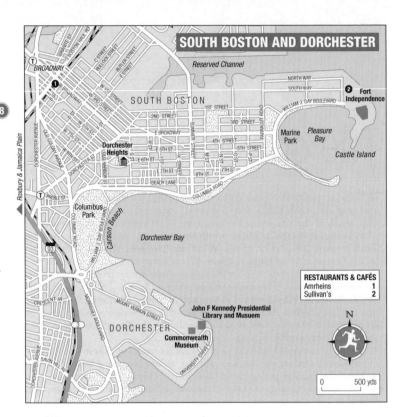

SOUTH BOSTON AND DORCHESTER

is allegedly based on real-life Irish-American Southie mob boss James "Whitey" Bulger, who fled Boston in 1995 after his thirty-year grace period as an FBI informant had come to an abrupt, indictment-related close.

More unfortunate is South Boston's lingering taint as a hotbed of racial tension, owing to friction between its old timers and the African-American students that were bussed here in the 1970s in compliance with court-mandated **public-school desegregation**. On South Boston's first day of desegregation busing (September 13, 1974), stones, eggs and tomatoes were thrown at arriving schoolchildren; amidst the fracas, nine black South Boston High School students were injured when white students shattered the windows of their bus. These days, while still a little rough in spots, South Boston has softened. Visitors (who generally head this way to imbibe in the neighbourhood pub culture) may be surprised to learn that Southie is home to a number of scenic beaches – easily Boston's best.

Castle Island

South Boston narrows to an end in Boston Harbor on a 22-acre strip of land called **Castle Island**. The island was once only connected to the mainland via a causeway bridge, but landfill projects in the nineteenth century fashioned it into a peninsula. Castle Island lies just off the terminus of William J. Day Boulevard, and is a favourite leisure spot for many Bostonians. Its appeal is easy to see: parks and beaches run for miles, parking is free and the swimming is accompanied by spectacular views of Downtown and the harbour. It's all best appreciated via the two-mile walkway that, thanks to its circular shape, is known as the "Sugar Bowl". Adjacent to Fort Independence, *Sullivan's*, a snack bar founded in 1951, is a local institution, with a seasonal army of employees serving tasty portions of french fries and grilled fare; enjoying one of their $1.60 hot dogs is the perfect way to cap off a summer's day.

Fort Independence

Fort Independence (guided tours Sat & Sun noon–3.30pm; free; Broadway **T**, then bus #9 or #11), a stout granite edifice that's the dominating feature of Castle Island, was one of the earliest redoubts in the Americas, originally established in 1634. The fort has been rebuilt several times since – what you see today is actually a thicker rendition of the 1801 version. Its hulking stone walls tempt exploration, a desire that can be fulfilled on summer weekends when free ranger-led tours provide history and folklore about the dank interior corridors; one legend has it that friends of an officer shot dead in a duel sealed his killer alive in a chamber in the fort's dungeons. Ten years later, Edgar Allan Poe, while assigned to duty here as an officer in the US Army, heard the tale and used it as the basis for his story, *The Cask of Amontillado*. Outside, picnicking abounds, with views of the beach and the planes of nearby Logan Airport.

Dorchester

Occupying the southeast corner of the city, **Dorchester** lies beneath South Boston, below Columbia Road. North Dorchester was from its earliest days a centre of trade and is still a largely industrial area. South Dorchester has seen more turbulence over the years – once a coveted spot for upper-class country homes, it followed the streetcar suburb pattern of the southern districts and remained relatively affluent until after World War II, when the middle class left; property values soon plummeted, and crime and unemployment rose. While it's still rough in parts, things are brighter today, and it's home to a broad ethnic mix, notably Irish, Haitians, Latinos, Vietnamese, Caribbeans and African-Americans, as well as a young student blend. Most visitors come here for the **John F. Kennedy Presidential Library and Museum** (JFK's mother lived in Dorchester as a girl); there are also some worthwhile restaurants and shops along "Dot" (Dorchester) Avenue. Just across the parking lot from the JFK Museum, it's worth popping by the new **Commonwealth Museum**, if only to spy the original 1780 Massachusetts Constitution, still used in the governance of the state.

John F. Kennedy Presidential Library and Museum

The **John F. Kennedy Presidential Library and Museum**, at Columbia Point (daily 9am–5pm; $12, CityPass accepted; ☎1-866/JFK-1960, ⓦwww.jfklibrary .org; JFK/UMass **T**; free shuttle every 20min, free parking), stands out for providing a fascinating glimpse into the culture of a recent, storied, era, while being spectacularly situated in a stunning, glass-fronted, curvilinear I.M. Pei-designed building – allegedly the architect's favourite commission – offering panoramic views over Boston Harbor.

The museum opens with a well-done eighteen-minute **film** covering Kennedy's political career up until the 1960 Democratic National Convention, and is narrated with soundbites from Kennedy himself. On leaving the auditorium and entering the exhibition space, other displays cover the presidential campaign of 1960 and the highlights of the brief Kennedy administration against a backdrop of stylized recreations of his campaign headquarters, the CBS studio that hosted the first televised presidential debate between him and Richard Nixon, and the main White House corridor. The campaign exhibits are most interesting for their television and radio ads, which illustrate the squeaky-clean self-image America possessed at that time. The section covering the Kennedy administration is more serious, animated by a 22-minute film on the Cuban Missile Crisis that evokes the tension of the event, while possibly exaggerating Kennedy's heroics. Most sobering is the darkened hallway towards the end where a televised announcement of the president's assassination on November 22, 1963, plays in a continuous loop. Lighter fare is on display in the **Jackie Kennedy exhibits**, which trace her evolution from young debutante to First Lady-cum-popular icon; items on display include her outfits, her camera and her baby brush.

The final section of the museum is perhaps the best: a 115ft-high glass **atrium** overlooking the harbour, where a majestic American flag presides over modestly presented excerpts from Kennedy's *Profiles on Courage* – affecting enough to move even the most jaded JFK critic. The research **library**, open to any member of the public with advance notice of specific archival requests, holds JFK's papers (some 8.4 million pages in all) from his curtailed term in the Oval Office. The archive is also the repository for Ernest Hemingway's original manuscripts; Kennedy helped Hemingway's wife get the papers out of Cuba following her husband's 1961 suicide (call ☎ 1-866/JFK-1960 for an appointment to see them).

Commonwealth Museum

Upon entering the **Commonwealth Museum** (Mon–Fri 9am–5pm; free; ☎ 617/727-9268, ⓦ www.sec.state.ma.us/sec/mus/museum; JFK/UMass **T**; free shuttle every 20min, free parking) just across the car park from the JFK Museum and sited inside the Massachusetts Archives building, it's easy to feel you're in the wrong place – a workaday government office rather than a historical museum entrusted with the state's most valuable treasures. Put these misgivings aside and head straight to the Treasures Gallery, a dark, guarded *Mission Impossible*-esque alcove where five of the state's most priceless documents lie encased under pressure-sensitive glass. This set of archives includes one of the fourteen original copies of the Declaration of Independence, the 1691 Charter of the Province of Massachusetts Bay (which endearingly depicts a hand-drawn, curly-wigged King William in its upper-left corner) and the "Constitution of the Commonwealth of Massachusetts in 1780", the oldest written document still used for governance in the world and the museum's most notable possession. All are scripted in an ornate, florid cursive, and, except for the papery Declaration of Independence, were scribbled onto animal skin (check out the sewn-up tear on the Constitution's lower-left side). While the rest of the museum – really just a handful of exhibits – is quite small, and lacks the wow-factor of the Treasures Gallery, it contains copies of a number of fascinating state archives (which is fitting, considering the museum's location). One such document is the 1637 decree banishing religious dissident Anne Hutchinson from the Massachusetts Bay Colony; you can also view her friend Mary Dyer's written plea to end Quaker prosecution (soon after the letter was drafted in 1659, Dyer was hanged on Boston Common, see p.79). You'll also find the 1679 deed for Cape Cod, "purchased" from Native Americans at the giveaway price of "two brass kettles, six coats...a box...and five pounds and ten shillings".

On your way out, ask the front desk for a viewing of your own historical documents – the office can look up the records of any family that came over to Massachusetts.

Dorchester Heights Monument

At the convergence of South Boston and Dorchester rises the incline of **Dorchester Heights** (Broadway **T** to bus #11 to G St stop), a neighbourhood of three-storey rowhouses whose northernmost point, Thomas Park, is crowned by a 70ft tall square marble Georgian revival **tower** commemorating George Washington's bloodless purge of the Brits from Boston. After the Continental Army had held the British under siege here for just over a year, Washington wanted to put an end to the whole thing. On March 4, 1776, the general amassed all the artillery around and placed it on the towering peak of Dorchester Heights, so the tired Redcoats could get a good look at the patriots' firepower. Intimidated, they swiftly left Boston – for good.

Thomas Park, generally empty and pristine, still commands the same sweeping views of Boston and its southern communities that it did during the Revolutionary War. The best vista is from the top of the monument itself, though it's only open by appointment (free; ☎617/242-5642). Next to the park is South Boston High School, the location of nationally televised racial turmoil during desegregation busing in the 1970s.

Roxbury

Roxbury, a historically African-American neighbourhood, occupies much of south central Boston below the South End, between Dorchester and Jamaica Plain. This formerly pastoral region was one of the city's most coveted addresses in the seventeenth and eighteenth centuries, when wealthy families built sumptuous country homes here. Around the 1950s, the area hit hard times, and the urban blight has left its scars, although ongoing attempts to restore some of the impressive, if neglected, properties in the area have been slowly successful, drawing in former South Enders who've been pushed out by that neighbourhood's skyrocketing property prices. For exploring by day, the area holds some historical interest around **Dudley Square**, where a couple of Revolutionary War-era sites have been preserved. Another attraction here, especially if you have children in tow, is the **Franklin Park Zoo**, located in yet another of Frederick Law Olmsted's green spaces. To learn more about Roxbury's history, or to hop on a tour of its best sights, check in with "Discover Roxbury" (☎617/427-1006, ⊛www.discoverroxbury.org), run by a group of well-informed Roxbury residents, whose themed trolley ($25), bike ($5) and walking ($5) tours usually take in the Dillaway-Thomas House as well the home of Ella Collins Little, where a young Malcolm X spent a number of formative years.

Dudley Square and around

Roxbury's commercial centre is **Dudley Square** – the intersection of Dudley and Warren streets – which is little more than the usual mix of restaurants and shops. If you're in the area, check out the **Dillaway-Thomas House**, at 183 Roxbury St between Dudley Square and the Roxbury Crossing **T** stop (open by appointment only; donations welcome; ☎617/445-3399), a structure built in 1750 as a parsonage and subsequently used as the main headquarters for Brigadier General Thomas and the continental army in the Revolutionary War. Its first floor is remarkably well preserved, featuring many details of its original construction, such as exposed beams; the best part, though, may be the serene apple orchard surrounding it, enhanced by incredible skyline views. Across the street is John Eliot Square, from where William Dawes began his ride to Lexington on April 18, 1775, to warn of the British arrival by "sea".

8 Franklin Park and Franklin Park Zoo

The southernmost link in the Emerald Necklace (see box, p.103), **Franklin Park** was one of Olmsted's proudest accomplishments when it was completed, owing to the sheer size of the place, and its scale is indeed astounding: 527 acres of green space, with countless trails for hikers, bikers and walkers leading through the hills and thickly forested areas. It's quite easy to get lost among all the greenery and forget that you're still in the city. In the not-so-distant past, Franklin Park was considered shaggy and even unsafe, but its administrators have worked hard to change this perception. Aside from the zoo, the park sports a golf course, basketball and tennis courts and, in summer, frequent live music and movie showings.

The **Franklin Park Zoo**, on the far eastern edge of Franklin Park (April–Sept Mon–Fri 10am–5pm, Sat & Sun 10am–6pm; Oct–March daily 10am–4pm; $14, kids $8; ☎617/541-LION, ⓦwww.zoonewengland.org; Forest Hills **T**) is much like any other zoo, and is really only essential if you're travelling with kids, who'll definitely get a kick out of the Serengeti Crossing, where they'll interact with zebras, ostriches, and ibex along four-acres of rolling, wooded hills. Adults may enjoy the array of exotic fauna, much of which is contained in the African Tropical Forest, an impressively recreated savanna that's the largest indoor zoo design in North America, housing gorillas, warthogs and pygmy hippos. More fun is had at Bird's World, a charming relic from the days of Edwardian zoo design: a huge, ornate wrought-iron cage you can walk through while birds fly overhead.

Jamaica Plain

Walking around **Jamaica Plain** – "JP" in local parlance – you'll probably come across a bumper sticker slogan to the tune of "ban Republican marriage" or "Make Levees, Not War". Such is the left-leaning bent of this funky, artsy neighbourhood, populated by a good mix of students, Hispanic and African-American enclaves and young middle-class families. Located between Roxbury and Brookline, the area's activity centres on, appropriately, **Centre Street**, which holds some inventive cafés and restaurants; the northern part of the street (just past its intersection with S. Huntington Ave) in particular plays host to a stronghold of excellent Latin food eateries (see Chapter 11). Free and inexpensive activities abound in JP: call in for a free tour at the **Samuel Adams brewery**, spend a couple of hours picnicking or canoeing on Jamaica Pond, stroll around **Forest Hills Cemetery** or pay a visit to the neighbourhood's star attraction, the **Arnold Arboretum**, on its southwestern edge.

Arnold Arboretum

The 265-acre Harvard University-run **Arnold Arboretum**, 125 Arborway (daily dawn–dusk; donations welcome; ☎617/524-1718, ⓦwww.arboretum.harvard .edu; Forest Hills **T**), is the most spectacular link in the Emerald Necklace. Its collection of over 15,000 flowering trees, vines and shrubs has benefited from more

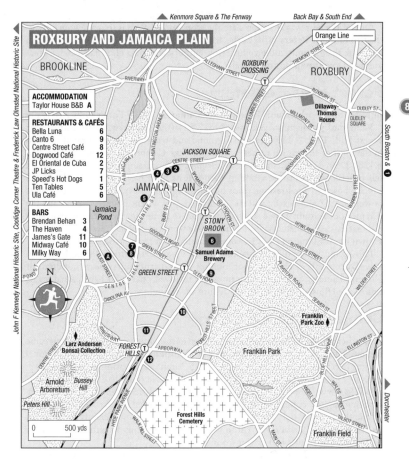

than 100 years of both careful grooming and ample funding, and is now one of the finest in North America. The plants are arranged along a series of paths populated by runners and dog-walkers as well as serious botanists, though it certainly doesn't require any expert knowledge to enjoy the grounds.

The array of Asian species – considered one of the largest and most diverse outside Asia – is highlighted by the **Larz Anderson Bonsai Collection**, brilliantly concentrated along the Chinese Path walkway at the centre of the park. The arboretum also has more than seven hundred trees that are over a hundred years old; eighteen of them (including an 1881 silver maple that, at over 120ft, is the tallest tree here) have been chosen as part of a self-guided Centenarian tour (the trees and plants are labelled with a gold tag, and you can pick up helpful guide maps from the visitor's centre).

Although the staff does an impressive job of keeping the grounds looking fabulous year-round, it's best to visit in spring, when crab-apples, lilacs and magnolias complement the greenery with dazzling chromatic schemes. "Lilac Sunday", the third Sunday in May, celebrates the arboretum at its most vibrant (and busiest), when its collection of **lilacs**, the second largest in the US, is in full bloom. **Fall** is also a good time to visit, when the arboretum becomes a glorious mass of blazing oranges, reds and browns.

One of the best ways to appreciate the scope of the place is to make your way to the top of 240ft **Peters Hill**, in the arboretum's southern section, where you can overlook the grounds in their impressive entirety and, on a clear day, catch a great view of Downtown Boston as well.

Forest Hills Cemetery

Just east of the arboretum, **Forest Hills Cemetery**, at 95 Forest Hills Ave (daily 8.30am–dusk; donations welcome; ☎617/524-0128, Ⓦwww.foresthillstrust.org; Forest Hills **T**), is a 250-acre burial ground and sculpture garden created in 1848 in the spirit of the garden cemetery tradition, like Cambridge's Mount Auburn (see p.128). Dotted with Victorian stone carvings and contemporary art, the park – a self-proclaimed "romantic vision of nature at its most harmonious and abundant" – was chosen as final resting place by an intriguing roster of Bostonians: poetic powerhouses Anne Sexton and e.e. cummings, playwright Eugene O'Neill and the inventor of the fountain pen, Lewis Waterman, to name a few. But it's the cemetery's elaborately carved memorials – including five works by Daniel Chester French (best known for Washington DC's Lincoln Memorial) that really stand out.

This scenic necropolis is also known for its annual Lantern Festival, held in July. During this celebratory (not sombre) event, participants release hundreds of glowing lanterns, inscribed with messages to loved ones who have passed away, onto Lake Hibiscus, which float away into the twilight.

Samuel Adams brewery

In northern Jamaica Plain, a cavernous nineteenth-century brewery building came full circle in 1985 when the **Boston Beer Company** (the brewer behind Samuel Adams beer; Mon–Sat 10am–3pm, Fri till 5.30pm; $2 donation given to charity; persons 21 and over must bring valid ID or passport in order to drink; ☎617/368-5080, Ⓦwww.samueladams.com; Stony Brook **T**), and generally credited with kick-starting the country's microbrew revolution, settled here at 30 Germania St. While this is really only the company's half-pint facility (used mainly for research and development), that doesn't stop visitors from attending its extremely popular hour-long brewhouse and tasting-room tours.

The guided tours begin by crunching samples of barley malt and passing around handfuls of hops – their pungent aroma redolent of evergreen trees – before heading downstairs to discuss the fermentation process. The last twenty minutes are spent beer guzzling, civilized-style: free pitchers of brew are passed around, poured into complimentary seven oz souvenir glasses, and then pontificated upon by the world's luckiest tour guides.

After you've finished, check out the brewery building's other offerings, including *Ula Café* and *Bella Luna* (see p.147 & p.158).

Cambridge

J ust across the Charles River from Boston, **Cambridge** is more unbuttoned and laidback than its big city counterpart, and populated by a younger, more bohemian type of resident. Highlighted by two of the most illustrious institutions of higher learning in the country, its denizens, including clean-cut college students, trendy teenagers, starched business people and street musicians and artists, manage to support a buzzing streetlife and café culture that can either be seen as a refreshing change from provincial Boston or just a continuation of it – it's still Boston, but Boston letting loose.

A walk down Cambridge's colonial-era brick pavement and narrow, crooked roads takes you past plaques and monuments honouring literati and revolutionaries who lived and worked in the area – some hailing from as early as the seventeenth century. Nevertheless, Cambridge manages – perhaps even better than Boston itself – an exhilarating mix of colonial past and urban present; the extensive range of residents and activities, and the sheer energy that pervades its classrooms and coffeehouses, are all enough to make it an essential stopover on your trip.

Cambridge resembles a bow tie, with Harvard Square forming the knot. On its southern border is the sinuous Charles River, with Boston on the opposite bank, while the concave northern side is shared with the large, mostly residential city of **Somerville**, popular with locals for its restaurant and café scene centring on the alternative vibe of **Davis Square**. Cambridge proper, meanwhile, is loosely organized around a series of squares – actually confluences of streets that are the focus of each area's commercial activity. By far the most famous of these is **Harvard Square**, which radiates out from the **T** stop along Massachusetts Avenue, JFK Street and Brattle Street. Roughly coterminous with Harvard Square is **Harvard University**; together, these two areas make up the cultural and academic heart of Cambridge. This is where people converge to check out the famous Ivy League institution, historical monuments, a lively coffeehouse-and-bookstore scene and a disgruntled counterculture. Its total area – only a single square mile – is small in comparison with the entirety of Cambridge, but the density of attractions here make it one part of town not to be missed.

Old Cambridge, the clean, impeccably kept colonial heart of the city, is easily accessible from Harvard Square; sights here include impressive mansions – most notably the **Longfellow House** – and peaceful **Mount Auburn Cemetery**. East from here, on the other side of the university, **Central** and **Inman squares** represent the core of **Central Cambridge**, and are of primary interest for their atmospheric bar scene. As with Central Cambridge, **Eastern Cambridge** grew up around industry rather than academia. Today, it draws most of its interest from the **Massachusetts Institute of Technology**, one of the world's premier science and research institutions. Home to some innovative – if at times peculiar – architecture

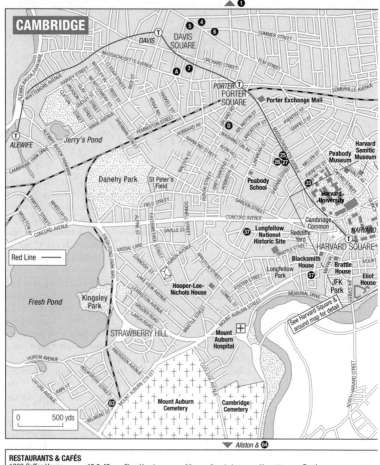

RESTAURANTS & CAFÉS							
1369 Coffee House	19 & 42	Chez Henri	26	flour bakery + café	55	Rendezvous	49
Alive and Kicking Lobsters	61	Christina's	20	Friendly Toast	28	Salts	39
All-Star Sandwich Bar	17	Cuchi Cuchi	38	Helmand	8	Sofra	63
Andala Coffee House	56	Craigie on Main	35	Hungry Mother	23	Soundbites	1
Baraka Café	58	Dalí	10	Koreana	34	Ten Tables	37
BerryLine	27	Darwin's Ltd.	57	Olé Mexican Grill	13	Toscanini's	40
Blue Room	30	Diesel Café	6	Oleana	29	True Grounds	3
Blue Shirt Café	4	East Coast Grill	15	Punjabi Dhaba	22	Tupelo	9
Central Kitchen	45	Emma's Pizza	31	Redbones	7		

and an excellent museum, MIT spreads out below **Kendall Square**, which itself is home to a cluster of stalwart high-tech companies. Finally, you'll find some good shopping and restaurants along **Huron Avenue** and around **Porter Square**, the area that makes up **Northwest Cambridge**.

Some history

Cambridge began inauspiciously in 1630, when a group of English immigrants from Charlestown founded **New Towne** village on the narrow, swampy banks of the Charles River. These Puritans hoped New Towne would become an ideal

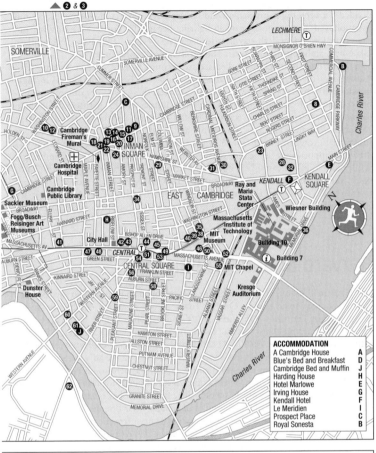

SOMERVILLE

LECHMERE Ⓣ

Charles River

CAMBRIDGE

Ray and Maria Stata Center

KENDALL SQUARE

Wiesner Building

Massachusetts Institute of Technology

Building 10

Building 7

MIT Chapel

Kresge Auditorium

Cambridge Fireman's Mural

Cambridge Hospital

Cambridge Public Library

Sackler Museum

Fogg/Busch Reisinger Art Museums

City Hall

Dunster House

EAST CAMBRIDGE

KENDALL SQUARE

CENTRAL

CENTRAL SQUARE

ACCOMMODATION

A Cambridge House	A
Blue's Bed and Breakfast	D
Cambridge Bed and Muffin	J
Harding House	H
Hotel Marlowe	E
Irving House	G
Kendall Hotel	F
Le Meridien	I
Prospect Place	C
Royal Sonesta	B

BARS & CLUBS

Atwood's Tavern	11	Green Street	54	Olde Magoun's Saloon	2	Thirsty Scholar Pub	12
Bukowski's Tavern	16	Johnny D's	5	Paradise	52	Trina's Starlite Lounge	18
Cantab Lounge	43	Lily Pad	14	People's Republik	48	T.T. the Bear's Place	53
The Cellar	41	Lizard Lounge	33	Phoenix Landing	51	Western Front	60
The Druid	21	The Middle East	53	Plough & Stars	47		
Enormous Room	45	Middlesex Lounge	50	River Gods	59		
The Field	44	Miracle of Science		Ryles	24		
Flat Top Johnny's	32	Bar & Grill	46	Scullers Jazz Club	62		
Great Scott	64	Muddy Charles Pub	36	Temple Bar	25		

religious community; to that end, they founded a college in 1636 for the purpose of training clergy. Two years later, the college took its name in honour of a local minister, **John Harvard**, who bequeathed his library and half his estate to the nascent institution. New Towne was eventually renamed **Cambridge** after the English university where many of its founders were educated, and became one of the largest publishing centres in the New World after the importation of the printing press in the seventeenth century. Its university and printing industry established Cambridge as an important centre of intellectual activity and political thought, and during the late eighteenth century its population became sharply divided between the many artisan and farmer sympathizers of the revolution and the moneyed Tory minority; when fighting began, the Tories were driven from their mansions on modern-day Brattle Street (then called "Tory Row"), their place taken by Cambridge intelligentsia and prominent Revolutionaries.

In 1846, the Massachusetts Legislature granted a city charter linking Old Cambridge (the Harvard Square area) and industrial East Cambridge as a single municipality. Initially, there was friction between these two very different neighbourhoods; in 1855, citizens from each area unsuccessfully petitioned for them to be granted separate civic status. Though relations improved, the distinctive characters remain. The late nineteenth and early twentieth centuries brought substantial growth to the town. A large, mainly Irish immigrant population was drawn to opportunity in the industrial and commercial sectors of East Cambridge, while academics increasingly sought out Harvard, whose reputation continued to swell, and the **Massachusetts Institute of Technology**, which moved here from Boston in 1916. The fact that nearly half of its 90,000-plus residents are university affiliates ensures that it will remain one of America's most opinionated cities.

Harvard Square and around

The Harvard **T** station marks Cambridge's centre, opening up onto **Harvard Square** and the square's main tenant, Out of Town News, where an enthusiastic youth brigade (led by Harvard's "Unofficial Tours" guides) rallies visitors in the shadow of the Harvard Yard buildings. A small **tourism kiosk** run by the Cambridge Tourism Office (daily 9am–5pm; ☎617/441-2884 or 1-800/862-5678, ⓦwww.cambridge -usa.org) faces the station exit, but more of the action is in the adjacent sunken area known as **The Pit** – teens can spend entire days sitting here admiring each other's green hair and body piercings, while homeless locals hustle for change. This is also the beginning of the **street music scene**, where folk diva Tracy Chapman (a graduate of Tufts University, in nearby Somerville) and country star Bonnie Raitt (a Radcliffe alumna) both got their starts. The square reaches its most frenetic state on Friday and Saturday nights and Sunday afternoons, when all the elements converge – crowds mill about while performers do their thing on every corner.

The Old Burying Ground

Facing Harvard Square to the north along Massachusetts Avenue is one of Cambridge's first cemeteries, the **Old Burying Ground** (daily 9am–5pm; if the gate is locked, pop in and ask the sexton if he can open it), whose environs have scarcely changed since the seventeenth century. To enter the grounds, look for the gate beside the simple, grey-washed, eighteenth-century **Christ Church**.

The epitaphs have an archaic ring to them ("Here lyes…"), and the stone grave markers are adorned in a style blending Puritan austerity and medieval superstition: inscriptions praise the simple piety of the staunchly Christian deceased, but are surrounded by death's-heads carved to ward off evil spirits. Its most famous occupants include several of Harvard's first presidents as well as two black veterans of the Revolutionary War, Cato Stedman and Neptune Frost. Be sure to check out the **milestone** marker (at the northeast corner, where Garden Street meets Massachusetts Avenue) found just inside the gate, whose 270-year-old inscription is still readily visible. Originally set to mark the then-daunting distance of eight miles to Boston, the letters A.I. identify the stone's maker, Abraham Ireland.

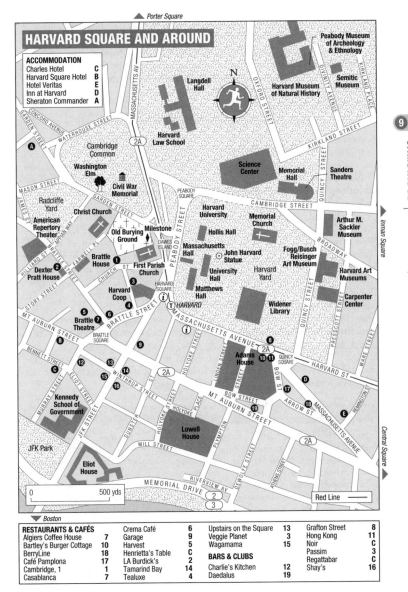

HARVARD SQUARE AND AROUND

ACCOMMODATION
Charles Hotel	C
Harvard Square Hotel	B
Hotel Veritas	E
Inn at Harvard	D
Sheraton Commander	A

Peabody Museum of Archeology & Ethnology

Langdell Hall

Semitic Museum

Harvard Museum of Natural History

Harvard Law School

Cambridge Common

Washington Elm

Civil War Memorial

Science Center

Memorial Hall

Sanders Theatre

Radcliffe Yard

Christ Church

American Repertory Theater

Old Burying Ground

Milestone

Harvard University

Memorial Church

Arthur M. Sackler Museum

Hollis Hall

Brattle House

Dexter Pratt House

First Parish Church

Massachusetts Hall

John Harvard Statue

Fogg/Busch Reisinger Art Museum

Harvard Art Museums

University Hall

Harvard Yard

Harvard Coop

Matthews Hall

Widener Library

Carpenter Center

Brattle Theatre

Adams House

Kennedy School of Government

JFK Park

Lowell House

Eliot House

MEMORIAL DRIVE

Red Line

Boston

RESTAURANTS & CAFÉS					
Algiers Coffee House	7	Crema Café	6	Upstairs on the Square	13
Bartley's Burger Cottage	10	Garage	9	Veggie Planet	3
BerryLine	18	Harvest	5	Wagamama	15
Café Pamplona	17	Henrietta's Table	C		
Cambridge, 1	1	LA Burdick's	2	**BARS & CLUBS**	
Casablanca	7	Tamarind Bay	14	Charlie's Kitchen	12
		Tealuxe	4	Daedalus	19

Grafton Street	8		
Hong Kong	11		
Noir	C		
Passim	3		
Regattabar	C		
Shay's	16		

Dawes Island

A triangular traffic island squeezed into the intersection of Massachusetts Avenue, Garden Street and Peabody Street, **Dawes Island** is anything but bucolic – the wedge of concrete serves as a bus stop. The island is named after the patriot who rode to alert residents that the British were marching to Lexington and Concord on April 19, 1775 – the *other* patriot, that is, William Dawes (see p.52).

While Longfellow opted to commemorate Paul Revere's midnight ride instead, Cantabrigians must have appreciated poor Dawes's contribution just as much. To be completely accurate, there was also a third rider, Dr Samuel Prescott, who's generally credited as the only one to complete the ride. Bronze hoof marks in the pavement mark the event, and several placards provide information on the history of the Harvard Square/Old Cambridge area.

Cambridge Common and Radcliffe Yard

A trapezoidal patch of green between Massachusetts Avenue, Garden Street and Waterhouse Street, **Cambridge Common** has been a site for recreation and community events since the area's earliest settlers used it as a cow pasture. Visitors flock here for its historical interest, but locals congregate for Frisbee and sunbathing – although after dusk it can be an altogether lonelier, and somewhat dodgier, place.

Early Harvard commencements took place here, as did public debates and training exercises for the local militia. You can retrace a portion of the old **Charlestown–Watertown path**, along which the British Redcoats beat a sheepish retreat to Watertown during the Revolutionary War, and which still transects the park from east to west. A broad range of **statuary** dots the southeast corner of the park, and you can't miss the towering monument to Lincoln and the Civil War dead, which all but overshadows the tableau of two emaciated figures nearby, wrought as an unsettling memorial to the Irish Potato Famine.

Just across Garden Street from Cambridge Common is a less crowded park, **Radcliffe Yard**, originally the centre of Radcliffe College, established in 1878 to give women access to (then exclusively male) Harvard; the two colleges merged in the 1970s. The yard itself is a picturesque, impeccably preserved quadrangle; enclosed by brick buildings upheld by Ionic columns, it's dotted with statues and pathways, making it a great place for a summer picnic or stroll.

The Washington Elm

Perhaps the prettiest feature on Cambridge Common is the revered **Washington Elm**, under which it's claimed George Washington took command of the Continental Army. The tree is at the southern side of the park, almost facing the intersection of Garden Street and Appian Way, and is predictably accompanied by a wealth of commemorative objects: three cannons captured from the British when they evacuated Boston, an engraving of Washington standing in the shade of the elm and monuments to two Polish army captains hired to lead revolutionary forces. What the memorials don't tell you is that the city of Cambridge cut down the original Washington Elm in 1946 when it began to obstruct traffic; it stood at the intersection of Mason and Garden streets. The present tree is actually the offspring of that tree, raised from one of its branches. To further confuse the issue, the Daughters of the American Revolution erected a monument commemorating the southeast corner of the park as the spot where Washington did his historic thing. And recently, American historians have uncovered evidence strongly suggesting that Washington never commissioned the troops on the common at all, but rather in Wadsworth House at Harvard Yard.

For another, more curious memorial to the tree, check out the **Washington Elm marker** embedded in the intersection of Mason and Garden streets. What looks like an ordinary manhole actually bears the inscription "Here Stood the Washington Elm" – just be careful not to get honked at (or injured) by oncoming traffic.

Along JFK Street

The stretch of **JFK Street** below Harvard Square holds more of the city's many public spaces, including **Winthrop Square**, site of the original New Towne marketplace and since converted into a tiny, well-shaded park, presided over by restaurants and shops and strewn about with benches. Cross the park and walk down Winthrop Street to the right to get a sense of the sloping topography and narrow street design of early Cambridge.

Harvard Yard and the university

The transition from Harvard Square to **Harvard Yard** – the proper centre of the university – is brief and dramatic: in a matter of only several feet, the buzz of car traffic and urban life gives way to grassy lawns, towering oaks and an aura of intellectualism. The atmosphere is more illusory than real, however, as the Yard's narrow footpaths are constantly plied by preoccupied students and camera-clicking tour groups, who make the place seem more like an amusement park than a university campus. You can join the hullabaloo by taking a free one-hour student-guided tour from the Harvard Information Center in the **Holyoke Center Arcade**, 1350 Massachusetts Ave (June–Aug Mon–Sat 10am, 11.15am, 2pm & 3.15pm; Sept–May Mon–Fri 10am & 2pm, Sat 2pm; no tours during breaks in the academic calendar; ☎617/495-1573, ⓦwww.harvard.edu/visitors). The centre also provides limited free internet use, as well as **maps** and brochures detailing everything Harvard-related. Alternatively, you could hop on one of the lively "Unofficial Tours" (daily 10.45am, 11.30am, 12.30, 1.30pm, 2.30pm & 3.30pm; $10 suggested donation; ☎617/674-7788, ⓦwww.harvardtour .com), departing from the Cambridge information kiosk, just outside the Harvard **T** station; its student guides are easily spotted in their humorously misspelled "Hahvahd" T-shirts.

The Old Yard

Enter through Johnston Gate, across Massachusetts Avenue from the Common, and you're in **Old Yard**, a large, rectangular area dating from 1636, when it was created as a grazing field for university livestock. Opposite the gate, in front of symmetrical, marble-hued **University Hall**, is the yard's trademark icon, the **John Harvard statue**, around which chipper student guides inform tour groups of the oft-told "three lies" (it misdates the college's founding; erroneously identifies John Harvard as the college's founder; and isn't really a likeness of John Harvard at all). While it's a popular spot for visitors to take pictures, male students at the college covet the statue as a site of public urination, so you might want to stay away from rubbing the toe (supposedly good luck).

Along the northwest border of the yard, stout **Hollis Hall** is the dormitory where Henry David Thoreau lived as an undergraduate. The architectural contrast between modest Hollis, which dates from 1762, and its grandiose southern neighbour, **Matthews Hall**, built around a hundred years later, reflects Harvard's transition from a training ground for ministers to a cosmopolitan university. The **indentations** in Hollis's front steps also hold some historical interest: students used to warm their rooms by heating cannonballs, and, when it came time to leave for the summer, they would dispose of them by dropping them from their windows. Harvard's first chapel, the charming 1744 **Holden Chapel** to the rear, is also worth a quick peek for its attractive Georgian architecture and provincial blue-and-white pediment.

Tercentenary Theatre and around

To the east of the Old Yard lie the grander buildings of the grassy enclave known as the **Tercentenary Theatre**, where a vast set of steps leads up to the enormous pillars of **Widener Library**. Named after Harvard grad and *Titanic* victim Harry Elkins Widener, whose mother paid for the project, it's the centre of the largest private library collection in the US, boasting 65 miles of bookshelves, a first folio of Shakespeare and a Gutenberg Bible among its holdings (you'll need a Harvard ID to see them). At the opposite side of the New Yard is **Memorial Church** (T617/495-5508, Wwww.memorialchurch.harvard.edu), whose narrow, white spire strikes a balancing note to the heavy pillared front of Widener; its 172ft-high steeple, topped by a medieval pennant-shaped **weathervane**, is a classic postcard image of Harvard Yard. Inside the church, the nave bears the names of alumni who've died at war; woefully, the organ at the rear – adorned with gilded carvings of starfish, kelp, cod and crab – was removed in 2010; it's set to be replaced by a new custom-built organ in 2012.

The Science Center and Law School

The immense structure facing the New Yard is Harvard's **Science Center**. The big lecture halls on the first floor are home to some of Harvard's most popular classes; one celebrity professor who taught here was the late evolutionary biologist Stephen Jay Gould. A popular myth has it that the centre was designed to look like a camera, since one of its main benefactors was Polaroid magnate Edwin Land, but any likeness is purely accidental.

Up Massachusetts Avenue, on the east side of Cambridge Common, lies the main quad of the famed **Harvard Law School**, founded in 1817. The campus focuses on the stern grey pillars of **Langdell Hall**, an imposing edifice on its western border, whose entrance bears the inscription *"Non sub homine, sed sub deo et lege"* ("Not under man, but under God and law"). Inside is the renovated **Harvard Law Library**, where you can practically smell the stress in the air.

Memorial Hall and the Carpenter Center

The rest of the campus lies east of the Science Center, starting at 45 Quincy St with the pointed arches and flying buttresses of **Memorial Hall**, built to commemorate the Harvard students who died during the Civil War. While it resembles a church, right down to its central vaulted **narthex**, which is bathed in filtered sunlight through Tiffany and La Farge stained-glass windows, the space actually serves as **Sanders Theatre**, undoubtedly Harvard's most impressive concert space.

The conspicuously modern **Carpenter Center** is hard to miss as you continue past Memorial Hall and look down Quincy Street: the slate-grey granite slab stands out amidst Harvard's ever-present brick motif. Completed in 1963 as a centre for the study of visual art at Harvard, the Carpenter Center is the only building in America designed by modernist French architect Le Corbusier (known for Zurich's Centre Le Corbusier and avant-garde furniture design), and its jarring difference from its surroundings has drawn some criticism from traditionalists. Still, it's a striking space; be sure to traverse its trademark feature, a **walkway** that leads through the middle of the building, meant to reflect the path worn by students on the lot on which the centre was constructed. The modest **Sert Gallery**, on the third floor (Tues–Sun 1–5pm; free; ☎617/495-3251), puts on rotating contemporary art exhibits culled from Harvard's collections, while the lower floors of the building frequently display student art exhibits. Also downstairs is the **Harvard Film Archive** (☎617/495-4700, ⓦ//hcl.harvard.edu/hfa), which screens old-school, foreign and contemporary classics such as *Whatever Happened to Baby Jane* or *La Femme Infidèle* – check their website for scheduling, or pick up a calendar from inside the building.

Harvard University art museums

Harvard's three art museums – the **Fogg**, the **Sackler** and the **Busch-Reisinger** – have benefited from years of scholarly attention and donors' financial generosity. All three are currently closed for a major renovation that will merge them into one single collection at 32 Quincy St (formerly the building of the Fogg and Busch-Reisinger museums). Set to open in 2013, the new **Harvard Art Museum** will encompass over 150,000 works of art, including highlights of Harvard's substantial gathering of Western art, a small yet excellent collection of German Expressionists and Bauhaus works, and sensuous Buddhas and gilded bodhisattvas from its Asian and Islamic art collections. During the renovation, you can check out a sampling of some of the university's finest works at 485 Broadway, formerly the **Arthur M Sackler Museum** (Tues–Sat 10am–5pm; $9; ☎617/495-9400, ⓦwww.harvardartmuseum.org).

Harvard Museum of Natural History and Peabody Museum of Archeology and Ethnology

North of the Sackler Museum, Divinity Avenue holds the beloved **Harvard Museum of Natural History** (☎617/495-3045; ⓦwww.hmnh.harvard.edu), as well as a separate entity, the **Peabody Museum of Archeology and Ethnology** (☎617/496-1027; ⓦwww.peabody.harvard.edu), linked to the HMNH via a walkway. Entry to both is provided with a common ticket (daily 9am–5pm; $9, free to Massachusetts' residents Sun 9am–noon year round and Wed 3–5pm Sept–May). Favoured by children, but also worth a visit for adults, the museums are the public front for Harvard University's natural history institutions and as such feature comprehensive collections of North American and Mayan archeology, interactive exhibits related to meteorites, gemstones and climate change, and lots of funhouse-sized dinosaur skeletons and bones.

The Peabody Museum of Archeology and Ethnology

Considered a separate body from the Museum of Natural History, the **Peabody Museum of Archeology and Ethnology**, 11 Divinity Ave, displays materials culled from the university's anthropological and archeological expeditions. The strength of the museum lies in its collection of pieces from **Mesoamerica**, ranging from digs in the pueblos of southwestern United States to artifacts from Incan civilizations. Best are the enormous, carved Copan stelæ on which practical information such as birth, death and bloodletting are all recorded in ancient Mayan. The ground-floor exhibits centre on the indigenous cultures of North America. Here you'll find the only surviving Native American artifacts collected by Lewis and Clark, as well as colourful kachina dolls crafted by Arizona Hopi for their children and stupendous examples of Northwestern ceremonial masks with pronounced bird beaks.

Harvard Museum of Natural History

A second-floor passageway connects the Peabody with the **Harvard Museum of Natural History**, set in a nineteenth-century Victorian building at 26 Oxford St. Begin your visit at **Minerals, Gems and Meteorites,** a visual feast of rocks and gemstones with a stunning 1600lb amethyst-encrusted cavity serving as its centre piece. Reputed to be one of the world's finest mineral collections, most of the gems are truly exquisite; even for geological laymen, there's plenty of eye candy to keep you occupied. Seek out the small display devoted to **meteorites**: in addition to outlasting a fall from outer space, these mighty rocks have seen 4.5 billion years and counting.

The adjacent gallery houses the museum's *pièce de resistance,* the stunning **Ware Collection of Glass Models of Plants.** This project, the work of a father-and-son team from Dresden, Germany, began in 1887 to serve as a teaching collection and concluded almost fifty years later in 1936, leaving the museum with an absolutely unique and visually awesome collection of flower models constructed to the last detail, entirely from glass; it's really not to be missed. Down the hall, the **zoological galleries** are home to some gloriously huge dinosaur fossils, including a 42ft-long prehistoric marine reptile, the *Kronosaurus*, the teeth of which (as the museum proudly proclaims) "are the size of bananas". Around the corner is the *Glyptodont*, which looks like an inflated armadillo.

The Harvard Semitic Museum

Diagonally opposite the Peabody Museum entrance is the **Harvard Semitic Museum**, 6 Divinity Ave (Mon–Fri 10am–4pm, Sun 1–4pm; free; ☎617/495-4631, Ⓦwww.fas.harvard.edu/~semitic), which lacks the magnetism of its neighbours but holds some Near Eastern archeological artefacts that are worth a look. Pieces range from Egyptian tombs to Babylonian cuneiform, and include a particularly appealing collection of tiny stone-cut votive figurines from ancient Cyprus. There is also a set of Egyptian amulet and funerary figurines, which were buried with the dead along with a magical charm so that they could later reawaken and "perform the agricultural labor that was required in the afterlife".

Harvard houses

Harvard's attractive upperclassmen residences, most of which are nested in the area east of JFK Street and south of Massachusetts Avenue, are a visible reminder of the university's legacy. Nearest the Yard, at 26 Plympton St, **Adams House** has the most rebellious history of the lot, having been used as a revolutionary prison for General "Gentleman Johnny" Burgoyne, and later serving as a raucous undergraduate residence (1901–1931), complete with indoor rifle and pistol practice, water fights and a pet monkey. Just south of Adams juts the graceful, blue-topped bell tower of **Lowell House**, at 2 Holyoke Place, which boasts one of Harvard's most beautiful courtyards, surrounded by a compound of sober brick dormitories and fastidiously manicured grounds. Further southwest, along the banks of the Charles, rises the purple spire of **Eliot House**, at 101 Dunster St, once a blueblood bastion of social privilege that can count Jay Rockefeller and Leonard Bernstein as former residents. To the east, at 945 Memorial Drive, lies **Dunster House**, whose red Georgian tower top is a favourite subject of Cambridge's tourist brochures; it was modelled after Christ Church College's Big Tom in Oxford. Alongside Adams, Dunster was historically considered a centre for radical culture: while the other residences were often praised for their building of a "house spirit", Dunster had no rules or regulations, but rather a reputation for "extreme informality".

Old Cambridge: Upper Brattle Street

After the outbreak of the American Revolution, Cambridge's patriot dissidents ran their Tory neighbours out of town, but left their sumptuous houses along "Tory Row" (now **Brattle Street**, the main drag of **Old Cambridge**) more or less unharmed. Extending west from Eliot Street and Harvard Square, the area has remained a neighbourhood of stately mansions, although only three of the houses are open to the public; the rest you'll have to view from across their expansive, impeccably kept lawns.

The Brattle House and Farwell Place

The first of several noteworthy residences along Brattle Street, the **Brattle House**, at no. 42, doesn't reflect the unabashedly extravagant lifestyle of its former resident, the Revolutionary War commander General William Brattle. Dwarfed as it is by surrounding shops and restaurants, it currently houses the Cambridge Center for Adult Education; they don't mind if you pop in for a look.

Down the street and to the right, tiny **Farwell Place** features several modest Federal-style houses dating to the early nineteenth century and is the best (and only remaining) example of the square's residential character before it became a teeming centre of activity. The restored house at no. 17 is one of the best examples of the genre; it now houses Christ Church's thrift shop (☎617/492-3335).

The Dexter Pratt House

A marker on the corner of Brattle and Story streets commemorates the site of a tree that once stood near the **Dexter Pratt House**, at 56 Brattle St. The house is the former home of a village blacksmith celebrated by Longfellow in a popular poem that began, "Under a spreading chestnut tree/The village smithy stands..." In 1876, the chestnut was cut down, despite Longfellow's vigorous opposition, because it was spreading into the path of passing traffic. The city of Cambridge fashioned a chair out of the felled tree and presented it as a birthday present to Longfellow, who then composed a mawkish poem about the whole affair ("From My Easy Chair"), and all was forgiven. These days the Federal-style building is home to the *Hi-Rise Bread Company* sandwich shop. Beyond the house, at the intersection of **Mason** and **Brattle streets**, a string of distinguished mansions signals the edge of Old Cambridge proper.

Longfellow National Historic Site

One house you can visit for more than just a look is the recently renovated **Longfellow National Historic Site**, 105 Brattle St (May–Oct Wed–Sun 10am–4.30pm, tours hourly 10.30–11.30am & 1–4pm; $3; ☎617/876-4491, Ⓦwww.nps.gov/long; Harvard **T**). Erected for Royalist John Vassal in 1759, who promptly vacated it on the eve of the Revolutionary War, and used by George Washington as headquarters during the Siege of Boston, it later became home to poet Henry Wadsworth Longfellow, who moved in as a boarder in 1837. When he married the wealthy Fanny Appleton, her father purchased the house for them as a wedding gift in 1843, and Longfellow lived here until his death in 1882.

The house is preserved in an attempt to portray it as it was during Longfellow's residence, and the halls and walls are festooned with his furniture and art collection, including portraits of fellow writers Ralph Waldo Emerson and Nathaniel Hawthorne. Most surprising is the wealth of nineteenth-century pieces from the

Far East amassed by Longfellow's son, Charlie, on his world travels; four of his Japanese screens are included, the best of which, a two-panel example depicting geishas in spring and winter costumes, is in an upstairs bedroom. His other son, Ernie, stayed at home to make a name for himself as a landscape and portrait painter; a number of his works adorn the walls of the house. Just outside, a lovely garden features labyrinthine shrubs, snapdragons and roses all laid out with historical accuracy from plans dating to 1904.

Hooper-Lee-Nichols House

The second Brattle Street mansion open to the public is the bluewashed **Hooper-Lee-Nichols House** at no. 159 (tours Mon & Wed 1–5pm; $5; ☎617/547-4252, Ⓦwww.cambridgehistory.org), half a mile west of the Longfellow House. While a bit out-of-the-way, the house – one of the area's oldest residences – does give an intimate sense of colonial Cambridge life. It's particularly unusual for its various architectural incarnations: it began as a stout, post-medieval farmhouse and underwent several renovations until it became the Georgian mansion it is today. Rooms have been predictably restored with period writing tables and canopy beds, but knowledgeable tour guides spice things up a bit, opening secret panels to reveal centuries-old wallpaper and original foundations.

Mount Auburn Cemetery

Past the Hooper-Lee-Nichols House, at the intersection of Brattle and Mount Auburn streets, is the **Mount Auburn Cemetery** (daily 8am–5pm, summer till 7pm; Ⓦwww.mountauburn.org), an unexpected treasure. Laid out in 1831 as America's first "garden cemetery", its 175 acres of stunningly landscaped grounds, complete with ponds and fountains, are more like a beautifully kept municipal park than a necropolis; locals love it for strolling and jogging (it's also, rather incongruously, a great date spot). The best way to get a sense of the cemetery's scope is to ascend the **tower** that lies smack in its centre atop a grassy bluff; from the top you can see not only the entire grounds but all of Downtown Boston and its environs. Like most cemeteries in the Boston area, Mount Auburn has its share of resting luminaries, among others, the painter Winslow Homer and art patron Isabella Stewart Gardner are buried here; ask the folks in the main office for a map of famous graves if you're interested.

Central Square

A mile east of Brattle Street, **Central Square**, marked by the convergence of Massachusetts Avenue, Prospect Street and Western Avenue, is roughly in the geographical centre of Cambridge, and is the city's civic centre as well. The square is an interesting mix of cultural and industrial Cambridge – a working-class area that's steadily populated by students and young families, with an ethnically diverse population, good places to shop and eat, and some of the best **nightlife** in Cambridge. Indeed, you'll find substantially more activity here after dark, especially along Massachusetts Avenue, as denizens flock to hear live music.

In 2004, the Gothic quarters of **City Hall**, at 795 Massachusetts Ave, were the first in the nation to issue same-sex marriage licenses, an event heralded at the stroke of midnight on May 17 with rice-throwing and impromptu bursts of the

Star-Spangled Banner. Across the street, the imposing marble **Clifton Merriman Building**, 770 Massachusetts Ave, houses a beautiful and historic post office (Mon–Fri 7.30am–6.45pm, Sat 7.30am–2pm; ☎617/575-8700).

Inman and Kendall squares

Inman Square marks a hip stretch directly north of Central Square that's centred on the confluence of Cambridge, Beacon and Prospect streets. There's not many sights here per se – just a pleasant, mostly residential neighbourhood where much of Cambridge's working-class, Portuguese-speaking population resides alongside students and hipster types. What does make Inman worth a visit, though, is its café culture and broad range of excellent restaurants, where you can enjoy some of the town's finest food without breaking the bank. Look out for *Punjabi Dhaba*, one of the best Indian spots around (see p.161). While in the area, check out the **Cambridge Firemen's Mural**, on the front of the Inman Square Firehouse at 1384 Cambridge St. This piece of public art was painted by a young local artist named Ellary Eddy in 1976 and depicts then-members of Engine No. 5; it also includes images of Benjamin Franklin, who founded the country's first volunteer fire department, and George Washington, who stayed in Cambridge during the Siege of Boston.

Adjacent to the Massachusetts Institute of Technology, **Kendall Square** grew from the ashes of the post-industrial desolation of East Cambridge in the 1960s and 1970s to become a glittering testament to the economic revival that sparked Massachusetts in the 1980s. By day, Kendall bustles with students and programmers lunching in low-key eateries; at night, the business crowd goes home and the place becomes largely quiet, although a sampling of brave new bars and eateries have moved in here of late. The long-time exception to this is the Kendall Square Cinema (see p.178), which draws large crowds to see some of the best art-house and second-run movies in the area.

The Massachusetts Institute of Technology

The geography of Eastern Cambridge is dominated by the **Massachusetts Institute of Technology** (**MIT**), which covers more than 150 acres alongside the Charles River, providing the area with its intellectual backbone and imbuing it with some delightfully curious modern architecture. Originally established in Back Bay in 1861, MIT moved to this more auspicious campus across the river in 1916 and has since risen to international prominence as a major centre for theoretical and practical research in the sciences. Both NASA and the US Department of Defense pour funds into MIT in exchange for research and development assistance from the university's best minds.

The campus buildings and geography reflect the quirky, brainy character of the institute, emphasizing function and peppering it with a peculiar notion of form. Everything is obsessively numbered and coded: you can, for example, go to 1-290 (the Pierce Laboratory) for a lecture in 1.050 (Engineering Mechanics 1), which gets you closer to a minor in Course 1 (Civil and Environmental Engineering). MIT students are also notoriously mischievous and famed for their "hacks" – or pranks. Some of the best-known include the installation of a police car on top of the Great Dome (complete with a cruiser number, π), the explosion of an enormous weather balloon that read "MIT" from the 46-yard line of the annual Harvard-Yale football game and the confiscation of a cannon from rival school Caltech (3000 miles west), subsequently bedecked with one of MIT's signature gold rats and displayed in time for Campus Preview Weekend.

Buildings 7 and 10

Behind the massive pillars that guard the entrance of MIT's main building, **Building 7**, at 77 Massachusetts Ave, you'll find a labyrinth of corridors – known to Techies as the **Infinite Corridor** – through which students can traverse the entire east campus without ever going outside. Just inside the building's entrance you'll find the **MIT Information Center** (Mon–Fri 9am–5pm, campus tours at 11am & 3pm; ☏617/253-4795), while atop the nearby Maclaurin Building (aka "Building 10") is MIT's best-known architectural icon, a massive gilt hemisphere called the **Great Dome**.

Ray and Maria Stata Center

Looking like a set of egg timers designed by Salvador Dalí, the **Ray and Maria Stata Center**, at 32 Vassar St, is the $200 million work of renowned architect Frank Gehry and was partly funded by Bill Gates of Microsoft. Opened in May 2004, self-guided tours of the public spaces on the first and third floors are possible Mon–Fri 9am–5pm. There are several entrances to the building, all of which lead to Student Street, bizarrely located *in* the building. An information desk is conspicuous by its location under a huge question mark hanging from the ceiling.

Kresge Auditorium and MIT Chapel

MIT has drawn the attention of some of the major architects of the twentieth century, who have used the university's progressiveness as a testing ground for some of their more experimental works. Two of these are located in the courtyard across Massachusetts Avenue from Building 7. The **Kresge Auditorium**, designed by Finnish architect Eero Saarinen, resembles a large tent, though its real claim to fame is that it puzzlingly rests on three, rather than four, corners; the architect

---

364.4 Smoots + 1 Ear

if you walk from Back Bay to Cambridge via the **Harvard Bridge** (which leads directly onto MIT's campus), you might wonder about the peculiar marks partitioning the sidewalk. Doled out into "Smoots", these units of measure represent the height of **Oliver R. Smoot**, an MIT Lambda Chi Alpha fraternity pledge in 1958. At 5'7", Smoot was the shortest member of the group, and part of his pledge initiation included the (quite willing) use of his body as a measuring tape, across the length of the Harvard Bridge – resulting in the conclusive "364.4 Smoots + 1 Ear" at the bridge's terminus. While the marks continue to be repainted each year by LCA pledges, the Smoot itself has gone global: in addition to the ample press devoted to Smoot and gang, the "Smoot" measurement has made it all to way to a conversion calculator on Google.

allegedly designed it over breakfast by cutting into his grapefruit. In the same courtyard is the red-brick **MIT Chapel**, also the work of Saarinen, and shaped like a stocky cylinder with an abstract sculpture crafted from paper-thin metals serving as a rather unconventional spire; inside, a delicate metal screen scatters light patterns across the floor.

A couple of blocks back toward Kendall Square, at 20 Ames St, the I.M. Pei-designed **Wiesner Building** hosts the **List Visual Arts Center** (Tues–Sun noon–6pm, Thurs till 8pm; free), which displays contemporary artworks that utilize a wide range of media.

MIT Museum

While it only takes up two small floors of gallery space, the **MIT Museum**, near Central Square at 265 Massachusetts Ave (daily 10am–5pm; $7.50; ☎617/253-5927, ⓦweb.mit.edu/museum), packs a nice punch with its exhibits. The museum has a number of standout permanent displays, including "Holography: the Light Fantastic", a collection of seriously cool eye-trickery. There is also "Robots and Beyond", where those of the humanoid persuasion can view robotic displays such as *Kismet*, a "sociable robot" who has the ability to utilize an eye-opening range of emotional expression and physical gestures. The museum's best exhibit, however, is Arthur Ganson's "Gestural Engineering", a fascinating display of ingenious mini-machines combining Ganson's imaginative brand of engineering and sculpture. In *Machine with Wishbone*, a lone wishbone ambles along, pulling behind it a mass of wiry wheels. *Cory's Yellow Chair* flings itself into a six-pointed star, then repositions back into shape with a snap. Perhaps the most poignant sculpture is *Alone*, where, unlike the other works, a solitary figure sits high upon a platform, motionless and still. Far below, underneath the figure, wheels speedily turn.

Northwest Cambridge and Somerville

Off any university-oriented or colonial heritage sightseeing circuit, **Northwest Cambridge** has more local charms on offer. The area's centre, **Porter Square**, is a mile north of Harvard Square along Massachusetts Avenue, and, among its assets, has a great bookstore (*Porter Square Books*, at 25 White St), and the region's largest concentration of Japanese eateries. The walk from Harvard will take you past some of Cambridge's most chic restaurants and boutiques, while Porter Square itself is hard to miss – look for the 46ft red kinetic sculpture *Gift of the Wind*, by Susumu Shingu; it's right outside the subway stop.

Davis Square

Just beyond Porter Square lies **Davis Square**, the convergence of a mind-boggling six streets, and the beating heart of the city of **Somerville**. A former working-class stronghold, Davis currently shares space with students, young families and some funky public art. One of the area's best features is its scenic **Minuteman Bike Trail**, which begins nearby, at the Alewife **T** stop, and continues through Arlington and Lexington to Bedford (☎617/542-BIKE, ⓦwww.massbike.org). By night, head over to a performance at the stellar **Somerville Theatre** at 55 Davis Square (☎617/625-5700, ⓦwww.somervilletheatreonline.com), which screens first- and second-run films in a former 1914 vaudeville house. The square itself is a fun place to kick around for an afternoon, and easily accessed from the Davis **T** stop on the Red Line. A sleek coffee shop, restaurants and the live-music landmark *Johnny D's* (see p.171) face the square's central plaza, which, on warm weather weekends, is typically occupied by strumming musicians.

Listings

Listings

⑩

Accommodation

D
espite the opening of some new hotels and B&Bs over the last few years, Boston has a surprisingly limited range of reasonably priced **accommodation**. Though there are still bargains to be found, prices at many formerly moderate hotels have inched into the expense-account range: you're looking at spending upwards of $200 just to stay the night during **high season** – which, while not unanimously agreed upon, is often deemed summer and early fall.

Your best bet to save money is to make your booking online: most hotels offer discounted rates on their websites, as do discount **booking agencies** like Orbitz (ⓦwww.orbitz.com), Expedia (ⓦwww.expedia.com) and Priceline (ⓦwww.priceline.com). If calling a hotel directly, be sure to inquire about special packages when reserving a room. Additional discounts of around ten percent can often be had with an AAA membership. Your other option, if you don't mind braving the sharp East Coast winter, is to come in the **off-season**, usually November to April, when many hotels not only have more vacancies but also offer weekend package discounts. At any other time of year, be sure to make reservations well in advance. May and June (graduation) and September (start of the school year) are particularly busy months, due to the large student population here. October, when leaf-peeping season is in full bloom, is also expensive.

In response to the hotel crunch, some visitors turn to less-expensive **B&Bs**, many of which are tucked into renovated brownstones in Back Bay and the South End; other good choices can be found outside the city centre, in Brookline and Cambridge. Short-term **furnished apartments**, spread throughout the city, are another option, though most have two-week minimum stays. There are also a handful of decent **hostels** if you're looking for truly budget accommodation.

Prices in this chapter reflect the lowest listed **price** for a standard double room in summer – depending on availability and season, you may end up paying more, or you might pay half the listed price by finding a great deal online.

Finally, all accommodations are **keyed** to the relevant **chapter maps** in the "Guide" portion of this book.

Hotels

Hotels in Boston range from the usual assortment of chains to some excellent independently run hotels, the highest concentration of which – including some of the best – are in **Back Bay**. Not surprisingly, most of the business hotels are located in or around the **Financial District**.

Modestly cheaper rates can be found at **Cambridge**'s hotels, though rates at these, too, go sky-high around college commencement and during the fall. A handful of gay-friendly hotels and B&Bs, mostly in the **South End**, are listed on p.181.

Downtown

Ames Hotel 1 Court St ☎617/979-8100, ⓦwww.ameshotel.com; **State** T.
Currently one of Boston's "it" spots, the *Ames* is a 114-room contemporary boutique hotel located inside the city's first skyscraper, built in 1893. Luxurious rooms are furnished in tones of white and grey (with the occasional citrus burst), and enhanced by flat-screen TVs, iPod docks and great views of downtown. There's also a stylish on-site restaurant, *Woodward*, designed to feel like a chic museum of curios. $305.

Langham Hotel 250 Franklin St ☎617/451-1900, ⓦwww.boston.langhamhotels.com; **State** T.
This stern granite building in the heart of the Financial District is the former Federal Reserve Bank of Boston, built in 1922. The hotel's spacious rooms are decorated in a contemporary French style, and each one features iPod docks, internet access, and Italian marble bathrooms. Ask about the hotel's exquisite Saturday morning chocolate buffet. $310.

Marriott's Custom House 3 McKinley Sq ☎617/310-6300 or 1-888/236-2427, ⓦwww.marriott.com; **Aquarium** T. All the rooms at this Downtown landmark-turned-hotel are high-end, one-bedroom suites with spectacular Boston Harbor and city views; there's also a great gym on the top floor. $399.

Millennium Bostonian Hotel Faneuil Hall Marketplace ☎617/523-3600 or 1-866/866-8086, ⓦwww.millenniumhotels.com; **State** T. Right in the heart of Downtown, the *Millennium Bostonian* has splendid quarters, some with fireplaces and – unusual for Boston – balconies. The lobby and guestrooms recently underwent a $24 million makeover, and the result – Frette linens, flat-screen TVs and a funky-looking library with zebra seating – is fabulous. $234.

Nine Zero Hotel 90 Tremont St ☎617/772-5800 or 1-800/434-7347, ⓦwww.ninezero.com; **Park St** T. Executive-class boutique hotel with 190 polished quarters equipped with wi-fi, CD players, plush linens, and a complimentary morning paper. $260.

Omni Parker House 60 School St ☎617/227-8600 or 1-800/843-6664, ⓦwww.omniparkerhouse .com; **Park** T. Though the present building only dates from 1927, the *Omni Parker House* is the oldest continuously operating hotel in the US. The lobby, decorated in dark oak with carved gilt mouldings, recalls the splendour of the original nineteenth-century building. Rooms, given their historic nature, run on the small side, but are pleasingly furnished and equipped with flat-screen cable TVs. $233.

XV Beacon 15 Beacon St ☎617/670-1500 or 1-877/XVBEACON, ⓦwww.xvbeacon.com; **Park St** T. Ultra-decadent boutique hotel across from the Boston Athenæum, with 61 spectacular rooms complete with marble bathrooms, Kiehl toiletries, a CD player, beautiful upholstery, and working gas fireplaces; some rooms even have four-poster beds. All rates include access to your own chauffeured Lexus for the length of your stay. $325.

Waterfront and Seaport District

Boston Harbor Hotel 70 Rowes Wharf ☎617/439-7000 or 1-800/752-7077, ⓦwww .bhh.com; **Aquarium** T. Opulent accommodation in an atmosphere of studied corporate elegance, right on the water. There's a health club, pool, gracious concierge staff, and rooms with harbour and city views; the former are substantially pricier. $445.

Fairmont Battery Wharf 3 Battery Wharf ☎617/994-9000, ⓦwww.fairmont.com /batterywharf; **Haymarket** T. Opened in 2008, this 192-room property (including 42 elegant suites) is superbly sited on a wharf bordering the North End. Which means a waterfront location, plus access to all the Italian restaurants, pastries and espresso for which the North End is famed. Rooms are spacious, with huge marble bathrooms enhanced by rain showerheads; the *Fairmont* also stands out for its impeccable service. $250.

Harborside Inn 185 State St ☎617/723-7500, ⓦwww.harborsideinnboston.com; **State** T. This small hotel is housed in a renovated 1890s mercantile warehouse across from Quincy Market. The (relatively) reasonably priced rooms – with exposed brick, hardwood floors, and cherry furniture – are a welcome surprise for this part of town. They also run a great sister property, the *Charlesmark Hotel*, in Back Bay (see p.137). $149.

InterContinental Hotel 510 Atlantic Ave ☎617/747-1000, ⓦwww.intercontinentalboston .com; **South Station** T. Swanky, skyline-altering hotel that caused quite a buzz when it opened in 2006. Seen as a harbinger of the Waterfront's rejuvenation,

the *InterContinental* offers deluxe amenities (including a fitness centre with a 45ft heated pool), a tempting spa, and spacious, modern rooms overlooking the water. $349.
Seaport Hotel 1 Seaport Lane ⊤617/385-4000, ⒲www.seaportboston.com; **South Station T**. A luxurious Boston newcomer in the Seaport District, this hotel offers access to the Institute of Contemporary Art and convention centre, as well as business travel standards like crisp linens and internet access. $380.

Charlestown

Marriott Residence Inn Boston Harbor 34–44 Charles River Ave ⊤617/242-9000, ⒲www.residenceinnboston.com; **Community College T**. The Marriott's *Residence Inn* is an all-suiter close to some of the main sights along the Freedom Trail. Comfortable rooms offer free wi-fi and generous kitchen amenities (stove, fridge, toaster), plus there's an amazing view of Boston's skyline over the river. $249.

Beacon Hill

Beacon Hill Hotel 25 Charles St ⊤617/723-7575 or 1-888/959-BHHB, ⒲www.beaconhillhotel.com; **Charles T**. Pampered luxury in the heart of Beacon Hill, these thirteen small but sleek chambers occupy a regal mid-1800s brick building, and come with flat-screen TVs, DirectTV, wi-fi and individually stylized rooms. The hotel is also home to a fantastic bistro and fireplace bar (see p.153). $225.

🏃 **The John Jeffries House 14 David G Mugar Way** ⊤617/367-1866, ⒲www.johnjeffrieshouse.com; **Charles T**. This little gem has some of the best prices in town, and clean and tasteful rooms to match. A mid-scale spot at the foot of Beacon Hill, it features a cosy lounge and Victorian-style rooms, in addition to cable TV, wi-fi, and a/c; single-occupancy studios include kitchenettes. Singles from $113.

🏃 **Liberty Hotel 215 Charles St** ⊤617/224-4000, ⒲www.libertyhotel.com; **Charles T**. The *Liberty Hotel* has taken over the labyrinthine digs of an 1851 prison and fashioned it with stylish furnishings and lush details such as a fitness and business centre, a 90ft lobby, phenomenal city views, and overnight shoe-shines. It also houses *Scampo* restaurant and the *Alibi* lounge (see p.153 & p.164); the latter is currently one of the places to see and be seen in Boston. $315.

The West End

Bulfinch Hotel 107 Merrimac St ⊤617/624-0202, ⒲www.bulfinchhotel.com; **North Station T**. A beautiful and fresh addition to the West End, this sleek newbie housed in a vintage triangular – or flatiron-shaped – building has small but pretty wool-toned rooms brightened with contemporary paintings, internet access, and an exercise room. $169.
Onyx Hotel 155 Portland St ⊤617/557-9955, ⒲www.onyxhotel.com; **North Station T**. The stark, glass-panelled front of this small luxury hotel belies an opulent interior, though avoid the "Britney Spears" room – designed by her mother, it looks as you would expect the singer's childhood room to look, complete with pink bible and fairy statuettes. Very pet-friendly, and the in-hotel *Ruby Room* bar is great for a nightcap. $209.

Back Bay

Back Bay Hotel 350 Stuart St ⊤617/266-7200, ⒲www.doylecollection.com; **Arlington T**. Set in a 1920s building that used to be the Boston Police headquarters, the 220 smallish rooms in this lavishly furnished hotel have huge beds, marble bathrooms, multi-head showers, and heated towel racks. The function rooms are named after the celebrated Irish writers Shaw, Yeats, Beckett, Joyce, and Wilde; displays in the lobby show old police memorabilia. $275.
Boston Park Plaza Hotel & Towers 64 Arlington St ⊤617/426-2000 or 1-800/225-2008, ⒲www.bostonparkplaza.com; **Arlington T**. This hotel's old-school elegance and hospitality – plus its central location – make it stand out; the high-ceilinged rooms, complete with internet access, are comfortable, too. $200.

🏃 **Charlesmark Hotel 655 Boylston St** ⊤617/247-1212, ⒲www.thecharlesmark.com; **Copley T**. Forty smallish, contemporary rooms with cosy beechwood furnishings, good rates, a lively bar and modern amenities such as wi-fi and CD/DVD players (plus the sound system is hooked into your bathroom so you can sing as you shower). $145.
The College Club 44 Commonwealth Ave ⊤617/536-9510, ⒲www.thecollegeclubofboston.com; **Arlington T**. The College Club was founded in 1890 by 19 women wanting to create a space of "sociability and companionship" for college-educated women. Now the oldest women's club in the country, it

plays host to eleven well-priced guestrooms (available to both male and female visitors), many with shared baths, all decorated with antique furnishings. The smart location by the Public Garden and Newbury Street goes a long way. In summer, single rooms with shared baths start at $109; doubles with private baths $219.

The Colonnade 120 Huntington Ave ℡617/424-7000 or 1-800/962-3030, ⊛www .colonnadehotel.com; Prudential **T**. With its beige poured-concrete shell, the *Colonnade* looks weirdly like a parking garage. The interior, however, is a very different story since its reinvention in 2008 (to the tune of $25 million): expect stylish rooms with high thread-count linens, wi-fi, flat-screen HDTVs and iPod alarm clocks. Rooms are spacious, and in summer months there's access to a rooftop pool – the only one in Boston. $300.

Copley Square Hotel 47 Huntington Ave ℡617/536-9000 or 1-800/225-7062, ⊛www .copleysquarehotel.com; Copley **T**. Situated on the eastern fringe of Copley Square, this recently renovated space has become something of a luxe hotspot. Rooms are spacious and come complete with iPod docks, wi-fi and contemporary bathrooms. Downstairs buzzes with the clientele of *minibar* (see p.165), an uber-sleek martini lounge. $275.

Eliot Hotel 370 Commonwealth Ave ℡617/267-1607 or 1-800/442-5468, ⊛www.eliothotel .com; Hynes **T**. West Back Bay's answer to the *Four Seasons*, this independent, plush, nine-floor suite hotel has sizable rooms with kitchenettes, luxurious Italian marble baths, huge beds with Egyptian cotton sheets, and wi-fi. It also hosts two great restaurants, *Clio* (see p.138) and *Uni Sashimi*. $250.

Fairmont Copley Plaza 138 St James Ave ℡617/267-5300 or 1-800/795-3906, ⊛www .fairmont.com/copleyplaza; Copley **T**. Built in 1912, the iconic *Fairmont* has long boasted Boston's most elegant lobby, with its glittering chandeliers, mirrored walls, and *trompe l'oeil* sky. Most rooms are decorated in a French Neoclassical style and have full marble bathrooms and wi-fi. Even if you don't stay here, be sure to have a martini in the fabulous *Oak Bar* (see p.165), with its high-coffered ceilings and mahogany chairs. $259.

Four Seasons 200 Boylston St ℡617/338-4400 or 1-800/332-3442, ⊛www.fourseasons.com; Arlington **T**. The tops in city accommodation,

with 288 large rooms. The penthouse-level health spa has an indoor pool that seems to float over the Public Garden. $350.

Hotel 140 140 Clarendon St ℡617/585-5600, ⊛www.hotel140.com; Back Bay **T**. Appealing, affordable accommodation in the heart of Back Bay. A self-proclaimed "boutique hotel", the amenities won't blow your mind, but the hotel does have a sense of style, and it's tough to beat the price for its location. $160.

Inn @ St. Botolph 99 St. Botolph St ℡617/236-8099, ⊛www.innatstbotolph .com; Back Bay **T**. On a quiet side street on the western cusp of the South End, this stylish hideaway features sixteen oversized suites with kitchenettes, bold houndstooth patterns and black and brown striped furniture, wi-fi, an on-site laundry room and gym and continental breakfast. $160.

The Lenox 61 Exeter St ℡617/536-5300 or 1-800/225-7676, ⊛www.lenoxhotel.com; Copley **T**. Billed as Boston's version of the New York's *Waldorf-Astoria* when its doors first opened in 1900, the *Lenox* – after a recent renovation – remains one of the most upscale hotels in the city, with a renowned staff and 212 exquisite rooms featuring high ceilings, walk-in closets, and, in some, working fireplaces. $250.

Mandarin Oriental 776 Boylston St ℡617/535-8888, ⊛www.mandarinoriental.com; Copley **T**. Boston is all abuzz with the opening of this glamorous, extremely expensive hotel. Spacious rooms are accompanied by luxurious details such as silk window treatments, personal trainers and the city's best spa. The romantic *L'Espalier* (see p.154), long a darling of Boston's restaurant scene, has moved from its brownstone digs into a space adjacent to the hotel. $600.

Taj Boston 15 Arlington St ℡617/536-5700, ⊛www.tajhotels.com; Arlington **T**. Replacing (albeit lovingly) Boston's historic Ritz-Carlton, *Taj Boston* is the ultimate in luxurious, old-school Boston accommodation, with wood-burning fireplace suites, gilded antique furniture, and a not-to-be-beaten location across from the Public Garden. $249.

W Hotel 100 Stuart St ℡617/261-8700, ⊛www.starwoodhotels.com; Boylston **T**. Smack in the Theater District, this super trendy newcomer is adding some spice to Boston's hotel scene. Floor-to-ceiling windows, 350-thread-count sheets, munchie boxes, immodest but stylish bathrooms, a Bliss spa and the renowned *Market* restaurant (run by the famed Jean-Georges Vongerichten) are a sampling of the amenities that await. $339.

The South End

Chandler Inn 26 Chandler St ⏣617/482-3450 or 1-800-842-3450, ⓦwww.chandlerinn.com; **Back Bay T**. Contemporary yet cosy, the *Chandler Inn* offers 55 petite rooms in a European-style hotel above the popular *Fritz* bar (see p.182); perks like plasma satellite TVs, iPod docks, wi-fi and marble bathrooms are included in the rates. $175.

Kenmore Square and the Fenway

Gryphon House 9 Bay State Rd ⏣617/375-9003 or 1-877/375-9003, ⓦwww.innboston.com; **Kenmore T**. This hotel-cum-B&B around the corner from Fenway has eight wonderfully appointed suites equipped with working gas fireplaces, cable TV, a handy DVD library, wi-fi, continental breakfast, and free parking (a big plus in Boston). $179.

Hotel Commonwealth 500 Commonwealth Ave ⏣617/933-5000, ⓦwww .hotelcommonwealth.com; **Kenmore T**. Old-world charm mixed with modern decor makes this a welcome addition to Boston's luxury hotel scene, with nice touches like choice linens and L'Occitane products, as well as the *Eastern Standard* restaurant (see p.166). $400.

Cambridge

Charles Hotel 1 Bennett St ⏣617/864-1200 or 1-800/882-1818, ⓦwww.charleshotel.com; **Harvard T**. A Harvard Square landmark with clean, bright rooms – some overlooking the Charles River – that come with an array of amenities: cable TV, Shaker furniture, access to the adjacent Le Pli Spa and even an ice skating rink (in winter). There's also an excellent jazz club, *Regattabar* (see p.171), iconic restaurant, *Henrietta's Table* (see p.159), and a sultry bar, *Noir* (see p.168), on the premises. $299.

Harvard Square Hotel 110 Mt Auburn St ⏣617/864-5200 or 1-800/222-8733, ⓦwww .hotelsinharvardsquare.com; **Harvard T**. Rooms here are pretty basic – clean, plain, and on the small side – although there is wi-fi throughout, and its namesake is so close you can practically smell the ivy. $150.

Hotel Marlowe 25 Edwin H Land Blvd ⏣1-800/825-7140, ⓦwww.hotelmarlowe .com; **Kendall T**. The funky decor at this hotel is cosy and plush, with faux leopard print rugs and bright, boutique-y designs in all the rooms. Pet friendly (they'll even order a birthday cake for your pup), with an evening wine hour, an on-site fitness centre, and complimentary kayak and bicycle rentals. $200.

Hotel Veritas 1 Remington St ⏣617/520-5000, ⓦwww.thehotelveritas .com; **Harvard T**. Right in Harvard Square, this chic thirty-room European-style hideaway really puts the "ooh" into boutique hotel: posh linens, silk drapes, fresh flowers, inventive cocktails crafted in a seductive lounge, locally farmed charcuterie and even access to the yoga studio across the street. Service is stellar, and the classy concierges all sport Brooks Brothers' suits. $269.

Inn at Harvard 1201 Massachusetts Ave ⏣617/491-2222 or 1-800/222-8733, ⓦwww .hotelsinharvardsquare.com; **Harvard T**. Harvard University owns this red-brick, European-influenced hotel, set directly on its campus. Its four-storey atrium was inspired by a Venetian piazza, and its rooms, while small, look out onto Harvard Square and come with huge writing desks. A wide range of rates, from $179 to $419.

Kendall Hotel 350 Main St ⏣617/577-1300, ⓦwww.kendallhotel.com; **Kendall T**. This independent hotel near MIT occupies a former 1894 fire station. Its 73 quaint rooms are country-chic with quilts and reproduction antiques; amenities include wi-fi, a full breakfast buffet and gym access. $200.

Le Méridien 20 Sidney St ⏣617/577-0200, ⓦwww.starwoodhotels.com; **Central T**. Contemporary hotel anchoring an office tower near MIT. The modern rooms have white and grey colour schemes and come with internet access, both wired and wi-fi; there's also a fitness centre and rooftop garden on-site. $233.

Royal Sonesta 40 Edwin H Land Blvd ⏣617/806-4200, ⓦwww.sonesta.com; **Kendall T**. Luxury quarters with good views of the Boston skyline, and a free on-site shuttle available to whisk you around town. The rooms have big, sparkling bathrooms, and the hotel's public spaces are festooned with striking (and some strikingly bad) art. The *Sonesta* is also notable for its atrium-style pool (equipped with a handy retractable roof and sun deck). $209.

Sheraton Commander 16 Garden St ☎617/547-4800 or 1-800/535-5007, ⓦwww .sheraton.com/commander; Harvard **T**. The hotel's name refers to George Washington, who, legend has it, took command of the Continental Army on nearby Cambridge Common. Rooms are luxurious and enhanced by charming frills such as terrycloth robes, nightlights, an umbrella service (should you have forgotten to pack yours), in-room video games and wi-fi. The *Commander* is located just around the bend from Harvard University, in a building that dates to 1927. $239.

Bed and breakfasts

The **bed and breakfast** industry in Boston is thriving, for the most part because it is so difficult to find a hotel room here for under $200 a night – and some B&Bs offer just that, at least in the off-season. On the other hand, many B&Bs cash in on the popularity of their old-world charm, meaning their prices may hover near those of the swankier hotels. One plus is that breakfast is included with the price of your stay; while this can vary greatly (from self-serve milk and cereal to fresh omelettes with home-made scones), it's still a thrifty perk.

A number of the best B&Bs are outside the city, in either **Cambridge** or **Brookline**, though a handful of stellar in-town options have recently sprung up (generally in the **South End**). You can make reservations directly with the places we've listed; there are also numerous B&B **agencies** that can do the booking for you and find you a room in an unlisted house (see box below).

Charlestown

Green Turtle Floating B&B Shipyard Quarters Marina, 13th St, Charlestown ☎617/337-0202, ⓦwww.greenturtlebb.com; North Station **T**. A special place: two well-appointed rooms situated on a peaceful marina in scenic Charlestown. Wake up to fresh pastries, your own private harborfront patio and the sound of waves lapping at your door. $195.

Beacon Hill

Charles Street Inn 94 Charles St ☎617/314-8900, ⓦwww.charlesstreetinn.com; Charles **T**. An intimate nine-room inn with lavish rooms styled after the (presumed) tastes of various Boston luminaries; the Isabella Stewart Gardner room features a Rococo chandelier, while Oliver Wendell Holmes's chamber boasts a king-sized sleigh bed. All rooms come with working

B&Bs and short-term rental agencies

Bed & Breakfast Agency of Boston ☎617/720-3540 or 1-800/248-9262, UK ☎0800/ 895 128, ⓦwww.boston-bnbagency.com. Can book you a room in a brownstone, a waterfront loft, or even aboard a yacht.

Bed & Breakfast Associates Bay Colony ☎781/449-5302 or 1-888/486-6018, ⓦwww.bnbboston.com. Features some real finds in Back Bay, the South End, and Cambridge. Friendly and helpful staff.

Bed & Breakfast Reservations ☎617/964-1606, ⓦwww.bbreserve.com. Lists B&Bs in Greater Boston, North Shore, and Cape Cod.

Boston Reservations/Boston Bed & Breakfast, Inc ☎617/332-4199, ⓦwww.boston reservations.com. Competitive rates at B&Bs in Boston and Cambridge as well as at leading hotels. Will also book rooms in many other cities worldwide.

Greater Boston Hospitality ☎617/393-1548, ⓦwww.bostonbedandbreakfast .com. Rentals in homes, inns, and condominiums. Good for booking out-of-town accommodation.

fireplaces – it's one of Boston's best romantic getaways. $300.

Back Bay

Copley Inn 19 Garrison St ☎617/236-0300, ⓦwww.copleyinn.com; **Prudential T**. Comfortable, clean rooms (with a slightly corny decor), full kitchens, friendly staff and a great location on the South End border make this an ideal place to stay in Back Bay. If you stay six days, the seventh night is free. $165.

Newbury Guest House 261 Newbury St ☎617/670-6000, ⓦwww.newburyguesthouse .com; **Copley T**. Big, popular Victorian brownstone that fills up frequently, so be sure to call ahead. The 32 rooms were thoroughly renovated in 2009 and range from spacious bay-windowed quarters with hardwood floors to tiny digs well suited for the discerning economic traveller. All rooms offer fluffy white beds, wi-fi, a DVD library, a hot continental breakfast buffet and an unbeatable location at the heart of Newbury Street. $200.

The North End

La Cappella Suites 290 North St ☎617/523-9020, ⓦwww.lacappellasuites .com; **Haymarket T**. Accommodation has come to the North End with this lovely new arrival – three cosy, modern rooms, two with private balconies, and all with wi-fi, cable TV, and a public seating area. Be prepared for a five-floor walk-up and minimal breakfast service. $150.

The South End

82 Chandler Street 82 Chandler St ☎617/482-0408, ⓦwww.82chandler.com; **Back Bay T**. Four basic rooms with minimal service in a restored, 1863 brownstone that sits on a tree-lined street in the South End. Breakfast is served on the sunny top floor – where you'll also find the best room in the house, with a working fireplace and great views. Wi-fi access is available throughout the premises. $135.

Aisling Bed and Breakfast 21 East Concord St ☎617/206-8049, ⓦwww.aisling-bostonbb.com; **Massachusetts Ave T**. Three basic rooms with cable TV and wi-fi in a Victorian rowhouse blessed with its original mouldings and marble fittings. The owners are incredibly

accommodating (they'll even pick you up at the airport); guests rave about the fabulous breakfasts. $200.

Caj House 45 Worcester St ☎617/803-4279, ⓦwww.cajhouse.com; **Massachusetts Ave T**. Fourteen carefully renovated short-term rental apartments featuring modern amenities (flat-screen TVs with cable, wi-fi) in brightly, individually decorated spaces with full kitchens. One-week minimum stay; four weeks is the norm. They also maintain nine apartments at 677 Tremont St. $425–550 per week.

Clarendon Square Inn 198 West Brookline St ☎617/536-2229, ⓦwww.clarendon square.com; **Prudential T**. Gorgeous, well-loved bed and breakfast on a pretty residential street, with great attention paid to design details and indulgent perks like heated bathroom tiles, limestone floors, a private garden, and a 24hr roof-deck hot tub. $195 to $395.

Encore B&B 116 West Newton St ☎617/247-3425 ⓦwww.encorebandb .com; **Back Bay T**. On a pleasant side street, you'll get pampered at this cheerful B&B with contemporary decor, wi-fi and a sitting area or balcony in all three of the rooms. $140–240.

Gilded Lily 4 Claremont Park ☎617/877-3676, ⓦwww.thegildedlily-boston.com; **Massachusetts Ave T**. Two spacious, elegant, carefully restored suites (which still retain their original crown mouldings and marble mantles) equipped with flat-screen TVs and DVD players; the rooms, which are set in a pretty brick rowhouse, share a roof deck with great views of Downtown. $200.

Kenmore Square and the Fenway

Oasis Guest House 22 Edgerly Rd ☎617/267-2262, ⓦwww.oasisgh.com; **Symphony T**. Sixteen comfortable, basic, very affordable rooms, some with shared baths, in a renovated brownstone near Symphony Hall. Continental breakfast included in the rate. $99.

Brookline

Beech Tree Inn 83 Longwood Ave ☎617/277-1620, ⓦwww.thebeechtreeinn.com; **Coolidge Corner T**. Just two blocks from the **T** and around the corner from the restaurants and shops of Coolidge Corner, this welcoming turn-of-the-century Victorian has ten brightly decorated rooms, scrumptious breakfasts and baked goods throughout the day. $119.

Bertram Inn 92 Sewall Ave ☎617/566-2234, ⓦwww.bertraminn.com; Coolidge Corner **T**. Sixteen luxurious rooms (and one junior suite), some with wood-burning fireplaces, in a 1907 tobacco merchant's home on a quiet street close to Coolidge Corner. They also run the pretty *Samuel Sewall Inn*, just across the street. $149.

Longwood Inn 123 Longwood Ave ☎617/566-8615, ⓦlongwood-inn.com; Coolidge Corner **T**. Sprawling 1900s Victorian mansion with a beautiful mahogany-panelled dining room and fireplace. The 35 guestrooms vary in size and shape and offer basic (though bright) decor, free parking, kitchen access and wi-fi. $129.

On the Park 88 Columbia St ☎617/277-0910, ⓦwww.onthepark.net; Griggs or Winchester **T**. A little off the beaten path (but still near to Coolidge Corner), this one-hundred-year-old home has three delightful bedrooms decked out in warm tones, with a nice mix of contemporary and antique furnishings. Free parking, and full breakfasts in the morning. $135.

Jamaica Plain

Taylor House 50 Burroughs St, Jamaica Plain ☎617/983-9334, ⓦwww.taylorhouse.com; Green Street **T**. This delightful B&B, with two beautiful golden-retriever mascots, is superbly sited between JP's main drag – Centre Street – and scenic Jamaica Pond. Its three charming rooms, tucked away on the second floor of an 1855 Italianate house, offer queen-sized beds, free parking and wi-fi. Complimentary continental breakfast, which includes fresh baked bread, is served daily. $159.

Cambridge

A Cambridge House 2218 Massachusetts Ave ☎617/491-6300 or 1-800/232-9989, ⓦwww .acambridgehouse.com; Davis **T**. Located

in Porter Square, this classy B&B has two room styles: one contemporary, and one Victorian with canopy beds and period pieces. Rates, which include parking, range from $129 to $249.

Blue's Bed and Breakfast 82 Avon Hill St ☎617/354-6106 ⓦwww.bluesbedandbreakfast .com; Porter or Harvard **T**. Two sunny, folk-art-filled bedrooms in a cosy house that's one mile from Harvard Square. Blessed with welcoming, world-travelling owners, the rate includes free wi-fi and great breakfasts. $110 single, $140 double.

Cambridge Bed and Muffin 267 Putnam Ave ☎617/576-3166, ⓦwww.bedandmuffin.com; Central or Harvard **T**. Just one block from the river and close to Harvard and Central Squares, this tranquil B&B has a friendly owner and endearing little rooms with polished pine floors and handmade quilts. No en-suite bathrooms, and no TVs, but plenty of books and quiet. $100.

Harding House 288 Harvard St ☎617/876-2888, ⓦwww.cambridgeinns.com; Harvard **T**. This cosy Victorian home has fourteen bright rooms with hardwood floors, throw rugs, TV, a/c, wi-fi, limited free parking and museum passes; includes a tasty breakfast. In summer, rates begin at $115 shared bath, $175 private bath.

Irving House 24 Irving St ☎617/547-4600, ⓦwww.cambridge inns.com; Harvard **T**. Excellent, friendly, popular option near Harvard Square that shares the same management with the *Harding House* (see above). Laundry facilities (coin-operated), wi-fi, limited free parking and tasty breakfasts are included. In summer, rates begin at $115 shared bath, $125 private bath.

Prospect Place 112 Prospect St ☎617/864-7500 or 1-800/769-5303, ⓦwww.prospectpl.com; Central **T**. This Italianate edifice holds a restored parlour, along with nineteenth-century period antiques – including two grand pianos – and floral-decor rooms. $120.

Hostels

There are a fairly limited number of **hostel** accommodations in Boston, and if you want to stay in one, you should definitely book ahead, especially in the summertime. Unless otherwise stated, the listings below are marked on the map on p.101.

40 Berkeley 40 Berkeley St ☎617/375-2524, ⓦ www.40berkeley.com; Back Bay **T**. Clean and simple rooms in a convenient South End location; full breakfast included. Singles ($58), doubles ($70) and triples ($105).

HI–Boston 12 Hemenway St ☎617/536-1027, ⓦ www.bostonhostel.org; Hynes **T**. Around the Back Bay–Fenway border, this clean and safe hostel offers standard dorm accommodation, but stands out for its fun management (who plan a lot of field trips), internet access and Sunday pancake breakfasts. $32–39.

HI–Fenway Summer Hostel 575 Commonwealth Ave ☎617/267-8599, ⓦ www.bostonhostel .org; Kenmore **T**. A summer-only hostel (June to mid-Aug) that functions as a BU dorm in winter months. There are both private rooms and three-bed dorms with en-suite baths and a/c available; there's also laundry and internet access on-site, and Red Sox tickets available on a first-come first-serve basis. $39 dorm bed, $99 private room.

Eating

Historically, weather-beaten Yankees have tended to favour hearty meals made from native ingredients without a lot of fuss. Today, though, while outsiders may see menu items like boiled lobster, clam chowder and Yankee pot roast as quintessentially New England, most Bostonians take pride in their city's contemporary, diverse palate (while retaining a certain nostalgia for the classic dishes as comfort food). The city's dining scene mirrors the increasing diversity of Boston's population itself, with innovative restaurants taking root everywhere – particularly in the South End, where French and fusion cuisine (in a fashionable setting, of course) are the *mots du jour*. Indeed, Tremont St, the South End's main thoroughfare, is known as "Restaurant Row". Happily, too, there is no shortage of places to eat in Boston: the city is packed with bars and pubs that double as restaurants, cafés that serve affordable meals, plus plenty of higher-end, dinner-only options.

As for Boston's culinary landscape, there are ever-popular **Italian** restaurants – both traditional southern and fancier northern – that cluster in the North End, mainly on Hanover and Salem streets. The city's tiny **Chinatown** packs in not only a fair number of Chinese spots, but Japanese, Vietnamese and Taiwanese, too. Dim sum, where you choose selections from carts wheeled past your table, is especially big for Sunday brunch. At the other end of the spectrum, Boston's trendiest restaurants, many serving voguish **New American fusion cuisine**, tend to cluster in Back Bay and the South End. Meanwhile, across the Charles, Cambridge's eating options, mostly laid out along Massachusetts Avenue between Central, Harvard, and Porter squares, run the gamut from budget **Indian and Mexican eateries** to high-end American cuisine. Funky (if slightly out-of-the-way) Inman Square, just below Cambridge's border with Somerville, has a few good spots as well, many of them specializing in contemporary twists on **American classics**.

To keep things manageable, we've broken down the listings within this chapter into two categories: **coffee shops** and **restaurants**. While many coffee shops offer filling food alongside their caffeinated wares, for the sake of simplicity we've grouped cafés that have extensive food menus under "restaurants".

Coffee shops

Boston's status as a university town is reflected in its well-established **café** scene. The swankiest spots are those that line Back Bay's **Newbury Street**, where people-watching is sometimes included in the price tag. Value is better in the **North End**, where Italian cafés serve excellent beverages and desserts, plus provide a lively atmosphere. The most laidback cafés are across the river in **Cambridge**, catering to the large student population.

Eating maps

We've plotted the eating establishments in this chapter on maps within the neighbour-hoods portion of the Guide. These maps can be found on the following pages:

Downtown, pp.40–41
The North End, p.64
Beacon Hill & the West End, p.78
Back Bay, p.86

The South End, p.95
Kenmore Square & the Fenway, p.101
Roxbury & Jamaica Plain, p.115
Cambridge, pp.118–119

Downtown

Flat Black Coffee Company 50 Broad St
T617/951-1440; State **T**. While the *Starbucks* invasion has done some real damage to Downtown's coffee culture, this Australian-inspired newcomer (in Australianese, a flat black is an espresso) offers up free-trade coffee to happy Financial District patrons. Tasty pastries on offer as well as free wi-fi.
Sip Café 0 Post Office Square T617/338-3080; **Downtown Crossing T**. Nestled in a little glass house in the centre of Post Office Square, this café shines with its floor-to-ceiling windows, friendly staff, locavore sandwiches and artful lattes flourished with a fern or heart.

The North End

Boston Common Coffee Co. 97 Salem St
T617/725-0040; Haymarket **T**. Among a neighbourhood of historic espresso joints this mini coffee-chain still stands out for its quality beverages (with fun latte flavours like "junior mint"), bright environs, window seating that overlooks Salem Street and fast, free wi-fi. There are two other locations in town: 515 Washington St and 10 High St (Downtown Crossing and the Financial District, respectively).
Caffé dello Sport 308 Hanover St
T617/523-5063; Haymarket **T**. A continuous stream of Rai Uno soccer matches is broadcast from the ceiling-mounted TV sets, making for an agreeable din amongst a very local crowd. Along with espresso, beer, wine, and sambuca are served.
Caffé Paradiso 255 Hanover St T617/742-1768; **Haymarket T**. Simple but great little neigh-bourhood hangout with rugby and soccer matches on the TV. Drink options include espresso, wine, and cocktails, but come for the tasty pastries and wickedly good gelato.
Caffé Vittoria 290-296 Hanover St
T617/227-7606; Haymarket **T**. A Boston institution, the *Vittoria* is one of the city's

most authentic Italian cafés. Its dark wood panelling, pressed tin ceilings, murals of the Old Country, and Sinatra-blaring Wurlitzer are all vintage North End. The café is only open at night, though a street-level addition next door is open by day for cappuccinos. Cash only.

Beacon Hill

Caffe Bella Vita 30 Charles St T617/720-4505; **Charles T**. A casual, linger-worthy café with fine cups of coffee, decent pastries and low-key lunch options, free wi-fi and a smart location, location, location right in the heart of Beacon Hill's main thoroughfare.

Back Bay

L'Aroma Café 85 Newbury St T617/412-4001; **Copley T**. This amiable, European-style café has a friendly staff, standout baked goods (try the "everything cookie"), and tasty cappuccinos good for refuelling after shopping in the trendy boutiques of Newbury Street. There's outdoor seating, too, perfect for spying on other shoppers.
Wired Puppy 250 Newbury St T857/366-4655; **Copley T**. Free Trade beans are served by skilled *baristas* at this community-minded spot in the heart of Boston's main shopping district. Puppies are encouraged on the patio, and the café's free wi-fi invites keyboard clacking.

The South End

Francesca's Café 564 Tremont St T617/482-9026; **Back Bay T**. A great place to check out the Tremont Street crowd passing by the plate-glass windows. The coffee shop gets packed in the evenings, with a largely gay clientele caffeinating itself for a night out.
Uptown Espresso Caffe 563 Columbus Ave
T617/236-8535; **Massachusetts Ave T**. This brownstone café offers free wi-fi (no outlets, however), home-made chicken salad

sandwiches, berry scones and, of course, tempting espresso drinks, sipped in their sunroom or serene outdoor patio.

Kenmore Square and the Fenway

Espresso Royale Caffe 736 Commonwealth Ave ⑦617/277-8737; Kenmore **T**. Kenmore's a little thin on coffeeshops, but this funky little chain will do. Alongside traditional cups of java, original blends like a zesty orange cappuccino are served; the cheerful decor is enhanced by abstract wall paintings, free wi-fi, and cosy seats. Other locations at 44 Gainsborough St, and in Back Bay at 268 Newbury St.

Brookline

Café Fixe 1642 Beacon St, Brookline ⑦617/879-2500; Washington Square **T**.

A sleek white-walled space augmented by jazz on the stereo and high-quality espresso drinks swirled through with latte art. Free wi-fi (no outlets).

🏃 **Japonaise Bakery & Café 1020 Beacon St,** Brookline ⑦617/566-7730; St. Mary's **T**; 1815 Massachusetts Avenue, Cambridge ⑦617/547-5531; Porter Sq **T**; 1032 Commonwealth Ave ⑦617/738-7200; Babcock Street **T**. A life changer: French pastries with a Japanese twist such as the habit-forming An doughnut, a sugary puff filled with sweet red-bean paste; the savoury curry doughnut – filled with beef, carrots and onions – is another one of the many worthy treats on offer.

KooKoo 7 Station St, Brookline Village ⑦617/730-5525; Brookline Village **T**. Adorable neighbourhood café with local pastries, espresso drinks and falafel roll-ups made with love.

Boston's Best Ice Cream

There's a rumour going around town that Boston scoops up more **ice cream** than any other US city. While this statistic remains unconfirmed, there's no question that Bostonians love their cones, and the city is home to a notable set of ice cream purveyors. The following are the cherries-on-tops – six great shops for getting your sweet on.

BerryLine 3 Arrow St, Cambridge ⑦617/868-3500; Harvard **T**; 1668 Massachusetts Avenue, Cambridge ⑦617/492-3555; Porter Sq **T**; 1377 Boylston St ⑦617/236-0082; Fenway **T**. This local homage to the national tangy-frozen-yogurt craze features fresh-fruit toppings and intriguing yogurt flavours like green tea and honey graham in addition to the classic "plain".

BonBon 197a Massachusetts Ave ⑦617/904-0770; Hynes **T**. Across the street from the Christian Science complex, this Willy Wonka candyland serves up addictive *gelato* with flavours like cinnamon toast crunch and hazelnut chocolate. Lighter yet more flavourful than your regular ice cream.

Christina's 1255 Cambridge St, Inman Square, Cambridge ⑦617/492-7021; Central **T**. Inspiring well-deserved devotion amongst a legion of fans, people endure rush-hour traffic to get their hands on a scoop of *Christina's* Adzuki bean, burnt sugar, or honey lavender – ingredients procured from the owner's spice shop right next door.

Emack & Bolio's 255 State St ⑦617/367-0220; Aquarium **T**. 290 Newbury St ⑦617/536-7127; Copley **T**. Though this pint-sized parlour with a rocker past has grown into a national purveyor, Boston is still very much its home. Try a scoop each of Chocolate Moose and Vanilla Bean Speck in a chocolate-dipped waffle cone to get hooked. Also known for its fruit smoothies.

JP Licks 659 Centre St, Jamaica Plain ⑦617/524-6740; Green St **T**; 352 Newbury St ⑦617/236-1666; Hynes **T**. A beloved institution that's named for its original Jamaica Plain location, this funky, Jersey cow-themed café has home-made hot fudge sauce and tempting flavours like coconut almond chip. Good house-roasted coffee, too.

Toscanini's 899 Main St, Cambridge ⑦617/491-5877; Central **T**. The New York Times has called it "the best ice cream in the world". Their inventive, ever-changing ice cream list includes original flavours like khulfee – a concoction of pistachios, almonds, and cardamom.

Jamaica Plain

 Canto 6 3346 Washington St, Jamaica Plain ☎617/983-8688; Green St **T**. Tasty espresso drinks and some of Boston's best baked goods served from a tiny storefront. Try the "bostok," a brioche with orange blossom cream, or the sweet, caramelized *canneles*.

Ula Café 284 Amory St, ☎617/524-7890; **Stonybrook T**. Located inside the labyrinthine brewery building, hip *Ula* has knockout sandwiches such as sweet potato with avocado and Monterey jack ($7.30), in-house pastries, and fresh popovers throughout the day – a hot item in more than just tempera- ture. Limited free wi-fi, and strong coffee beverages, too.

Cambridge

1369 Coffee House 757 Massachusetts Ave ☎617/576-4600; Central **T**. The *1369* mixes earnest thirty-something leftists with youthful hipsters in a relaxed environment. Your best bets are the standard array of caffeinated beverages. There's a second and similarly snug location at 1369 Cambridge St (☎617/576-1369; #69 bus).

Algiers 40 Brattle St ☎617/492-1557; **Harvard T**. Delightfully atmospheric North African café popular with the artsy set. Its cosy nooks are usually populated by Harvard bookworms taking advantage of the restorative powers of the signature mint coffee. Free wi-fi.

Andala Coffee House 286 Franklin St ☎617/945-2212; Central **T**. Israeli-inspired brownstone café that's renowned for its Arabic coffee and authentic Mediterranean dishes like the "foole plate" – fava beans, lemon juice and parsley blended and served alongside warm bread.

Café Pamplona 12 Bow St ☎617/492-0352; **Harvard T**. Spanish-style basement café and patio that hasn't budged since 1959. Drop in for a *media noche* (ham, pork and muenster cheese on a mini French roll) and linger over a cappuccino.

Crema Café 27 Brattle St ☎617/876-2700; **Harvard T**. Popular café in the heart of Harvard Square that clamours with a clientele seeking *Crema's* potent espresso drinks and made-entirely-from-scratch food offerings. Breakfast sees the likes of the "maximillion" (scrambled eggs with sweet potato and rosemary goat cheese on a homemade English muffin; $4.75); lunch fare includes a great spinach and artichoke chicken sandwich ($6.95).

Tealuxe 0 Brattle St ☎617/441-0077; Harvard **T**. Smaller than a teacup, this endearing spot still manages to stock over a hundred varieties of tea, including crème de la Earl Grey, which some connoisseurs think tastes like birthday cake. Good bubble teas, too.

Somerville

Diesel Café 257 Elm St ☎617/629-8717; **Davis T**. They take their caffeine seriously at this trendy, garage-like coffee shop where patrons get revved on High Octane (double shots). Best is the photo booth where you can document your transformation from morning slob into caffeinated go-getter.

True Grounds 717 Broadway ☎617/591-9559; **Davis T**. Well-loved neighbourhood café with free wi-fi, cosy quarters, seriously good sandwiches, and espresso drinks born out of love and knowledge. They also stock *Christina's* ice cream (see box, p.146).

Restaurants

There is no shortage of places to **eat** in Boston, and the city has price ranges and cuisines to please every palate. Head to Boston's **North End** for tasty **Italian** food served amidst authentic and romantic environs. Or pop by the gay-friendly **South End**, the city's foodie district and Boston's best spot for contemporary New American fare. **Chinatown** has a number of tasty Asian-inspired eateries; it also stays open late and manages to get up early enough to serve dim sum brunch. **Kenmore Square** has a number of late-night hangouts to please its student and club-going population; the block where Boylston Street meets up with Mass Ave (technically in **Back Bay**) is also popular for after-hours pizza slices and the like. **Downtown** and the **Waterfront** are good for seafood, and the former has a lot of quick lunch options for feeding its workday regulars. Rounding out the Boston food tour, **Back Bay** has a great café culture that encourages outdoor seating and people watching. Across the river, **Cambridge** and **Somerville** have an impressive collection of Indian and Mexican eateries, as well as contemporary fusion fare that easily rivals Boston's.

Downtown

Defining "downtown" Boston can be a little nebulous (some say it's strictly the Financial District and Government Center, while others expand it to include everything from the Financial District down to the Theater District). To keep things simple, we've sub-divided the Downtown restaurants section into smaller sub-headings, so that no matter where you are, you're always near good food.

Boston Common and Downtown Crossing

Chacarero 26 Province St ⓣ617/367-1167, ⓦwww.chacarero.com; Downtown Crossing **T**. Fabulous and fresh, the *chacarero* is a Chilean sandwich built upon warm, soft bread that's filled with avocado, chicken, green beans, muenster cheese, and hot sauce. It's the gold standard of Downtown lunch fare, with good veggie options as well. Closed weekends, cash only. There's a second option nearby at 101 Arch St (ⓣ617/542-0392; both Downtown Crossing **T**).

Falafel King 48 Winter St ⓣ617/338-8355; Downtown Crossing **T**. You'll know you've found this hidden gem, nestled within an unappealing, semi-sketchy food court, when you come across a long line of gleeful regulars. Quick, cheap, and tasty, the *Falafel King* offers up traditional *shawarma* sandwiches ($5.50) made better with pickles, *baba ghanoosh* (aubergine), and salad ($6.30), and, if the *King* deems you worthy, free samples of his well-loved falafel. Closed weekends, cash only.

Kingston Station 25 Kingston St ⓣ617/482-6282; Downtown Crossing **T**. Doubling as a late-night bar and bistro joint, this noisy, white-tiled restaurant is also great for lunch and after-work drinks. Done up in the style of a train station, the reason-ably priced menu features an awesome "station burger" (sunnyside egg, bacon, gruyere and fixings; $15) and a number of fresh, creative cocktails.

Locke-Ober 3 Winter Place ⓣ617/542-1340; Park **T**. A Boston legend, this blue-blooded institution consists of traditionalist fancy fare like steak *au poivre* and oysters on the half shell (although the recent takeover by star chef Lydia Shire has infused a much-appreciated flair into the menu). Old-school, expensive, and lovingly indulgent, patrons should dress to impress and prepare to be wowed by a mahogany-and-chandelier setting that once served JFK and has seen many a marriage proposal. Reservations recommended.

Marliave 10 Bosworth St ⓣ617/422-0004; Park St **T**. Dating to 1875, this storied Boston landmark has been recently reborn by the owner of *Grotto* (see p.153). There's a bistro menu with tuna niçoise salad ($9) and steak frites ($19.50) served in an atmospheric nineteenth-century space. The second-floor dining room is entirely enclosed in glass and has great views, while the restaurant's basement level offers up coffee beverages and home-made truffles.

No. 9 Park 9 Park St ⓣ617/742-9991, ⓦwww .no9park.com; Park St **T**. Well-loved Boston landmark with serene green walls and plates busy with southern French and Italian entrees ranging from day boat scallops with rock shrimp ($39) to Peking duck with blackberries ($39). A seven-course tasting menu ($112; with wine, add $74) allows you to try almost everything.

Sam La Grassa's 44 Province St ⓣ617/357-6861; Downtown Crossing **T**. Quite possibly Boston's best deli, complete with home-made pickles and tasty, bulging sandwiches such as the "fresh from the pot" corned beef ($8). Only open during weekday lunch hours (11am–3.30pm).

Silvertone 69 Bromfield St ⓣ617/338-7887; Park Street **T**. Nostalgia runs high at this bustling basement bar and eatery with standout comfort foods like mashed potatoes and meatloaf and a super-cheesy mac and cheese. Rightly popular with the afterwork crowd, *Silvertone* also has cocktails, and a good selection of beers on tap. Closed Sun.

Zo 2 Center Plaza ⓣ617/227-0101; Government Center **T**. A bit tricky to find (it's unfairly hidden behind the massive, curved Center Plaza building), during weekday lunch hours *Zo* serves up Boston's best gyro sandwiches – crafted with pork, tomatoes, onion, home-made *tzatziki* sauce and warm flatbread ($7).

Faneuil Hall and around

Durgin Park **Faneuil Hall Marketplace** ☏617/227-2038; Haymarket **T**. A Boston landmark, in operation since 1827, *Durgin-Park* has a no-frills Yankee atmos- phere and a waitstaff known for its surly charm. Formerly hailed as a great place to go for iconic New England fare like roast beef, baked beans and warm Indian pudding, in recent years, the food quality has dipped; nowadays, it's best for drinks and ambience only.

Quincy Market **Faneuil Hall Marketplace** ☏617/523-1300; Haymarket **T**. The *doyenne* of Faneuil Hall marketplace, the historic *Quincy Market building* houses a better- than-normal food court on its first floor that's packed with tempting stalls serving everything from seafood and Italian pastries to sushi and Greek food.

Union Oyster House **41 Union St** ☏617/227-2750, ⊛www.unionoysterhouse .com; Haymarket or State **T**. The oldest conti- nuously operating restaurant in America has two big claims to fame: King Louis-Philippe lived over the tavern during his youth, and, perhaps apocryphally, the toothpick was first used here. The restaurant's food is so-so; the real draw is the charming raw bar – six oysters will set you back around $12.

Wagamama **Quincy Market in Faneuil Hall Marketplace** ☏617/742-9242, ⊛www .wagamama.com; Haymarket or State **T**. A reliable option in a touristy setting, this British noodle joint has fresh juices and cheap and filling ramen fare like the *moyashi soba* in a vegetable soup with squash, snow peas, and bean sprouts ($10). There are other locations in Harvard Square (57 JFK St, ☏617/499-0930) and in the Prudential Center (800 Boylston, ☏617/778-2344).

The Financial District and around

Milk Street Café **50 Milk St** ☏617/542-3663; State **T**. Kosher and quick are the key words at this Downtown eatery, popular with business folks and vegetarians for the large designer sandwiches and salads.

Mr Dooley's Boston Tavern **77 Broad St** ☏617/338-5656; State **T**. One of the many Irish pubs downtown, though with a quieter, more laidback feel than the rest. It's known for both its live music acts and traditional Irish Breakfast Sundays (bacon, eggs, black pudding, and baked beans), the latter a particularly useful bit of know-how as finding anything open around here on Sun can be a challenge.

Radius **8 High St** ☏617/426-1234; South Station **T**. Housed in a former bank, this ultramodern French restaurant injects a dose of minimalist industrial chic to the cautious Financial District. The tasty nouvelle cuisine is complemented by an extensive wine list, although some would say that a trip here is wasted if you don't order (surprisingly) the burger ($19), considered the best in town.

Sakurabana **57 Broad St** ☏617/542-4311; State **T**. Sushi restaurant that bustles by day with Financial District regulars hankering after its tasty bento-box lunch specials ($12). The environs are pretty basic (and there's generally a wait); you may be better off getting your meal to go, or coming at dinnertime when the staff is less harried.

Sultan's Kitchen **116 State St** ☏617/560-9009; State **T**. A great little Turkish joint, this lunch spot is favoured by businessmen who line up for the agreeably spicy Ottoman classics. Take a table in the casual upstairs room and you'll feel miles away from nearby tourist- laden Quincy Market.

The Theater District

Finale Desserterie **1 Columbus Ave** ☏617/423-3184; Boylston or Arlington **T**. Devil- ishly good desserts are the mainstay at this extremely cushy sweet-tooth emporium; the top-notch wines and cordials that go with them are a treat, too. There's another location in Harvard Square, Cambridge at 30 Dunster St (☏617/441-9797; Harvard **T**).

Jacob Wirth **31 Stuart St** ☏617/338-8586; Boylston **T**. A German-themed Boston landmark, around since 1868. Even if you don't like bratwurst washed down with a hearty lager, something is sure to please. There are sing-alongs on Fri.

Montien Thai **63 Stuart St** ☏617/338-5600; Boylston **T**. Situated on the cusp of the Theater District bordering Chinatown, *Montien* is a pleasant merging of the two neighbourhoods. Great for a quiet before- show meal, the menu is authentic Thai (think *Massaman* curry with coconut milk, $12) pleasing locals and visitors alike.

Teatro 177 Tremont St ☎617/778-6841; Boylston **T**. A gorgeous space with high arched ceilings and serene blue lighting, pre- and post-show patrons file in here for Italian fare, or simply antipasti ($8–24) and drinks. Be sure to order the calamari with lemon aioli ($14), considered to be some of the best squid in town; the rigatoni with bolognese sauce ($21) is another standout. Although noisy, it's still a great date spot.

Troquet 140 Boylston St S ☎617/695-9463; Boylston **T**. Breeze into *Troquet* and settle yourself in for a romantic evening of indulgent French fare overlooking Boston Common. The perfect conclusion to a night at the theatre (they're open until 10.30pm) – try the marinated beet salad with hazelnuts and goat cheese ($14), or the slow-roasted Vermont lamb with fig ($39). Known for its extensive wine list, *Troquet* is worth visiting for its bar alone; there's also an exquisite in-house *patisserie*, downstairs.

Chinatown

Dongh Khanh 81 Harrison Ave ☎617/426-9410; Chinatown **T**. During the summer, people line up to get their hands on *Dongh Khanh's* bubble tea, made from fresh fruit, tapioca, and tasty fixings (the avocado is to die for). Their traditional Vietnamese dishes are good as well.

Gourmet Dumpling House 52 Beach St ☎617/338-6222; Chinatown **T**. Tables fill up quickly at this Chinese restaurant known for its dumplings (try the mini juicy variety with pork; $6.50) and extensive, fresh, authentic menu.

Mei Sum Inc. 36 Beach St ☎617/357-4050; Chinatown **T**. Don't sweat the gritty environs or lack of menu; beyond *Mei Sum's* dingy exterior lie the neighbourhood's best *bánh mí* (Vietnamese sandwiches on toasted French bread). While it's best if you know what you want beforehand (pork pâté, cold cuts, spicy beef or tofu; all $2.75), kindly counter-folks do their utmost to help out sandwich neophytes. If you prefer a point-and-order approach, head to *New Saigon Sandwich*, down the street at 696 Washington (☎617/542-6296).

Peach Farm 4 Tyler Street ☎617/482-3332; Chinatown **T**. A Chinatown seafood standby with unfashionable digs but fresh seafood fare that you'll see swimming in tanks moments before it arrives on your plate. Go for the oysters in black bean sauce ($13) or the pea leaf sprouts with garlic ($8). Open late.

Shabu-Zen 16 Tyler St ☎617/292-8828; Chinatown **T**. Test your culinary skills at this fun and healthy spot which lets you cook your own thinly sliced meats and veggies tableside. Entrees include rice or noodles, a side of raw veggies, and dessert; the chicken platter is $11.

Taiwan Café 34 Oxford St ☎617/426-8181; Chinatown **T**. Foodies swoon over this busy, authentic Taiwanese eatery which serves up mustard greens with edamame ($7.95), clams with spicy black bean sauce, and steamed pork buns ($5.95) done just right. Cash only, open until midnight.

Winsor Dim Sum Café 10 Tyler St ☎617/338-1688; Chinatown **T**. Tired of waiting until the weekend to satisfy your dim sum brunch fix? Wait no more. *Winsor* provides menu-based dim sum offerings (as well as other tasty Chinese fare) throughout the week. The only downside is the menu setting means you'll have to forego a nostalgic cart-pushing experience (for that, head around the bend to *Hei La Moon* at 88 Beach St, ☎617/338-8813).

Xinh Xinh 7 Beach St ☎617/422-0501; Chinatown **T**. The ample "Best of Boston" awards in the window are the first clue that you're in for some superlative Vietnamese food. While the menu is extensive, most people just come for the big bowls of piping-hot *pho* noodle soup ($6.50).

The Leather District and around

Les Zygomates 129 South St ☎617/542-5108, ⓦ www.leszygomates.com; South Station **T**. Busy French bistro with good wine selections (there's more than a hundred international varieties) and gourmet *frites* that's located just a few blocks from South Station. Try the lamb with fava beans ($28) for dinner, and for dessert indulge in rhubarb and mango crisp. Good lunches, too. Live jazz nightly.

O Ya 9 East St ☎617/654-9900; South Station **T**. The portions are petite and the sushi prices sky high, but patrons swoon over *O Ya's* exquisite fare such as wild bluefin tuna *tataki* and roasted beet sashimi. One of Boston's great foodie hangouts, in a sleek, intimate space.

Sorriso Trattoria 107 South St ☎617/259-1560; South Station **T**. Exposed brick and lofty ceilings complement the tasty Italian fare at this hip trattoria convenient to South Station. Entrees ($17–25) are prepared with local ingredients when available, such as the arugula and Vermont goat cheese ravioli ($18); lunch is less expensive and just as good.

South Street Diner 178 Kneeland St ⊤617/350-0028; **South Station** ⊤. The stools at the counter have been spinning since 1947 when this Boston landmark opened its doors for local factory workers. Now known more for being a late-night hangout, folks head here for burgers, sandwiches, and the like. Open 24hr. There's also a jukebox and beers on tap.

Waterfront, Fort Point Channel, and the Seaport District

The Barking Crab 88 Sleeper St (at the Northern Avenue Bridge) ⊤617/426-CRAB; **South Station** ⊤. This endearing, touristy seafood shack aims to please with its homey atmosphere (it looks like a circus tent), friendly service, and unpretentious menu. Pretty much anything that can be pulled from the sea is served, including their "barking crab" cakes ($10), but really, it's more about the ambience. The prime waterfront location attracts quite a crowd in the warmer months (the upside is you get to hold onto a "lobster beeper" until your table is ready).

Channel Cafe 300 Summer St ⊤617/426-0695; **South Station** ⊤. Creative chalkboard lunch offerings (such as shaved sirloin tacos for $12.95) in a high-ceilinged, artsy space adjacent to a number of galleries. Regulars rave about the sweet-potato fries with five-spice aioli ($5). Good breakfast burritos, too, if you're in the area.

flour bakery + café 12 Farnsworth St ⊤617/338-4333; **South Station** ⊤. An offshoot of the well-loved South End institution (see p.155), this eatery is tucked inside a brick warehouse around the corner from the Children's Museum. Bursting with fantastic pastries, sandwiches and salads, they're best known for their life-changing BLTs and house-made raspberry seltzer. Top off your meal with a home-made pop tart or peanut butter Oreo cookie. There's also a new Cambridge location in Central Square at 190 Massachusetts Ave (⊤617/225-2525).

James Hook & Co. Lobsters 15 Northern Ave ⊤617/423-5500; **South Station** ⊤. Like a phoenix from the ashes (or a boiled lobster leaping from its shell), the seafood wholesaler

James Hook survived its 2008 fire and is back to serving up some of Boston's best lobster rolls (and at only $12, they're some of the city's best-priced rolls, too). Very casual – you serve yourself at a picnic table.

Sportello 348 Congress St ⊤617/737-1234; **South Station** ⊤. Boston super chef Barbara Lynch (*No.9 Park*, the *Butcher Shop*) has done it again with this simple yet sumptuous modern interpretation of a lunch counter. Italian-inspired dishes range from Roman gnocchi with polenta and lamb ragu ($14) to swordfish with prosciutto ($21); there's also a neat little take-away section filled with sandwiches, pastries and the like.

Sel de la Terre 255 State St ⊤617/720-1300; **Aquarium** ⊤. *Sel de la Terre* honours its name (salt of the earth) with rustic Provençal fare like hearty bouillabaisse, lamb and aubergine dishes, and what are perhaps the best french fries in Boston. They also have a new location adjacent to their sister restaurant, *L'Espalier*, in Back Bay at 774 Boylston St (⊤617/266-8800).

Yankee Lobster Fish Market 300 Northern Ave ⊤617/345-9799; **Silver Line Way** ⊤. Right by the water in the Seaport District, this casual, noteworthy seafood spot serves up fried-fish fare and lobster rolls ($16) ordered from a takeout counter. It's a hike from Downtown – you might want to hop on the Silver Line. Good beers available, too.

The North End

Antico Forno 93 Salem St ⊤617/723-6722; **Haymarket** ⊤. Cosy, down-home restaurant serving impressive Italian standards that won't break the bank. Known for their oven-fired pizzas ($11.50–12.50), *Antico* also serves up a top-notch *caprese* salad ($11).

Carmen 33 North Sq ⊤617/742-6421; **Haymarket** ⊤. With its intimate size and pretty, exposed brick walls, *Carmen* is perhaps the North End's most romantic spot. No dessert, but their signature small plates such as the roasted red beets with mint and ricotta ($6) or entrees like *crespelle bolognese* ($20) make sure you don't leave hungry.

The Daily Catch 323 Hanover St ⊤617/523-8567; **Haymarket** T; **2 Northern Ave** ⊤617/772-4400; **South Station** ⊤. Ocean-fresh seafood – notably calamari and shellfish (Sicilian-style, with mega doses of garlic) – draws big lines to this tiny storefront restaurant.

⑪

Galleria Umberto 289 Hanover St ☎617/227-5709; Haymarket **T**.
North End nirvana. There are fewer than a dozen items on the menu, but the lines are consistently to the door for Umberto's perfect pizza slices and savory *arancini* (fried and stuffed rice balls). Lunch only, and get there early as they always sell out.

Giacomo's 355 Hanover St ☎617/523-9026; Haymarket **T**. Will you have to wait in line for an hour before getting a seat at this modest Italian restaurant? Probably. Do neighbourhood residents ever eat here? Not really. But that doesn't stop the crowds from coming, nor does it prevent Giacomo from turning out consistently lauded Italian classics like chicken marsala ($14) and fettucini with peas ($14). Cash only.

La Summa Cucina Italiana 30 Fleet St ☎617/523-9503; Haymarket **T**. If you're looking for simple Italian food as good as your *nona* used to make, look no further than *La Summa*, named for the chef-owner's grandma, who taught her to cook while she was growing up in the North End. Their baked manicotti ($16) will make your day.

Marco 253 Hanover St ☎617/742-1276; Haymarket **T**. The hustle and bustle of Hanover Street fades away inside this secluded gem, perched on the second floor of a historic building. The excellent (albeit pricey) Italian entrees (such as chicken with sage and fontina; $28) are served on rustic wooden tabletops amidst antique ceiling beams and exposed brick walls.

Maria's Pastry 46 Cross St ☎617/523-1196; Haymarket **T**. The best pastries in the North End, and inexplicably under-rated. Her chocolate *cannoli* with fresh ricotta filling is the mandatory first choice.

Mike's Pastry 300 Hanover St ☎617/742-3050; Haymarket **T**. Attended by locals and tourists alike, in many ways *Mike's is* the North End. The full rainbow of pastries is represented here (eclairs, *cannoli*, marzipan, *gelato* et al), and lining up for one of these twine-wrapped boxes is a quintessential Boston experience.

Modern Pastry 257 Hanover St ☎617/523-3783; Haymarket **T**. You can't miss *Modern's* glorious vintage sign out front, nor would you want to – inside is fresh *torrone, cannoli* and little marzipan fruits. Family-owned for seventy years.

Monica's Trattoria 67 Prince St ☎617/720-5472; Haymarket **T**. Some of the most intensely flavoured Italian fare around, prepared and served by Monica's three sons, who grew up in the North End. Monica herself has a gourmet shop around the corner, at 130 Salem St.

Neptune Oyster 63 Salem St ☎617/742-3474; Haymarket **T**. Snazzy little raw bar filled with fans who swear by the fantastic shucked shellfish and best-in-town lobster rolls (served hot with butter or cold with mayo).

Pizzeria Regina 11 1/2 Thacher St ☎617/227-0765, ⓦ www.reginapizzeria.com; Haymarket **T**. Visit this North End legend for tasty, cheap pizza, served in a neighbour-hood feed station where the wooden booths haven't budged since the 1940s. Don't be fooled by chains bearing the *Regina* label in other parts of town, this is the original, vastly superior location. Cash only, and be prepared for a wait.

Ristorante Damiano 307-309 Hanover St ☎617/742-0020; Haymarket **T**. Open-air little *piattini* (small plates) spot offering up a welcome alternative to the traditional Italian red-sauce thing. No dessert served, but that's hardly a problem in this neighbourhood.

Taranta 210 Hanover St ☎617/720-0052, ⓦ www.tarantarist.com; Haymarket **T**. *Taranta* is a mix of Italian and Peruvian flavours, which translates into pork chops with sugar cane and giant Peruvian corn ($30) and lobster ravioli with mascarpone tomato sauce ($25). Located on busy Hanover St, *Taranta* remains a bit of a secret among locals, although the folks who go once usually wind up becoming regulars.

Volle Nolle 351 Hanover St ☎617/523-0003; Haymarket **T**. Chic lunchtime sandwich eatery with standout combinations, such as the pesto chicken with prosciutto and fresh mozzarella ($8.95). The charismatic owner also stocks her counter with mind-blowing cookies and great coffee beverages. Cash only.

East Boston

Santarpio's 111 Chelsea St ☎617/567-9871; Airport **T**. People generally head out to East Boston for two reasons: either to go to the airport or to eat pizza at *Santarpio's*. Outside is a dark, unappealing house; inside sees booths, slow table service and chewy, much-lauded pies. An Eastie institution.

Scup's in the Harbour 259 Marginal St, Building 16 ☏617/569-7287; Airport **T**. Fantastic BLT sandwiches with pesto mayo, a rotating selection of home-made empañadas, and Thalia's famed sweets tempt you at this everyone-knows-your-name spot nestled in the Boston Harbor Shipyard. *Scup's* is best known for its weekend brunch, and with tidbits like "millionaire's bacon" (made better with maple syrup and hot sauce) and baked eggs with breadcrumbs and cream, it's not hard to fathom why. Seating is limited; try to avoid the rush times.

Charlestown

Figs 67 Main St ☏617/242-2229; Community College **T**. New-school pizzeria serving excellent thin-crust pies topped with such savoury items as figs and prosciutto or caramelized onions and arugula. Another location is at 42 Charles St in Beacon Hill (☏617/742-3447; Charles **T**).

Navy Yard Bistro & Wine Bar Corner of 1st Ave and 6th St ☏617/242-0036; Community College **T**. Close to the USS *Constitution*, but a bit tricky to find, this neighbourhood restaurant nicely toes the line of elegance and approachability. New American favourites like lamb chops ($22) and seared sea scallops ($22) are served at dinnertime from the open kitchen.

Sorelle Bakery and Café 1 Monument Ave ☏617/242-2125; Community College **T**; 100 City Sq ☏617/242-5980; Community College **T**. Two locations: one a welcome oasis after crossing the Charlestown Bridge, the other more tucked away, with a delightful hidden patio. Both have stellar muffins and cookies, plus lemonade and other lunch fare.

Tangierino 83 Main St ☏617/242-6009, ⓦwww .tangierino.com; Community College **T**. Super-romantic Moroccan restaurant with authentic entrees like *ka'dra* lamb with figs and cheese-filled aubergine ($27). Next door, patrons puff contentedly on hookahs and ogle the belly dancers at their *Casbah Lounge*.

Zumes Coffee House 223 Main St ☏617/242-0038; Community College **T**. A bit out of the way from Charlestown's major sights (but just around the corner from the Phipps Street Burying Ground), *Zume's* ("Zoo-mees") offers knockout doughnuts, great sandwiches (try the roast beef with gorgonzola and horse-radish sauce for $7.50), coffee beverages and free wi-fi. Enjoy it all from one of the cushy leather seats.

Beacon Hill and the West End

75 Chestnut 75 Chestnut St ☏617/227-2175; Charles/MGH **T**. Tucked away off Beacon Hill's main thoroughfare (Charles St), this neighbourhood go-to serves American classics like Nantucket seafood stew ($20) and steak tips ($16). The bar scene buzzes most nights, and patrons receive complimentary cheese and crackers while waiting for a table. A good date spot, but also favoured by families.

Beacon Hill Bistro 25 Charles St (in the Beacon Hill Hotel) ☏617/723-7575; Charles/MGH **T**. Sleek New American and French bistro with an upscale feel. Short ribs with prunes ($9) share counter space with cod with capers and tomatoes ($18.50); breakfast is traditional American.

Grotto 37 Bowdoin St ☏617/227-3434; Government Center **T**. Romance is on the menu at this brick-walled, subterranean Italian spot that's close to Government Center. The petite dining room is well suited for close conversation, and its hearty offerings (such as fontina fondue with truffle oil; $10) are sure to please your date.

Lala Rokh 97 Mount Vernon St ☏617/720-5511, ⓦwww.lalarokh.com; Charles **T**. Have the waitstaff help you with the inscrutable menu at this exotically plush Azerbaijani restaurant, where you can fill up on the appetizers (such as roasted aubergine *kashk-e-bademjan*) and *torshi* (condiments) alone; locals rave about the *morgh pollo* (saffron chicken with cumin and rose petals). Main courses for $15–22.

Osteria Rustico 85 Canal St ☏617/742-8770; North Station **T**. An inexpensive hole-in-the-wall lunch spot that's a welcome break from the West End's many sports bars. *Osteria's* regulars rave about the gnocchi with fresh tomatoes and basil, the *tonno* (tuna) salad, and anything made with their addictive tomato cream sauce.

Paramount 44 Charles St ☏617/720-1152; Charles **T**. The Hill's neighbourhood diner serves Belgian waffles ($6) and omelettes ($5.50–8.50) to brunch regulars by day, and American standards like hamburgers ($12) and steak tips ($19) by night. Expect long waits on weekends.

Scampo 215 Charles St (in the Liberty Hotel) ☏617/536-2100; Charles/MGH **T**. Set in the *Liberty Hotel*, a sprawling, cruciform-shaped 1851 prison that was re-fashioned in 2007 as a luxury hotel, *Scampo* is an Italian-inspired restaurant helmed by star chef Lydia Shire. The imaginative menu includes a "mozzarella bar", eight different riffs on caprese salad ($13–26), creative breads and pizza and handmade pasta dishes.

Toscano 47 Charles St ☏617/723-4090; Charles/ MGH T. Classy, open-air Tuscan restaurant pleasing lunch and dinner diners alike with its superb renditions of *pappa al pomodoro* soup ($8) and margherita pizza ($13).

Upper Crust 20 Charles St ☏617/723-9600; Charles T. A popular pizza joint with fresh and tasty offerings; there's generally a slice of the day (such as spinach with pesto and tomato; $3). There are other locations at 222 Newbury St ☏617/262-0090; Copley **T**. 245 Summer St ☏617/367-0066; South Station **T**, and at 683 Tremont St ☏617/927-0090; Massachusetts Ave **T**.

Whole Foods 181 Cambridge St ☏617/723-0004; Bowdoin T. This supermarket franchise pops up like a foodie oasis on a strip that's thin on good eateries. Inside, you'll find Boston's best salad bar, and casual tables standing ready for diners.

Zen 21 Beacon St ☏617/371-1230; Government Center T. Close to the State House, this cheerful orange eatery buzzes at lunch time with 9-to-5ers seeking out Zen's affordable, well-executed sushi. Also doubles as a casual dinner spot.

Back Bay

Atlantic Fish Co. 761 Boylston St ☏617/267-4000; Copley T. Smack in the middle of busy Boylston Street, the wooden dining room of this seafood restaurant feels like it was lifted straight out of the belly of a yacht. Its menu changes daily according to what's fresh; entrees, which run about $27 for dinner, are stellar.

Burritos and Tacos to Go! 145 Dartmouth St (in the Back Bay T station) no phone; Back Bay T. This quick Mexican take-out stand, located inside of Back Bay station, serves cheap and exceptionally tasty burritos ($3.75) and tacos ($2.25) to grateful straphangers and area workers. Mon–Fri 11am–7pm.

Café Jaffa 48 Gloucester St ☏617/536-0230; Hynes T. Some of the city's best falafel and other Middle Eastern staples are served in this cool, inviting space with polished wood floors.

Douzo 131 Dartmouth St ☏617/859-8886; Back Bay T. A sexy, modern decor coupled with

standout sushi make this a great new option along the Back Bay-South End border. The service is hit or miss, but the food is consistently top-notch.

Grill 23 161 Berkeley St ☏617/542-2255; Arlington T. This carnivore-fest has outstanding steaks that are aged in-house, fish from exotic locales, and myriad mouthwatering wines. As with most big city steak houses, be prepared for expensive price tags.

India Samraat 51A Massachusetts Ave ☏617/247-0718; Hynes T. Casual Indian outpost that has been serving up aromatic *rogan josh* (lamb cubes cooked with yogurt and almonds; $13) and other tasty mainstays to Back Bay patrons for close to two decades.

Legal Seafoods Park Plaza Hotel, 26 Park Park Plaza ☏617/426-4444, ⊛www.legalseafoods .com; Arlington T; 255 State St ☏617/742-5300; Aquarium T; 100 Huntington Ave, Level Two, Copley Place ☏617/266-7775; Copley T; 800 Boylston St, Prudential Center ☏617/266-6800; Prudential T; 5 Cambridge Center ☏617/864-3400; Kendall T; 20 University Rd ☏617/491-9400; Harvard T. The *Starbucks* of the sea: it seems you can't turn a corner in Boston without encountering one of these ubiquitous eateries. As they claim, the seafood is fresh, and the clam chowder is loved by many, but the chain feel of the place may shiver your timbers.

L'Espalier 774 Boylston St ☏617/262-3023; Copley T. A ravishing French restaurant now happily situated in its new location adjacent to the *Mandarin Oriental*. A great date spot, *L'Espalier* serves a first-rate seasonal menu; the dinner *prix fixe* runs a steep $82.

The Other Side Cosmic Café 407 Newbury St ☏617/536-9477; Hynes T. This ultracasual hipster hangout on "the other side" of Newbury Street (it's across Mass Ave), offers gourmet sandwiches, creative green salads, and fresh juices. They also have pitchers of quality beer. Open late.

Mike & Patty's 12 Church St ☏617/423-3477; NE Medical Center T. Located in Bay Village (see p.92), a residential satellite of Back Bay, *Mike & Patty's* is a teensy breakfast and lunch spot serving some of the best sandwiches in the city. While it's not on the road to any major sights, those who make the trek out will feel amply rewarded by *M&P*'s fried green tomato BLTs ($7.25) and grilled banana sandwiches ($6.50).

Mistral 223 Columbus Ave ☎617/867-9300; **Arlington T**. The dining room of *Mistral* feels like a designer's fairy-tale creation – all arched floor-to-ceiling windows, high ceilings, potted shrubbery and fanciful chandeliers. Its acclaimed French menu features Mediterranean dishes such as Atlantic swordfish with "aubergine" ($35).

Parish Café & Bar 361 Boylston St ☎617/247-4777, **Arlington T**. The ambience isn't much, but who cares when you're eating one of the best sandwiches in Boston? *Parish Café* formed when a number of esteemed Boston chefs decided to create a fancy rotating sandwich menu, such as Ming Tsai's "Blue Ginger" (rare tuna with teriyaki glaze and avocado wasabi aioli; $13). Also at 493 Massachusetts Ave ☎617/391-0501; **Massachusetts Ave T**.

Sonsie 327 Newbury St ☎617/351-2500, ⊛www.sonsieboston.com; **Hynes T**. This Newbury Street staple is good for contemporary bistro fare, swanky sandwiches, pastries, and a killer chocolate bread pudding. In the summertime, aim for their Sunday brunch when the restaurant opens onto the street, jazz filters lazily through the air, and of course the food is fabulous.

Sorellina 1 Huntington Ave ☎617/412-4600; **Copley T**. Kid sister to *Mistral* (see above), this contemporary Italian restaurant often steals the limelight from her more established sibling. Service is outstanding, and the home-made pasta ($13–30) is the stuff dreams are made of.

Stephanie's on Newbury 190 Newbury St ☎617/236-0990, ⊛www.stephaniesonnewbury .com; **Copley T**. Though they pride themselves on their yellowfin tuna salad ($17), what sets *Stephanie's* apart is the outdoor dining in the prime people-watching territory of Newbury Street. Open until 11pm.

Summer Shack 50 Dalton St ☎617/867-9955; **Hynes T**. Spacious seafood locale with kitschy maritime decor and lots of seating. The raw bar is tops (around $1.75 per clam), and the grilled fish (market price hovers around $20) is also quite good. Plus they have corn dogs ($5.50).

Trident Booksellers & Café 338 Newbury St ☎617/267-8688; **Copley T**. Great little neighbourhood café featuring a "perpetual breakfast" and tasty, vegetarian-friendly lunch and dinners. Set inside one of Boston's best independent bookstores, plates include a breakfast burrito with

mushrooms and avocado ($8.25) and pan-seared salmon over sweet potato hash ($13). Pick up an obscure magazine and read it while gazing out onto Newbury Street. Open until midnight.

Via Matta 79 Park Plaza ☎617/422-0088; **Arlington T**. This romantic Italian restaurant beckons patrons from the Theater District and offers a great range of dining environs: al fresco on the patio, inside the white-walled dining room, or even smack in the centre of the animated kitchen. The range of seating and the seasonal menu guarantee a different experience every visit.

The South End

Addis Red Sea 544 Tremont St ☎617/426-8727; **Back Bay T**. An intimate Ethiopian eatery with carved wooden stools, communal plates and *injera* (a warm spongy bread) served alongside *gomen wat* (collard greens with onions and garlic; $8). A welcome affordable option right on Boston's "Restaurant Row".

Aquitaine 569 Tremont St ☎617/424-8577; **Back Bay T**. Settle into an enveloping leather banquette at this elegant French *brasserie*, gape at the astonishing array of wines and feast on the best steak frites ($26) and foie gras in town. They also have a more affordable brunch (the prix fixe option is $10).

B&G Oysters 550 Tremont St ☎617/423-0550; **Back Bay T**. If you can manage to get a table at this tiny pearlescent restaurant, you're in luck. The oysters (from $2.50 each) are simply the best Boston has to offer.

Butcher Shop 552 Tremont St ☎617/423-4800; **Back Bay T**. Not your grandpa's butcher shop, this sleek offspring of the Barbara Lynch empire (the woman behind *B&G Oysters* and *No. 9 Park*) offers small plates set with seasonal fruits and fancy charcuterie. There's also a swanky wine bar and gourmet hot dogs.

Charlie's Sandwich Shoppe 429 Columbus Ave ☎617/536-7669; **Back Bay T**. This historic hole-in-the-wall diner (established in 1927) was one of the first racially-integrated restaurants in Boston. Standouts include the decadent banana and pecan griddlecakes and their justly famous turkey hash. Closed Sundays, cash only, and beware – no customer toilets.

flour bakery + café 1595 Washington St ☎617/267-4300; **Back Bay T**. This bakery has a drool-worthy array of *brioche au* *chocolat*, old-fashioned sour cream coffee cake, gooey caramel nut tarts, savoury sandwiches, home-made breads, and thirst-quenching drinks. Choosing just one can be torture. There's also a new location in the Seaport District (see p.151) and in Central Square at 190 Massachusetts Ave ☎617/225-2525; Central **T**.

Franklin Café 278 Shawmut Ave ☎617/350-0010; Back Bay **T**. New American cuisine at very reasonable prices, enjoyed by a hip, unpretentious clientele. There are only eleven tables, so be prepared to wait at the bar for at least two martinis.

Gaslight, Brasserie du Coin 560 Harrison Ave ☎617/536-9477; Broadway **T**. Run by the masterminds behind *Aquitaine* (see above), this buzzing brasserie has an authentically French white-tile-and-mirror interior. Fun for brunch, dinner sees classic dishes like steak frites ($20) and steamed mussels ($16.75). Reservations recommended.

Hamersley's Bistro 553 Tremont St ☎617/423-2700, ⓦwww.hamersleysbistro .com; Back Bay **T**. *Hamersley's* is widely regarded as one of the best restaurants in Boston, and with good cause. Every night star chef (and owner) Gordon Hamersley dons a baseball cap and takes to the open kitchen, where he dishes out unusual – and unforgettable – French-American fare that changes with the season, such as pan-roasted lobster with leeks, roasted chestnuts, and black truffles ($38).

Metropolis Café 584 Tremont St ☎617/247-2931; Back Bay **T**. Presided over by star-shaped lanterns, this cosy spot (a former ice cream parlour) has a loosely mediterranean menu by night (think roasted chestnut soup or sardines over garlicky escarole), but they're best known for their tasty Sunday brunch featuring the likes of mimosas with fresh strawberries and grilled blueberry muffins.

Myers + Chang 1145 Washington St ☎617/542-5000; Back Bay **T**. This "indie diner" with an open kitchen serves Asian fusion dishes, such as braised short-rib tacos with pear ($13), *nasi goreng* (Indonesian fried rice with pork, pineapple and fried egg; $14), and an awesome scorpion bowl cocktail for two ($16). Bonus: your bill comes with complimentary coconut macaroons.

South End Buttery 314 Shawmut Ave ☎617/482-1015; Back Bay **T**. Impossible to

resist, this adorable neighbourhood café (now with an adjacent bistro) offers egg sandwiches on home-made biscuits, house-made soups and sandwiches, cappuccinos, and terrific cupcakes named for the owner's dogs.

Stella 1525 Washington St ☎617/247-7747; Back Bay **T**. Primo Italian fare, such as mouth-watering parmesan *arancini* balls ($8) and home-made gnocchi ($19), served in a beautiful white interior. Nice outdoor seating in summer, and you can catch the equally good late-night menu from 11pm–1:30am.

Teranga 1746 Washington St ☎617/266-0003; Massachusetts Ave **T**. Close to the Roxbury end of the South End, this Senegalese crowd pleaser serves up authentic fare like *thiebou djeun* (herb-stuffed white fish cooked in tomato stew with jasmine rice and pumpkin; $15) accompanied by innovative fresh juices.

Toro 1704 Washington St ☎617/536-4300; Massachusetts Ave **T**. A hip and lively tapas bar brimming with sassafras mojitos ($10) and inventive tapas plates such as the octopus ceviche ($9) and salt cod fritters with lemon ($9). Plates range from $5 to $12.

Tremont 647 647 Tremont St ☎617/266-4600; Back Bay **T**. Adventurous American cuisine by night (think sea bass in banana leaves), *Tremont 647* is best loved for their Sunday "pajama brunch" when locals and servers roll up in their Sunday morning finest.

Union Bar and Grille 1357 Washington St ☎617/423-0555; Broadway **T**. This elegant eatery has tremendously good food and deep, black leather banquettes. Dinners begin with a pitch-perfect skillet of cornbread, followed by better-than-mom's American food such as the pan roasted chicken with chorizo stuffing ($19). While the weekend brunch is very inexpensive, expect to spend $25 an entree for dinner.

Kenmore Square and the Fenway

Audubon Circle 838 Beacon St ☎617/421-1910; Kenmore **T**. The seemingly endless bar may grab your attention first, but it's the food that's worth staying for. Any of the appetizers are good bets, as are the grilled items – from burgers with chipotle ketchup to tuna steak with banana salsa and *fufu* (fried plantains mashed with coconut milk).

Expect to pay around $9 per dish. There's a limited selection of home-made desserts, as well.

Canestaro 16 Peterborough St ☎617/266-8997; Kenmore **T**. A worthwhile detour after a visit to the Museum of Fine Arts, this neighbourhood eatery offers inexpensive Italian-American cuisine, as well as soups, sandwiches and salads in a warm-toned dining room sited on a residential side street. Nice patio, too.

Clio 370 Commonwealth Ave (in the Eliot Hotel) ☎617/536-7200; Hynes **T**. Celebrity chef Ken Oringer shines with his stylish *Clio*, a French-inspired affair boasting a constantly rotating menu. Dishes include the likes of foie gras with bitter strawberry ($20) and sauteed diver scallops with butternut squash ($36), all served within warmly-lit surroundings.

Eastern Standard 528 Commonwealth Ave ☎617/532-9100; Kenmore **T**. A relaxed bistro serving up fairly fancy, pre-Red Sox game fare. The menu can be a bit hit or miss, so go for the spaghetti carbonara or veal schnitzel – or just to watch a game in their lofty, atmospheric bar.

India Quality 484 Commonwealth Ave ☎617/267-4499; Kenmore **T**. The decor may be shabby, but it's the spicy Indian food and great beer selection that keeps 'em coming back to this affordable restaurant.

La Verdad Taqueria 1 Lansdowne St ☎617/351-2580; Kenmore **T**. This Ken Oringer hangout (see *Clio* above and *Toro* on p.156) in the shadow of Fenway Park is perfect for watching a Red Sox game or for setting up your big night after with a taco, a beer, and a shot ($5 special).

Petit Robert Bistro 468 Commonwealth Ave ☎617/375-0699; Kenmore **T**. This sweet and petite French bistro boasts a chalkboard menu that's been priced for the little guy; entrees, such as the chicken *coq au vin* with buttered noodles, run $14–20. There's another location in the South End at 480 Columbus Ave (☎617/867-0600; Back Bay **T**).

Trattoria Toscana 130 Jersey St ☎617/247-9508; Kenmore **T**. Boston residents are cuckoo for this pricey Tuscan favourite, regaled for its antipasto, home-made pasta and lemon-drop ice cream. Great for a romantic dinner after museum hopping in the Fenway. Seating is tight.

Brookline

Anna's Taqueria 1412 Beacon St ☎617/739-7300; Coolidge Corner **T**. Exceptional tacos, burritos and quesadillas are the only things on the menu at this bright and cheap Mexican eatery. But they're so good that branches had to be opened around the corner at 446 Harvard St (☎617/277-7111; Coolidge Corner **T**), in Beacon Hill at 242 Cambridge St (☎617/227-8822; Charles/MGH **T**) and in Cambridge at 822 Somerville Ave (☎617/661-8500; Porter **T**), to accommodate the legions of devotees.

Dok Bua 411 Harvard St, ☎617/232-2955; Coolidge Corner **T**. There's often a wait to get into this no-frills Thai find, dotted with Christmas lights and miniature plastic-food displays. While the service is very welcoming, it's the food here that really stands out– try the *moo yang* (grilled pork marinated in Thai herbs; $7.95). The menu is extensive, and there are picture aids for Thai-food neophytes.

Genki Ya 398 Harvard St, ☎617/277-3100; Coolidge Corner **T**. While for many years *Fugakyu* (at 1280 Beacon St) was the reigning champ of Brookline's sushi scene, this organic newcomer makes a creditable claim to the throne. The ambience is simple, but the sushi rolls are darn complicated – there's a huge range of combinations, such as the "Hawaii roll" (mango, sweet potato, banana, avocado, cucumber and cream cheese; $11.95). A healthful spot, with brown rice rolls encouraged.

La Morra 48 Boylston St, ☎617/739-0007; Brookline Village **T**. People come from all around to savour this Italian gem's sausage risotto and romantic hole-in-the-wall ambience. Good for couples, or just to catch up with friends; there are $25 family-style dinners on Sunday nights.

Orinoco 22 Harvard St, ☎617/232-9505; Brookline Village **T**. Stylish Venezuelan cantina that starts things off right (with phenomenal cocktails – the *caipiroja* with blood orange is stellar; $9.50). Dinner here is also superb: begin with a *reina pepiada arepa* with chicken ($6) followed by the *cordero tradicional* (plaintain-crusted lamb chops with mint *mojo*; $19). Reservations are not taken, so get there early to avoid the wait. There is another (cocktail-less) location in the South End at 477 Shawmut Ave (☎617-369-7075).

Washington Square Tavern 714 Washington St, ☎617/232-8989; Washington Square **T**. Cosy, off-the-beaten-path restaurant/ bar with an eclectic menu that turns out inventive meals like pork tenderloin with fig glaze and sweet potatoes ($18). Just hanging out and absorbing the vibe at the bar is worthwhile, too.

Zaftig's 335 Harvard St, ☎617/975-0075; Coolidge Corner **T**. Famed Jewish deli with a lengthy menu and excellent reuben and pastrami sandwiches. *Zaftig's* is best-known for their Sunday brunch, and rightly so – the banana stuffed French toast in a bourbon vanilla batter ($9) is extraordinary.

Allston

Ariana 129 Brighton Ave, ☎617/208-8072; Harvard Ave **T**. Locals rave about this new Afghani restaurant, a superlative option in a neighbourhood that's known for its ethnic cuisine. Kind staffers guide you through the menu, which offers standout vegetarian fare as well as plenty of meat dishes (like leg of lamb with tomatoes and lentils; $13). The decor is spartan but elegant.

Super 88 1095 Commonwealth Ave, ☎617/787-2288; Packards Corner **T**. This spacious Asian supermarket houses a tasty, inexpensive food court with a cornucopia of eastern cuisines – Vietnamese, Chinese, Thai, Japanese, and Taiwanese.

Jamaica Plain

Bella Luna 284 Amory St, ☎617/524-6060; Stonybrook **T**. Nouvelle pizza with a funky array of fresh toppings. You can order from their list of combinations or design your own; prices start from $7.

Centre Street Café 669A Centre St, ☎617/524-9217; Green St **T**. At weekend brunch time, the line stretches down the street in front of this laidback, institution serving locally sourced California-style cuisine. Lunch and dinner are less of a big deal and are just as good; expect creative American fare such as the potatoes Santa Cruz with fresh veggies or sesame noodles with coconut-peanut sauce (both $10).

Dogwood Café 3712 Washington St, ☎617/522-7997; Forest Hills **T**. Great for a meal after a trip to the Arnold Arboretum (see p.114), the dark wood-panelled *Dogwood* pleases families, hipsters and elderly couples alike. Brick-oven pizzas (named after trees in

the arboretum) run $9–19; there are also pastas, burgers and other comfort food fare available, in addition to indie beers on tap. Open till 1am.

El Oriental de Cuba 416 Centre St, ☎617/524-6464; Green St **T**. Popular, inexpensive, casual Cuban joint with an extensive menu and crowd-pleasing favourites like beans, rice and plantains ($8.95) and paella ($17).

Ten Tables 597 Centre St, ☎617/524-8810; Green St **T**. This inviting date spot was designed to feel like an intimate dinner party – there really are only ten tables – although they've recently added a low-lit bar. The seasonal French and American fare (entrees $19–26), such as pan-seared bass with summer greens ($22), is made from local ingredients, and is great for wooing a love interest. Reservations recommended. Another location has opened up in Cambridge at 5 Craigie Circle, ☎617/576-5444.

South Boston

Amrheins 80 W Broadway, South Boston ☎617/268-6189; Broadway **T**. A Southie landmark and a favourite of local politicians for generations. The good-ole' American comfort food is terrific, and you get plenty of it. *Amrheins* also offers a free shuttle taking you safely to and from the **T** station.

Roxbury

Speed's Hot Dogs 42 Newmarket Sq, ☎617/839-0102; Andrew Sq **T**. Road-trip aficionados will want to track down this unassuming food truck - located in a dusty, semi-sketchy part of Roxbury - which has been cranking out the city's best hot dogs since 1975. The humongous dogs ($7) are marinated in apple cider and brown sugar, grilled once you order, and then stuffed into giant toasted buns. Top it all off with vidalia onions and special sauce. *Speed's* has variable hours; if it's raining, call to make sure they're open. Get there early to avoid a long wait or a dog shortage.

Cambridge

Harvard Square and around

Bartley's Burger Cottage 1246 Massachusetts Ave ☎617/354-6559; Harvard **T**. A must-visit in Cambridge. Boston's best burgers, washed down with raspberry lime rickeys. The Americana-festooned environs poke fun at politicians of the hour, and a noisy waitstaff shouts out your order. Good veggie burgers, too. Cash only, and funky hours, but that's all part of the appeal.

Cambridge, 1 27 Church St, ☏617/576-1111; Harvard T. Sleek thin-crust-pizza spot in the heart of Harvard Square, which derives its name from the early 1900s brick firehouse building in which it's sited.

Casablanca 40 Brattle St, ☏617/876-0999; Harvard T. Stellar Mediterranean entrees ($25–28 at dinner) and tapas ($8-15) at this Harvard hangout nestled underneath the Brattle cinema. A bright mural of *Rick's Cafe* peruses the scene from on high.

Chez Henri 1 Shepard St ☏617/354-8980; Harvard or Porter T. Fantastic French fare with a strong Cuban accent, which translates into crispy duck with a tamarind-rum glaze ($15) and adds up to some of Cambridge's best cuisine. Most folks (looking to spend less cash) head straight to the adjacent bar for the amazing Cuban pressed sandwich ($13).

Darwin's Ltd 148 Mt Auburn St ☏617/354-5233; Harvard T. The rough-hewn exterior conceals a delightful deli serving the best sandwiches on Harvard Square – wonderfully inventive combinations include roast beef, sprouts, and apple slices served on freshly baked bread. No credit cards. There's another location at 1629 Cambridge St (☏617/491-2999; Harvard T).

Garage 36 JFK St no phone ; Harvard T. A sort of mall with hipster stores (records, tattoos and hemp clothing), this landmark spot also has good cheap eats - pizza, Mexican, Vietnamese, and ice cream.

Harvest 44 Brattle St ☏617/868-2255; Harvard T. Upscale, white-tableclothed Harvard Square institution with an oft-changing menu of rich New American cuisine; the outdoor courtyard is another fine feature. Go for the fish of the day (market price) or the tuna bolognese with fresh tomatoes and gnocchi ($16).

Henrietta's Table Charles Hotel, 1 Bennett St ☏617/661-5005; Harvard T. One of the few restaurants in Cambridge serving classic New England fare. Rich entrees such as roasted duck ($15) or pork chops ($16) work well with side dishes of wilted greens or mashed potatoes. Some would say a trip to *Henrietta's* is wasted if it's not for their famous brunch, served every Sunday from noon to 3pm; it costs $45 per person but

allows unlimited access to a cornucopia of farm-fresh treats from around New England.

LA Burdick's 52D Brattle St ☏617/491-4340; Harvard T. Simply breathing in the aromas at this fabulous *chocolaterie* is an exercise in indulgence: iced chocolate, chocolate mousse cake, and little chocolate mice and penguins, all waiting to be consumed.

Tamarind Bay 75 Winthrop St ☏617/491-4552; Harvard T. This bright basement eatery serves up distinctively spiced Indian food, perhaps the area's best. Regulars coo about the banana dumplings and *lalla mussal dal* (black lentils simmered in spices; $13.50).

Upstairs on the Square 91 Winthrop St ☏617/864-1933, ⊛www.upstairsonthesquare .com; Harvard T. With a whimsical decor of animal-striped carpet patterns and winged light bulbs, it's no surprise that *Upstairs on the Square* serves imaginative food. Located somewhere between New American and Old Colonial, figure on entrees like Nantucket sea scallops with porcini marmalade and tarragon ($37). Their carved pink bar mixes up fanciful cocktails accented with gummi sharks. Reservations recommended.

Veggie Planet 47 Palmer St ☏617/661-1513; Harvard T. This casual eatery underneath *Passim* (see p.171) has creative vegetarian and vegan pizzas, soups and salads. Try the vegan peanut curry (tofu, broccoli, peanuts and Thai red curry sauce; $11) on their slow-rise organic dough.

Central Square and around

Alive & Kicking Lobsters 269 Putnam Ave ☏617/876-0451; Central T. Walk too fast and you'll miss this crustacean shack, heavy on New England charm. Bulging lobster "sandwiches" (made on two slices of toasted bread instead of the traditional hot dog bun; $13.95 with chips) are served from behind a counter and eaten on picnic tables. Wash it all down with a home-made root-beer soda.

Baraka Café 80 1/2 Pearl St ☏617/868-3951; Central T. A hidden jewel, this North African eatery just off Central Square is loved by neighbourhood residents. Known for its signature lemonade (boosted with rose water and orange essence), *Baraka Café* offers small plates like *bedenjal mechoui* (smoky aubergine with garlic) and entrees like *m'satel* (lamb chops served with almond tartlet and saffron shallots; $16). Cash only.

Central Kitchen 567 Massachusetts Ave ☎617/491-5599; Central T. Hip Central Square bistro with a chalkboard menu offering delightful European classics (*moules frites* for $12) and contemporary American twists (mushroom ragout with ricotta dumplings for $17) in an intimate, stylish setting.

Craigie on Main 853 Main St ☎617/497-5511; Central T. A culinary dream-team, this French-inspired favourite, known for its "refined rusticity", rotates seasonal plates like grilled Spanish octopus ($18) and confit-roasted pig's head to share ($60 for two). The staff treats patrons like family, and their kindly attitude and thoroughness contributes to the restaurant's success as much as the cuisine. Reservations are a must.

Cuchi Cuchi 795 Main St ☎617/864-2929; Central Square T. Start by lingering over fantastic cocktails at the bar to soak in *Cuchi Cuchi's* Gatsby-esque fabulousness. The waitresses are decked out in vintage flapper dresses, and gilded mirrors and painted lampshades abound. The international menu reflects a similar attention to detail; savoury cornets with tuna tartare and avocado (five for $20) are lovingly prepared, as is the beef stroganoff with shallot and mushroom sauce ($12).

Koreana 154 Prospect St ☎617/576-8661, ⊛www.koreanaboston.com; Central Square T. Tables here have a built-in grill, allowing you to barbecue your own tasty meats and veggies (prices start from $16). The sushi bar (from $4.50 per piece) is also pretty good.

Rendezvous 502 Massachusetts Ave ☎617/576-1900; Central T. A welcome addition to Central Square, *Rendezvous* serves Mediterranean-inspired fare with a locally-grown flavour. Although the dishes rotate, sample plates include swiss chard dolmas with cucumber-purslane salad ($20) and roast chicken with Moroccan spices ($23). The Sunday prix fixe menu ($38) is highly recommended.

Kendall Square and around

Blue Room 1 Kendall Sq ☎617/494-9034, ⊛www.theblueroom.net; Kendall T. Unpretentious restaurant with superlative grilled fusion cuisine; pan-seared skate ($21) and braised lamb ($23) are common, but what accompanies them – cumin and basmati yogurt or tomatillos – isn't. The menu changes with what ingredients are available, so the food is always fresh and innovative.

Emma's Pizza 40 Hampshire St ☎617/864-8534; Kendall T. This tasty, local pizzeria has signature thin pies and slices featuring fun toppings like roasted sweet potatoes and ricotta. Consistently listed at or near the top of "best in Boston" lists.

Friendly Toast 1 Kendall Sq ☎617/621-1200; Kendall T. A delightful riot of bright green paint, '50s kitsch, a jukebox and vinyl seating, this breakfast-all-day funhouse serves pumpkin pancakes with whipped cream ($7.75) and "King Cakes" in honour of Elvis (banana and chocolate-chip pancakes with peanut butter in between; $10.25). Expect a wait on weekends.

Hungry Mother 233 Cardinal Medeiros Ave ☎617/499-0090; Kendall T. This south of the Mason-Dixon line, special-occasion spot serves salted boiled-peanut appetizers ($4), cornmeal catfish mains ($19) and poured cocktails in mason jars. Come dessert, you'll be saying an "Amen" to the *Mother*. Very popular; reservations recommended.

Salts 798 Main St. ☎617/876-8444; Central T. Foodies are awhirl with *Salts'* merging of local ingredients with exquisite French technique and presentation. The glazed duck for two ($65) is incredibly popular – you almost need to order it in advance – but you can't really go wrong with anything on the menu.

Inman Square and around

All Star Sandwich Bar 1245 Cambridge St ☎617/868-3065; Central T. A wrap-free zone, the menu at this sandwich utopia crosses many borders - *cubanos*, muffalettas, and reubens are all well represented. The meat loaf meltdown is a spicy standby ($9); they also make good chili ($3.95) and fries "from hell" ($4.95).

East Coast Grill 1271 Cambridge St ☎617/491-6568, ⊛www.eastcoastgrill.net; Harvard or Central Square T. A bright and funky atmosphere (think shades of *Miami Vice*) in which to enjoy fresh seafood and Caribbean side dishes such as grilled avocado, pineapple salsa, and fried plaintains. The Sunday serve-yourself Bloody Mary bar is reason enough to visit, and there is a raw bar tucked into one corner.

Olé Mexican Grill 11 Springfield St ☎617/492-4495; Central T. Widely regarded as one of Boston's best Mexican eateries, this pricier-than-a-taqueria-spot is worth it for the *tacos de atún asado* (rare tuna steak in handmade tortillas for $19), jicama salad ($9), and guacamole ($9). Across the street you'll find their *Olecito*, an adorable takeaway taco joint (cash only; T617/876-1374).

Oleana 134 Hampshire St T**617/661-0505; Central** T. If you can, secure a table here on the blissful, wisteria-laden patio, where you can linger over Mediterranean-fused lamb steak with fava-bean moussaka ($25) and Armenian bean and walnut paté with home-made string cheese ($4). Be sure to save room for the Baked Alaska, served with coconut ice cream and passion fruit-caramel sauce ($14). *Oleana* also runs a Middle Eastern bakery and café, *Sofra*, worth seeking out at 1 Belmont St, Cambridge (T617/661-3162).

Punjabi Dhaba 225 Hampshire St T**617/547-8272; Central** T. This unassuming Indian eatery inspires almost maniacal devotion among its fans, who trek across Cambridge for quick and cheap *palak paneer* and chicken *tikka masala*.

Tupelo 1193 Cambridge St T**617/868-0004, Central** T. Leave your diet at the door for owner Petsi's "comfort food with a southern drawl" - Cajun gumbo with andouille sausage, fried oysters with remoulade, cheddar grits, biscuits and sausage gravy - you name it, she's got it, and she does it good. Tupelo is the mastermind behind Petsi's Pies; so as hard as it may be, try and save room for an order of pecan pie with bourbon ice cream to top off your meal.

East Cambridge

Helmand 143 1st St T**617/492-4646; Lechmere** T. The interior won't win any style

awards, but this beloved Afghan dinner restaurant is favoured by everyone from Harvard students to families to couples on a first date. Don't miss the *kaddo borawni*, baked baby pumpkin seasoned with sugar and served on yogurt garlic sauce ($7.50).

Somerville

Blue Shirt Café 424 Highland Ave T**617/629-7641; Davis** T. Right in the heart of Davis Square, this teensy café is a great spot for picking up healthful items like fresh juices, salads, and sandwiches before hopping on to the T. They also do a great breakfast.

Dalí 415 Washington St T**617/661-3254,** W**www.dalirestaurant.com; Harvard** T. An upscale tapas restaurant featuring energetic Spanish music, excellent sangria, and most importantly superlative tapas (from $4.50). Start with the Spanish white asparagus, farm trout with red wine sauce, and braised rabbit in sweet-and-sour sauce.

Redbones 55 Chester St T**617/628-2200,** W**www.redbones.com; Davis** T. A variety of American barbecue ($10–21) is represented in huge portions, accompanied by delectable sides such as collard greens and Cajun "dirty rice". In the unlikely case that you have room for dessert, the pecan pie is top-notch. Gets busy at dinner, so arrive early.

Soundbites 708 Broadway T**617/623-8338 ; Davis** T. The staff will hustle you in and out of this local breakfast eatery, but in between you'll savour challah French toast loaded with fresh fruit ($8), as well as some of the best pancakes in town. Be prepared for a wait on weekends, although you can grab a cup of coffee while still in line.

⑫

Drinking

D espite – or, perhaps, because of – the lingering Puritan ethic that pervades Boston, people here tend to **drink** more than they do in the rest of the country, with the consequence that few American cities offer as many bars per capita in which to knock back a few beers. Before you start planning a big night out, however, it's worth knowing that drinking in Boston is not without its headaches – and we don't just mean the morning after.

While the number of watering holes in Boston is high, most **stop serving alcohol at 2am**. Another sticking point is that the city's university culture means the US **drinking-age minimum of 21** is strictly enforced; even if you're obviously of-age, you'll still be required to show at least one form of valid photo **identification**, either in the form of a driver's licence or passport, to gain entrance to any place serving drinks. Smokers will find themselves marginalized thanks to the **smoking ban**, which prohibits smoking even on outdoor patios. If you must smoke indoors, there are a handful of cigar lounges in town; your best bet is Cigar Masters at 745 Boylston St (☎617/266-4400, ⓦwww.cigarmasters.com; Copley **T**), where patrons puff contentedly and relax in leather armchairs; cigars from $3 to $30. Finally, the **T** shuts down at 12am, making it harder to get home if you're out late; you may want to call a cab (see p.25), as it can be difficult to find one when the exodus of drinkers are let out of the bars.

As for types of places, it's not surprising that, given the city's Irish heritage, **pubs** make up the majority of Boston's drinking establishments. Especially high concentrations of these are found in the **West End**, **Cambridge**, and **Downtown** around Quincy Market; many are unextraordinary, but several are the real deal, drawing as many Irish expats as they do Irish-American locals.

More hip are the **bars** and **lounges** of **Back Bay**, especially those along Newbury and Boylston streets, which occasionally offer as much attitude as atmosphere. Some of the most popular bars in this area are actually adjuncts of restaurants and hotels; still others cater to the city's gay population, although most of the gay bars can be found in the **South End** (see Chapter 15 for the best).

Drinking maps

We've plotted the drinking establishments in this chapter on maps within the neighbourhoods portion of the Guide. These maps can be found on the following pages:

The rest of the city's neighbourhood bars, pick-up joints and yuppie hotspots are differentiated by their crowds: **Beacon Hill** tends to be older and stuffier; **Downtown**, mainly around Quincy Market and the Theater District, draws a healthy mix of tourists, business people and sporty types; in addition to its student-oriented clientele, **Kenmore Square** brims with Red Sox fans of all styles. Across the river, **Cambridge** is perhaps the most fun, with a let-loose population of creative types and eclectic Ivy Leaguers.

Downtown and the Waterfront

Bell in Hand Tavern 45 Union St ☏617/227-2098; **State or Government Center T**. The oldest continuously operating tavern in Boston, established in 1795 by Boston's last town crier, draws a fairly exuberant mix of tourists and young professionals.

Biddy Early's 141 Pearl St ☏617/654-9944; **South Station T**. If there's such a thing as an "upscale dive", this is it; cheap beer (buckets of five bottles for $15), inexpensive (and surprisingly tasty) bar food, colourful regulars, a juke box and a happy after-work crowd.

Cheers Faneuil Hall Marketplace ☏617/227-0150, ⓦwww.cheersboston.com; **Haymarket T**. A replica of the NBC set (the original inspiration is on Beacon Street; see p.164), this place is little more than an overpriced tacky tourist trap that's good for a photo-op.

Corner Pub 162 Lincoln St ☏617/542-7080; **South Station T**. Recently remodelled local dive that's been hunkered down outside of Chinatown for over twenty years. Vinyl seating, a concrete bar, greasy food and a cheap-drinks-sipping crowd.

Drink 348 Congress St ☏617/695-1806; **South Station T**. A zigzagging bar and painstakingly constructed cocktails (they even chip their own ice) from three different centuries (the 1800s to today) are highlights of this subterranean hotspot. Don't be fooled by the limited cocktail menu – expert bartender-therapists will lend an ear to your drinking desires and then concoct the perfect customized beverage. It's a bit of a hike from downtown; take a cab.

Felt 533 Washington St ☏617/350-5555; **Downtown Crossing T**. *Felt* is an upscale pool hall and dance lounge full of the young and beautiful willing to pay $15 an hour for a table. A place to be seen; no sports wear, T-shirts or sneakers allowed.

Good Life 28 Kingston St ☏617/451-2622; ⓦwww.goodlifebar.com **Downtown Crossing T**. Part of the pleasing night-out triangle that includes *Kingston Station* (see p.148) and *JJ Foley's* (see below) This stylish bar generates quite a buzz, owing as much to its martinis as it does to its old-school hip-hop nights. Choose between full meals ($12–25), dozens of vodkas, or getting your groove on downstairs.

Green Dragon Tavern 11 Marshall St ☏617/367-0055; **Government Center T**. Another tavern that dates to the colonial era, this was a popular meeting place for patriots during the Revolution. There's a standard selection of tap beers, a raw bar, and a full menu rife with twee historical humour ("One if by land, two if by seafood").

Hillstones 60 State St ☏617/573-9777; **State Street T**. Part of a swanky restaurant chain, *Hillstones* doubles as the sleekest bar in Faneuil Hall. In summer, a low deck opens out into the evening air; close enough to feel the energy from Faneuil Hall, but far enough removed so you can swill your martini in peace.

JJ Foley's 21 Kingston St ☏617/695-2529; **Downtown Crossing T**. Attended by bike messengers and businessmen during the day, this little Irish gem plays host to a casual scene of locals and students by night. Friendly and recommended.

Les Zygomates 129 South St ☏617/542-5108; **South Station T**. This elegant wine bar (also reviewed on p.163) has an exceptional selection of varietals. Neophytes might want to get their palates wet at the weekly wine-tasting sessions (Tues 7–8.30pm; $30).

Limelight 204 Tremont St ☏617/423-0785; ⓦwww.limelightboston.com; **Boylston T**. A karaoke utopia where you can opt for the stage (fee hovers at around $6) and perform in American Idol-esque environs (you even get to choose your own background imagery), or the studios ($12 per person an hour) where you and your friends can belt out "Like a Virgin" in privacy.

Lucky's 355 Congress St ☏617/357-5825; **South Station T**. Over the water in the Fort Point Channel (and across the street from *Drink*; see above), this lounge bar is one of Boston's best-kept secrets – mainly because it's off the beaten tourist path (the fact that there's no sign out front adds to its in-the-know vibe). Inside is a swinging '50s pad complete with martini-swilling patrons and frequent live jazz; on Sunday, Frank Sinatra impersonators get the crowd dancing.

Mr Dooley's Boston Tavern 77 Broad St ☏617/338-5656; **State T**. One of Downtown's many Irish pubs, though with a more laidback feel than the rest. Known for its live music acts and traditional Irish Breakfast Sundays (bacon, eggs, black pudding, and baked beans).

Charlestown

Casbah Lounge 83 Main St ☏617/242-6009, ⓦwww.tangierino.com; **Community College T**. While couples get romantic next door at *Tangierino's* Turkish restaurant (see p.153), partiers head to the adjacent *Casbah Lounge* where they can puff contentedly on hookahs and watch the belly dancers.

Tavern on the Water 1 8th St Pier 6, ☏617/242-8040, ⓦwww.tavernonthewater .com; **Community College T**. Located right on the water (the USS *Constitution* is anchored nearby), the *Tavern* sports what is possibly Boston's best skyline view. The food is forgettable, so stick with whatever's on tap.

Warren Tavern 2 Pleasant St ☏617/241-8142; **Community College T**. Paul Revere and George Washington were both regulars here, and the oldest standing structure in Charlestown is still decent for a drink. Also has a generous menu of dependable tavern food.

Beacon Hill and the West End

21st Amendment 150 Bowdoin St ☏617/227-7100; **Government Center T**. This dimly lit, down-home watering hole, which gets its name from the amendment that repealed Prohibition, is a favourite haunt of legislators from the adjacent State House and students from nearby Suffolk University. You might even run into Senator John Kerry.

Alibi 215 Charles St, in the *Liberty Hotel* ☏857/241-1144; **Charles/MGH T**. Currently *the* place to see and be seen in Boston, and there's generally a wait to get in. A dressed-up clientele soaks up the vibe cast by leather seating, candlelight and mug shots.

Bin 26 Enoteca 26 Charles St ☏617/723-5939; **Charles T**. Lovingly run by the proprietors

of *Lala Rokh* (see p.153), this classy wine bar has up to 250 bottles in its rotation and 50–60 varieties available by the glass. Helpful servers can assist you in matching your drink up with its perfect food counterpart, perhaps a marinated olive plate ($7) or a slice of gorgonzola ($6).

Boston Beer Works 112 Canal St ☏617/896-BEER; **North Station T**. Originally a Fenway spot, this Boston institution has since opened up additional digs in the West End. With over 15 micro-beers on tap (made on the premises), billiards, and reasonable bar food, it makes for a great spot to kick back and watch the game.

Cheers 84 Beacon St ☏617/227-9605, ⓦwww.cheersboston.com; **Arlington T**. As the conspicuous banners outside proclaim, this is the bar that served as the inspiration for the TV show *Cheers*. If you must go, be warned – it's packed with camera-toting tourists and the inside bears little resemblance to the NBC set. The food, though cutely named (eNORMous burgers), is pricey and mediocre, and it's almost certain that nobody will know your name.

Emmet's Pub and Restaurant 6-B Beacon St ☏617/742-8565; **Park Street T**. Named after the Irish rebel Robert Emmet, this cosy watering hole tucked in the quieter section of Beacon Street is one of the more relaxed places to have a beer in town; the bulk of its business comes from government workers from the nearby State House during happy hour. The kitchen serves decent staples, such as fish and chips.

Fours 166 Canal St ☏617/720-4455, ⓦwww .thefours.com; **North Station T**. The classiest of the West End's sports bars, with an army of TVs broadcasting games from around the globe, as well as paraphernalia from the Celtics, Bruins, and other local teams.

McGann's 197 Portland St ☏617/227-4059; **North Station T**. An authentic Irish bar, but with a more upmarket, restaurant-like feel. Inside its cheerful bright red exterior there's a very active world rugby-watching crowd in addition to the usual Red Sox fans.

Sevens Ale House 77 Charles St ☏617/523-9074; **Charles T**. While the tourists pack into nearby *Cheers*, you can drop by this cosy, wood-panelled joint to watch a game or shoot darts in an authentic Boston neighbourhood bar. Positives include a wide selection of draft beers, daily specials, and substantial portions.

Back Bay

Bukowski's Tavern 50 Dalton St ☎617/437-9999; Hynes T. Arguably Boston's best dive bar, this parking garage watering hole has views over the Mass Pike and such a vast beer selection that a home-made "wheel of indecision" is spun by waitstaff when patrons can't decide what to drink. Excellent rock 'n' roll jukebox, too. There's a smaller, equally cool location in Inman Square, Cambridge 1281 Cambridge St (☎617/497-7077; Central T).

City Bar 61 Exeter St, in the *Lenox Hotel* ☎617/933-4800; Copley T. Located inside one of Back Bay's poshest addresses, *City Bar* is great for a tasteful glass of wine or a cognac to begin the night. No raucous crowd here; instead, a thirty-something coterie mingles pleasantly amidst expansive leather couches and candlelight. There's another location on the waterfront, in the *Westin Hotel* at 425 Summer St (☎617/443-0888).

Corner Tavern 421 Marlborough St ☎617/262-5555; Hynes T. With its bistro-style tiled floor, warm-toned wood bar and jukebox, this inviting neighbourhood joint oozes nostalgia. Tucked inside a brownstone that's located on one of Boston's most beautiful streets, expect a relaxed atmosphere, affordable drinks and good bar food.

Flash's 310 Stuart St ☎617/574-8888; Arlington T. A nice laidback alternative for Back Bay, with a beer-drinking crowd as well as lots of girly drinks on offer, such as the "Nordic Nectar" (vodka, fresh orange juice, Cointreau and a splash of champagne; $8). Easy to find by its retro neon sign.

Minibar 51 Huntington Ave, in the *Copley Square Hotel* ☎617/424-8500; Copley T. Reminiscent of a European lounge, this contemporary all-white bar serves up "mini cuisine" (sandwiches and *pizzettes* sized for elves) to a young and stylish crowd. One of Boston's places to see and be seen.

Oak Bar 138 St James Ave in the *Fairmont Copley Plaza* ☎617/267-5300; Copley T. Rich wood panelling, high ceilings and excellent martinis (including the "engaging martini," replete with an $11,000 diamond credit and deluxe suite) make this one of the more genteel Back Bay spots to drink.

Saint 90 Exeter St ☎617/236-1134; Copley T. Posh bar/club where the young and beautiful come to dance on weekends. Three modish lounge spaces, including a white leather vodka bar (with exotic flavours like lychee and cardamom) and a red-toned "bordello" room, complete with ample plush furnishings and mirrors for checking yourself out.

TC's Lounge 1 Haviland St ☎617/247-8109; Hynes T. Divey to the max, with photos of half-naked ladies on the ceiling, video games of the Buck Hunter ilk and a carnival game with porn prizes, this dark hideaway is popular with students and those who want to get a little crazy. Cash only.

Top of the Hub 800 Boylston St ☎617/536-1775; Prudential T. An atmospheric space on the 52nd floor of the Prudential Center, *Top of the Hub* features a snazzy jazz lounge, swanky cocktails, and fancy food. A great date spot, although you have to go through an unromantic security check first.

The South End

28 Degrees 1 Appleton St ☎617/728-0728; Back Bay T. The food is Italian-inspired fare, but the drinks (like the frozen bellini or blueberry basil martini) are a safer bet at this gay-friendly, candle-lit lounge replete with leather seating, wispy curtains at your table and underwater toilets.

Anchovies 433 Columbus Ave ☎617/266-5088; Back Bay T. This dim, cosy spot has a great "gang's-all-here" vibe with standout fixings: $3 tallboys, a rubber chicken and a Virgin Mary on the walls, a friendly neighbourhood crew and a kitchen serving a full menu of worthy Italian fare until 2am.

The Beehive 541 Tremont St ☎617/423-0069; ⊛www.beehiveboston .com; Back Bay T. Snuggled inside the Boston Center for the Arts is this spacious newcomer to the city's bar scene. With chandeliers dripping from the ceiling, a red-curtained stage and knock-you-down cocktails, the *Beehive* exudes a vaudeville vibe, complete with jazz, cabaret or burlesque shows playing nearly every night of the week.

Delux Café & Lounge 100 Chandler St ☎617/338-5258; Back Bay T. This retro hideaway has all the fixings of a great dive: kitschy decor; constant cartoon viewing; and a Christmas-lit Elvis shrine. The menu is funky American fusion with old standbys like grilled cheese sandwiches and split-pea soup. Cash only.

Jacque's Cabaret 79 Broadway ☎617/426-8902; Arlington T. *Priscilla, Queen of the Desert* invades New England at this drag dream where divas lip-synch *I Love the Nightlife*. There's a nice melting pot of patrons, including frequent bachelorette parties. Showtime is 10.30pm nightly (Tues is Karaoke night), but beware – the festivities end at midnight, Cinderella. Cover $6–10, and you should consult a map before you head over as it's a little tricky to find.

Masa 439 Tremont St ☎617/338-8884; **Arlington T**. Next to *28 Degrees* (see above), the glistening bar at this softly lit Southwestern restaurant buzzes with a dressed-up crew eager to get their hands on *Masa's* composed $1 tapas – try the Habanero meatball with blue cheese – and spiced watermelon margaritas ($10).

Kenmore Square and the Fenway

An Tua Nua 835 Beacon St ☎617/262-2121; **Kenmore T**. Despite its Gaelic name ("the new beginning") this popular Boston University hangout is just as much dance bar as it is Irish pub. Weekend dance nights get especially crowded with BU and Northeastern undergrads (ladies, be prepared for youthful oglers); Wed is karaoke and salsa night.

Audubon Circle 838 Beacon St ☎617/421-1910; **Kenmore T**. Sleek, modern bar, where a well-dressed crowd gathers for cocktails and fancy bar food (see review, p.156) before and after games at Fenway Park.

Bleacher Bar 82A Landsdowne St ☎617/262-2424; **Kenmore T**. Beneath the bleachers in centre field is the newest addition to Fenway Park, and you don't need a ticket to get in. Here, you'll find a pub festooned with vintage memorabilia and a window with a direct view of the diamond – quite thrilling on game night.

Cask 'n Flagon 62 Brookline Ave ☎617/536-4840; **Kenmore T**. While some say the recently expanded *Cask* has lost its former low-key greatness, this sports pub has been an iconic Fenway spot since 1969. With a great location (right behind Fenway Park's Green Monster) and landmark stature, there may be no better place to watch the game. Be kind to the moody bouncers, who won't hesitate in barring your entrance if you seem too "drunk" or not to their liking.

Cornwall's 654 Beacon St ☎617/262-3749; **Kenmore T**. A British-style pub smack in the heart of Kenmore Square that serves a largely student population and carries an excellent beer selection.

Eastern Standard 528 Commonwealth Ave (in the *Hotel Commonwealth*) ☎617/532-9100; **Kenmore T**. Set inside a gorgeous, high-ceilinged dining room, this Boston favourite pulls in a nice mix of clientele, both age-wise and style-wise. The knowledgeable bartenders are just as quick to mix up a swanky highball as they are to pull you a pint, and there's a pretty patio in the summer.

Lansdowne Pub 9 Lansdowne St ☎617/247-1222; **Kenmore T**. Breeze into this authentic Irish pub adjacent to Fenway Park and imbibe the accommodating atmosphere, standout pub grub with cheesy fries ($3) and fish and chips ($14), and gleeful regulars enjoying a Sox game.

The Lower Depths Taproom 476 Commonwealth Ave ☎617/266-6662; **Kenmore T**. A welcome newcomer to the ballpark scene, this pub is known for its extensive beer knowledge (16 on tap, plus plenty in bottles), pretzels, and excellent $1 hot dogs. Cash only; beer and wine only.

Squealing Pig 134 Smith St ☎617/566-6651; **Longwood T**. A bit further out (it's in Mission Hill), this affable spot has a neighbourhood pub vibe, complete with friendly bartenders, live music, and tasty comfort food à la their "toasties" sandwiches (chicken, pesto, brie, and tomato all grilled to perfection for $9).

Brookline

The Publick House 1648 Beacon St ☎617/277-2880; **Washington Square T**. Stouts, ales, and porters are all well represented at this dark wood-panelled Belgian brewfest with a seriously hefty beer list. Wooden pews and throne-like seats fill the roomy quarters, and there are good steak salads and veggie burgers on offer.

Matt Murphy's 14 Harvard St ☎617/232-0188, ⓦwww.mattmurphyspub.com; **Brookline Village T**. Pulled pints here are served alongside Irish comfort food such as potato and leek soup with warm brown bread and shepherd's pie with a crispy potato crust. The place is tiny, but the waits are worth it. They also have occasional live music. No credit cards.

Allston-Brighton

Model Café 7 North Beacon St ☎617/254-9365; **Harvard Ave T**. If you enjoy drinking pilgrimages, dive bars characterized by ironic facial hair, free popcorn, wall-mounted fish, and Buck Hunter, then the *Model* will worm its way into your drunken heart.

Silhouette Lounge 200 Brighton Ave ☎617/206-4565; Allston St **T**. Another beloved Allston dive, "the Sil" is where salty locals rub elbows alongside beer-guzzling hipsters. There are darts, pool, free popcorn and cheap pitchers of PBR.

Jamaica Plain

Brendan Behan 378 Centre St ☎617/522-5386; Green St **T**. The godfather of Boston's Irish pubs, this dimly lit institution has the usual friendly staff all week long, as well as live music available on most weekends.

The Haven 2 Perkins St ☎617/983-2000; Stonybrook **T**. This Scottish restaurant and bar packs a punch with its incredibly good food offerings (including haggis and neeps; $8), modern decor, and prickly thistles set in mason jars. At its centre, there's an eye-catching antler chandelier.

James's Gate 5–11 McBride St ☎617/524-2836; Forest Hills **T**. Beat Boston's harsh winter by sipping Guinness beside the blazing fireplace in this cosy pub, or by trying the hearty fare in the restaurant out back. Pub-quiz Mon nights at 8pm.

Cambridge

Atwood's Tavern 877 Cambridge St ☎617/864-2792; Central **T**. Off the beaten path, this Inman Square pub offers two-dozen beers on tap, tasty comfort food (such as crispy fish sandwiches for $9, and mac and cheese for $10), and live music most nights after 10pm ($5 cover). Pub-quiz Wed nights at 7.30pm.

The Cellar 991 Massachusetts Ave ☎617/876-2580; Harvard **T**. The two floors here, each with a bar, are regularly filled with a crowd of Harvard faculty members, older students, and other locals imbibing fine beers and killer Long Island iced teas.

Charlie's Kitchen 10 Eliot St ☎617/492-9646; Harvard **T**. While downstairs is a well-loved burger joint, upstairs is a buzzing bar, at its rowdiest on Tues karaoke nights. Fifteen beers on tap, a rocking juke box, and a good mix of patrons. They've recently expanded to include an outdoor beer garden.

Daedalus 45 1/2 Mount Auburn St ☎617/349-0071; Harvard **T**. While the rest of this restaurant/bar isn't bad-looking

(think dark wooden panelling and tables), the real draw here is the rooftop deck. Built in a former greenhouse, this pleasant building top comes with neighbourhood views and a nicely dressed twenty- and thirty-something crowd. Deck open to drinkers after 10.30pm.

The Druid 1357 Cambridge St ☎617/497-0965; Central **T**. Right in the heart of Inman Square, this well-loved, tightly squeezed Irish pub has reasonably priced indie beers (in addition to perfectly pulled pints of Guinness), kindly bartenders, standout burgers ($10) and fish and chips ($15), Sunday brunch and a popular trivia night on Wednesdays.

Enormous Room 567 Massachusetts Ave ☎617/491-5550; Central **T**. Walking into this tiny lounge tucked above *Central Kitchen* (see p.150) is tantamount to entering a swanky, opium-den-like slumber party. The clientele lounge, sans shoes (these are placed discreetly in cubbies), on a selection of plush couches. Good DJs.

The Field 20 Prospect St ☎617/354-7345; Central **T**. Although *The Field* is located between Harvard and MIT, this Irish pub attracts an eclectic non-college crowd. You can play pool or darts while you sip one of the variety of beers on tap.

Flat Top Johnny's 1 Kendall Sq ☎617/494-9565; Central **T**. Twelve tournament-sized pool tables, old-school pinball and dart boards in a casual space adjacent to the landmark Kendall Square movie theatre.

Grafton Street 1280 Massachusetts Ave ☎617/497-0400; Harvard **T**. Modern Irish pub atmosphere, home to an older, well-dressed set that enjoys smooth drafts and equally good food. Nicely situated in the heart of Harvard Square.

Green Street 280 Green St ☎617/876-1655; Central **T**. Really a restaurant serving dolled-up comfort food, *Green Street* is the kind of spot where discerning drinkers go to savour a Maker's on the rocks. Expect a twenty-and thirty-something clientele as well as drool-worthy concoctions such as the "Pearl White" (Bombay gin, *lillet blanc*, fresh lemon, simple syrup, and mint; $7). Makes a nice location for a first date.

Middlesex Lounge 315 Massachusetts Ave ☎617/868-6739; Central **T**. A slightly hipper-than-thou vibe, but with good reason - the gorgeous space (high ceilings, exposed brick, pretty wood panelling) makes you want to dress to impress. Lush lounge chairs on wheels and minimalist tables you can move around to design your own drinking environs. There are often lines out the door for their nights of electro-retro beat dance heaven (cover ranges from free to $10).

Miracle of Science Bar & Grill 321 Massachusetts Ave ☎617/868-ATOM; Central **T**. Surprisingly hip despite its status as an MIT hangout, this popular bar has recently added a full restaurant. There's science-themed decor and a laidback, unpretentious crowd, though the place can get crowded on weekend nights. The bar stools will conjure up memories of high-school chemistry class.

Muddy Charles Pub 142 Memorial Drive (MIT's Bldg 50) ☎617/253-2086; Kendall **T**. Right on the MIT campus, this popular student pub has incredible waterfront views, cheap pitchers of beer, and a casual, grandfatherly vibe. No food, but patrons are encouraged to use their phone for local restaurant hook-ups.

Noir Charles Hotel, 1 Bennett St ☎617/661-8010; Harvard **T**. With its sultry red lighting and tall black leather booths, *Noir* seems the perfect setting to carry on a discreet affair. Most patrons just come for the decadent martinis, however.

People's Republik 878 Massachusetts Ave ☎617/491-6969; Central or Harvard **T**. Smack dab between MIT and Harvard, *People's Republik* attracts a good mix of technocrats and potential world-leaders as a result. It takes its Communist propaganda seriously – with its posters on the walls, anyway; the range of tap offerings is positively democratic.

Phoenix Landing 512 Massachusetts Ave ☎617/576-6260; Central **T**. The *Phoenix* is about the only place in Cambridge you'll still catch European sporting events (shown on the weekends) but it's best known for its fun nightly dance parties.

Plough & Stars 912 Massachusetts Ave ☎617/576-0032, ⊕www.ploughandstars.com; Central or Harvard **T**. Under-the-radar neighbourhood spot that's very much worth a visit, whether for its animated cribbage games, pub grub, or its nightly live music.

Rialto 1 Bennett St, *Charles Hotel* ☎617/661-5050; Harvard **T**. The bar adjunct to the posh restaurant of the same name caters to a wealthy crowd that matches the plush atmosphere. Dress semi-formal and be prepared to pay big-time for the drinks and cocktails, which are, admittedly, excellent.

River Gods 125 Cambridge St ☎617/576-1881; Central **T**. Though a bit of an underground spot, it's worth the trip. An Irish bar with a twist, they serve good cocktails alongside Guinness, fantastic food and DJs spinning sweet tunes; patrons lounge in throne-like chairs and ogle the suits of armour.

Shay's 58 JFK St ☎617/864-9161; Harvard **T**. Unwind with grad students over wine and quality beer at *Shay's*, a relaxed contrast to the student-oriented bars elsewhere in Harvard Square.

Temple Bar 1688 Massachusetts Ave ☎617/547-5055; Harvard or Porter **T**. Cambridge's stand-out scenester bar attracts a chi-chi crowd to its smart digs outfitted with attractive touches like fancy floral arrangements and Martini Rosso advertising posters.

Somerville

Olde Magoun's Saloon 518 Medford St ☎617/776-2600; Central **T**. Quite a hike from any public transport, *Magoun's* is a lovable Irish pub with a sports-bar feel. Great seasonal beer selection, tasty bar food and a friendly staff that are heavy on the brogues.

Thirsty Scholar Pub 70 Beacon St ☎617/497-2294, ⊕www.thirstyscholarpub.com; Harvard **T**. One of the cosiest bars around, *Thirsty's* warm red-brick and burnished-wood interior is matched by a smiling waitstaff and down-home comfort food like shepherd's pie and baked beans. Bring a book to read, or listen up while distinguished writers declaim their own at the bar's oft-hosted readings.

Trina's Starlite Lounge 3 Beacon St ☎617/576-0006; Central **T**. Festooned with '50s-era rockabilly decor, the small bar at this indie hangout fills up quickly nearly every night of the week. The restaurant offers comfort food such as gravy fries ($5) and mac and cheese with Ritz crackers ($9).

Nightlife

I n recent years Boston's **nightlife** has received something of a wake-up call, although for a major American city, its scene still feels small and is geared primarily to a college crowd. **Lansdowne Street**, adjacent to Fenway Park and once queen of the clubbing scene, has unfortunately quietened down after the closing of mainstays *Axis* and *Avalon*; stay tuned, however – this area has a habit of reinventing itself, and something new could pop up here at any moment. A few stylish clubs have sprung up in areas, such as **Downtown Crossing**, that were previously ghost towns by night. Boylston Place – which links Boston Common with the Theater District and is known locally as "The Alley" – is where most of the action is found. Though the city is by no means a 24-hour one, these hotspots have breathed fresh air into a scene that once lived in the shadow of the city's so-called high culture.

Live music plays a huge role in the city's nightlife arena, with bars and clubs catering to a young crowd, especially in Cambridge around Harvard and Central squares, where you're as likely to hear a noisy rock band as a mellow DJ. Boston has spawned its share of enormous **rock** acts, from the ever-enduring dinosaur rockers Aerosmith to a smattering of post-punk and indie favourites such as the Pixies and Sebadoh. Boston is also home to a number of well-loved **jazz** and **blues** joints; you can usually find something cheap and to your liking almost any day of the week. If you're interested in hearing classical or opera, check Chapter 14.

For **club and music listings**, check Thursday's *Boston Globe* "Calendar," the *Boston Phoenix*, the *Improper Bostonian, Metro, Stuff@night* and *The Weekly Dig*. You'll also find a number of websites helpful for up-to-date listings; for details on media and websites, see p.30 and p.36.

Live music

The strength of Boston's **live music** is in the intimacy of its smaller venues, though superstar acts make the city a regular stop on their world tours as well. Two of the biggest **concert halls** are far out of town: the Comcast Center, south of the city in Mansfield (☎508/339-2333, ⓦwww.livenation.com), and the DCU Center, an hour or so west in Worcester (☎508/755-6800, ⓦwww.centrumcentre.com).

On a more human scale, plenty of **alternative venues** serve up everything from name bands to obscure new acts; if all else fails, there's always street music at "The Pit" in Harvard Square (p.120), where you're bound to hear some free amateur acts – whether you like it or not.

Rock venues

Agganis Arena 925 Commonwealth Ave
☎617/358-7000, ⓦwww.bu.edu/agganis;
Pleasant St **T**. See map on p.101. State-of-
the-art Boston University amphitheatre
that hosts a wide range of big-name live
entertainment, from college hockey games
to Alice and Chains to Sesame Street.

Bank of America Pavilion Fan Pier, Northern Ave
☎617/728-1600, ⓦwww.livenation.com; South
Station **T**. See map on pp.40–41. Concerts by
well-known performers from Harry Connick
Jr to Deep Purple are held here during the
summer under a huge white tent at Boston
Harbor's edge.

Bill's Bar 5 1/2 Lansdowne St ☎617/421-9678;
Kenmore **T**. See map on p.101. This self-titled
"dirty rock bar" books a "sleazy" line-up
that includes rock, metal, and indie bands
as well as reggae Sundays. There are also
a number of 18+ shows; covers generally
hover around $10.

Church 69 Kilmarnock St ☎617/236-7600;
Museum **T**. See map on p.101. Brand-new
225-person music lounge tucked away on
a residential Fenway street, which hosts
fifteen bands a week, from rock to metal
to folk (cover $7–10). Also runs an on-site
comfort-food restaurant with a renowned
weekend brunch.

Great Scott 1222 Commonwealth Ave, Allston
☎617/566-9014; Harvard Ave **T**. See map on
pp.118–119. Popular with students and older
hipsters alike, this well-loved space plays
host to local and national (read: national
acts you probably haven't heard of) rock
and indie bands. Cheap drinks, and a
pleasant patio where you can kick back and
play groupie. Friday night here is "The Pill",
a mixture of live rock and a DJ-spinning
dance-athon.

House of Blues 15 Lansdowne St
☎1-888/693-BLUE; Kenmore **T**. See map
on p.101. The Boston icon has returned,
hosting big-name acts like Cyndi Lauper,
BB King and She & Him in a glossy new
venue next to Fenway Park.

Lizard Lounge 1667 Massachusetts Ave,
Cambridge ☎617/547-0759; ⓦwww
.lizardloungeclub.com; Harvard or Porter **T**. See
map on pp.118–119. The downstairs portion
of the *Cambridge Common* restaurant is a
favourite among local students. Rock and
jazz acts are onstage almost nightly for a
fairly nominal cover charge (usually around

$8), while every Sunday there's a slamming
poetry hour.

Middle East 472 Massachusetts Ave, Cambridge
☎617/864-3278, ⓦwww.mideastclub.com;
Central **T**. See map on pp.118–119. Local and
regional bands of every sort – salsa to ska
and mambo to hardcore – stop in regularly
at this Cambridge institution. Bigger acts
are hosted downstairs; smaller ones ply
their trade in a tiny upstairs space. A third
venue, the *Corner*, has shows nightly that
are usually free, with belly dancing every
Sunday. The attached restaurant, *ZuZu*,
serves decent Middle Eastern food.

Museum of Fine Arts 465 Huntington Ave
☎617/369-3300, ⓦwww.mfa.org; Museum **T**.
See map on p.101. Better known for their
jazz and classical acts, the MFA is steadily
gaining rock fans thanks to their stellar
bookings of bands like The Sea and the
Cake and Mates of State. Intimate, pared-
down performances are held in the Remis
Auditorium and outdoors in the Calderwood
Courtyard; tickets run about $30.

Orpheum Theater 1 Hamilton Place ☎617/679-
0810; Park St or Downtown Crossing **T**. See
map on pp.40–41. Once an old-school movie
house, it's now a venue for big-name
bands. The small space ensures you're
closer to the action, and its retro environs
are a refreshing change from the new,
bigger box-styled venues.

Paradise Rock Club 967-969 Commonwealth
Ave ☎617/562-8800, ⓦwww.thedise.com;
Pleasant Street **T**. One of Boston's classic
rock venues. Lots of greats have played
here, including Blondie, Elvis Costello
and Tom Waits, to name a few. It's still as
happening as it was 25 years ago, only
now it has a restaurant-cum-rock lounge
next door.

TDBanknorth Garden 50 Causeway St
☎617/624-1000, ⓦwww.tdbanknorthgarden
.com; North Station **T**. See map on p.78. This
arena, up in the West End, attracts many
of the big-name acts that pass through
New England when the Celtics or Bruins
aren't playing.

T.T. the Bear's Place 10 Brookline St,
Cambridge ☎617/492-BEAR, ⓦwww
.ttthebears.com; Central **T**. See map on
pp.118–119. A downmarket version of the
Middle East: lesser-known bands, but in
a space with a grittiness and intimacy its
neighbour lacks. All kinds of bands appear,
mostly rock and punk.

Jazz, blues, and folk venues

The Beehive 541 Tremont St ☎617/423-0069; ⓦwww.beehiveboston.com; Back Bay **T**. See map on p.95. A vaudeville-esque space with jazz, cabaret, or burlesque shows playing nearly every night of the week; see p.165 for a full review.

Cantab Lounge 738 Massachusetts Ave, Cambridge ☎617/354-2685, ⓦwww.cantab -lounge.com; Central **T**. See map on pp.118–119. Although from the outside it looks like the kind of sleazy place your mother wouldn't want you to set foot in, it's actually one of the truly bohemian spots in town, with hopping live jazz and blues.

Johnny D's 17 Holland St, Somerville ☎617/776-2004; ⓦwww.johnnyds.com; Davis **T**. See map on pp.118–119. A mixed bag with talent ranging from the sublime to the ordinary, and a $10 cover charge for most shows. Acts include garage bands, progressive jazz sextets, traditional blues artists, and some uncategorizables.

Lily Pad 1353 Cambridge St, Cambridge ☎617/395-1393; Central **T**. See map on pp.118–119. This bare-bones space covers the musical spectrum – everything from early jazz to rock to electro-acoustic to chamber music and even (very popular) yoga classes can be found here.

Passim 47 Palmer St, Cambridge ☎617/492-7679, ⓦwww.clubpassim.org; Harvard **T**. See map on pp.118–119. Folkie hangout in Harvard Square where Joan Baez and Suzanne Vega got their starts. Acoustic music, folk, blues, jazz and spoken-word performances in windowed basement setting. Covers run around $12.

Regattabar 1 Bennett St, Cambridge ☎617/661-5000, ⓦwww.regattabarjazz.com; Harvard **T**. See map on pp.118–119. The *Regattabar* draws top national jazz acts, although, as its location in the swish *Charles Hotel* might suggest, the atmosphere and clientele are both decidedly formal. Dress nicely and prepare to pay at least a $20 cover.

Ryles 212 Hampshire St, Cambridge ☎617/876-9330, ⓦwww.rylesjazz.com; Central **T**. See map on pp.118–119. Two levels of live music – swing and salsa (dancing is encouraged) upstairs, and smooth jazz and blues downstairs. *Ryles* also does a good jazz brunch on Sun, where a plate of blueberry pancakes and sausage costs $10.

Scullers 400 Soldiers Field Rd, Allston ☎617/562-4111, ⓦwww.scullersjazz.com; Harvard **T**. See map on pp.118–119. Upscale jazz club in the *DoubleTree Guest Suites* draws five-star acts, including some of the stars of the contemporary jazz scene. You'll need to hop in a taxi to get here, as the walk along the river at night can be risky. The cover charge varies wildly – anywhere from $20 to $55.

Wally's Café 427 Massachusetts Ave, Roxbury ☎617/424-1408, ⓦwww.wallyscafe.com; Massachusetts **T**. See map on p.95. Founded in 1947, this is one of the oldest jazz clubs around, and some folks think it's one of Boston's best assets. Free live music every night, and a diverse crowd.

Western Front 343 Western Ave, Cambridge ☎617/492-7772; Central **T**. See map on pp.118–119. The *Front* puts on rollicking jazz, blues, and reggae shows for a dance-crazy audience. It's got a bit of a gritty underbelly; stay safe and take a cab here.

Nightclubs

Boston's **nightclubs** are mostly clustered around "The Alley" (Boylston Place), the Theater District and Kenmore Square with a few prominent ones in Back Bay and the South End. A handful of the venues in those two neighbourhoods are **gay clubs**, often the most happening places in town; for a complete listing, see Chapter 15.

The music at these clubs changes almost nightly, so to keep apprised of what's on, check the individual club websites, the "Calendar" section in Thursday's *Boston Globe*, or the listings in the weekly *Boston Phoenix* and daily *Metro*. **Cover charges** are generally in the $5–20 range, though sometimes there's no cover at all. Boston's venues tend to be easily entered – no New York–style selection at the door – though there is a tendency for bouncers to block sneakers and torn jeans. On weekends, clubs can be overrun with party-goers; come on a weeknight if you want to increase your elbow room.

Comedy central

Boston's **comedy clubs** can be a pleasant alternative to the club scene, especially when you factor in the lack of dress code and the top-notch comics who often headline as part of a cross-country tour.

Comedy Connection, recently moved to the historic Wilbur Theatre (☏617/248-9700, ⓦwww.thewilburtheatre.com; Boylston Ⓣ), is a high-calibre venue attracting both local and national acts such as Tom Green and Kevin Nealon. The city's only improv venue, the **ImprovAsylum Theater**, 216 Hanover St (☏617/263-6887, ⓦwww.improvasylum .com; Haymarket Ⓣ), often brings the house down with off-the-cuff sketches based on audience cues. **Dick's Beantown Comedy Vault**, in Remington's restaurant at 124 Boylston St (☏1-800/401-2221, ⓦwww.dickdoherty.com; Boylston Ⓣ), garners positive reviews for its inexpensive, intimate shows. In all cases, book your tickets ($10–40) ahead of time, as shows often sell out.

Downtown

Estate 1 Boylston Place (in "The Alley") ☏617/351-7000, ⓦwww.theestateboston.com; Boylston Ⓣ. Go-go dancers in lingerie, chandeliers hanging in a bumping ballroom and a wraparound balcony for enjoying the scene are some of the pleasures that await you at *Estate*. No cover for the ladies before 11pm; after that, it's a steep $20. There's an enforced dress code; Thurs is gay night.

Gypsy Bar 116 Boylston St ☏617/482-7799, ⓦwww.gypsybarboston.com; Boylston Ⓣ. Very posh lounge and dance club popular with the European set; you can watch schools of jellyfish pulsating behind the bar as you order an *Indulgence* cocktail. Prepare to dress snappy – no sneakers or sleeveless tees, as well as (weirdly) no polo shirts. DJ dance beats Fri and Sat, $10 cover after 9.30pm.

Liquor Store 25 Boylston Place ☏617/357-6800, ⓦwww.liquorstoreboston.com; Boylston Ⓣ. Though clubs tend to open and close every six months over here in "The Alley," the *Liquor Store* seems as though it could be here to stay. The young and beautiful steadily party hard here to current hits, R&B, and house while trying their luck on the mechanical bull. No sneakers, expect a cover of around $5.

Mojitos Latin Lounge 48 Winter St ☏617/988-8123, ⓦwww.mojitoslounge.com; Park St Ⓣ. The reggaeton dance scene gets going at around 10.30pm nightly, with Latin music such as merengue, bachata and salsa thrown in. The downstairs dance floor gets cramped, but the upstairs club is roomier and lined with murals of music legends like Tito Puente and Celia Cruz. $10 cover.

Royale 279 Tremont St ☏617/338-7699, ⓦwww .royaleboston.com; Boylston Ⓣ. This 1918 opera house has been re-imagined as a 33,000-square-foot club offering party-goers the chance to dance in a vintage ballroom. Thoroughly updated, the *Royale* features a modern sound system and stage, pricey cocktails and plenty of space (including a balcony) in which to mingle. Generally a $20 cover, but free for ladies before midnight.

Umbria 295 Franklin St ☏617/338-1000; State Ⓣ. One of the latest additions to the city's bar scene, *Umbria* breaks from the downtown Irish pub mould by dancing to an ultra-lounge beat – a hybrid of bar, nightclub, and restaurant. Stick by the bar, though, for the fabulous martinis.

Venu 100 Warrenton St ☏617/338-8061, ⓦwww .venuboston.com; Boylston Ⓣ. This slick Theater District club with different theme nights throughout the week gives you opulent eye candy for your hefty ($30) cover charge: Art Deco stylings, beautiful patrons, and a laser-lit dancefloor.

Back Bay

Saint 90 Exeter St ☏617/236-1134; Copley Ⓣ. High-end lounge and club with lush decor and chi-chi drinks – the tables tend to be occupied by people more famous than you, however. Popular with a swanky thirty-something crowd. Get there early to avoid the $20 cover charge. See full review on p.165.

Kenmore Square and the Fenway

An Tua Nua 835 Beacon St ☏617/262-2121; Kenmore Ⓣ. Despite its Gaelic name ("The New Beginning"), this popular neighbourhood hangout is just as much a dance bar as it is an Irish pub. Weekend dance nights get especially crowded with BU and North-eastern undergrads, who sweat it out on the dance floor or check each other out from the many ringside seats. Wed is karaoke and salsa night.

Jillian's 145 Ipswich St ☎617/437-0300, ⓦwww.jilliansboston.com; Kenmore Ⓣ. Clubbing utopia: a massive, three-storey entertainment club complex housing a pool hall, a raucous, spacious dance club, and a Lucky Strike bowling alley catering to a dressed-up, twenty-something clientele.

Cambridge

Hong Kong 1238 Massachusetts Ave ☎617/864-5311; Harvard Ⓣ. Downstairs is adequate Chinese food, upstairs is a Scorpion Bowl-guzzling ($16) funhouse of dance. It's sketchy, but Harvard heads still have a fondness for this late-night rite of passage.

Middlesex Lounge 315 Massachusetts Ave ☎617/868-6739; Central Ⓣ. This pretty wood-panelled space often has lines out the door for its nights of scenester electro-retro beat dance heaven (cover ranges from free on up to $10). (See p.167 for full review).

Performing arts and film

Boston's **cultural scene** is famously vibrant, and many of the city's artistic institutions are second to none in the US. Foremost among them is the Boston Symphony Orchestra, which gave its first concert on October 22, 1881. In fact, Boston is arguably at its best in the **classical music** department, and there are many smaller but internationally known chamber and choral music groups – from the Boston Symphony Chamber Players to the Handel & Haydn Society – to shore up that reputation. The Boston Ballet is also considered world-class, though it's probably best known regionally for its annual holiday production of *The Nutcracker,* with audience numbers ranking it as the most attended **ballet** production in the world.

The **theatre** here is quite active, too, even if it is a shadow of its 1920s heyday, when more than forty playhouses were crammed into the **Theater District** on the edge of downtown. It's a real treat to see a play or musical at one of the opulent old theatres such as the Wang or the Opera House. For current productions, check the listings in the *Boston Globe's* Thursday "Calendar" section, the *Boston Phoenix*, or the *Improper Bostonian.*

There is the usual big-city glut of multiplexes showing first-run **films**. For foreign, independent, classic, or cult cinema, you'll have to look mainly to other municipalities – Cambridge is best in this respect, though Brookline and Somerville also have their own art-movie and rerun houses.

Classical music

Boston prides itself on being a sophisticated city of high culture, and nowhere does that show up more than in its proliferation of **orchestras** and **choral groups** and the venues that house them. This is helped in no small part by the presence of four of the premier music academies in the nation: the Peabody Conservatory, the New England Conservatory, the Berklee College of Music, and, across the river in Cambridge, the Longy School of Music.

Most of the companies listed below perform at regular venues, which we've reviewed right after (and those performance spaces do put on additional concerts as well). Check the usual listings sources for concert information, or call the groups directly.

Symphonies and chamber music ensembles

Alea III and Boston Musica Viva ☏617/353-3340, ⊛www.aleaiii.com (Alea III) and ☏617/354-6910, ⊛www.bmv.org (Boston Musica Viva). Two regulars at BU's Tsai Performance Center (see below).

Boston Baroque ☏617/484-9200, ⊛www.boston baroque.org. The first permanent Baroque orchestra in the country (it was founded in 1973) is now a resident ensemble at Jordan Hall and Harvard's Sanders Theatre.

Boston Camerata ☏617/262-2092, ⊛www .bostoncamerata.com. Regular performances of choral and chamber concerts, from medieval to early American, at various locations in and around Boston.

Boston Chamber Music Society ☏617/349-0086, ⊛www.bostonchambermusic.org. This society has soloists of international renown who perform in Jordan Hall (Fri) and the Sanders Theatre (Sun) as well as in various venues throughout the city.

Boston Philharmonic ☏617/236-0999, ⊛www .bostonphil.org. Exuberant orchestra whose conductor prefaces performances with a discussion of the evening's composition. Performances take place at Jordan Hall (Sat) and the Sanders Theatre (Sun).

Boston Pops ☏617/266-1492, ⊛www.bso.org. A subsection of the Boston Symphony Orchestra, the Pops are considered to be lighter and "poppier" than their more formal counterpart, and are best known for their dynamic July 4th performance on the Esplanade.

Boston Symphony Chamber Players ☏617/266-1492 or 1-888/266-1200, ⊛www.bso.org. The only permanent chamber group sponsored by a major symphony orchestra and made up of its members; they perform at Jordan Hall as well as other venues around Boston.

Boston Symphony Orchestra ☏617/266-1492, ⊛www.bso.org. Boston's world-renowned orchestra performs in Fenway's acoustically perfect Symphony Hall; in summer, they ship out to the Tanglewood Festival in gorgeous Lenox, Massachusetts.

The Cantata Singers & Ensemble ☏617/868-5885, ⊛www.cantatasingers.org. Boston's premier choral group, which also performs regularly at Jordan Hall in addition to other venues in the Boston area.

Handel & Haydn Society ☏617/266-3605, ⊛www.handelandhaydn.org. Performing chamber and choral music since 1815, these distinguished artists can be heard at Symphony Hall, Jordan Hall, and the Cutler Majestic.

Pro Arte Chamber Orchestra ☏617/779-0900, ⊛www.proarte.org. Co-operatively run chamber orchestra in which musicians have full control. Gives Sun afternoon performances at Harvard's Sanders Theatre.

Performance venues

Berklee Performance Center 136 Massachusetts Ave ☏617/747-2261 for concert information and box office, ⊛www.berkleebpc.com; Symphony **T**. Berklee College of Music's main performance centre, known for its quality contemporary repertoire.

Isabella Stewart Gardner Museum 280 The Fenway ☏617/278-5150 for the music department, 617/278-5156 for the box office, ⊛www .gardnermuseum.org; Museum **T**. Chamber and classical concerts, including many debuts, are held regularly at 1.30pm on Sundays (Sept–May) in the museum's ornate Tapestry Room; there are also shows on Thurs evenings, including jazz concerts. The $23 ticket (available at the door or online from ⊛www.museumtix.com) includes museum admission.

Jordan Hall 30 Gainsborough St ☏617/585-1270, ⊛www.newenglandconservatory.edu; Symphony **T**. The impressive concert hall of the New England Conservatory, one block west from Symphony Hall, is the venue for many chamber music performances, as well as those by the Boston Philharmonic (☏617/236-0999, ⊛www.bostonphil.org).

Museum of Fine Arts 465 Huntington Ave ☏617/369-3300 for event information, ☏617/369-3306 for tickets, ⊛www.mfa.org; Museum **T**. During the summer, the MFA's jazz, folk, and world music "Concerts in the Courtyard" ($30) take place each Wed at 7.30pm; a variety of indoor performances – from tango to indie rock to opera recitals – are also scheduled for the rest of the year.

Sanders Theatre 45 Quincy St ☏617/496-2222, ⊛www.fas.harvard.edu/~memhall/sanders.html; Harvard **T**. Inspired by Christopher Wren's Sheldonian Theatre in Oxford, England, the 1875 Sanders is known for its 180-degree design. The Boston Philharmonic, the Boston Chamber Music Society, Master-works Chorale, and the Boston Baroque all perform here.

PERFORMING ARTS AND FILM | Classical music

Symphony Hall **301 Massachusetts Ave**
☎1-888/266-1492 for concert information,
☎1-888/266-1200 for tickets, ⓦwww.bso.org;
Symphony T. This is the regal, acoustically
perfect venue for the Boston Symphony
Orchestra, currently under the direction of
James Levine; the famous Boston Pops
concerts happen in May and June; in July &
August, the BSO retreats to Tanglewood, in
the Berkshires.

Tsai Performance Center **685 Commonwealth**
Ave ☎617/353-TSAI for event information or
☎617/353-8725 for box office, ⓦwww.bu
.edu/tsai; **Boston University T**. Improbably
tucked into Boston University's School
of Management, this mid-sized hall is a
frequent venue for chamber music performances, prominent lecturers, and plays;
events are often affiliated with BU and thus
can be very inexpensive.

Dance

The city's longest-running **dance** company is the world-class **Boston Ballet**
(☎617/695-6950 or 1-800/447-7400, ⓦwww.bostonballet.org); their biggest
blockbuster, the yearly performance of the *The Nutcracker*, has an audience attendance of more than 140,000. The troupe performs at the Citi Performing Arts
Center and the Opera House (see p.177).

In addition, smaller but still prominent troupes, like **World Music** (ⓦwww
.worldmusic.org) and Zoé Dance (ⓦwww.zoedance.org) put on music and dance
performances that are a bit less traditional and staid, in venues like the Berklee,
the Institute for Contemporary Art, and the Orpheum Theatre. The affable **Big
Moves** (ⓦwww.bigmoves.org) has a chub-loving dance chapter in town; they also
offer fun free dance classes like "Putting the Belly back into Belly Dance."

The **Boston Dance Alliance** has an informative website centred on Boston's
local dance scene (ⓦwww.bostondancealliance.org).

Theatre

It's possible to pay dearly for a night at the **theatre**. Tickets to the bigger shows
range from $25 to $125 depending on the seat, and there is, of course, the potential
of a pre- or post-theatre meal (see p.149 for restaurants in the Theater District).
Your best option is to pay a visit to **BosTix** (☎617/482-BTIX) – a half-price,
day-of-show ticket booth with two outlets: in Copley Square, at the corner of
Dartmouth and Boylston streets, and at Faneuil Hall Marketplace, (Mon–Sat
10am–6pm, Sun 11am–4pm) – tickets go on sale at 11am, and only cash is
accepted. Their website (ⓦwww.bostix.org) also has a number of discounted
show tickets available.

Full-price tickets can be had via **Ticketmaster** (☎1-800/745-3000, ⓦwww
.ticketmaster.com) or by contacting the individual theatre directly in advance of
the performance. If you have a valid school ID or ISIC card, a number of theatres
offer vastly cheaper **student rush** tickets on the day of the performance; call the
venue in question for more information. The **smaller venues** tend to showcase
more offbeat and affordable productions; shows can be under $10 – though you
shouldn't bank on that.

Geared toward local actors and theatre companies, **StageSource**, the Greater
Boston Theatre Alliance, has an informative website with information on the
Boston scene (☎617/720-6066, ⓦwww.stagesource.org).

Yankee cooking (and drinking)

Built on the unfussiness of the Puritan appetite and the city's proximity to the Atlantic Ocean, Boston's traditional cuisine – epitomized by pot roast, seafood chowder and cream pies – is as comforting as comfort food gets. While this nostalgic brand of Yankee cooking remains strong in public memory, nowadays it's seen on menus less and less. That said, its one essential component, fresh fish, remains commonplace, and even though the city prides itself on its diverse, contemporary palate, the occasional baked bean may still make an entrance onto your plate. Be it lobster or voguish fusion fare, pair your meal with a local brew for entry into Yankee food paradise.

Chowder, clams and sacred cod

Boston's greatest culinary tradition is, without a doubt, seafood. In the eighteenth and nineteenth centuries, cod fishing was a cornerstone of the regional economy (nearby Cape Cod got its name because of the white fish's profusion in its waters), and the city's connection to the sea continues to this day, cropping up everywhere from menu items to furry animal toys. So strong is Boston's love for fish that a wooden "Sacred Cod" hangs in the Massachusetts State House (see p.80) as a testament to the fishing industry's importance. When Harvard pranksters stole the emblem in the 1930s, the House refused to reconvene until it was recovered.

Lobster roll ▲

Chowder ▼

Five superb seafood spots

If you're new to seafood, these worthwhile eateries are sure to get you hooked.

▶▶ **B & G Oysters** Fancy South End foodie spot with some of the best (and priciest) fish fare in town. See p.155

▶▶ **The Barking Crab** The Crab's waterfront location and accompaniments (paper plates and greasy French fries) keep this seafood shack buzzing throughout summer. See p.151

▶▶ **Daily Catch** Smaller than a barnacle, they still manage to pack people into this endearing Sicilian-style restaurant. See p.151

▶▶ **Neptune Oyster** Sleek and petite, it's where top Boston chefs (and everyday laymen) sate their lobster-roll fix. A must-do. See p.152

▶▶ **Summer Shack** Kitschy and kid-friendly, this spacious spot is part clam shack, part raw bar heaven. See p.155

New England offers a stellar variety of maritime morsels. Perhaps the most iconic is lobster, served as a "roll" wherein sweet lobster meat, a touch of mayo, salt and pepper is blended together and stuffed into a buttered and toasted hot dog bun. Boiled lobster is easy enough to make (you just stick it in piping hot water), but eating it is a labour of love, requiring nutcrackers, miniature forks, a rather camp plastic bib and lots of napkins. It helps if you bring an experienced lobster aficionado with you for your first go-around to ensure that you dig out every succulent morsel. Clams are another staple, showing up in creamy chowders or on their own steamed (also called "steamers") and eaten straight from the shell, or fried to a crispy perfection. Other shellfish specialities include scallops, baked with a butter-crumb topping, and raw oysters, splayed on the half-shell and served on a bed of ice, accompanied by lemon juice, horseradish and hot sauce.

▲ Grilled oyster

▼ Ice cream is a Boston passion

Sweet teeth

If no meal is truly complete without dessert, then Boston is a fine place to be, home to everything from kid-fuelled candy shops to upscale dessert spots. The North End rules for after-dinner delights, laced as it is with incredible late-night Italian pastry joints where espresso and sambuca are offered alongside crisp *cannoli* and custard-filled eclairs. *Gelato* is scooped in the neighbourhood as well, though the entire city is truly crazy about ice cream. Fine ice cream parlours are all over town, but *Toscanini's* (p.146), across the river in Cambridge, churns out the stuff of legend with flavours like burnt caramel, cocoa pudding and Earl Grey, all freshly-crafted from inside their glassy storefront. That said, the city's most historic dessert, delicious

venues on a single South End property. Its major tenant is the Calderwood Pavilion, home of the luxurious Wimberly Theatre, and the Roberts Theatre – a contemporary, black-box, flexible stage set-up.

Hasty Pudding Theatre 12 Holyoke St, Cambridge T617/495-5205, W www.hasty pudding.org; **Harvard** T. Harvard University's Hasty Pudding Theatricals troupe, dating to 1795, mounts one show per year (usually an eclectic musical comedy with Harvard guys in drag as the centrepiece; Feb & March), then hits the road – after which the Cambridge Theatre Company moves in. That said, the troupe is best known for its priceless "Man and Woman of the Year" awards, in which big-time actors lead a

parade through Cambridge, are awarded a pot of pudding and then get "roasted" by troupe producers.

Institute of Contemporary Art Theater 100 Northern Ave T617/478-3100, W www.ica boston.org; **Courthouse Station** T. Count on the unconventional at the theatre of the ICA, Boston's leading venue for all things postmodern and cutting-edge. The World Music dance troupe (see p.176) performs here regularly.

Lyric Stage 140 Clarendon St T617/437-7172, W www.lyricstage.com; **Copley** T. Both premieres and modern adaptations of classic and lesser-known American plays take place at this intimate theatre within the renovated YWCA building.

Film

In Boston, as in any other large American city, it's easy enough to catch general-release **films** – the usual listings sources carry all the details you need. If you're looking for out-of-the-ordinary film fare, however, you'll have to venture from the centre – the best second-run theatres are clustered around Cambridge. Whatever you're going to see, admission will cost you about $11, though matinees before 6pm can be cheaper. You can call T617/333-FILM for automated film listings.

AMC Fenway 13 401 Park Drive T617/424-6111; **Fenway** T. Multiplex showing usual blockbuster fare for popcorn munchers with the occasional off-beat flick thrown in. Student discounts on offer.

AMC Loews Boston Common 19 175 Tremont St T617/423-5801; **Park** T. There are nineteen screens at this plush megaplex right by Boston Common; the armrests move back so you can hold hands with your honey.

AMC Loews Harvard Square 10 Church St, Cambridge T617/864-4581; **Harvard** T. A nice blend of vintage environs (it opened in 1926) and modern flicks, this petite Loews location hosted the first live US performance of the *Rocky Horror Picture Show*, a beloved stage tradition that continues to this day (Sat at midnight; prepare for a rowdy live cast in addition to the film; $10).

Brattle Theatre 40 Brattle St, Cambridge T617/876-6837, W www.brattlefilm.org; **Harvard** T. A historic indie cinema that pleasantly looks its age. Hosts a thematic film series plus occasional author appearances and readings; beer, wine and fresh popcorn are available for purchase.

Coolidge Corner Moviehouse 290 Harvard St, Brookline T617/734-2500, W www.coolidge .org; **Coolidge Corner** T. Film buffs flock to this classic theatre for foreign and independent movies. The Coolidge also runs ingenious programmes like "Box Office Babies", baby-friendly movie screenings where gurgling noises are encouraged. The interior is adorned with Art Deco murals.

Harvard Film Archive Carpenter Center, 24 Quincy St, Cambridge T617/495-4700, Whcl.harvard.edu /hfa; **Harvard** T. A mixed bag of artsy, foreign and experimental films are shown here.

Institute of Contemporary Art 100 Northern Ave T617/478-3100, W www.icaboston.org; **Courthouse Station** T. Inventive, eclectic and (of course) contemporary, the ICA screens indie fare such as Japanese animation and video installations amidst its glassy environs.

Kendall Square Cinema One Kendall Square, East Cambridge T617/499-1996, W www .landmarktheatres.com; **Kendall** T. All the neon decoration and small screens of your average multiplex, but this beloved spot has the area's widest selection of first-rate foreign and independent films. It's actually located on Binney Street, near Cardinal Medeiros Avenue.

Mugar Omni Theater Boston Museum of Science ⊤617/723-2500, www.mos.org; Science Park **T**. Daytime-only showings ($9), mainly of documentaries dealing with the natural world and science, all viewed on a five-storey IMAX wraparound screen. There's also a planetarium ($9) and a 3D cinema where you get to wear cool retro glasses ($5, plus $21 museum admission fee).

Museum of Fine Arts Theater 465 Huntington Ave ⊤617/267-9300, www.mfa.org/film; Museum **T**. Offbeat art films and documentaries, mostly by locals, often accompanied by lectures from the filmmaker. Also hosts several showcases, such as the Boston Jewish Film Festival.

Somerville Theatre 55 Davis Square, Somerville ⊤617/625-5700, ⓦwww.somervilletheatre online.com; Davis **T**. Wacky home for camp, classic, cult, independent, foreign and first-run pictures. Also doubles as a venue for live music. It's way out there – in more ways than one – past Cambridge, but worth the trip.

Stuart Street Playhouse 200 Stuart St ⊤617/426-4499, ⓦwww.stuartstreetplayhouse .com; Boylston **T**. When this 1970s cinema was re-converted back to a movie theatre in 2009 it signalled the return of art-house films to Downtown. Tucked away in the Theater District, there's an elegant lobby and (endearingly) only one screen, generally lit up with an indie flick.

⑭

PERFORMING ARTS AND FILM | Film

⑮

Gay Boston

For a town with a Puritan heritage and long-entrenched Blue Laws, it may come as some surprise that Boston is one of the more gay-friendly cities on the East Coast. Boston was one of the first cities in the US to endorse same-sex marriage, and in 2007 this sentiment was reaffirmed when state senators and representatives voted, by a landslide, against an anti-gay marriage amendment.

Much of the action centres around the **South End**, a largely residential area whose gay businesses (primarily restaurants, galleries and cafés) are concentrated on a stretch of Tremont Street above Union Park. Adjacent to the South End, on the other side of Arlington Street, is tiny **Bay Village**, a smaller gay enclave with one very well-known cabaret joint, *Jacque's* (see p.182). Largely leftist **Cambridge** is also gay-friendly, with a few established gay nights to show for it, while **Jamaica Plain**, a neighbourhood south of Boston proper, is quietly carving out a reputation for itself as a lesbian-friendly community.

Although the city's **gay nightlife** ranges from leathermen at the Ramrod to cocktail-swilling guppies at Club Café, it remains small and fairly concentrated; the lesbian club scene, meanwhile, despite gaining more of a foothold in recent years, is still vastly under-represented in comparison. That said, in general Boston is so liberal in many ways the entire city is a playground for the LGBT community.

Information and resources

Boston's free **gay newspaper** is *Bay Windows* (Ⓦ www.baywindows.com), a good source for **club information** – the other being the gay-friendly alternative paper *The Boston Phoenix*. All can be found in various venues and bookstores, notably Calamus and the Center for New Words (see p.183). These two noteworthy vestibules also have gay and lesbian community **bulletin boards**, with postings for apartment rentals, club happenings and so forth.

General resources and support groups

Boston Glass Community Center 93 Massachu-setts Ave ☏617/266-3349, Ⓦ www.jri.org/glass; Hynes **T**. Drop-in center for people aged 13–25.
Fenway Community Health Center 1340 Boylston St ☏617/267-0900, Ⓦ www.fenway health.org. All manner of health care for the gay community.
Gay and Lesbian Helpline ☏617/267-9001. General information source.

Online

EDGE Boston Ⓦ www.edgeboston.com. LGBT local and national news with good coverage of local gay clubs and bars.
Link Pink Ⓦ www.linkpink.com. Definitive "pink pages" for businesses, hotels, shops, and services catering to the New England LGBT community.
The List Ⓦ www.queeragenda.org. Sign up to receive free weekly emails about upcoming gay and lesbian events in the Boston area.

Out In Boston ⊛ www.outinboston.com.
Extensive and fun LGBT website with
events listings, local and national news and
"homoscopes."

Sports

Boston Sports Club 560 Harrison Ave
☏ 617/482-1266. A good gay-friendly gym
with pool in the South End.

Pride Sports Boston ⊛ www.pridesportsboston
.com ☏ 617/937-5858. An alliance of gay-
and lesbian-friendly gyms that organizes
numerous sporting groups as well as
Boston's team in the Gay Games.
Revolution Fitness 209 Columbus Ave
☏ 617/536-3006. Stylish gym with exposed
brick, standout yoga classes, and lots of
state-of-the-art equipment.

Accommodation

All of Boston's **accommodations** are gay-friendly but none endorse a strict gay-only
clientele policy. That said, you're likely to find more gay visitors than straight ones
sleeping in the city's few gay-run guesthouses and bed and breakfasts. Most are
situated in **the South End** and Back Bay, putting you within walking distance of
the city's best gay bars and cafés; a quieter option in **Jamaica Plain** may appeal to
members of the lesbian community, given its proximity to lesbian-friendly spots
like the Midway Café. The **rates** below refer to the lowest cost of a standard double
room in summer.

Chandler Inn 26 Chandler St ☏ 617/482-3450
or 1-800/842-3450, ⊛ www.chandlerinn.com;
Back Bay T. Contemporary yet cosy, the
Chandler Inn offers 55 petite rooms in a
European-style hotel above the popular
Fritz bar (see p.182); perks like plasma
satellite TVs, iPod docks, wi-fi and marble
bathrooms are included in the rates. $175.
Clarendon Square Inn 198 West Brookline St
☏ 617/536-2229, ⊛ www.clarendonsquare.com;
Prudential T. Gorgeous, well-loved bed and
breakfast on a pretty residential street, with
great attention paid to design details and
indulgent perks like heated bathroom tiles,
limestone floors, a private garden and a
24hr roof-deck hot tub. $195 to $395.
Encore B&B 116 West Newton St ☏ 617/247-3425
⊛ www.encorebandb.com; **Back Bay T**. On a
pleasant side street, you'll get pampered at
this cheerful B&B with contemporary decor,
wi-fi and a sitting area or balcony in all three
of the rooms. $140–240.

Inn @ St. Botolph 99 St. Botolph St
☏ 617/236-8099, ⊛ www.innatstbotolph.com;
Back Bay T. On a quiet side street on the
western cusp of the South End, this stylish
hideaway features 16 oversized suites with
kitchenettes, bold houndstooth patterns and
black and brown striped furniture, wi-fi, an
on-site laundry room and gym and continental breakfast. $160.
Taylor House 50 Burroughs St, Jamaica Plain
☏ 617/983-9334, ⊛ www.taylorhouse.com;
Green Street T. This delightful B&B, with
two beautiful golden-retriever mascots,
is superbly sited between JP's main drag
(Centre Street) and scenic Jamaica Pond.
Its three charming rooms, tucked away
on the second floor of an 1855 Italianate
house, offer queen-sized beds, free parking
and wi-fi. Complimentary continental
breakfast, which includes fresh baked
bread, is served daily. $159.

Bars, clubs and cafés

In a sense, Boston's **gay scene** is less of a "scene" these days, largely due to the fact
that Boston is such a gay-friendly town – LGBT folk should feel welcome all over
the city. That said, Boston has a good variety of gay bars and clubs, ranging from the
sophisticated (dbar) to the low-key (Fritz) – and, of course, a number of bumping
dance clubs (Machine, Thursday nights at Estate); see Chapter 13 for further details
on these and other venues.

Gay and lesbian events calendar

Boston Pride (June) A week-long festival that culminates in a parade starting at Boston Common. ⓦwww.bostonpride.org.

Fantasia Fair (Oct) The US's longest running continuous transgender event has been in Provincetown (see p.239) since 1975. ⓦwww.fantasiafair.org.

Out on the Edge (Oct) Held at the Boston Center for Arts, this is one of the world's premier queer theatre fests. ⓦwww.thetheateroffensive.org.

Holly Folly (Dec) Provincetown's (see p.239) big gay Yuletide fest draws the crowds back to the Cape Cod seaside town. ⓦwww.hollyfolly.com.

The hottest lesbian ticket around is Thursday night's Queeraoke at Midway Cafe, in Jamaica Plain; the ever-shifting Dyke Night is also a great event (ⓦwww.dykenight.com). For those night owls who haven't gotten their fill of dancing after the clubs close, ask around for an invite to Boston's secretive after-hours private party at Rise (306 Stuart St; ☎617/423-7473); the members-only stomping ground for gays and straights only gets going at 2am.

28 Degrees 1 Appleton St ☎617/728-0728; **Back Bay T**. The food is swanky Italian-inspired fare, but the drinks (like the frozen bellini or blueberry basil martini) are a safer bet at this candle-lit lounge replete with contemporary leather seating, wispy curtains at your table, and underwater toilets.

Club Café 209 Columbus Ave ☎617/536-0966, ⓦwww.clubcafe.com; **Back Bay T**. This combination restaurant/video bar popular among South End guppies has two back lounges, *Moonshine* and *Satellite*, showing the latest videos with signature martinis like the Pouty Princess and the Dirty Birdie.

dbar 1236 Dorchester Ave, Dorchester ☎617/265-4490, ⓦwww.dbarboston.com; **Savin Hill T**. Although Dorchester's *dbar* is a bit removed from the city centre, it's worth the trip – most locals think it's the best gay bar in town. Set amidst an inlaid mahogany interior, dbar serves fancy fusion fare like seared diver scallops ($19) from 5.30–10pm; after that it's all about pomegranate cosmos ($8.50) and getting your groove on to Top 40 and house tunes.

The Eagle 520 Tremont St ☎617/542-4494; **Back Bay T**. Generally tends to be the last stop of the night, with a cruise-y, dive-y flavour, and long lines at the boys' toilets. Prepare for salty bar service.

Fritz 26 Chandler St ☎617/482-4428; **Back Bay T**. This South End sports bar below *Chandler Inn* (see "Accommodation" p.181) is often likened to the gay version of *Cheers* due to its friendly staff and mix of casually attired locals and visitors. Good for Sun brunch.

Guerrilla Queer Bar First Friday of every month; ⓦwww.bostonguerrilla.com. Once a month, the Guerrilla kids take over a classically hetero bar, shake it up and make it queer for the evening. It's an awesome event with a splash of politics mixed in; check out their Facebook page if you want to get in on the action.

Jacque's Cabaret 79 Broadway ☎617/426-8902; **Arlington T**. *Priscilla, Queen of the Desert* invades New England at this drag dream where divas lip-synch "I Love the Nightlife." There's a nice melting pot of patrons, including frequent bachelorette parties. Showtime is 10.30pm nightly (Tues is Karaoke night), but beware – the festivities end at midnight, Cinderella. Cover $6–10, and you should consult a map before you head over as it's a little tricky to find.

Machine 1254 Boylston St ☎617/536-1950; **Kenmore T**. A favourite with the gay crowd on Fri & Sat when the club's large dancefloor and top-notch music has the place pumping. The pool tables, video screens, and bar near the dancefloor let you take a breather and soak up the scene. Cover $8–10.

Milky Way 284 Amory St, Jamaica Plain ☎617/524-6060; **Stonybrook T**. Situated in lesbian-friendly JP, on fourth Fridays the Milky Way hosts "Dyke Night," one of the most happening lesbian dance-athons in town. The lounge is set inside Bella Luna pizzeria, and offers Wii bowling and old-school Galaga.

Midway Café 3496 Washington St, Jamaica Plain, ☎617/524-9038, ⓦwww.midwaycafe.com; **Green Street T**. Neighbourhood live music hangout with a popular Thurs Queeraoke Night; complete with costumes and wigs; afterwards there's a dance party till 2am. $5 cover.

Paradise 180 Massachusetts Ave, Cambridge ⓣ617/868-3000, ⓦ www.paradisecambridge .com; Central **T**. Upstairs, male dancers (almost) bare it all; those who want to keep some clothes on stay downstairs where a smallish dancefloor rocks out to Top 40

tunes. Open till 1am Mon–Wed & Sun, 2am Fri & Sat.

Ramrod 1254 Boylston St ⓣ617/536-1950, ⓦwww.ramrodboston.com; Kenmore **T**. This Fenway meat market attracts a pretty hungry crowd with its strictly enforced Levi/leather dress code (Fri & Sat) – no dress shirts or "colognistas" allowed. Not quite as hardcore as it sounds, as it's directly upstairs from the harmless *Machine* (see above).

Bookstores

Calamus Bookstore 92B South St ⓣ617/338-1931, ⓦwww.calamusbooks.com; South Station **T**. Born from the ashes of the much-lamented Glad Day bookstore, Calamus is owned by former Glad Day manager John Mitzel and is easily recognized by the Rainbow flag outside.

Center for New Words 7 Temple St, Cambridge ⓣ617/876-5310, ⓦwww.centerfornewwords .org; Central Square **T**. This feminist bookstore caters to all aspects of the literary scene with reading rooms, a host of workshops, and regular discussions like "feminism and dessert."

🔟

Shopping

Though Boston has its share of chain stores and typical mall fare, there are plenty of unusual and funky places to **shop** here. The city is perhaps best loved for its bookstores, having established a reputation as a literary haven and academic centre.

No matter what you're looking for, Boston is an extremely pleasant place in which to shop for it, with unique, high-quality stores clustered on charming avenues like Beacon Hill's Charles Street and Back Bay's Newbury Street. The former has a dense concentration of **antique shops**, while the latter is an eight-block stretch that starts off with upscale clothing purveyors, and then begins to cater to more of a student population as it moves west past Exeter Street; here, **record stores** and **novelty shops** take over, a theme continued out to Kenmore Square. This span also has a handful of good **bookstores** – though the best are clustered in and around Harvard Square, across the Charles River in Cambridge. In recent years, the North End has become a magnet for boutique wear, with tempting designer shops popping up on and around Hanover Street; the South End has a number of fashionable clothing and home decor stores as well.

The rest of the action takes place in various downtown quarters, such as **Faneuil Hall Marketplace**. This area has become more commercialized over the years, but its lively atmosphere makes a trip to this outdoor mall worthwhile. To the south, **Downtown Crossing**, at Washington and Summer streets, is great for bargain-hunting, albeit in slightly seedy environs. Stores are generally open 9.30 or 10am to 6 or 7pm Monday to Saturday and from noon to 6pm on Sunday.

Antiques

Cambridge Antique Market 201 Monsignor O'Brien Hwy, East Cambridge ☎617/868-9655; **Lechmere T**. Slightly off the beaten track, but the 150 dealers at this five-floor co-operative-style market have everything from nineteenth-century furniture to vintage clothing.

Consignment Galleries 363 Highland Ave, Somerville ☎617/629-4900; **Davis T**. Affordable spot crammed with all sorts of delightful antique goodies: drop-leaf tables, quality china, mahogany mirrors and jewellery, to name a few.

Marcoz Antiques 177 Newbury St ☎617/262-0780; **Copley T**. Boutique with eighteenth- and nineteenth-century French, English and American furniture and accessories.

Twentieth Century Limited 73 Charles St ☎617/742-1031; **Charles/MGH T**. A glittering selection of antique jewellery with a focus on earlier twentieth-century pieces; don't leave without locating the treasure trove filled with fabulous names like Chanel and Kenneth Jay Lane.

Bookstores

Boston has a rich history as a literary city, enhanced by its numerous universities as well as the many authors and publishing houses that have called the town home. This legacy is well reflected in the quality and diversity of **bookstores** found both in Boston and neighbouring Cambridge. For books with a Boston connection, along with a history of literature in nineteenth-century Boston, see pp.276–280.

New

Ars Libri Ltd. 500 Harrison Ave ☎617/357-5212; **Broadway T**. Tall shelves of rare art, architecture and ethnography books are the centrepiece of this tranquil, off-the-beaten-path South End dealer.

Barnes & Noble Prudential Center, 800 Boylston St ☎617/247-6959; **Prudential T**; **660 Beacon St** ☎617/267-8484; **Kenmore T**. Two large outposts of the national bookstore chain, with decent newsstands and good selections of bargain books and calendars. The one on Beacon Street is topped off by the neon Citgo sign (see p.100).

Borders 10-24 School St ☎617/557-7188; **State T**; **511 Boylston St** ☎617/236-1444; **Copley T**; **CambridgeSide Galleria, 100 CambridgeSide Place, Cambridge** ☎617/679-0887; **Lechmere T**. Another comprehensive bookstore chain. The School Street location, with its 40ft ceilings and columned entranceway, is particularly tempting.

Brookline Booksmith 279 Harvard St, Brookline ☎617/566-6660; **Coolidge Corner T**. This cosy shop with hardwood floors has a friendly staff that welcomes browsing; holds a good author reading series, too.

Calamus Bookstore 92B South St ☎617/338-1931; **South Station T**. Boston's only gay bookstore, with a good selection of reasonably priced books and cards, plus a vast community bulletin board at the entrance.

Globe Corner Bookstore 90 Mt. Auburn St, Cambridge ☎617/497-6277; **Harvard T**. These travel specialists are well stocked with maps, travel literature and guidebooks, including an especially strong section on New England.

Grolier Poetry Bookstore 6 Plympton St, Cambridge ☎617/547-4648; **Harvard T**. With 14,000 volumes of verse, this tiny shop has gained an international following among poets and their fans. Frequent readings.

Harvard Book Store 1256 Massachusetts Ave, Cambridge ☎617/661-1515; **Harvard T**. Three huge rooms of new books upstairs, with a basement for used volumes and remainders downstairs. Academic and critical work in the humanities and social sciences dominate, with a healthy dose of fiction thrown in.

Harvard Cooperative Society 1400 Massachusetts Ave, Cambridge ☎617/499-2000; **Harvard T**. Founded in 1882 by a group of students, the Coop carries an extensive range of textbooks, fiction and travel guidebooks; it's also the best place to buy Harvard and MIT insignia clothing. Some of its charm was lost during the recent takeover by Barnes & Noble, but it remains a Harvard Square mainstay.

Lame Duck Books 12 Arrow St, Cambridge ☎617/868-2022; **Harvard T**. This literary treasure chest sells rare books that date from the seventeenth century. It's pricey, but the collection is incredible, with plenty of first editions, and delights like a portrait of Dostoevsky scribbled on by the author.

Lucy Parsons Center 549 Columbus Ave ☎617/267-6272; **Mass Ave T**. The Far Left lives on in this South End sanctuary, with a particular bent toward feminist lit, labour issues and radical economics. They also have free pamphlets on local demonstrations, plus occasional readings and lectures.

MIT Press Bookstore 292 Main St, Cambridge ☎617/253-5249; **Kendall T**. Lots of fascinating science and tech stuff, much of it surprisingly accessible, and racks of discounted and remaindered books as well. Also organizes the authors@MIT series of talks, usually held in the Kirsch Auditorium at the Stata Center (32 Vassar St).

Nini's Corner/Out of Town News Harvard Square, Cambridge; Harvard T. Few published magazines cannot be found at one of these two old-fashioned newsstands that stand across from each other in the heart of Harvard Square.

Schoenhof's Foreign Books 76A Mount Auburn St, Cambridge ☎617/547-8855; **Harvard T**. Well-stocked foreign-language bookstore that's sure to have that volume of Proust you're looking for, as well as any children's books you might be after.

Trident Booksellers & Café 338 Newbury St ☎617/267-8688; **Hynes T**. One of the last great independent bookstores in Boston proper. Has a bit of an alternative vibe; buy some funky stationery and write letters home over a cup of coffee in their superb café (see p.155). Also carries a knockout magazine selection, with lots of indie and foreign titles.

Used

Brattle Book Shop 9 West St ☎617/542-0210; **Park St T**. One of the oldest antiquarian bookstores in the country. You can buy a book for $1 outside, or find one for $10,000 inside; they recently sold a first-edition Walden for a few grand.

Bryn Mawr Book Store 373 Huron Ave, Cambridge ☎617/661-1770; **Harvard T**. This neighbourhood bookstore vends titles in a relaxed Cambridge setting. Weather permitting, there are pavement displays for pedestrian browsers.

Lorem Ipsum 1299 Cambridge St, Cambridge ☎617/497-7669; **Central T**. A magnetic space, Lorem Ipsum is the epitome of the local bookstore, well stocked with every-thing from art and children's lit to "pirates" and "tiny books". Best is the TV at its entrance on which a taped note decries: "read instead".

Raven Used Books 52-B JFK St, Cambridge ☎617/441-6999; **Harvard T**. Readers rave about Raven, and rightly so. This tidy little bookstore stocks scholarly (but not pretentious) reads covering everything from anarchism and poetry to jazz and physics. It's nearly impossible to leave without a book under your arm. There's a new location at 263 Newbury St (☎617/578-9000; Copley **T**).

Comics

Million-Year Picnic 99 Mt Auburn St, Cambridge ☎617/492-6763; **Harvard T**. For the comic-obsessed. Features Japanese anime, Superman, Tank Girl and more, (it's stronger on current stuff than older material). The staff has encyclopedic knowledge, and is tolerant of browsers.

New England Comics 14a Eliot St, Cambridge ☎617/354-5352; **Harvard T**. Back issues of classic comics, new editions and graphic novels fill this Cambridge stalwart. There are seven other locations in New England, including Allston (131 Harvard Ave ☎617/783-1848; Harvard Ave **T**) and Brookline (316 Harvard St ☎617/566-0115; Coolidge Corner **T**).

Clothes

Boston is a great place for **clothes shopping**, with options running the gamut from dollar-per-pound vintage duds to extravagant boutique and designer threads. The North End has been getting particular attention lately for its up-and-coming boutiques, while the gay-savvy South End has been accruing its own smart selection of clothing and home stores. Cobblestoned Charles Street is long on location charm as well as swanky shops to match its upscale address. Newbury Street (ⓦwww .newbury-st.com) remains the go-to standard for big-name designer stores such as Marc Jacobs, Armani and Chanel, although it also has funky affordable wear with youthful spots like Johnny Cupcake.

Designer stores

Alan Bilzerian 34 Newbury St ☎617/536-1001; **Arlington T**. Tri-level store with international haute couture from Jean-Paul Gaultier and Comme des Garçons alongside the owner's own label. Menswear and accessories occupy the first floor and womenswear the second.

Armani 22 Newbury St ☎617/267-3200; **Arlington T**. The Boston outpost of this power-suit mainstay displays the classic no-fuss designs of its Italian workaholic

namesake. A go-to spot if you have a big interview coming up (and plenty of money to spend). Further down (in the Copley Mall) is the more affordable Armani Exchange (☎617/247-5910) and the sportswear-brand Emporio Armani (☎617/262-7300).

Chanel 5 Newbury St ☎617/859-0055; **Arlington T**. A great start to Boston's shopping boulevard, this branch sells everything Chanel, from Karl Lagerfeld's ready-to-wear collections to cosmetics.

J. Press 82 Mt Auburn St, Cambridge ☎617/547-9886; **Harvard T**. Old Harvard lives on in J. Press's classic collection of high-quality men's suits; rates are mid-level ($695–1300 per suit), and the courteous staff makes shopping here a joy.

Louis 60 Northern Ave ☎617/262-6100; Courthouse Station T. A Boston landmark (pronounced "Looeez"), this fashionista funhouse is loaded with perfect pieces (men's and women's clothing, shoes, jewels) by fabulous names like Zac Posen and Jason Wu. In 2010, Louis moved from its stately Back Bay digs into a glassy new home out in the Seaport District.

Marc Jacobs 81 Newbury St ☎617/425-0707; Arlington T. Busy Marc Jacobs namesake (filled as much with eager college students as style gurus) downstairs offers the affordable Marc by Marc Jacobs line, while upstairs is fashion heaven (with equally sky-high prices).

Riccardi 116 Newbury St ☎617/266-3158; Copley T. This, one of the hippest designer schmatta shops in Boston, could hold its own just fine in Paris or New York. A few of the labels on parade are Dolce & Gabbana, Prada and Jean-Paul Gaultier. Good spot for fancy jeans.

Local and boutique stores

Bobbles & Lace 26 Prince St ☎617/248-0419; Haymarket T. Don't sweat the corny name. Known for its affordable selection of trendy clothing, Bobbles & Lace is particularly favoured for well-priced party dresses and jewellery.

Bodega 6 Clearway St ☎617/421-1550; Hynes T. A truly fantastic original. Out front stocks your favourite bodega mainstays (think Cheerios and toilet paper); walk towards the vending machine door to reveal a secret backroom filled with covetous designer sneakers and stylish hip-hop wear.

City Sports 480 Boylston St ☎617/267-3900; Copley T, 11 Bromfield St ☎617/423-2015; Downtown Crossing T; 44 Brattle St, Cambridge ☎617/492-6000; Harvard T. Established in 1983 by two friends upset about the lack of sports gear in Boston, this local standby has grown into a healthy chain with shops up and down the east coast. It's still a Boston landmark, however, and worth popping in for any athletic gear you might need (or to pick up one of their eponymous T-shirts).

Dress 221 Newbury St ☎617/424-7125; Copley T. A bonafide Boston best. This trendsetting yet friendly boutique has stylish T-shirts (Adam + Eve), jeans (Lofli), separates, and droolworthy dresses (Vena Cava, Vanessa Bruno) to sate even the most discerning fashionista. Ultrachic but very welcoming.

Holiday 53 Charles St ☎617/973-9730; Charles/ MGH T. An adorable little shop distinguished by its plush interior and great sense of wit (evidenced by a "closed" sign that reads "ta-ta for now"), Holiday offers pretty dresses and ensembles by Loeffler Randall and Tory Burch that'll put you in good stead for either a Parisian getaway or a Sunday stroll on Charles Street.

In-jean-ius 441 Hanover St ☎617/523-5326; Haymarket T. Stylish North End boutique filled with high-end women's denim like Rock & Republic and Goldsign; best are the helpful staffers that magically steer you toward that perfect pair of jeans. Its owner also runs a stellar dress store, Twilight, around the corner at 12 Fleet St (☎617/523-8008).

Karmaloop 301 Newbury St ☎617/369-0100; Hynes T. A refreshing change from the upscale Newbury Street shop theme, Karmaloop hocks men's streetwear and bright kicks in a space accented by elegant velvet wallpaper and bumping tunes.

Looc Boutique 12 Union Park St ☎617/357-5333; Back Bay T. Crisp and clean, this whitewashed shop offers breezy, French-inspired numbers like structured coats and striped nautical tees. It'll make you want to take a romantic bicycle ride along the Seine with flowers in your basket.

Passport 43 Brattle St, Cambridge ☎617/576-0900; Harvard T. Possessed with wanderlust but afraid of airports? Get thee to Passport, where an inviting array of stylish luggage, chic-yet-packable clothing, cashmere wraps and other delightful travel sundries stand at the ready to boost your "full body scanner" morale.

Johnny Cupcakes 279 Newbury St ☎617/375-0100; Hynes T. Every hipster in town has a Johnny Cupcakes T-shirt, but why shouldn't they when Johnny prints each one with catchy slogans like "Make Cupcakes Not War"? Endearing with an edge, pick up one of their cupcake and crossbones shirts to show your support for this local boy with a dream.

Stel's 334 Newbury St ☎617/262-3348; Hynes **T**. Browsing the wares along handcrafted tables and exposed brick walls, this slouchy boutique feels a bit like your grandparents' attic, complete with soft, neutral cardigans and woollen separates. Pricier than your grandparents would like, but Stel's is a master of throw-it-together chic.

Twilight 12 Fleet St ☎617/523-8008; Haymarket **T**. Run by the same lovely mastermind behind In-jean-ius, Twilight opened up when trendy denim wearers started asking about things to wear for a big night out. Filled with chi-chi dresses (think Betsey Johnson), heels and well-priced sparkly jewellery, this delightful space has friendly staffers that welcome both browsers and buyers with equal warmth.

Uniform 511 Tremont St ☎617/247-2360; Back Bay **T**. If you know a guy who needs a little style kick, march him into Uniform where kindly South End staffers will transform him into an "after" photo sporting casually chic brands like Penguin and Ben Sherman.

Vintage, thrift and consignment

40 South Street 40 South St, Jamaica Plain ☎617/522-5066; Green St or Forest Hills **T**. Rocking little vintage shop packed with racks of checked button-down shirts, denim and tops for both men and women. Good selection of leather boots, too.

Bobby from Boston 19 Thayer St ☎617/423-9299; NE Medical or Broadway **T**. Long adored by local rockers and professional movie stylists, Bobby's is an artful South End loft long on Union Jacks, shoes, ties, suspenders, dapper hats and clothing from the 1920s to the 1960s. It's an incredible fashion dream world, and a must-visit for vintage lovers. Cash or cheque only.

Dame 68 South St, Jamaica Plain ☎617/935-6971; Green St or Forest Hills **T**. A treasure-trove of pristinely kept dresses, heels and men's button-downs, all carefully displayed alongside antique wood floors and pressed-tin ceilings.

The Garment District/Dollar-a-Pound 200 Broadway, Cambridge ☎617/876-5230; Kendall **T**. Warehouse full of bins crammed with used togs. If you have the time to sift through the leftovers of twentieth-century fashion, you'll happen upon some great

bargains – all at the rate of $1.50 per pound of clothing. On Fridays, it's reduced to 75¢ per pound. In 2008, the building saw the addition of Boston Costume, affirming the property's status as the go-to place for Halloween ensembles.

Karma 26 Prince St ☎617/723-8338; Haymarket **T**. Not your grandmother's consignment store: a stylish little North End spot carrying vintage designer threads like Prada and Chanel. There's also an inviting array of inexpensive jewellery and a solid sales rack in the back.

Oona's 1210 Massachusetts Ave, Cambridge ☎617/491-2654; Harvard **T**. Since 1972, Oona's has been the place to find vintage "experienced clothing" – in this case kimonos, flapper dresses, leather jackets and various accessories.

Poor Little Rich Girl 166 Newbury St ☎617/425-4874; Copley **T**; also 121 Hampshire St, Cambridge ☎617/873-0809; Central **T** and 374 Somerville Ave, Somerville ☎617/684-0157; Harvard **T**. A funky little consignment shop with rock star roots (the owner is in a band called "Heavy Stud"), this vintage gem has well-priced goods in a teensy locale.

Second Time Around at nos. 176, 219 & 324 Newbury St ☎617/247-3504 (for no.176); Copley **T**; 82 Charles St ☎617/227-0049; Charles/MGH **T**; 8 Eliot St, Cambridge ☎617/491-7185; Harvard **T**. Great prices on barely worn, albeit conservative, clothing, predominantly from Banana Republic, the Gap, Anne Taylor and Abercrombie & Fitch.

Velvet Fly 28 Parmenter St ☎617/557-4359; Haymarket **T**. Dubbed "modern vintage", this North End boutique offers both contemporary and re-worked dresses alongside handbags, jewellery and other wardrobe staples.

Hats

Salmagundi 765 Centre St, Jamaica Plain ☎617/522-5047; Green St **T**. Derbys, porkpies, homburgs, straw weaves – even just the *names* sound fun at this modern-day millinery, known for its selection of classic hat styles in contemporary colours and stripes.

Shoes

Leokadia 667 Tremont St ☎617/247-7463; Back Bay **T**. Designed to feel like you're stepping inside your mother's stylish shoe closet, this smart boutique loves putting ladies in the big girl's shoes – Dolce Vita, Pucci, Givenchy and more. It's expensive, but there are frequent sales.

Moxie 51 Charles St ☎617/557-9991; Charles/MGH **T**. Put your feet up on a pedestal at this swish shoe store selling high-end brands like Tory Burch and Marc by Marc Jacobs.

Cosmetics

The Beauty Mark 33 Charles St ☎617/720-1555; Charles/MGH **T**. They say it's what's on the inside that counts, and if that's the case, then the Beauty Mark must be feeling pretty good about itself. Decked out in tones of white and French blue, this girly-girl heaven is filled with rows of luxurious cosmetics, all enjoyably explored with the aid of kindly staffers.
Colonial Drug 49 Brattle St, Cambridge ☎617/864-2222; Harvard **T**. Family-owned since 1947, this landmark apothecary features an extensive selection of hard-to-find perfumes, colognes and high-end shave brushes and lathers. An aromatic time capsule, it's easy to lose an hour here browsing the curious merchandise (think elm lozenges, imported toothpaste and "Colonel Ichabod Conk's moustache wax"). Cash only.

Malls and department stores

The major **malls** quite obviously cobble together all your needs in one convenient location; unfortunately, with the loss of Filene's Basement in Downtown Crossing, none here particularly stand out.

Malls

CambridgeSide Galleria 100 Cambridgeside Place, Cambridge ☎617/621-8666; Lechmere **T**. Not too different from any other large American shopping mall. The haze of fluorescent lights and packs of teens can be draining, but there's no similarly dense and convenient conglo-meration of shops in Cambridge.
Copley Place 100 Huntington Ave ☎617/369-5000; Copley **T**. This upscale office-retail-cum-residential-complex features more than a hundred stores, including Jimmy Choo, Salvatore Ferragamo and Tiffany & Co., with Barney's and Neiman Marcus as its department-store anchors.
Faneuil Hall Marketplace Faneuil Hall ☎617/523-1300; Government Center **T**. The city's most famous market, with a hundred or so shops, plus next door's Quincy Market. It's a bit tourist-oriented, but still worth a trip.
The Heritage on the Garden 300 Boylston St ☎617/423-0002; Arlington **T**. Not so much a mall as a very upscale mixed-use complex across from the Public Garden, consisting of condos, restaurants and boutiques.

The Shops at Prudential Center 800 Boylston St ☎617/236-3100; Prudential **T**. This conglo-meration of a hundred or so mid-market shops is heavily patronized by local residents and conventioneers from the adjacent Hynes Convention Center.

Department stores

Barneys New York 100 Huntington Ave, in Copley Place ☎617/385-3300; Copley **T**. Boston gets tired of being compared to New York. But when this luxe Manhattan landmark opened here in 2006, there were cries of fashion glee heard around the city. Worth popping by just to glimpse its sleek design; Barneys is best loved for its women's shoes, jeans and menswear departments. Take note: it's very pricey.
Lord & Taylor 760 Boylston St ☎617/262-6000; Copley **T**. Excellent place to stock up on high-end basics, from sweaters and suits to jewellery and cosmetics.
Macy's 450 Washington St ☎617/357-3000; Downtown Crossing **T**. Much the generic urban department store, with all the basics covered, including a better-than-average cosmetics section and a worthwhile men's department.

Neiman Marcus 5 Copley Place ☎617/536-3660; Copley **T**. Along with nearby Barneys, this is Boston's most luxurious department store, with prices to match. Three levels, with an impressive menswear collection on the first.

Saks Fifth Avenue 786 Boylston St ☎617/262-8500; Copley **T**. Another Back Bay beauty, with plenty of posh clothes, shoes and accessories (including Boston's best selection of sunglasses) to please every style obsessive.

Crafts

Boston Bead Company 23 Church St, Cambridge ☎617/868-9777; Harvard **T**. With so many kinds of beads, it's a good thing the sales staff can assist you in creating a "distinctly personal adornment." Great afternoon activity for older children.

The Cambridge Artists' Cooperative 59 Church St, Cambridge ☎617/868-4434; Harvard **T**. Three floors fill this Harvard Square shop with all kinds of crafts, from woodcarvings and glass sculptures to wearable art and beaded bags.

Magpie 416 Highland Ave, Somerville ☎617/623-3330; Davis **T**. Hip crafts boutique that's stocked with handmade goods like knitted iPod cases and irreverent needlework. A great way to support your local artist.

Rugg Road Paper Co. 105 Charles St ☎617/742-0002; Charles/MGH **T**. They've got high-end paper products of all kinds, including lovely cards, stationery and wrapping paper.

Food and drink

Look no further than the North End for all manner of tasty **pastries**; for gourmet-style **take-home eats**, Cambridge is especially strong in variety.

Bakeries

Bova's Bakery 134 Salem St ☎617/523-5601; Haymarket **T**. A 24-hour bakery in the North End, selling delights like plain and chocolate *cannoli*, oven-fresh cakes and whoopie pies; famously cheap, too, with most items around $5.

ChocoLee Chocolates 23 Dartmouth St ☎617/236-0606; Back Bay **T**. Inventive sweets abound at this well-loved *choco-laterie* known for its outstanding cupcakes, salted caramel truffles, made-to-order chocolate beignets and, come summertime, in-house popsicles.

Clear Flour Bread 178 Thorndike St, Brookline ☎617/739-0060; Packards Corner **T**. Locals line up here religiously for Boston's best artisan breads, brioche and pear ginger coffee cake. Worth the trek out.

Eldo Cake House 36 Harrison Ave ☎617/350-7977; Chinatown **T**. The best bakery in Chinatown, replete with candied plums and ginger, tasty egg tarts and fluffy mango sponge cake.

Maria's Pastry Shop 46 Cross St ☎ 617/523-1196; Haymarket **T**. The place doesn't look like much, but Maria's has the best Neapolitan treats in town; her custard-filled *sfogliatelle* and *ossa di morti* (bones of the dead) cookies are to die for.

Mike's Pastry 300 Hanover St ☎617/742-3050; Haymarket **T**. The famed North End bakery is one part Italian and two parts American, meaning in addition to *cannoli* and tiramisu, you'll find counters full of brownies and cookies. The endless array of eclairs is not to be missed – but expect to wait in line for one.

Party Favors 1356 Beacon St, Brookline ☎617/566-3330; Coolidge Corner **T**. Entering Party Favors immediately triggers a mouth-watering Pavlovian response – you can smell the baked goods, but you can't see them. Hidden amongst the birthday balloons and decorations lies a secret reserve of Boston's best cupcakes.

Tatte 1003 Beacon St, Brookline ☎617/232-2200; Saint Mary's **T**. Meticulously baked brioche and cheesecake as well as Tatte's signature tarts and "nut boxes" – rows of toasted nuts nestled inside a buttery, caramelized crust. Lovely to gaze upon, they're equally wonderful to consume.

Gourmet food and wine shops

Cardullo's 6 Brattle St, Cambridge
T617/491-8888; Harvard **T**. Gourmet
products from just about anywhere are
available at this well-stocked Harvard
Square store; if nothing else, be sure to
stop in for a sample. Depending on the
weather, you can sit at one of the sidewalk
tables with a fresh sandwich and watch the
people go by.

Formaggio Kitchen 244 Huron Ave, Cambridge
T617/354-4750; Harvard **T**; 268 Shawmut
Ave, T617/350-6996; Back Bay **T**. One of the
best cheese shops in Boston; the gourmet
meats, salads, sandwiches and baked
goods are also worth sampling.

Haymarket Blackstone St, no phone;
Haymarket **T**. Although it's not very classy
(and certainly not gourmet), Haymarket
is a Boston institution, and the best
place in town to score ridiculously cheap
produce. On warm weather Friday and
Saturday mornings, farm and fish stands
set themselves up all along Blackstone
Street (near Faneuil Hall); prepare for lots of
heckling and haggling.

Monica's Salumeria 130 Salem St
T617/742-4101; Haymarket **T**. Lots of
imported Italian cheeses, cooked meats,
cookies and pastas.

New Deal Fish Market 622 Cambridge St,
Cambridge T617/876-8227; Lechmere **T**.
Top-notch, sashimi-grade seafood with
a wide selection of fish ranging from the
crowd pleasers (crab, lobster and shrimp) to
more specialized fare like maguro tuna and
stickleback. Very fairly priced.

Polcari's Coffee 105 Salem St
T617/227-0786; Haymarket **T**.
Established in 1932, this adored old-world
coffee vendor is nicely stocked with a wide
variety of blends as well as every spice you
could think of. Worth going inside for the
aroma alone, or just to hear the local gossip
from the guys behind the counter.

Salumeria Italiana 151 Richmond St
T617/523-8743; Haymarket **T**. Arguably the
best Italian grocer this side of Rome. Stocks
only the finest cheeses, meats, balsamic
vinegars and more.

Savenor's 160 Charles St T617/723-6328;
Charles/MGH **T**; 92 Kirkland St, Cambridge
T617/576-6328; Harvard **T**. Known for its
meats, this small gourmet food shop in
Beacon Hill also has a better-than-average
produce selection (Julia Child used to shop
here), in addition to prepared foods – ideal
for taking to the nearby Charles River
Esplanade for a picnic.

V. Cirace & Sons 173 North St T617/227-3193;
Haymarket **T**. A great liquor store, with the
expected range of Italian wines – it's in the
North End, after all – and much more.

Health food

Trader Joe's 899 Boylston St T617/262-6505;
Hynes **T**. Everyone's favourite Hawaiian-
themed grocery store, well-stocked with
good deals on day-to-day items like
imported cheeses, juice and baked goods
in addition to more eclectic fare like Masala
veggie burgers and wasabi mayonnaise.
Conveniently located in Back Bay; well-
situated for a picnic in the Public Garden.

Whole Foods 181 Cambridge St T617/723-0004;
Bowdoin **T**. 15 Westland Ave T617/375-1010;
Symphony **T**. The Boston branches of this
pricey, organic-friendly chain have all the
alternative foodstuffs you'd expect, plus
some of Boston's best salad bars.

Galleries

Dozens of Boston's major **art galleries** can be found on Newbury Street; most
are generally browser-friendly. SoWa, in the South End, tends to feature the most
contemporary work, as does the Seaport District.

Alpha Gallery 38 Newbury St T617/536-4465;
Arlington T. Pale pine wood floors and
spacious white walls are the hallmarks of
this inspired contemporary gallery. Focused
primarily on paintings by emerging and
mid-career artists, there are occasionally
master shows as well.

Barbara Krakow Gallery 10 Newbury St,
5th floor T617/262-4490; Arlington T. This
A-list multimedia gallery attracts the hottest
artists from New York City and around the
globe; Kiki Smith and Annette Lemieux are
but two of the stars that have shown here in
recent years.

SoWa Artists Guild 450 Harrison Ave
℡617/482-2477; ⊛www.fortpointarts.org;
Broadway T. Boston's contemporary art
stronghold, 450 Harrison Avenue is home to
fifteen galleries and over fifty artist studios.
Gallery heavyweights Carroll and Sons,
Chase Young and Samsøn Projects all
exhibit their wares here, and everything from
painting, photography, drawing, sculpture,
video and prints is on view. Aim your visit for
one of the monthly "First Friday" evenings,
when the space is abuzz with wine, cheese
and art appreciators.

Fort Point Arts Community 300 Summer St
℡617/423-4299; ⊛www.fortpointarts.org;
South Station T. Founded in 1980, this
cavernous warehouse space is the public
front for the Fort Point Arts Community.
Contemporary painting and mixed media is
viewed in a gallery downstairs; upstairs has
historically been a workspace sanctuary for
scores of local artists. Twice a year, they
host a wildly popular open studios event
(check website for dates).

Gallery NAGA 67 Newbury St ℡617/267-9060;
Arlington T. Contemporary painting,
sculpture, studio furniture and photography
from Boston and New England artists,
located in the Gothic Revival Church of
the Covenant.

The Hallway 66a South St, Jamaica Plain
℡617/818-5996; **Green St T**. Skinny little
alleyway of art exhibiting works by local
painters, sculptors and dreamers. The
Hallway also squeezes in enthusiastic
patrons for frequent live-music shows and
JP's ever-popular "First Thursdays" event.

Robert Klein 38 Newbury St ℡617/267-7997;
Arlington T. The only major art gallery
in New England devoted exclusively to
fine-art photography, Robert Klein peddles
beautiful imagery by Cartier-Bresson and
Penn, in addition to works by emerging
photographers.

The Society of Arts and Crafts 175 Newbury St
℡617/266-1810; **Copley T**. The oldest
non-profit crafts group in America has
two floors here. The first is its commercial
outpost, with a wide range of ceramics,
glass and jewellery; the second floor is
reserved for themed (and free) special
exhibitions.

Music

In Your Ear Records 957 Commonwealth Ave,
Allston ℡617/787-9755; **Pleasant Street T**,
72A Mount Auburn St, Cambridge ℡617/481-
5035; **Harvard T** Indulge in the Ear's massive
collection of used CDs, records and other
agreeable esoterica to sate your vintage
music cravings. The Cambridge location is
smaller but equally appealing.

Looney Tunes 1106 Boylston St ℡617/247-2238;
Hynes T. The way a record store should be
– walls festooned with vintage jazz records,
a great selection of CDs and a hip staff that's
not snooty.

Newbury Comics 332 Newbury St
℡617/236-4930; **Hynes T** ; **Faneuil Hall**
Marketplace ℡617/248-9992; **Government**
Center T. Boston's biggest alternative
record store carries lots of independent
labels you won't find at the national
chains, along with a substantial array of
vinyl, posters, zines and kitschy T-shirts.
There's a branch in Cambridge at the
Garage mall, 36 JFK St ℡617/491-0337,
Harvard T.

Nuggets 486 Commonwealth Ave
℡617/536-0679; **Kenmore T**. American jazz,
rock and R&B are the strong suits at this
venerable new and used record store.

Planet Records 54B JFK St, Cambridge
℡617/492-0693; **Harvard T**. Unpretentious
and well-priced with a good selection of
used CDs. It doesn't get more rock 'n'
roll than the charred guitar they have
hanging by the register – a remnant
from the fire that gutted their Kenmore
Square location.

Skippy White's 1971 Columbus Ave, Roxbury
℡617/524-4500; **Stonybrook T**. Excellent
collection of jazz, blues, R&B, gospel, funk
and hip hop. Hum a few bars and the
knowledgeable salesfolk will guide you to
the right section.

Stereo Jack's 1686 Massachusetts Ave,
Cambridge ℡617/497-9447; **Porter Square T**.
Jazz and blues specialists selling mostly
used wares, but some new stuff, too.

Underground Hip Hop 234 Huntington Ave
℡617/262-0200, ⊛www.undergroundhiphop
.com; **Symphony T**. One of the best
selections of hip hop here or anywhere. It's
well-organized too – sit on a comfy stool,
listen all you want to the tunes on their

extensive website, and then they'll grab you what you need from the back.

Weirdo Records 844 Massachusetts Ave, Cambridge ☏857/413-0154; Central T. A lovingly culled mix of everything from undiscovered local bands to "squares and outsiders" to Iranian psychedelic rock. Lots of hard-to-find sounds, imports and other stuff you can't pick up anywhere else.

Home decor

Abodeon 1731 Massachusetts Ave, Cambridge ☏617/497-0137; Porter Square T. A terrific trove of classic twentieth-century design, with furniture by top modern designers as well as assorted new bric-a-brac. Pretty expensive, but most things are cheaper than they would be in New York or LA.

Acquire 61 Salem St ☏857/362-7380; Haymarket T. Curiosity shop meets furniture boutique at Acquire, a carefully curated collection of framed vintage prints, armchairs, jewellery, antique bookshelves and other pleasing home decor goodies all artfully displayed by the store's charismatic owner.

Hudson 312 Shawmut Ave ☏617/292-0900; Back Bay T. A hip South End home store with a chic summer-cottage vibe – think oversized mirrors bordered with sparkling seashells and white sofas accompanied by silk-screened pillows.

Koo de Kir 65 Chestnut St ☏617/723-8111; Charles/MGH T. The goal at this stylish, modern spot is to make even the most everyday objects artistic and gorgeous. For a pretty penny, you can buy such beautified home furnishings and accessories here.

Gift shops

Aunt Sadie's 18 Union Park St ☏617/357-7117; Back Bay T. General store-themed South End shop with delightfully campy items such as vintage Hawaiian postcards and scented candles with original aromas like beach (coconut oil) and amusement park (popcorn).

🏃 **Black Ink 101 Charles St ☏617/723-3883; Charles/MGH T; 5 Brattle St, Cambridge ☏617/497-1221; Harvard T**. Eclectic assortment of bits and bobs you don't really need but are cool anyway: rubber stamps, a smattering of hand-printed wrapping paper, amusing refrigerator magnets and a wide assortment of vintage postcards. They also run The Museum of Useful Things, full of whimsical yet utilitarian items, around the corner from their Cambridge location (49B Brattle St, Cambridge ☏617/576-3322; Harvard T).

Front 25 Channel Center St ☏617/670-3782; Broadway T. Front helps you get organized while still keeping things fun – their designed-in-house paper goods range from luggage tags to file folders to punctuation page markers; the eight days-a-week calendar thoughtfully adds in a "someday" column.

Good 88 Charles St ☏617/722-9200; Charles/MGH T. Within this petite, white-walled gift boutique Good's countless pretty *objets* take on a found-treasure quality, with seashells, gemstone necklaces, summery totes and framed nautical butterflies to dazzle even the most discerning browser.

Matsu 259 Newbury St ☏617/266-9707; Hynes T. A hip little shop featuring a medium-sized range of sleek Japanese clothing, knick-knacks (desk clocks, stationery, funky pens) and contemporary home-decor items.

Shake the Tree 67 Salem St ☏617/742-0484; Haymarket T. A good spot for a little retail therapy, with offerings that include bright, chunky gemstone necklaces, funky sock monkeys, aromatic candles and other modern, sweet *objets* that you will never need but simply must have.

Games

Eureka Puzzles 1349 Beacon St, Brookline
T617/738-7352; Coolidge Corner **T**. Take your kids (or your inner child) on a field-trip to this charming little puzzle and game store, filled to the gills with refreshingly cordless brain entertainment.

Specialist shops

Leavitt and Peirce 1316 Massachusetts Ave, Cambridge T617/547-0576; Harvard **T**.
Old-school tobacconists that have been around almost as long as Harvard. An outstanding selection of cigars, imported cigarettes and smoking paraphernalia (lighters, rolling papers, ashtrays), plus an upstairs chess parlour right out of the carefree past.

The Original Tremont Tearoom 101 Tremont St, Suite 609 T617/338-8100; Park St **T**.
An unusual way to spend an afternoon, the country's oldest "psychic salon" offers tea-leaf, palm and Tarot readings as well as mediumship – conversations with "the other side". A 30min Tarot reading will set you back $55; there are specials on Sunday.

Polka Dog Bakery 256 Shawmut Ave
T617/338-5155; Back Bay **T**; 42 South St, Jamaica Plain T617/522-1931; Green St **T**.
Terrific gourmet dog food shop – stop in for a gift for the furry one you left back home, or bring your pet with you to nosh on free samples.

Ward Maps 1735 Massachusetts Ave, Cambridge T617/497-0737; Porter Square **T**. Antique map Mecca with an extensive set of incredible vintage city cartography. The old-school map theme continues to tote bags, coasters and the like, and, additionally, there's a very cool collection of transit memorabilia.

Sports and outdoor activities

B ostonians have an acute love-hate relationship with their professional **sports** teams, obsessing over the four major franchises – baseball's Red Sox, football's Patriots, basketball's Celtics and hockey's Bruins – with evangelical fervour. After years of watching their teams narrowly miss championship bids, all their Christmases came at once with the Red Sox finally ending 86 years of hurt by taking the 2004 World Series and the Patriots earning their third title in four seasons just a few months later. The city's sports renaissance was cemented with the Celtics bringing home the NBA championship in 2008.

Local sports fans have an admirable tenacity, following their teams closely through good seasons and bad. This lively, vocal fan base makes attending a game a great way to get a feel for the city, though fans of an opposing team who might be inclined to root against Boston, be warned: you're in store for censure from the local faithful.

While the Patriots' colossal **Gillette Stadium** is located out of town, the **TD Banknorth Garden**, where the Celtics and Bruins play, is conveniently accessible by **T**, even if it lacks the history of the classic Boston Garden that it replaced (demolished in 1997). For fans of baseball, there is no more essential pilgrimage than the one to the Red Sox' idiosyncratic Fenway Park, accessed by the Green Line's Kenmore **T**.

In terms of participatory sports, there are more than a number of good areas for jogging, biking, rollerblading and the like, especially around the Esplanade, not to mention the possibility of getting out on the water that surrounds the city. The **Department of Conservation and Recreation** (**DCR**), 251 Causeway St (☎617/626-1250, ⓦwww.mass.gov/dcr), oversees most facilities.

Boston also hosts two iconic annual sporting events. The **Head of the Charles Regatta** is the world's largest two-day rowing competition, luring thousands of cheering spectators to the Charles River when its crews hit the water in October. The equally popular **Boston Marathon** dates all the way back to 1897; every third Monday in April, its 26.2-mile route is lined with thousands of fans who pass out water and urge runners on – particularly around the notoriously steep segment known as "Heartbreak Hill".

Baseball

The Boston **Red Sox** finally stopped tormenting fans when they won the 2004 World Series against the St Louis Cardinals, breaking the infamous "Curse of the Bambino" (see p.102). The ongoing rivalry between the Sox and Yankees is legendary, though Boston's need to define themselves relative to the Yankees' success has eased a bit thanks to recent breakthroughs. This is due in part to having one of the largest payrolls in the business – including paying a staggering $51 million in 2006 just for the rights to negotiate a contract with Japanese pitcher Daisuke Matsuzaka. The lavish spending paid off with another World Series victory in 2007.

Even if the Red Sox aren't performing so well, it's worth going to a game just to see **Fenway Park**, at 24 Yawkey Way, one of America's sports treasures. Dating from 1912, it's the oldest professional baseball stadium in the country, much more intimate than most, and one of bizarre dimensions, best represented by the abnormally tall (37ft) left-field wall, dubbed the "Green Monster". Tickets can cost upwards of $300 for the finest seats, but bleacher seats start from $12 and put you amid the raucous fans; there are few better ways to spend a Sunday summer afternoon in Boston. The stadium is near the Kenmore **T** stop; for ticket information, call ☎617/482-4SOX or 1-877/RED-SOXX or visit Ⓦwww.redsox.com.

The **season** runs from April to September, with playoffs in October. Tickets for the regular season are sold in two increments – generally once in December, and then again at a larger sale in January. Playoff tickets are acquired via a random drawing in mid-September; check Ⓦwww.redsox.com for exact sale dates. Even though tickets sell out extremely fast, don't give up hope; if you're desperate to see a game, check local Sox blogs or Ⓦboston.craigslist.org to see if any locals have tickets (be sure to meet the seller in person and ensure that they have paper tickets – not just an online printout). Fenway Park also sells a small number of one-per-person tickets at Gate E on game day; be sure to get there five hours early (but no earlier – this is enforced), follow all the rules (no leaving the line, no saving a place for your friends, etc) and hope to get lucky.

Basketball

While Boston's other sports franchises once had a reputation for falling short of victory, basketball's **Celtics** have won seventeen NBA championships – more than any other North American professional sports team except baseball's New York Yankees and hockey's Montréal Canadiens. But while they enjoyed dynastic success in the 1960s and 1980s, when they played on the buckling parquet floors of the beloved Boston Garden, the Celts fell on hard times in the 1990s. The team returned to their winning ways in 2008, capturing yet another NBA title, and nearly added their eighteenth trophy in 2010, narrowly losing to the Los Angeles Lakers, their bitter rivals.

The Celtics play in the sleek if soulless **TD Banknorth Garden**, 150 Causeway St (☎617/624-1000, Ⓦwww.nba.com/celtics), located at the North Station **T** stop in the West End. Most tickets are pricey – good seats run $50 to $200 – but you can snag a seat in the rafters for as little as $10. The season begins in late October and continues all the way through June, playoffs included.

Football

For years, the New England **Patriots** were saddled with the nickname "Patsies", and generally considered to be a laughing stock. Not any longer. One of the pre-eminent teams in the NFL, their championship dynasty includes Super Bowl wins in 2002, 2004 and 2005. Led by quarterback Tom Brady and the top coach in the business, Bill Belichick, the team completed a 21-game winning streak from 2003 to 2004, setting a record in the process.

New England's nearly 130-year-old **Harvard–Yale** football rivalry is also worth noting: dubbed simply "The Game", this legendary skirmish takes place each November and draws throngs of Ivy Leaguers to Cambridge's Harvard Stadium on alternating years (☎617/495-2211; ⓦwww.gocrimson.com).

Even before they won all those Super Bowls, going to a game wasn't a reasonable goal unless you had connections or were willing to pay a scalper upwards of $100 – tickets sell out far in advance. If you can get your hands on a pair the old-fashioned way, expect to pay $50 to $125 a head. The stadium is located in distant Foxborough, just north of the Massachusetts–Rhode Island border (for information, call ☎1-800-543-1776; for tickets, dial ☎617/931-2222 or visit ⓦwww.patriots.com). Better to drop by a sports bar on a Sunday afternoon during the fall season (late Aug–Dec); the best ones are located in the West End and Kenmore Square (see Chapter 12).

Soccer

While certainly not as popular here as it is elsewhere on the globe, soccer is beginning to catch on in Boston. The city's dynamic team, the **New England Revolution** ("Revs"), snagged a North American SuperLiga trophy in 2008, and tickets to their games tend to be fairly inexpensive ($20–40). Plus, unlike other Boston pro sports, seats are easy to come by. The season runs from April to October (☎508/543-8200, ⓦwww.revolutionsoccer.net).

Ice hockey

The Boston **Bruins** are one of the most storied teams in professional ice hockey with five Stanley Cup titles and a history going back to the founding of the National Hockey League. At one point, the "Big Bad Bruins" ran up a streak of 26 straight winning seasons – the longest in professional sports. A series of retirements, injuries, and bad luck turned things around and by the mid-90s they were posting the worst records in the NHL. The squad has recouped in recent years with strong showings in the playoffs, but they have not recaptured their glory days.

An equally entertaining, and cheaper, alternative to the Bruins is **college hockey**. The biggest event is the "Beanpot" (ⓦwww.beanpothockey.com), an annual competition that takes place on the first two Mondays in February, wherein the four big local teams – the **Boston University Terriers**, **Harvard Crimson**, **Boston College Eagles**, and **Northeastern Huskies** – compete for city bragging rights.

You can catch the Bruins at the **TD Banknorth Garden**, 150 Causeway St (North Station **T**; ☎617/624-1000, ⓦwww.bostonbruins.com), where tickets can be expensive ($17–300), especially if a good opponent is in town. The long regular season begins in October and continues, with playoffs, into June.

Beanpot tickets ($26–38; available from team websites or Ticketmaster ☎1-800-745-3000; ⓦwww.beanpothockey.com) are hard to come by, but regular season seats go for around $20, and the games are generally a good time.

Running, rollerblading and cycling

When warm weather hits Boston, residents take full advantage of it, turning up in droves to engage in **outdoor activities**. The most popular of these are **running**, **rollerblading**, and **cycling**, and they all pretty much take place along the banks of the Charles River, where the Esplanade provides eighteen miles of well-kept, picturesque trails stretching from the Museum of Science all the way down to Watertown and Newton.

On the Cambridge side of the Charles is Memorial Drive, closed off to traffic between Western Avenue and Eliot Bridge (May to mid-Nov Sun 11am–7pm); it's a prime place for blading and tanning.

Three of the most popular **bike trails** in the area are the Dr Paul Dudley White Bike Path (really just another name for the Esplanade loop), the South End's five-mile Southwest Corridor Park and the Minuteman Bikeway, which runs 10.5 miles from Alewife **T** station on the Red Line in Cambridge through Lexington to Bedford.

Rental shops

Blade rentals generally start at around $20/day; bike rentals around $30/day.

Back Bay Bicycles 366 Commonwealth Ave ⊤617/247-2336, ⊛www.backbaybicycles.com; Hynes **T**.

Beacon Hill Skate Shop 135 Charles St South ⊤617/482-7400; Boylston **T**.

Cambridge Bicycle 259 Massachusetts Ave, Cambridge ⊤617/876-6555, ⊛www.cambridge bicycle.com; Kendall **T**.

Community Bicycle Supply 496 Tremont St ⊤617/542-8623, ⊛www.communitybicycle.com; Copley **T**.

Information and tours

The DCR (see p.199) has information about bike trails as well.

Charles River Wheelmen ⊛www.crw.org. Coordinates regular, and usually free, bike tours on weekends from April to November.

InLine Club of Boston ⊛www.sk8net.com. Organizes community skates and other in-line events.

Massachusetts Bicycle Coalition 171 Milk St, suite 33 ⊤617/542-BIKE, ⊛www.massbike.org. Provides information about bike trails, and sells a Boston bike map ($6).

Urban AdvenTours 103 Atlantic Ave ⊤617/670-0637, ⊛www.urbanadventours.com; Aquarium **T**. Leads leisurely two-and-a-half hour tours around the city by bike. They also do rentals.

Golf

Boston isn't long on great golf courses, but the following two spots should do the trick if you're hankering to get out on the green.

Brookline Golf Club at Putterham 1281 West Roxbury Parkway, Brookline, ⊤617/730-2078, ⊛www.brooklinegolf.com. Decent, eighteen-hole municipal course adjacent to a country club. $39-50.

Fresh Pond Golf Club 691 Huron Avenue, Cambridge, ⊤617/349-6282, ⊛www.freshpond golf.com. Right on the reservoir, this pretty nine-hole course offers good rates and adequate playing conditions. $22–38.

Ice skating and skiing

The DCR operates several **ice-skating rinks** in the Boston area between mid-November and mid-March, of which the best-kept and most convenient to downtown is the **Steriti Memorial Rink**, 561 Commercial St (⊤617/523-9327) in the North End. When it's cold enough, the lagoon in the Public Garden offers free (unmonitored) skating, while the **Frog Pond** in Boston Common (Mon 10am–4pm, Tues–Thurs & Sun 10am–9pm, Fri & Sat 10am–10pm; $4; ⊤617/635-4505; Park St **T**) charges for the sport but also rents skates ($4, children under 13 free; rentals are $8, $5 for kids). The Larz Anderson skating rink at 23 Newton St in Brookline has gorgeous digs nested in the Anderson family's sprawling former estate; there are rentals on offer as well as skyline views (Tues & Thurs 10am–noon, Fri 7.45pm–9.45pm, Sat & Sun noon–5pm; $7 non-resident adults, $4 kids; rentals $5; ☏617/739-7518). To keep tabs on skating conditions throughout the city, visit the DCR website (🖥www.mass.gov/dcr).

Aside from gliding around Boston's pavements after a snow storm, you'll have to head out of the city if you're looking to **ski**. The petite Blue Hills Ski Area, at 4001 Washington St in Canton (about 30min south of Boston), offers ten different trails including a "magic carpet" beginner's slope ($18-36; ☏781/828-5070, 🖥www.ski-bluehills.org). Weston Cross-Country Ski, at 200 Park Rd, Weston, is the place to go for skiing of the horizontal variety ($15; ☏781/891-6575, 🖥skiboston.com). Both facilities rent equipment.

Water sports

The image of white sails dotting the Charles River Basin and Boston Harbor may be inviting; alas, you'll be stuck watching them from shore unless you have recognized **sailing** credentials or are willing to take a class. Should you have the former, present them to the Boston Harbor Sailing Club on Rowes Wharf (☏617/720-0049, 🖥www.bostonharborsailing.com; Aquarium **T**) and you can rent yourself a variety of boats from a daysailer ($75/day) to a cruiser ($425/day).

Classes are available through a number of outfits, the best being Community Boating (April–Oct; learn to sail package $100; ☏617/523-1038, 🖥www.community-boating.org) which also offers unlimited craft access to experienced seadogs. Piers Park Sailing Center, 95 Marginal St (April–Oct; ☏617/561-6677, 🖥www.piersparksailing.org; Maverick **T**), does a 21-hour course for $595. Child sailors get the best deal of all, though, through Community Boating (see Chapter 18).

Possibly an easier way to get on the water is renting a **canoe** or **kayak** from the Charles River Canoe and Kayak Center, Soldiers Field Road (May–Oct Fri 1pm–dusk, Sat–Sun 10am–dusk; ☏617/462-2513, 🖥www.ski-paddle.com; Harvard **T**), which maintains a green-roofed kiosk 200 yards from the Eliot Bridge on the Boston side of the Charles. Equipment is rented by the day or hour (canoes and kayaks $15–96); lessons are also available, but certainly not required.

If you'd prefer to landlub on a beach, look no further than South Boston's Castle Island (see p.110), where you can feast on grilled hot dogs from the landmark *Sullivan's* and cavort along three miles of sand.

Gyms

If you're staying at a hotel without a gym and are in need of a workout, a number of **gyms** and **fitness centres** offer one-time daily memberships for out-of-towners. The Beacon Hill Athletic Clubs (🖥www.beaconhillathleticclubs.com), with locations at 261 Friend St (☏617/720-2422; North Station **T**), 3 Hancock St (☏617/367-2422; Park St **T**), and 85 Atlantic Ave (☏617/742-0055; State St **T**), offers $15 walk-in day passes for use of its basic gym set-up. In the South End, the superlative Revolution Fitness, at 209 Columbus Ave (☏617/536-3006; 🖥revfitboston.com; Back Bay **T**), offers day passes for $15 with proof of hotel stay, $20 without. The Boston Athletic Club, located in South Boston at 653 Summer St (☏617/269-4300, 🖥www.bostonathleticclub.com; Downtown Crossing **T**), charges a walk-in rate of $25 a day for full use of its facilities, which include a sauna and pool; alternatively, a free pass can be printed from its website.

Paintball

Among all the miscellaneous forms of sports-like entertainment in the city, perhaps the oddest (and most fun, if you're into this type of thing) is **paintball** – a kind of simulated warfare where you shoot paintballs (and they do sting) at members of the opposing team, all while scampering around an area full of bunkers and obstacles. The proceedings take place in Everett at Boston Paintball, 111 Boston St (reservations ☏617/941-0123, ⊛www.bostonpaintball.com; $30 and up).

Otherwise, women can pay $20 ($60 for a weekly pass) to take advantage of Health-works Fitness Center, 441 Stuart St (☏617/859-7700; Back Bay **T**), a spa-like gym with a relaxed female-only environment. Both sexes can practice their downward dogs at the intensive drop-in **yoga** classes led by Baron Baptiste Power Yoga Institute (☏617/661-6565, ⊛www.baronbaptiste.com); its two locations, at 25 Harvard St, Brookline ($15 per class; Brookline Village **T**), and 2000 Massachusetts Ave, Cambridge ($15; Porter **T**), also rent mats ($4). Back Bay Yoga Studio, 364 Boylston St ($15 per class; ☏617/375-9642), and Karma Yoga, 778 Tremont St and 1120 Massachusetts Ave in Cambridge ($15 per class; ☏617/547-9642), are two other excellent drop-in yoga options.

Spas

If lying down on a massage table is your idea of exercise, jump-start your day with one of the blissful listings below.

étant **524 Tremont St** ☏617/423-5040, ⊛www.etant.com; Back Bay **T**. Facials, mud wraps, salt glows, massage – the gang's all here at this stylish South End hideaway. Thoughtful staffers even feed your parking meter.
The Spa at Mandarin Oriental **776 Boylston St** ☏617/535-8820, ⊛www.mandarinoriental.com;

Copley **T**. Lavish sanctuary nestled inside one of Back Bay's poshest hotels.
MiniLuxe **296 Newbury St** ☏857/362-7444, ⊛www.miniluxe.com; Hynes **T**. What better place to get a manicure than on swanky Newbury Street? MiniLuxe is glamorous, clean, and full of your favourite polishes.

Bowling

Massachusetts's variation on tenpin bowling is **candlepin bowling**, in which the ball is smaller, the pins narrower and lighter, and you have three rather than two chances to knock the pins down. It's somewhat of a local institution that is sadly on the wane in the city itself. The best places to find it in the Greater Boston area are Lanes and Games, 195 Concord Turnpike, Somerville (daily 9am–midnight; ☏617/876-5533, ⊛www.lanesgames.com; Alewife **T**) and Sacco's Bowl Haven, 45 Day St, Somerville (Mon–Sat 10am–midnight, Sun noon–11.30pm; ☏617/776-0552, ⊛www.saccosbowlhaven.com; Davis **T**). Suburban and regional venues still abound; visit ⊛www.masscandlepin.com for more information.

The local demise of candlepin bowling has been countered by a renaissance of the more conventional form of the game. Kings at 50 Dalton St in Back Bay (Mon 5pm–2am, Tues–Sun 11.30am–2am, over 21s after 6pm; ☏617/266-BOWL, ⊛www.backbaykings.com; Hynes **T**) is an upscale 16-lane bowling alley/bar usually packed to the rafters; Lucky Strike, inside Jillian's nightclub at 145 Ipswich St

(Mon–Sat 11am–2am, Sun noon–2am, over 18s after 8pm Mon–Thurs, over 21s after 8pm Fri–Sun; ☎ 617/437-0300, ⓦ www.luckystrikeboston.com; Kenmore **T**) is of the same sleek ilk.

Pool

There are plenty of places to shoot **pool** in the Boston area, and not just of the dive-y variety you'll invariably find in some of the city's more down-and-out bars. Flat Top Johnny's, at One Kendall Square in Cambridge (☎ 617/494-9565, ⓦ www.flattopjohnnys.com; Kendall **T**), pulls in a diverse young clientele to its casual environs. Felt, at 533 Washington St (☎ 617/350-5555; Downtown Crossing **T**) draws well-heeled scenesters and ardent pool players. The touristy Beantown Pub, 100 Tremont St (☎ 617/426-0111; Park Street **T**) offers adequate pool turf in the heart of Downtown.

Horse racing

While it's hardly the Kentucky Derby, East Boston's **Suffolk Downs** is a scenic, entertaining, and inexpensive ($2 admission fee) venue for throwing back a few beers with your friends; plus you'll hear a lot of Boston accents. Open from May to November, with four races a week in season. (☎ 617/567-3900, ⓦ www.suffolkdowns.com; Suffolk Downs **T**).

(18)

Kids' Boston

O ne of the best aspects of **travelling with kids** in Boston is the feeling that you're conducting an ongoing history lesson. While that may grow a bit tiresome for teens, younger children tend to eat up the colonial-period costumes, cannons and the like. Various points on the Freedom Trail are, of course, best for this, though getting out of the city to Lexington and Concord (see Chapter 20) will lead you along a similar path.

The city's **parks**, notably Boston Common, the Rose Kennedy Greenway, Franklin Park and the Public Garden – where you can ride the Swan Boats in the lagoon during summer, or climb on the sculpture Mrs Mallard and Her Eight Ducklings – make nice settings for an afternoon with the children, too. Boston Common in particular is known for its grandiose Tadpole Playground, complete with swings, jungle gym and kid-sized fountain. Wisteria-laden Christopher Columbus Park, right on the waterfront in the North End, is another good bet, with a splashy little fountain where kids can beat the heat on summer days. The best outdoor option, however, may be a Red Sox game at Fenway Park, as the country's oldest baseball stadium is easily reached by the **T** and games here are relatively affordable – if you can get tickets. **Harbour cruises** are also a fairly popular and unique way to see Boston, as is ascending to the top of one of the city's skyscrapers. There are, as well, a number of stellar **museums** in Boston aimed specifically at the younger set.

Two good family-oriented resources in town are the informative Ⓦ www.boston central.com, with listings on everything from arts and crafts to zoos and aquariums, and the *Boston Globe's* website (Ⓦ www.boston.com), the local go-to site for area listings and events.

Museums and sights

Though kids might not have **historical attractions** at the top of their list of favourite places, most of Boston's major **museums** manage to make the city's history palatable to youngsters. This is true at the USS *Constitution*, the old warship moored in the Charlestown Navy Yard (see p.72), and the **USS Constitution Museum**, where kids can test their seamanship skills in hands-on exhibits.

The **Children's Museum**, the **Museum of Science**, the **MIT Museum,** and the **Harvard Museum of Natural History** (p.58, p.83, p.131 & p.125 respectively) are four other places to let the little ones loose for a while; all provide a lot of interactive fun that's as easy for adults to get lost in as it is for kids. For animal sightings, the **Franklin Park Zoo** and the **New England Aquarium** (p.114 & p.57, respectively) can't be beaten. Finally, views from the dizzying heights of the Back Bay's **Prudential Tower** (p.91) are always sure to thrill.

Activities

For a different kind of education, America's oldest public boating set-up, Community Boating, 21 Embankment Rd (☎617/523-1038, ⓦwww.community-boating.org), between the Hatch Shell and Longfellow Bridge, offers youngsters aged 10 to 18 who can swim 75 yards the cheapest **sailing lessons** around – a mere dollar. The fee also allows summer-long access to the boathouse and entry to a number of one- to five-day classes, including kayaking and windsurfing.

If that seems like too much work, your children can learn things sitting down at the Museum of Science's **Charles Hayden Planetarium** and **Mugar Omni Theater** ($9, kids $7; ☎617/723-2500, ⓦwww.mos.org; Science Park **T**), which feature IMAX movies, laser shows set to the music of various rock and pop bands, and documentaries about cosmic phenomena that are screened onto a 57ft-high dome. Afterwards, the kids can check out the **Gilliland Observatory**, which, weather permitting, opens its roof and points its telescopes heavenwards on Friday nights (March to Nov, 8.30–10pm; free; ☎617/589-0267; Science Park **T**).

Another activity that makes learning fun is the **Museum of Fine Arts**' "Art Cart" (free with admission; July & Aug Wed 10am–8pm, Thurs & Sat 10am–4pm; Oct–June Sat & Sun 10am–4pm; ☎617/267-9300, ⓦwww.mfa.org; Museum **T**), which sets families up with tote bags full of museum-oriented goodies – drawing supplies, puzzles, Egyptian mysteries and the like – and then lets them loose in the museum. Check the website or call the museum directly for additional goings-on throughout the year. The last Saturday of each month is "Playdate" at the **Institute of Contemporary Art** (10am–4pm; free to up to two adults accompanied by children 12 and under; ☎617/478-3100, ⓦwww.icaboston.org; Courthouse Station **T**), when children hang out with artists, immerse themselves in creative play such as painting, designing, or sketching, and then let loose in an interactive performance on the ICA's phenomenal stage.

Shops

If and when the history starts to wear thin, there's always the failsafe of Boston's **malls** to divert the kids' attention (see p.189). To combine history with shopping, you could head to Faneuil Hall and Quincy Market, which are both hundreds of years old. One worthwhile store here is the **Build-A-Bear Workshop** (☎617/227-2478; Government Center **T**), where kids can pick out a teddy or doll, fill it with fluff, and then take it home in its own Cub Condo carrying case.

Red pops, warheads, and other delightful **candies** can be had at Irving's Toy and Candy Shop, 371 Harvard St, Brookline (☎617/566-9327; Coolidge Crossing **T**). If the kids are screaming for **ice cream**, load them up with home-made scoops of Hydrox cookie and cocoa pudding at Toscanini's, 899 Main St, Cambridge (☎617/491-5877; Central **T**), while you indulge in sophisticated flavours like burnt caramel and Earl Grey (there are a number of other standout ice cream purveyors in town; see p.146 for listings).

Few kids can resist Stella Bella (ⓦwww.stellabellatoys.com) at 1360 Cambridge St, Cambridge (☎617/491-6290; Harvard **T**), and 1967 Massachusetts Ave, Cambridge (☎617/864-6290; Porter **T**), one of the best **toy stores** in the area. Children are encouraged to sample the merchandise in a toy-strewn play space, while parents can kick back at the new parent's coffee hour on Fridays at 10.30am; Mondays have sing-along time at 11am. Another worthy toy store is Henry Bear's Park (ⓦwww.henrybear.com), whose extensive array of toys, games, and picture books has been pleasing families for over thirty years at 17 White St, Cambridge

Kids' tours

Boston Duck Tours ⊤617/723-3825, ⓦ www.bostonducktours.com. See p.27.

Boston Harbor Cruises May–Nov ⊤617/227-4321, ⓦ www.bostonharborcruises.com. Themed harbour cruises (including one to Boston Light) in addition to rides on *Codzilla*, a madcap speedboat with wild steering and a toothy grin.

Boston by Little Feet May–Oct Mon & Sat 10am, Sun 2pm; $8; ⊤617/367-2345, ⓦ www.bostonbyfoot.org; State St ⊤. One-hour Freedom Trail walk for ages 6 to 12. Tours begin in front of the statue of Samuel Adams at Faneuil Hall and include a map and kids' Explorer's Guide.

Boston Gliders Segway $60; ⊤1-866/611-9838, ⓦ www.bostongliders.com. Cruise Boston's pavements on your own set of wheels.

Freedom Trail Players July–Aug daily, call for times; $11, kids $6; ⊤617/227-8800, ⓦ www.thefreedomtrail.org. This troupe dresses in colonial garb and acts out Revolutionary historiana along the trail; tours last ninety minutes.

Liberty Schooner June–Sept noon, 3pm & 6pm; $30, kids $15; ⊤617/742-0333, ⓦ www.libertyfleet.com. This 125ft-tall ship departs from Long Wharf and sails for two hours around Boston's Harbor Islands.

New England Aquarium April–Oct daily, times vary; $40, kids $32; ⊤617/973-5200, ⓦ www.neaq.org. Three- to four-hour whale-watching excursions into the harbour.

(⊤617/547-8424, Porter **T**) and 19 Harvard St, Brookline Village (⊤617/264-2422; Brookline Village **T**).

Pixie Stix' petite boutique, 131 Charles St (⊤617/523-3211, Charles/MGH **T**) is a stylish godsend for girls in their tween years, with **clothes** that strike the right balance between cool-enough-for-school and parent approved. The Red Wagon has good duds and toys for the younger set at 69 Charles St (⊤617/523-9402, Charles/MGH **T**). Lester Harry's, at 115 Newbury St is the place to go in town for coo-worthy (albeit pricey) baby clothes (⊤617/927-5400, Copley **T**).

There's no shortage of **bookstores** catering to children in Boston either; the Children's Book Shop (237 Washington St, Brookline (⊤617/734-7323, ⓦ www .thechildrensbookshop.net; Brookline Village **T**), Curious George Goes to Wordsworth, 1 JFK St (⊤617/498-0062, ⓦ www.curiousg.com; Harvard **T**) and Barefoot Books, 2067 Massachusetts Ave, Cambridge (⊤617/576-0660, ⓦ www .barefoot-books.com; Porter **T**), are sure to have the latest titles, and others you didn't know existed. For **board games**, look no further than Eureka Puzzles, 1349 Beacon St, Brookline (⊤617/738-7352; Coolidge Corner **T**), a nostalgic speciality shop that's filled with cordless brain entertainment.

Theatre, puppet shows and other entertainment

If you want to get the tots some (kindergarten) culture, try the Boston Children's Theatre, 316 Huntington Ave (in the YMCA; ⊤617/424-6634, ⓦ www.boston childrenstheatre.org), whose productions of kids' classics are performed at the Grand Lodge of Masons, 186 Tremont St. Otherwise, head out to Brookline for the Puppet Showplace Theatre, 32 Station St (generally Wed & Thurs 10.30am, Sat & Sun 1pm & 3pm; ⊤617/731-6400, ⓦ www.puppetshowplace.org); tickets are $10 a head, big or small. While adults will probably find it corney, kids in the 7–13 age range go bonkers for Tomb at 5Wits, 186 Brookline Ave ($20, kids $16; ⊤617/375-9487, ⓦ www.5-wits.com), an Indiana Jones-esque "adventure experience" that leads problem-solving participants through a faux-Egyptian dig site.

Festivals and events

t's always good to know ahead of time what **festivals** or **annual events** are scheduled to coincide with your trip to Boston – though even if you don't plan it, there's likely to be some sort of parade, public celebration or seasonal shindig going on. For detailed information, call the Boston Convention and Visitors Bureau (☎1-888/SEE-BOSTON, ⓦwww.bostonusa.com) or check out the *Boston Globe's* helpful website (ⓦwww.boston.com); for a look at public holidays in Boston, see p.34.

The schedule below is not meant to be exhaustive but picks out some of the more fun and notable events happening throughout the year. If you're looking for specific **highlights**, note that a few nationwide events more or less reach their apotheosis here, such as St Patrick's Day (March) and Independence Day (July); tops in Boston-only happenings include the Boston Marathon (April), the Head of the Charles Regatta (Oct) and the Boston Tea Party Re-enactment (Dec).

January

First Night Jan 1. The New Year's celebration begins on New Year's Eve but carries into the first day of the year; see "December", below.

Chinese New Year Usually late Jan ☎1-888/SEE-BOSTON. Dragon parades and firecrackers punctuate the festivities throughout Chinatown. The New Year can fall in Feb, too, depending on the Chinese lunar calendar.

Moby Dick Marathon First weekend ☎508/997-0046. Non-stop read-aloud of the seaman's classic *Moby Dick*, held in the New Bedford Whaling Museum (see p.225). It takes about 25hrs to complete the tome; light whaleship fare, such as grog, helps propel you through the night.

February

The Beanpot First two Mondays ⓦwww .beanpothockey.com. Popular college hockey tournament, between Boston University Harvard, Boston College and Northeastern.

March

St Patrick's Day Parade and Festival Sun closest to March 17 ☎1-888/SEE-BOSTON. Boston's substantial Irish-American community, along with much of the rest of the city, turns out for this parade through South Boston (see Chapter 8) and buzzes with Irish folk music, dance and food. March 17 also happens to be "Evacuation Day," or the anniversary of the day that George Washington drove the British out of Boston during the Revolutionary

War, which gives Bostonians another excuse to tie one on.

New England Spring Flower Show Second or third week in March ☎617/933-4900, Ⓦwww.masshort.org. Winter-weary Bostonians turn out in droves to gawk at hothouse greenery in this week-long horticultural fest. Tickets cost $20.

April

Boston Marathon Third Mon ☎ 617/236-1652, Ⓦwww.bostonmarathon.org. Runners from all over the world gather for this 26.2-mile affair, one of America's premier athletic events. It crosses all over the Boston area, ending in Back Bay's Copley Square.

Patriots' Day Third Mon ☎781/862-1450. A celebration and re-creation of Paul Revere's famous ride from the North End to Lexington that alerted locals that the British army had been deployed to confiscate rebel armaments.

Independent Film Festival Last week in April Ⓦwww.iffboston.org. New England's biggest film Festival, IFFBoston screens over 120 features, documentaries and shorts – many followed by a Q&A with the director – in the city's art-house cinemas.

May

Lilac Sunday Third Sun ☎617/524-1718, Ⓦwww.arboretum.harvard.edu. You can view more than three hundred lilac varieties in full bloom at the Arnold Arboretum during this early summer event – a Boston institution.

June

Jimmy Fund Scooper Bowl First week ☎1-888/SEE-BOSTON. For a modest donation of around $8, you're allowed unlimited samples of the city's best ice creams.

Boston Pride Festival First week ☎617/262-9405, Ⓦwww.bostonpride.org. The celebration kicks off with a rainbow flag-raising at City Hall and culminates a week later with a gay pride parade, festival and block parties.

Dragon Boat Festival Variable weekend in early June Ⓦwww.bostondragonboat.org. A colourful Chinese festival whose highlight, dragon boat racing on the Charles River, is accompanied by the thundering sound of Taiko drums.

Bunker Hill Day Sun nearest June 17 ☎617/242-5601. The highlight of this festival in Charlestown is the parade celebrating the Battle of Bunker Hill (even though the bout was lost by the Americans).

Cambridge River Festival Third week ☎617/349-4380, Ⓦwww.cambridgema.gov/CAC. Memorial Drive is closed off from JFK St to Western Avenue for music shows, dancing and eclectic food offerings, all along the Charles River.

Boston Early Music Festival Every odd-numbered year ☎617/661-1812, Ⓦwww.bemf.org. This huge, week-long Renaissance fair with a strong music theme includes concerts and exhibitions throughout town.

July

Harborfest Late June to weekend nearest July 4 ☎617/227-1528, Ⓦwww.bostonharborfest .com. Includes a series of concerts on the waterfront (mostly jazz, blues and rock), and the competitive "Chowderfest," where area restaurants compete for the "Boston's Best Chowder" crown.

Boston Pops Concert and Fireworks July 4 ☎1-888-4th-POPS, Ⓦwww.july4th.org. The Boston Pops' wildly popular annual evening concert in the Oval area, in front of the Hatch Shell, is followed by thirty minutes of flashy pyrotechnics; people sometimes line up at dawn in order to get good seats.

Reading of the Declaration of Independence
July 4 ☎617/242-5642. Pretend it's July 4th, 1776, by attending the annual reading of the nation's founding document from the balcony of Old State House; the party continues on with speeches over at Faneuil Hall.

USS Constitution Turn-Around July 4
☎617/242-5601. Old Ironsides pulls up anchor and sails out (briefly) into Boston Harbor in this annual event that's a salute to the country's independence (and the ship's vitality).

Italian Feasts Throughout July and Aug
☎1-888/SEE-BOSTON. Features food and music throughout the North End; during the parades, locals pin dollar bills to the floats and statues of patron saints that are borne through the streets.

Shakespeare on the Common End of July to mid-Aug ⊕commshakes.org. It wouldn't be summer without the Common's free Shakespeare performances, held out in the elements or under the stars. Get there early for seats or bring a picnic blanket and snacks.

August

August Moon Festival Near the end of Aug
☎617/350-6303 ⊕www.chinatownmainstreet.org. During this festival, Chinatown's merchants and restaurateurs hawk their wares on the street amid dragon parades and firecrackers.

September

Arts Festival of Boston Around Labor Day weekend ☎617/635-3911, ⊕www.bostonartsfestival.com. Boston is transformed into a giant gallery, with three days of exhibits, arts and crafts pavilions, fashion shows, evening galas, receptions and outdoor musical performances at various locations.

Boston Film Festival Mid-Sept ☎617/523-8388. Week-long festival screening flashy major releases alongside independent shorts and documentaries with frequent discussions by directors and screenwriters.

BeanTown Jazz Festival Third week
☎617/747-3034, ⊕www.beantownjazz.org. Run by the Berklee College of Music, this ten-day festival offers free and ticketed (up to $30) jazz, Latin, blues and groove shows in venues around the South End and greater Boston.

Boston Fashion Week Late Sept to early Oct
⊕www.bostonfashionweek.com. Nothing on London, Paris, New York or Milan, but there are some fun events celebrating local designers.

October

Oktoberfest Early Oct ☎617/491-3434,
⊕www.harvardsquare.com. The usual beer, sauerkraut and live entertainment in Harvard Square, done Boston style – meaning the hops-fuelled shenanigans end at 6pm. If you're looking for a wilder time, head to the Harpoon Brewery's fest in the Seaport District (T1-888/HAR-POON ext. 3; $20).

Columbus Day Parade Second Mon
☎1-888/SEE-BOSTON. Kicked off by a

Open studios

Each fall, the **Boston Open Studios Coalition** arranges for local artists to showcase their paintings, pottery, photographs and other works of art to the public, on a neighbourhood-by-neighbourhood basis. Exhibitors include the United South End Artists (☎617/267-8862), the Jamaica Plain Artists (☎617/855-5767), ACT Roxbury (☎617/541-3900) and the Fort Point Arts Community (☎617/423-4299). Check ⊕www.cityofboston.gov/arts for listings.

ceremony at City Hall at 1pm, the raucous, Italian-flavoured parade continues into the heart of the North End.

Head of the Charles Regatta Penultimate weekend ☏617/868-6200, ⊛www.hocr.org. Hordes of locals and college students descend on the banks of the Charles River between Central and Harvard squares, ostensibly to watch the crew races, but also to picnic and pal around.

Pumpkin Festival Third Sat ☏617/635-4455 ⊛www.lifeisgood.com. The upbeat T-shirt company "Life is Good" rallies locals to

carve for a cause – Camp Sunshine – and attempts to beat its own mind-boggling record of lit up jack-o-lanterns (30,128). **Salem Haunted Happenings/Halloween ☏1-877/725-3662, ⊛www.hauntedhappenings .org.** Throughout Oct, Salem features autumnal, Halloween and witch-themed events up to and including the 31st; it all culminates with a costume ball and fireworks. A fun and easy day trip (via train – the traffic is terrible at this time of year) from Boston.

November

Annual Lighting Ceremony Late Nov ☏1-888/ SEE-BOSTON. Faneuil Hall Marketplace kick-starts the holiday season with the annual lighting of some 300,000 festive bulbs. **Thanksgiving Weekend before Thanksgiving ☏1-800/USA-1620, ⊛www.usathanksgiving.com.**

In Plymouth, Massachusetts, the first Thanks-giving ever is commemorated with parades, drum and bugle music and traditional feasts. For a celebration on the actual holiday (complete with trimmings), head to nearby Plimoth Plantation (⊛www.plimoth.org).

December

Boston Tea Party Re-enactment Sun nearest Dec 16 ☏617/482-6439 or 1-888/SEE-BOSTON. A lusty re-enactment of the march from Old South Meeting House to the harbour, and the subsequent tea-dumping that helped spark the American Revolution. **First Night Dec 31–Jan 1 ☏617/542-1399, ⊛www.firstnight.org.** A family-friendly festival

to ring in the New Year, featuring parades, ice sculptures, art shows, harbour cruises and live music throughout Downtown and Back Bay; culminates in a spectacular fireworks display over Boston Harbor. A button, granting admission to all events, tends to run around $18.

Out of
the City

Out of the City

Around Boston

W hile there's enough of interest in Boston itself to keep you going for several days at the very least, the city lies at the centre of a region concentrated with historic sights, and there's plenty to see and do within a relatively short distance. Perhaps the best inland day-trip you (or history buffs, at least) can make within a 25-mile radius of Boston is to the revolutionary battlegrounds of **Lexington** and **Concord**, but the city also makes an excellent base for visiting the numerous quaint and historic towns that line the North Shore of the Massachusetts coast. With its gruesome witch trials, **Salem**, around thirty minutes by train from North Station, is often travellers' first place of interest, and there's much more there besides, notably sights highlighting its prosperous days as a major port. Nearby **Marblehead** is pretty enough to merit a wander, too, if lacking any real must-sees; after a short stop there, you can continue on to the more rustic **Gloucester**, the setting of Sebastian Junger's book *The Perfect Storm*, and **Rockport**, an upscale seaside enclave with a great lobster shack and (surprisingly) Austrian strudel. Rte-1 is the quickest way up the coast, though coastal Rte-1A is more scenic. **Buses** run up this direction as well, operated both by the MBTA and by independent tour companies (see p.28) as does the MBTA commuter rail, with **trains** leaving regularly from Boston's North Station, on the Orange and Green lines.

On the South Shore, the 1627 Pilgrim village of **Plymouth** is the main tourist draw, though it has little to offer other than recreations of Pilgrim settlements and the vessel that brought them here, the *Mayflower II*. Further south, the famous old whaling port of **New Bedford** served as inspiration for Herman Melville's *Moby Dick*; today, the town docks ferries headed for Martha's Vineyard, and its salty wharves and cobblestoned streets still make for a worthy visit.

More removed from the greater Boston area, the peninsula of **Cape Cod** and its two sisters, the islands of **Nantucket** and **Martha's Vineyard**, are too far out for day-tripping; Chapters 21, 22 and 23 are devoted to this longstanding haunt of sun and sand.

Lexington and Concord

The serene New England towns of **Lexington** and **Concord**, almost always mentioned in the same breath, trade on their notoriety as the locations of the first armed confrontation with the British at the start of the American Revolution. Lexington is mostly suburban, while Concord, five miles west, is even sleepier, with a more bucolic feeling. Most of the towns' historical quarters have been incorporated into the **Minute Man National Park**, which takes in the Lexington Battle Green, North Bridge and much of Battle Road, the route the British followed on their retreat from Concord to Boston. These famous battles are evoked in a piecemeal but enthusiastic fashion throughout the park, with scale models, remnant musketry and the odd preserved bullet hole, all set amidst the area's pretty leafy environs. It's worth noting that, although beautiful at all times of the year, New England winters can put a damper on a trip out to the Lexington-Concord region – most of its major historical sites are closed come snow.

Just beyond the park's boundary lies another literary sight, **Walden Pond**, transcendental stomping ground for Henry David Thoreau, and now a beloved swimming hole. The whimsical **DeCordova Museum and Sculpture Park**, just over the town border in Lincoln, is very much worth a visit. Unfortunately, despite being accessible from Boston by train, a car or a tour bus is really necessary to visit the two towns, due to the distances between sites and the lack of decent public transport. That said, the best way to get around is via the Liberty Ride (June–Oct daily 10am–4.30pm; $25; ☎781/862-0500 ext.702, ⓦwww.libertyride.us), a hop-on, hop-off trolley tour that takes in the majority of the area's historical and literary sites, and is led by well-informed guides. While its route technically begins at the National Heritage Museum in Lexington, it's possible to take the commuter rail from North Station in Boston into Concord Station ($6.25 one-way); from there it's a ten-minute walk to the Liberty Ride stop in Concord centre.

Some history

On April 19, 1775, the first battle of the **American Revolution** began here when British troops marched to Concord to seize American munitions. Although the British had hoped to keep their plan of confiscation quiet; word of the operation had spread, and the American "Minute Men" – so called because they were prepared to fight at a moment's notice – were equipped with well-rehearsed plans for a British incursion. When the British set out from Boston Common, Paul Revere and William Dawes set out on separate routes to sound the alarm. Within minutes, church bells were clanging and cannons roaring throughout the countryside signalling the rebels to head for Lexington Green; hundreds more converged around the North Bridge area of Concord. Revere managed to give the final alarm to a sleeping John Hancock and Samuel Adams (who were in town to attend a provincial congress) at the Hancock-Clarke House.

John Parker, the colonial captain, was down the street at the Buckman Tavern, when he received word that the British were closing in on the Green. "Don't fire unless fired upon", he ordered the men, "but if they mean to have a war, let it begin here". With only 77 Americans pitted against 700 British regulars, it was more a show of resolve than a hope for victory. Who fired the first shot remains a mystery, but in the fracas that followed, eight Americans were killed, including Parker (the soldiers who died here are buried in a particularly affecting memorial at the northwest end of the Green). One wounded soldier crawled across the road to his home, only to die at his wife's feet – the still-standing house, on the corner of Harrington Road and Bedford Street, displays a commemorative plaque (Harrington Road is named after him). The British suffered no casualties, and marched three miles west to Concord.

By the time they arrived, it was already after sunrise on April 19, and hundreds more Minute Men had amassed on a farm behind North Bridge near where the lion's share of munitions were stored. When British officers began burning military supplies, the Americans saw the smoke and thought their houses were being torched. They fired on the British guarding the other side of the bridge – the "shots heard round the world", as history books have it. The British were now outnumbered four to one, and suffered heavily in the ensuing battle, which continued all the way back to Boston.

Lexington

The main thing to see in **LEXINGTON** is the wide-open space called **Battle Green**. The land serves as the town's common and is fronted by Henry Kitson's iconic *Minute Man* statue. This imposing bronze figure (popularly assumed to be that of Captain John Parker) is depicted bearing a musket, was built in 1899, and stands on boulders dislodged from the stone walls behind which the colonial militia fired at their British opponents on April 19, 1775.

On the eastern periphery of the green, the **visitor's centre** (daily: April–Nov 9am–5pm; Dec–March 10am–4pm, free; ℡781/862-1450, ⓦwww.lexington chamber.org) has a diorama that shows the detail of the battle and a helpful staff that can orient you historically and geographically. Facing the green, the **Buckman Tavern** (April–Oct daily 10am–4pm; tours every half-hour; $6; ℡781/862-5598, ⓦwww.lexingtonhistory.org), an eighteenth-century bar and hostelry that served as the Minute Men's headquarters while awaiting news of British incursion, looks like a typical pub, right down to its seven-foot-wide fireplace and lengthy tap bar on the first floor; the only bonafide vestige of revolutionary activity is the hole from a British bullet that's been preserved in an inner door near the taproom.

A couple of blocks north, at 36 Hancock St, a plaque affixed to the marigold, two-storey **Hancock-Clarke House** (June–Oct daily 10am–4pm; April to late May Sat & Sun 10am–4pm; tours hourly $6; ℡781/861-0928) solemnly reminds us that this is where "Samuel Adams and John Hancock were sleeping when aroused by Paul Revere"; the latter was the grandson of Reverend John Hancock, the man for whom the house was built in 1698. Exhibits on the free-admission museum floor include the drum on which William Diamond beat the signal for the Minute Men to converge and the pistols that British Major John Pitcairn lost on the retreat from Concord. Less interesting is the small wooden **Munroe Tavern**, somewhat removed from the town centre at 1332 Massachusetts Ave (June–Oct daily noon–4pm; April to late May Sat & Sun noon–4pm; tours hourly $6; ℡781/862-0295), which served as a field hospital for British soldiers, though for a mere hour and a half only. If you intend to visit all three sights, you'll save a bit by getting a combination ticket ($10), available at any of the three.

Just outside of Lexington town, a contemporary brick-and-glass building houses the unfairly overlooked **National Heritage Museum**, 33 Marrett Rd (Tues–Sat 10am–4.30pm, Sun noon–4.30pm; free; ⓦwww.monh.org), which has rotating displays on all facets of American history, daily life and culture; standouts include an amusing collection of cuckoo clocks, nostalgic board games and toys and a permanent exhibit on the battle events of Lexington.

If you need to **stay** in town, *aloft* at 727 Marrett Rd (℡781/761-1700, ⓦwww .starwoodhotels.com; $125) was created by *W Hotels* and features the sleek contemporary design and accoutrements (wi-fi, cable TV, Bliss soaps) for which the brand is known. Next door, its sister property, *Element*, is great for long-term stays, with spacious, eco-savvy rooms that come equipped with full-size kitchens (℡781/761-1750, ⓦwww.starwoodhotels.com; $155). If you're looking to have a **meal**, try *Via Lago*, 1845 Massachusetts Ave (℡781/861-6174), a casual counter-service spot that's good for fresh pastas, sandwiches and salads at lunch time; come nightfall, dinner is served by candlelight and a relaxed local crowd seeks sanctuary at the wooden bar. The *Upper Crust*, 41 Waltham St (℡781/274-0089), is a tasty outpost of the popular Boston pizza chain; after your meal, head down the block for home-made ice cream at *Rancatore's*, 1752 Massachusetts Ave (℡781/862-5090).

Concord

One of the few sizable inland towns of New England at the time of the Revolution, **CONCORD**, a fifteen-minute drive on Rte-2A west of Lexington, and a forty-minute train ride ($6.25 one-way) from Boston's North Station, retains a pleasant country atmosphere. Trains arrive at Concord Station, about half a mile from the city centre, and within walking distance of the rambling **Colonial Inn** (T 978/369-2373, W www.concordscolonialinn.com; $200), near the corner of Main and Monument streets. After a morning spent denouncing eighteenth-century British rule, it's customary to indulge in a quintessential British activity here – high tea – in its historic digs (reservations recommended for tea; $11–25). The inn also has a traditional dining room and a tavern that served as a makeshift revolutionary hospital during the war.

From the top of **Hill Burying Ground** to the west, you can survey Concord, as did Major Pitcairn when the Americans amassed on the far side of North Bridge. A few blocks behind it on Rte-62 is **Sleepy Hollow Cemetery** – though not the one of headless horsemen fame, which is located far from here in the Hudson River Valley. You will, however, find eminent Concord literati Emerson, Hawthorne, Thoreau and Louisa May Alcott buried atop the graveyard's "Author's Ridge", as signs clearly indicate. Fun fact: although the stones state that Sophia and Una Hawthorne are buried in Kensal Green, England, they were actually re-interred here in 2006 after their gravestones were, in a grand twist of fate, ruined by a hawthorn tree.

Concord Museum

A good place for orienting yourself with regards to Concord's literary and historical scene is the absorbing **Concord Museum**, at the intersection of the Cambridge Turnpike and Lexington Road (Jan–March Mon–Sat 11am–4pm, Sun 1–4pm; April–Dec Mon–Sat 9am–5pm, Sun noon–5pm; June, July & Aug Sun 9am–5pm; $10; T 978/369-9763, W www.concordmuseum.org). Located on the former site of Ralph Waldo Emerson's apple orchard, the museum houses nineteen galleries filled chock-a-block with prime cultural artefacts. One such prize is the famed "one, if by land, two, if by sea" signal lantern, hung from the Old North Church in Boston to warn of the impending British march at the outset of the Revolutionary War. If that's not enough to wow you, the museum also houses the entire personal study of Ralph Waldo Emerson, as well as Henry David Thoreau's personal effects, including the unassuming little green desk on which he wrote *Civil Disobedience* and *Walden*. Look closely at its keyhole; worn around the edges, you can tell Thoreau locked up his manuscript when guests came by.

Minute Man Historical Park and Old Manse

The best way get your Revolutionary War bearings in the area is to begin at the **Minute Man Visitor Center**, where Rte-2A intersects with Airport Road (daily: April to late-Oct 9am–5pm; Nov 9am–4pm; free; T 978/369-6993, W www.nps.gov/mima). Helpful rangers here will fill you in with a 24-minute film, and lead you to facts and maps directing you further down the five-mile "Battle Road Scenic Byway" (the April 19, 1775 route upon which 3500 British Regulars fought 1700 colonial militiamen; the Brits were later forced to retreat back to Boston on this same path). One highlight of the trail, just a bit west on Rte-2A from the visitor's centre, is the **Paul Revere Capture Site**, where, amidst a humble circle of stones a solemn plaque decrees "April 19, 1775, 1.30 am: at this point on the Old Concord road…ended the midnight ride of Paul Revere". Revere's horse was taken from him, and as he walked into Lexington he was just in time to hear the first shots of the American Revolution. It's worth stopping by **Hartwell Tavern** (west on Rte-2A) which still has its original 1733 brick and floorboards, for a chat with informative park rangers and the chance to witness a real-live musket firing demonstration (late-May to late-Oct daily 11.15am, 2.15pm, 3.15pm & 4.15pm; free); costumed rangers fire off a ¾ inch lead ball with help from their trusty seventeenth-century Brown Bess musket. The Minute Man Park culminates at the most hyped spot in Concord – **North Bridge** – the site of the first effective armed resistance to British rule in America. If you take the traditional approach from Monument Street, you'll be following the route the British took. Just before crossing the bridge, an inscription on the mass grave of some British regulars reads, "They came 3000 miles and died to keep the past upon its throne". The bridge itself, however, looks a bit too well-preserved to provoke much sentiment, and no wonder – it's actually the fifth replica of yet another replica of the original structure.

A stone's throw from North Bridge, the grey-clapboard **Old Manse**, at 269 Monument St (mid-April to Oct Mon–Sat 10am–5pm, Sun noon–5pm; guided tours only, every 30min; $8; ☎978/369-3909, ⊛www.oldmanse.org), was built for Ralph Waldo Emerson's grandfather, the Reverend William Emerson, who witnessed the hostilities from his window. The younger Emerson lived here on and off, and, in 1834, penned *Nature* here, the book that signalled the beginning of the Transcendentalist movement. Of the numerous rooms in the house, all with period furnishings intact, the most interesting is the small upstairs study, where Nathaniel Hawthorne, a resident of the house in the early 1840s, wrote *Mosses from an Old Manse*, a rather obscure essay that gave the place its name. Hawthorne passed three happy years here (although later getting evicted for non-payment of rent) shortly after getting married to his wife, Sophia, who, following a miscarriage, used her diamond wedding ring to etch the words "Man's accidents are God's purposes" into a window pane in the study. Another point of interest can be found on the first floor, where there's a framed swath of original English-made wallpaper with the British "paper tax" mark stamped on the back.

The Wayside

Another literary landmark, **The Wayside**, is east of the town centre at 455 Lexington Rd (April–Oct Wed–Sun 9.30am–5.30pm, last tour at 4.30pm; $5; ☎978/318-7825). The 300-year-old yellow wooden house was once home to both the Alcotts and the Hawthornes, though at different times. Louisa May Alcott's girlhood experiences here formed the basis for *Little Women* (though she actually penned the novel next door at the Orchard House, where the family lived from 1858 to 1867; there are tours here April to late-Oct daily 10am–4:30pm, Sun from 1pm, Nov to late-March Mon–Fri 11am–3pm, Sat 10am–4.30pm and Sun 1–4.30pm; $9; ☎978/369-4118, ⊛www.louisamayalcott.org). Among the antique furnishings, the most unusual is the slanted writing desk at which Hawthorne toiled standing up.

When hunger strikes, you can try the *Cheese Shop*, 29 Walden St (☎978/369-5778), a great place to stop for deluxe picnic fixings from paté and jellies to all manner of cheeses; locals swear by its "Friday Night Gourmet Dinner Club" – $75 for a three-course gourmet meal including wine (place your order by Wed to get in on the action). Over by the train station, *La Provence*, 105 Thoreau St (☎978/371-7428), is the place to go for authentic French **cooking** in an ultra-casual setting; great take-out options abound here as well. Top it all off with a sundae from *Bedford Farms* (☎978/341-0000), just across the street at no. 68, a quintessential New England ice cream purveyor that's been churning out the sweet stuff since 1880.

Walden Pond and DeCordova Sculpture Park and Museum

The tranquillity that Thoreau sought and savoured at **Walden Pond**, just two miles south of Concord proper off Rte-126 (daily dawn–dusk; $5 parking; ☎978/369-3254), is still present today – although now you'll have to share it with the happy sunbathers and hikers who pour in to retrace his footsteps. The pond has remained much the same since the author's famed two-year exercise in self-sufficiency began in 1845. "I did not feel crowded or confined in the least", he wrote of his life in the simple log cabin; and, though his semi-fictionalized account of the experience might have you believing otherwise, Thoreau hardly roughed it, taking regular walks into town to stock up on amenities and receiving frequent visitors at his single-room house.

The reconstructed **cabin**, complete with a journal open on its rustic desk, is situated near the parking lot (you'll have to content yourself with peering through the windows), while the site of the original structure, closer to the shores of the pond, is a peaceful spot commemorated with stones placed by visitors. The water looks best at dawn, when the pond still "throws off its nightly clothing of mist"; late-risers will still find it all quite lovely, however, and should come equipped with a swimsuit and comfortable shoes to maximize their transcendental experience.

Though technically a part of the town of Lincoln, the **DeCordova Sculpture Park and Museum**, 51 Sandy Pond Rd (Tues–Sun 10am–5pm; $12, sculpture park free when museum is closed; ☎781/259-8355, ⓦwww.decordova.org), is only a few miles south of downtown Concord and very much worth a visit. All manner of contemporary sculpture peppers the museum's expansive grounds, but most fascinating are the bigger works, like Jim Dine's *Two Big Black Hearts* and Paul Matisse's *Musical Fence*, which look like they've burst through the walls of a museum and tumbled into their present positions; Matisse's piece is interactive – tap it with a wooden stick like you would a xylophone. Most of the sculptures are by American (and in particular New England) artists, and are sufficiently impressive to make the **garden** overshadow the small on-site museum, whose rotating special exhibits are often just as eye-catching, with an emphasis on contemporary multimedia art.

Salem

Historic **SALEM**, easily accessed from Boston by both the North Station commuter rail station ($5.25 one-way) and by a 45-minute ferry from Central Wharf (by the Aquarium; ☎978/741-0220, ⓦwww.salemferry.com; $19 round-trip), is a great afternoon excursion from the city. Just sixteen miles from Boston on 128N, this quaint little town belies its grisly past, as the scene of the horrific **witch trials** of 1692, when Puritan self-righteousness reached its apogee. The place uses the stigma to its advantage by hyping up the correlating spookiness, especially around **Halloween**, which, despite some of the cheesiness on offer, is a great time to visit. Around the holiday, sites are open longer, myriad special events, talks and walking tours are held, and you get the chance to do some leaf-peeping during New England's spectacular fall season (ⓦwww.hauntedhappenings.org).

To gather **information**, head to the helpful Salem National Visitor's Center, at 2 New Liberty St (daily 9am–5pm; ☎978/740-1650, ⓦsalem.org), which also serves as the Salem Heritage Trail's unofficial starting point; you'll find public bathrooms here, too.

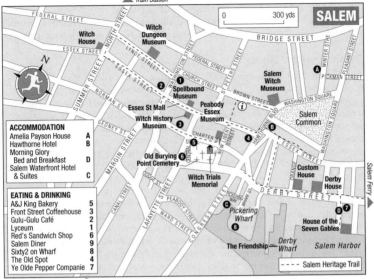

Map legend:

Train Station

SALEM

0 — 300 yds

BRIDGE STREET

FEDERAL STREET
Witch House
Witch Dungeon Museum
NORTH STREET
LYNDE STREET
ESSEX STREET
CHURCH STREET
FEDERAL STREET
ST PETERS STREET
BROWN STREET
WINTER STREET
PLEASANT STREET
PICKMAN STREET
Salem Witch Museum
A
WASHINGTON SQUARE
Salem Common
Spellbound Museum **1**
Essex St Mall
Peabody Essex Museum
Witch History Museum **3**
GEDNEY ST
MARGIN STREET
CHARTER
NEW LIBERTY STREET
4
5
B
HAWTHORNE BLVD
ESSEX STREET
Old Burying Point Cemetery **6**
Witch Trials Memorial
DODGE ST
Custom House
ORANGE STREET
Derby House
CANAL STREET
LAFAYETTE ST
PEABODY STREET
WARD STREET
DERBY STREET
C Pickering Wharf
8
House of the Seven Gables **D** **7**
The Friendship — Derby Wharf
Salem Harbor
Salem Ferry
- - - - Salem Heritage Trail

ACCOMMODATION

Amelia Payson House	A
Hawthorne Hotel	B
Morning Glory Bed and Breakfast	D
Salem Waterfront Hotel & Suites	C

EATING & DRINKING

A&J King Bakery	5
Front Street Coffeehouse	3
Gulu-Gulu Café	2
Lyceum	1
Red's Sandwich Shop	6
Salem Diner	9
Sixty2 on Wharf	8
The Old Spot	4
Ye Olde Pepper Companie	7

Accommodation

Salem is full of small **B&Bs** – some with no more than three rooms – in old historic houses with steep staircases. It is perhaps the only town in America where **hotels** are booked for Halloween months in advance; if you plan on coming any time in October, beware of high prices and full houses.

Amelia Payson House 16 Winter St ☎978/744-8304, ⊛www.ameliapaysonhouse .com. A sweet little B&B in a restored 1845 Greek Revival house run by friendly and accommodating owners. The rooms are clean and not too frilly, with wi-fi and snacks available. You'll eat a tasty breakfast in the morning set on pretty floral china. From $125.

Hawthorne Hotel 18 Washington Square W ☎978/744-4080, ⊛www.hawthornehotel.com. Built in 1925, this restored hotel, furnished with eighteenth-century reproduction furniture, is *the* place to stay in Salem. The 89 rooms are smart and comfortable, with iPod docks, wi-fi and flat-screen TVs. An adjoining four-room B&B and two restaurants are also on site. Free parking, too (a big plus around here). $129–259.

Morning Glory Bed and Breakfast 22 Hardy St ☎978/741-1703, ⊛www.morningglorybb.com. This three-room B&B down by the water (and the House of Seven Gables) has a friendly owner and a roof deck with water views. From $125.

Salem Waterfront Hotel & Suites 225 Derby St ☎978/740-8788, ⊛www.salemwaterfronthotel .com. This Best Western newcomer adds 86 much-needed rooms to Salem. Standard large hotel fare, with minimalist design, heated indoor pool, free wi-fi and prices to match. About $150.

The Town

Less known than its witch trials past were the many years Salem spent as a flourishing seaport (in 1790 it was the sixth biggest city in the country), and the remnants from this era only add to the town's aura, with abandoned wharves, rows of stately sea captains' homes and an astounding display of riches at the **Peabody Essex Museum**.

Today, the 1.7-mile **Salem Heritage Trail** (modelled after Boston's Freedom Trail, marked by a strip of red paint and all) links the town's principal historic sights, the majority of which are tied to the town's gruesome witch-hanging days.

Salem's witch sights

The **Salem Witch Museum**, 19½ Washington Square (daily 10am–5pm, July & Aug till 7pm; $8.50; ☎978/744-1692, ⊛www.salemwitchmuseum.com), provides some (kitschy) orientation on the witch trials. Its self-billing as a multimedia sound-and-light show makes it sound grander than it actually is: wax figures are used to depict the hysteria, a Darth Vader-esque voice narrates the show and, thanks to the museum's circular seating arrangement, there are significant portions of the performance where you can't actually see what's happening. Nonetheless, that it's housed in a suitably spooky former Romanesque church enhances the atmosphere, and it's still better and more official than the other "witch museums" in town – you'll learn that before the hysteria subsided nineteen were hanged, one man was pressed to death and hundreds of New England residents sent to jail where they had to pay for the food they ate; Salem citizen Rebecca Nurse was even charged for the chains she wore. In front of the museum is the imposing statue of a caped **Roger Conant**, founder of the town's original 1626 Puritan settlement, which was called Naumkeag after the eponymous river; the name was changed to Salem – a bastardization of "shalom" (meaning peace) – in 1629.

Salem's downtown thoroughfare, the car-free Essex Street Pedestrian Mall, is full of museums and boutiques selling witch-related paraphernalia with varying degrees of tact and taste. The **Spellbound Museum**, 192 Essex St (April–Nov 10am–7.30pm; Dec–March call for hours; $10; ☎978/745-0138, ⊛www.spellboundtours.com), is one of the best museums in town and displays a range of curios from around the world, like shrunken heads, vampire killing kits and tools used by practitioners of voodoo. The museum also hosts an entertaining evening ghost-hunting tour (daily 8pm; $13) around the town's supposedly haunted sights; visitors are encouraged to take as many pictures as possible in the hope of capturing light anomalies called "orbs" – supposedly the first manifestations of spirits – on camera. At the **Witch History Museum**, 197–201 Essex St (April–Nov daily 10am–5pm; $8; ☎978/741-7770, ⊛www.witchhistorymuseum.com), you can catch an impressive live presentation of the witch trials and tour a slightly corney recreation of "Old Salem" village. On the west side of town, the **Witch Dungeon Museum**, 16 Lynde St (April–Nov daily 10am–5pm; $8; ☎978/741-3570, ⊛www.witchdungeon.com), occupies a nineteenth-century clapboard church and treats visitors to farcical re-enactments of key witch trial-related events. Upstairs, it's the trial of Sarah Good – a pipe-smoking beggar woman falsely accused of witchcraft – based on actual court transcripts; after the show, actors escort you below ground to a re-created "dungeon" where you see that some of the prison cells were no bigger than a telephone booth.

On a less sensationalistic note, two blocks further west, at 310½ Essex Street, is Salem's only surviving house with an actual link to the trials. The misleadingly named **Witch House** (May–Nov 10am–5pm; $8.25; ☎978/744-8815, ⊛www.salemweb.com/witchhouse) is the former home of judge Jonathan Corwin. Furnished with antiques, the museum focuses more on Puritan life and architecture than on the trials themselves, which are only mentioned toward the end of the half-hour tour.

A pleasant respite from all the hysteria is the simple and moving **Witch Trials Memorial** at Charter and New Liberty streets, a series of elevated stones etched with the names of the hanged. The memorial is wedged into a corner of the **Old Burying Point Cemetery**, where one witch judge, John Hathorne, forebear of Salem's most famous son, Nathaniel Hawthorne, is buried, as well as Captain Richard More, a passenger on the *Mayflower*.

Peabody Essex Museum

Worth a trip to Salem alone, the sleek **Peabody Essex Museum**, at East India Square (Tues–Sun 10am–5pm; $15; ☎978/745-9500, ⓦwww.pem.org), is the oldest continuously operating museum in the US. The museum's vast, modern space incorporates more than thirty galleries displaying art and artefacts from around the world that illustrate Salem's past importance as a trading point between East and West. Founded by ship captains in 1799 to exhibit the items they obtained while overseas, the museum also boasts the biggest collection of nautical paintings in the world. Other galleries hold Chinese and Japanese export art, Asian, Oceanic and American decorative arts and a standout collection of contemporary paintings and photography.

On the ground level, creatively curated whaling exhibits include Ambroise Garneray's gruesome 1835 painting, *Attacking the Right Whale* (which depicts five sailors killing a whale, blood and all), as well as a fabulous scrimshaw collection that includes a nineteenth-century pie crimper and an 1829 etched sperm whale tooth that reads "Death to the living/long life to the killers/success to sailors wives & greasy luck to whalers" – it's the oldest documented scrimshaw in existence. You'll also find fanciful figureheads from now-demolished Salem ships, plus the reconstructed interior salon from America's first yacht, *Cleopatra's Barge*, which took to the seas in 1816. More contemporary exhibitions are found on the second floor, including the museum's stellar Asian collection.

The museum's prize possession, however, is **Yin Yu Tang** ($5 extra; reserve a time at the front desk), a sixteen-room Qing dynasty house that the museum purchased, dismantled and brought to Salem to foster awareness and appreciation of Chinese culture. This serene space features elaborately wrought scrollwork windows and two small fish ponds filled with Koi; keep an eye out for the little pink radio box high on the reception room wall – installed in millions of Chinese village homes in the 1960s, the radios played news, music and political announcements for twenty years, and could not be turned down or off.

Salem Maritime National Historic Site

Little of Salem's original waterfront remains, although the two-thousand-foot-long **Derby Wharf** is still standing, fronted by the imposing Federalist-style **Custom House** at its head. These two, and ten other mainly residential buildings once belonging to sea captains and craftsmen, make up the **Salem Maritime National Historic Site**, which maintains a **visitor's centre** at 193 Derby St and 2 New Liberty St (daily 9am–5pm; ☎978/740-1650, ⓦwww.nps.gov/sama). The Custom House is where Nathaniel Hawthorne worked as a surveyor for three years, a stint which he later described as "slavery". The office-like interior is rather bland, as is the warehouse in the rear, with displays of tea chests and such. Elias Derby received the nearby **Derby House** in 1762 as a wedding gift from his father; its position overlooking the harbour allowed him to monitor his shipping empire. The interior has been preserved in all its eighteenth-century finery. The original East Indiaman *Friendship* was launched in 1797 and captured by the British in 1812; the impressive 171-ft replica on the wharf was built by the Park Service and offers a fascinating insight into life at sea in the nineteenth century. Next to Derby House, the **West India Goods Store** emulates a nineteenth-century supply shop by peddling nautical accoutrements like fishhooks and ropes, as well as supplies like molasses candy and "gunpowder tea", a tightly rolled, high-grade Chinese green tea.

House of the Seven Gables

The most famous sight in the waterfront area is undoubtedly the **House of the Seven Gables**, 54 Turner St (guided tours daily: mid-Jan to June, Nov & Dec 10am–5pm; July–Oct 10am–7pm; $12.50; ☏978/744-0991, ⓦwww.7gables.org), a rambling mansion by the sea that served as inspiration for Hawthorne's epony-mous novel. Forever the "rusty wooden house with seven acutely peaked gables" that Hawthorne described, this 1668 three-storey dwelling has some other notable features, such as the bricked-off "Secret Stairway" that leads to the chimney and a small room. The author's birthplace, a small, barn-red house built before 1750, has been moved here from its original location on Union Street.

On your way out, pop into **Ye Olde Pepper Companie**, just across the way at 122 Derby St (☏978/745-2744) to sample their lemon "gibralters", the first candies to be made and sold commercially in the US (dating to 1806).

Eating and drinking

Salem has a good range of **pub grub** and casual American fare on offer; the fancier eateries lurk by the waterfront.

A&J King Bakery 48 Central St ☏978/744-4881. A decadent selection of walnut sticky buns, raspberry Danishes and fresh, overstuffed sandwiches.

Front Street Coffeehouse 20 Front St ☏978/740-6697. Endearing little coffeeshop with sandwiches freshly made to order, big salads, casual outdoor tables and free wi-fi.

Gulu-Gulu Café 247 Essex St ☏978/740-8882. Named for the Czech café where the owners met and fell in love, this bohemian spot serves crepes and paninis throughout the day and has an extensive beer selection. There's also live music and DJs most nights.

Lyceum 43 Church St ☏978/745-7665. Renovated in 2009, the historic lecture hall that once courted Emerson, Thoreau and Hawthorne now offers bistro fare like steak frites with shallot sauce ($27) and oysters on the half shell ($15 for six).

The Old Spot 121 Essex St ☏978/745-5656. Friendly English pub right in the centre of town with sixteen craft beers on tap and worthy bar fare like the ploughman's lunch (hardboiled eggs, three cheeses, pickle, ham, green apple and paté; $13).

Red's Sandwich Shop 15 Central St ☏978/745-3527. This lovable local spot serves hearty breakfast, lunch and dinner with bigger-than-your-plate pancakes and low-key American classics (meatloaf, pasta) in a little red house built in 1698. Cash only, very cheap.

Salem Diner 70 Loring Ave (Rte-1A), south of the centre ☏978/741-7918. This historic diner, serving inexpensive greasy spoon fare in an original 1941 Sterling Streamliner car (one of only four remaining in the US) is a must-visit for road-trip aficionados.

Sixty2 on Wharf 62 Wharf St ☏978/744-0062. Contemporary Italian *trattoria* known for its outstanding service; the menu offers savoury small plates (try the mozzarella-stuffed *arancini* for $6) alongside pricier entrees like gnocchi with sausage and peas ($22). Be sure to save room for the warm toffee pudding ($8).

Marblehead

Adjacent to Salem, the maritime town of **MARBLEHEAD**, about a thirty-minute drive on Rte-128 northeast of Boston, is filled with winding streets made up of well-preserved private sea captains' homes that lead down to the harbour. Once the domain of Revolutionary War heroes – it was Marblehead boatmen who rowed Washington's assault force across the Delaware River to attack Trenton – it's now a pleasant mix of Boston commuters and old-time residents. One thing that hasn't changed over the years is the town's dramatic setting on a series of rocky ledges overlooking the wide natural harbour, which makes it one of the East Coast's biggest **yachting centres**. Today, boating remains the lifeblood of the town, and Marblehead is at its most animated during the annual **Race Week** (last week of July).

You can get a good look at this picturesque port from **Fort Sewall**, which juts into the harbour at the end of Front Street; these are the remnants of fortifications the British originally built in 1644, which later protected the USS *Constitution* (on view in the Charlestown Navy Yard; see p.72) in the War of 1812. Closer to the centre of town is **Old Burial Hill**, which holds the graves of more than six hundred Revolutionary War soldiers and has similarly sweeping views. **Abbot Hall**, on Washington Street (Mon, Tues, Thurs & Fri 8am–5pm, Wed 8am–6pm, Sat 9am–6pm, Sun 11am–6pm; call to confirm hours, ☎781/631-0000), an attractive 1876 town hall which can be seen from far out at sea, houses Archibald Willard's famous patriotic painting *The Spirit of '76*.

The best of the central **hotels** is the elegant *Harbor Light Inn*, 58 Washington St (☎781/631-2186, ⓦwww.harborlightinn.com; $145–365), which has working fireplaces and a heated outdoor pool in summer. *One Kimball at Marblehead Light*, 1 Kimball St on Marblehead Neck (☎781/631-0010, ⓦwww.onekimball.com; $200), offers two deluxe suites overlooking the ocean and plays neighbour to a lighthouse. For **food**, *Jack Tar*, at 126 Washington St (☎781/631-2323), serves upscale pizza and fresh seafood dishes at dinnertime, whereas *Foodie's Feast* (daily 7am–4pm; ☎781/639-1104), just around the corner at no. 114, is a great café with inventive sandwiches, breakfast dishes and signature scones. Some would say that local institution *Maddie's Sail Loft*, 15 State St (☎781/631-9824), is Marblehead – head over here for a brew once you've finished your meal.

Gloucester

Founded in 1623, **GLOUCESTER**, just forty miles north of Boston up Rte-1 to 127, is the oldest fishing and trading boatyard in Massachusetts, and to this day it remains a salty, working-class port. The town's near-legendary fishermen are at the centre of Sebastian Junger's famous tale, *The Perfect Storm* (see p.276), which relays the true-life tragedy of a local swordfishing boat caught, and lost, in the worst storm in recorded history, when three simultaneous squalls merged off the coast in October 1991 and produced 100ft-high waves. The fate of all the sailors (some 100,000 total) who have perished offshore over the centuries is commemorated by an iconic 1923 statue, *Man at the Wheel*, overlooking the harbour. To learn a bit more about the port's fishing past, head to the excellent **Cape Ann Museum**, near the docks at 27 Pleasant St (Tues–Sat 10am–5pm, Sun 1pm–4pm; $8; ☎978/283-0455, ⓦwww.capeannmuseum.org), where the history of the region is well documented through old photographs, fishing and quarrying implements and paintings of mostly local scenes by a variety of artists including Winslow Homer, Milton Avery, Augustus Buhler and Gloucester-born marine artist Fitz Henry Lane.

Another lovely way to spend the day is to head east on East Main Street to the famed **Rocky Neck Art Colony**. While the Colony's quality of art varies, there are always a handful of standout galleries, and the area's unruly flowerbeds and pretty harbour views make for a pleasant (and free) meander.

Over in East Gloucester, at 75 Eastern Point Blvd off Rte-127A, lies the magical **Beauport** (tours hourly: mid-May to mid-Sept Mon–Fri 10am–4pm, mid-Sept to mid-Oct Mon–Sat 10am–4pm; $10; ☎978/283-0800), a 45-room mansion perched on the rocks overlooking Gloucester Harbor. Started in 1907 as a simple summer retreat for the collector and interior designer Henry Davis Sleeper (who designed Hollywood homes for Joan Crawford and Johnny Mack Brown), the house evolved over the following 27 years into a gabled, turreted villa filled with vast collections of European, American and Asian *objets*. The house is a fanciful mix of styles and themes, each room strikingly different from the next; keep an eye out for a room crafted to feel like the stern of a ship (with views over the water all the way to Boston), hand-painted wallpaper that has no repetitions, a red and gold "octagonal" room and an ingeniously lit-up collection of 130 pieces of amber glass.

Another compelling attraction is found a short drive south along the rocky coast of Rte-127: the imposing **Hammond Castle Museum**, 80 Hesperus Ave (June–Aug daily 10am–4pm; Sept–May Sat & Sun 10am–4pm; $8; ☎978/283-7673, ⓦwww .hammondcastle.org), whose builder, the eccentric financier and amateur inventor John Hays Hammond Jr, wanted to bring medieval European relics to the US. The austere fortress, which overlooks the ocean, is loaded with treasures, from armour and tapestries to, strangely enough, an elaborately carved wooden facade of a fifteenth-century French bakery and the partially crushed skull of one of Columbus's shipmates. The ultimate flight-of-fancy, however, is the 30,000-gallon pool whose contents can be changed from fresh to salt water at the switch of a lever – Hammond allegedly liked to dive into it from his balcony.

Practicalities

If you're looking to get out on the water, the **visitors' centre**, located just past the wistful *Fishermen's Wives Memorial* at Stage Fort Park, Rte-127 (June to mid-Oct daily 9am–5pm; ☎978/281-8865), can give you a map detailing area beaches; best is the Good Harbor Beach off Witham Street ($25 for parking). There is also ample information on **whale watches**, for which the region is known.

To **stay** in Gloucester, try the ✈ *Bass Rocks Inn*, 107 Atlantic Rd (☎1-888/802-7666, ⓦwww.bassrocksoceaninn.com; $199), outfitted with three beautiful properties that range from renovated suites in an 1899 house to a motel with a pool overlooking the sea. *Rocky Neck Accommodations*, 43 Rocky Neck Ave (☎978/283-1625, ⓦwww.rockyneckaccommodations.com; $134), offers basic (although some rooms have kitchens), clean, affordable digs with decks and outstanding views of the harbour. For a **meal**, stop by *Duckworth's Bistrot*, en route to Rocky Neck at 197 E. Main St (☎978/282-1919; closed Mon), for swanky fusion fare, or sip martinis at the fabulous *Franklin Cape Ann*, 118 Main St (☎978/283-7888), sister restaurant of Boston's beloved South End bistro (see p.156). *Virgilio's,* 29 Main St (☎978/283-5295), has incredible Italian sandwiches during the day; in the evening, grab dinner at ✈ *The Rudder,* at 73 Rocky Neck Ave (☎978/283-7967), an atmospheric "seafood chophouse" in a little wooden house next to the water on Rocky Neck (entrees around $22). For local **nightlife**, head to *The Crows Nest*, 334 Main St (☎978/281-2965), long the salty seadogs' hangout.

Rockport and around

Five miles north of Gloucester, scenically situated **ROCKPORT** is the more upscale and lively of the two towns, with children filling its many ice cream shops and couples crowding the bars and clamshacks. Its main drag is a thin peninsula called **Bearskin Neck**, lined with old salt-box fishermen's cottages transformed into restaurants and art galleries (a red lobster shed near the harbour's edge has been christened "Motif #1" because it's been painted so many times). The Neck rises as it reaches the sea, and there's a nice view of the rocky harbour from the end of it. **Dock Square**, at the town's centre, makes for pleasant shopping and meandering.

One of the best reasons for visiting Rockport is its access to the sea. One good way to get out on the waves is with **North Shore Kayak Outdoor Center**, 9 Tuna Wharf (☎978/546-5050), offering kayaking tours (around $40) led by affable guides.

North on Rte-127, **Halibut Point State Park** (late May to late Sept daily 8am–8pm; suggested donation) is a fantastic place to spend the afternoon. Formerly a nineteenth-century granite quarry, it's now a breathtaking rocky outcrop with sea views and craggy coastal access to the ocean (many a marriage proposal has taken place along the park's unruly shoreline). On your way back into town, stop by the consummate *Lobster Pool Restaurant*, on Folly Cove via Rte-127S (☎978/546-7808), for fresh lobster rolls eaten via picnic tables that overlook Ipswich Bay – there are rumblings that the *Pool*'s quality is beginning to dip, though, so ask a local for the latest input before heading out.

Practicalities

If you **stay** the night at the basic *Bearskin Neck Motor Lodge,* 64 Bearskin Neck (☎978/546-6677, ⓦwww.bearskinneckmotorlodge.com; $169), you'll wake up to lobstermen hauling in their buoys just outside your oceanfront porch. The pretty *Captain's House Inn*, 69 Marmion Way (☎978/546-3825, ⓦwww.captains house.com; $165), offers five charming guest rooms with ocean views; you can spot three lighthouses while eating home-made granola from its scenic porch.

For such a small space, Rockport offers a stellar array of **restaurants**. The most inviting is the *Roy Moore Lobster Company*, a tiny 1918 fish shack at 39 Bearskin Neck (☎978/546-6696), offering lobster by the pound, clam chowder and fish cakes on its sunny back porch; you can have a sit-down meal at the (less charming) related *Fish Shack Restaurant* (☎978/546-6667) at nearby Dock Square. Further down the neck is the upscale *My Place By the Sea* (☎978/546-9667), with a stupendous waterfront setting to complement its delicate entrees.

One minor practicality: **parking** in Rockport can be tough; unless you're staying in town, it's best to park and ride ($1 one-way) by Blue Gate Gardens florist at 124 Main St (Rte-127). Call the Chamber of Commerce (☎978/546-6575) for more information.

Plymouth

While most day-trippers from Boston head north first, Boston's South Shore, sweeping the coast from suburban Quincy to the former whaling port of New Bedford, has its own fair share of worthwhile destinations. It's best known for tiny **PLYMOUTH**, America's so-called "hometown", forty miles south of Boston. The town is mostly given over to commemorating the landing of the 102 Pilgrims here in December of 1620 and need only be visited by people with a real interest in the story.

The famous **Plymouth Rock**, where the Pilgrims are said to have touched land, is enclosed by a solemn, pseudo-Greek temple by the sea. As is typical with most sites of this ilk, the rock is of symbolic importance only – the Pilgrims had already spent several weeks on Cape Cod before landing here, and no one can be sure where they actually did land. Down the street is the recently expanded **Pilgrim Hall Museum**, 75 Court St (Feb–Dec daily 9.30am–4.30pm; $8; ☎508/746-1620, ⓦwww.pilgrimhall.org), with displays centring on pilgrim

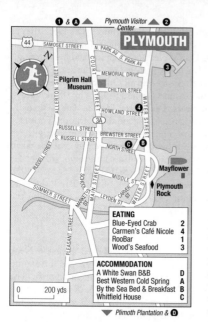

PLYMOUTH

EATING
Blue-Eyed Crab   2
Carmen's Café Nicole   4
RooBar   1
Wood's Seafood   3

ACCOMMODATION
A White Swan B&B   D
Best Western Cold Spring   A
By the Sea Bed & Breakfast   B
Whitfield House   C

0   200 yds

▼ Plimoth Plantation & ⒹⒸ

history and culture; you can touch a chunk of Plymouth Rock, view the last-known authentic pilgrim hat and eye the Hall's noteworthy collection of seventeenth-century century paintings.

A better way to spend your time is the replica of the *Mayflower*, called the **Mayflower II** (April–Nov daily 9am–5pm; $10; ☎508/746-1622, ⓦwww.plimoth.org), which was restored in 2000, and is berthed on the State Pier in Plymouth Harbor. Built in Britain by English craftsmen following the historically accurate plans of an American naval architect at MIT, the *Mayflower II* was ceremoniously docked in Plymouth in 1957 and given to America as a gesture of goodwill. You're free to wander the ship at leisure, and there are trained staff members – in contemporary clothing – available to answer any questions. Others in period costume will put on a well-presented pretence of ignorance of current events.

Similar in approach and authenticity is the **Plimoth Plantation**, three miles south of town off Rte-3 (same hours; $24; ☎508/746-1622, ⓦwww.plimoth .org). Everything you see in the plantation, such as the Pilgrim Village of 1627 and the Wampanoag Indian Settlement, has been created using traditional techniques; even the farm animals were "backbred" to resemble their seventeenth-century counterparts. Again, actors dressed in period garb try to bring you back in time; depending on your level of resistance, it can be quite enjoyable. If you intend to see both the Plantation and the *Mayflower II*, you'd do better to buy a combo ticket ($28) from the admissions desk.

Practicalities

Plymouth's **visitor centre** is on the waterfront at 130 Water St (☎508/747-7533, ⓦwww.visit-plymouth.com). Plymouth & Brockton provides a regular **bus** service to and from Boston ($14 one-way, $25 round-trip; ☎508/746-0378, ⓦwww.p-b.com). Once in Plymouth, a daily express **ferry** heads to Provincetown throughout the summer season (June to early Sept daily 10am; $40 round-trip; ☎508/747-2400 or ☎1-800/225-4000, ⓦwww.provincetownferry.com).

Should you need to overnight in town, a standout **motel** option is the clean and comfortable *Best Western Cold Spring*, 180 Court St (☎508/746-2222, ⓦwww.bw coldspring.com; $140). For a more homey choice, try *By the Sea*, 22 Winslow St (☎508/830-9643, ⓦwww.bytheseabedandbreakfast.com; $165), a harbourfront B&B with two spacious suites and private bath. *A White Swan B&B*, 146 Manomet Pond Rd (☎508/224-3759, ⓦwww.whiteswan.com; $135), is set in a historic farmhouse walkable to delightful White Horse Beach; while the 1782 *Whitfield House* has four Colonial-style rooms right in town at 26 North St (☎508/747-6735, ⓦwhitfieldhouse.com; $120).

America's hometown has a few favourable **food** options. Right on the water-front, *Blue-Eyed Crab*, 170 Water St (☎508/747-6776), offers fresh cuts of seafood, great cocktails and a bright outdoor patio. *Carmen's Café Nicole*, 114 Water St (☎508/747-4343) has a "taste for everyone" from breakfast till lunch – everything from salads and wraps to chili dogs and Mexican food is covered on its extensive menu. *RooBar,* 10 Cordage Park (☎508/746-4300), is adding a martini-infused kick to Plymouth's nightlife scene, with bistro-style entrees (around $18) come dinnertime. *Wood's Seafood*, 15 Town Wharf (☎508/746-0261), is a no-frills sea shack with counter service and delectable fried clams, lobster rolls and fish chowders.

New Bedford and around

The famous old whaling port of **NEW BEDFORD**, 60 miles due south of Boston, is still home to one of the nation's most prosperous fishing fleets: every year, they haul in the largest catch on the East Coast. And while it has its patches of grit, New Bedford has aged well, too. Recent preservation efforts, with an eye to the town's whaling heritage, have only served to heighten its aesthetic appeal.

The **downtown** area is now called the New Bedford Whaling National Historic Park, a collection of old buildings, art galleries and antique stores, the centrepiece of which is the remarkable **New Bedford Whaling Museum**, 18 Johnny Cake Hill (daily 9am–5pm, till 9pm every second Thurs of the month; $10; ⓦwww.whaling museum.org). Housed in a former church and presided over by a 66ft blue whale skeleton, the museum features the world's largest ship model and an evocative half-scale version of the whaling vessel *Lagoda*, as well as collections of scrimshaw, harpoons and artefacts retrieved by whalers from the Arctic and the Pacific.

More affecting is the **Seamen's Bethel**, directly opposite the museum, the famous "Whaleman's Chapel" that was built in 1832 and conjured up in Herman Melville's *Moby Dick* (May–Oct daily 10am–4pm; rest of year by appointment only; call ahead, though, as often closed on weekends and for private events; donation requested; ☎508/992-3295). The chapel features the ship-shaped pulpit described in Melville's tale, but this one is a replica built after a fire in 1866. More evocative are the memorials lining the walls for those who died at sea, a custom for lost sailors that's continued to this day. The park **visitor centre**, 33 William St (daily 9am–5pm; ☎508/996-4095), has interesting guides to local history – the Underground Railroad went through here – as well as maps of the park, working waterfront and nearby **mansions**, remnants of the town's whale-derived wealth. Chief among these are the old Federalist and Victorian houses around **County Street**, of which Melville commented:

Had it not been for us whalemen, that tract of land would this day perhaps have been in as howling condition as the coast of Labrador...all these brave houses and flowery gardens came up from the Atlantic, Pacific, and Indian oceans. One and all, they were harpooned and dragged hither from the bottom of the sea.

The Greek Revival **Rotch-Jones-Duff House & Garden Museum**, 396 County St (Mon–Sat 10am–4pm, Sun noon–4pm; $5; ☎508/997-1401, ⓦwww .rjdmuseum.org), built by a Quaker whaling captain in 1834, retains many of its original decorations and furnishings and is festooned with decadent marble fireplace mantles and Oriental rugs. The formal gardens, laid out in their original style, with boxwood hedges, roses and wildflowers, occupy an entire city block. On many Friday nights here in the summer you can hear low-key live music (as well as at the Whaling Museum); check the website for a calendar. Neighbouring **Madison**, **Maple** and **Orchard streets** also contain a number of fanciful, brightly repainted mansions. It's worth driving by – about all you can do, as they're all private – before heading out of town.

Practicalities

If you want to **stay** in New Bedford, the *Orchard Street Manor*, 139 Orchard St (☎508/984-3475, ⓦwww.the-orchard-street-manor.com; $125), is an atmospheric B&B replete with pool table, Moroccan accoutrements and great breakfasts, all set in a nineteenth-century former whaling captain's home. For **food**, *No Problemo*, right downtown at 813 Purchase St (☎508/984-1081; open late), serves whale-sized burritos, tasty *taquitos* and sangria (cash only). For more local flavour, try the authentic Portuguese dishes at *Antonio's*, 267 Coggeshall St (☎508/990-3636), where long lines often stretch out the door (cash only). For a little **nightlife**, the Zeiterion Theatre (☎508/994-2900, ⓦwww.zeiterion.org) hosts fantastic dance, theatre and music performances in a glorious vintage vaudeville space.

New Bedford is also a docking point for **ferries** to **Martha's Vineyard**; for more information, see p.253.

Cape Cod

O ne of the most celebrated slices of land in America, **Cape Cod** boasts a consistently stunning quality of light that shines over some of the best beaches in New England. The slender, crooked Cape gives Massachusetts an extra three hundred miles of coastline, easily accessed from the region's snug villages, many of which have been preserved as they were a hundred or more years ago with town green, white steeple church and lighthouse. **Provincetown**, at the very tip, is far out in more than just geography; known for being a vibrant gay resort, it is also an historic artist's colony, and as such is host to galleries and an esteemed art museum. "P-Town" is perched on the best stretch of the extensive **Cape Cod National Seashore**, adding to its seemingly endless natural beauty, though tiny towns like **Falmouth**, **Sandwich** and upscale **Chatham** have an appeal all their own; you may find that the charms of these scenic stops are enough to lure you away for the whole of your trip.

Some history

Martha's Vineyard and the Cape received their English designations in 1602, when explorer **Bartholomew Gosnold** visited the area: he named the island after his daughter, while the arm's moniker was inspired by the profusion of the white fish in local waters. By the early 1800s, **whaling** had become the Cape's primary industry, with the towns of the Outer Cape doing particularly well; fishing and agricultural ventures, including the harvesting of **cranberries**, were also lucrative.

Cape Cod's rise as a **tourist destination** is mainly attributable to the development of the railroad in the nineteenth century (Provincetown was connected to Boston by rail in 1873). Wealthy Bostonians and New Yorkers were, for the first time, able to get to the Cape with relative ease, and many purchased land to build summer homes. Today, the Cape's population more than doubles in the summer, when more than 80,000 cars a day cross the **Cape Cod Canal**.

For the foreseeable future, however, nature will be the real arbiter of the Cape's fate. Without the rocky backbone of other parts of the coast, the land is particularly vulnerable to **erosion**: between Wellfleet and Provincetown the land is scarcely one mile wide, and it's shifting all the time. The one benefit of the environmental situation is that it keeps development in check, especially in the vicinity of the protected **National Seashore**.

The shape of the Cape

The Cape is shaped like a **flexed arm**, with Sandwich at the shoulder, Chatham at the elbow and Provincetown the clenched fist at the very end. According to local parlance, the "Upper Cape" is the area you come to after crossing the Sagamore or Bourne bridges from the mainland, the "Lower Cape" is the forearm that stretches

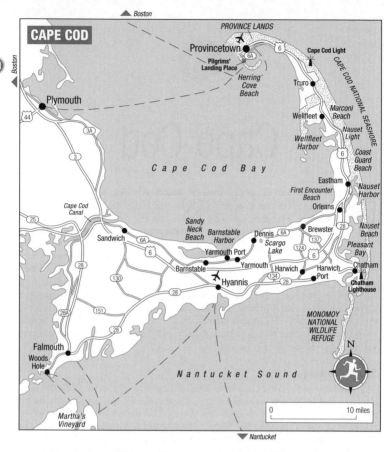

CAPE COD

PROVINCE LANDS

Provincetown

Pilgrims'
Landing Place

Herring
Cove
Beach

Cape Cod Light

Truro

CAPE COD NATIONAL SEASHORE

Plymouth

Marconi
Beach

Wellfleet

Nauset
Light

Wellfleet
Harbor

Coast
Guard
Beach

C a p e   C o d   B a y

Eastham

Nauset
Harbor

First Encounter
Beach

Orleans

Cape Cod
Canal

Nauset
Beach

Sandy
Neck
Beach

Barnstable
Harbor

Dennis

Brewster

Sandwich

Scargo
Lake

Pleasant
Bay

Yarmouth Port

Barnstable

Yarmouth

Harwich

Chatham

Hyannis

Harwich
Port

Chatham
Lighthouse

MONOMOY
NATIONAL
WILDLIFE
REFUGE

Falmouth

Woods
Hole

N a n t u c k e t   S o u n d

N

0   10 miles

Martha's
Vineyard

▼ Nantucket

approximately from Orleans to Provincetown and the "Mid-Cape" is everything in between, including the main commercial centre of Hyannis. From a traveller's perspective, however, things make more sense in terms of the **north coast** of the Cape from Sandwich to Brewster, the **south coast** from Falmouth to Chatham and the **outer Cape** (Eastham, Wellfleet, Truro and Provincetown).

Arrival and information

The main way of reaching the Cape is by **car**, though if you're heading there on a summer weekend, you may well regret this choice. On a fairly quiet day, it takes an hour to get from downtown Boston to the Sagamore Bridge via Rte-3, but this can double on summer weekends and holidays – if possible, try to start your trip on a weekday or a Sunday night, or aim to leave the Boston area by 2pm on Friday for a weekend trip. The bridge gets similarly crowded on Sunday returns; plan on getting out early in the morning or in the evening once the traffic has thinned. If you're heading directly to Falmouth, note that it's faster to aim for the Bourne Bridge, three miles south of Sagamore, and take Rte-28. Peter Pan's subsidiary Bonanza (one-way $21 to Bourne, slightly more to elsewhere; ☏1-800/343-9000, ⓦwww.peterpanbus.com) operates a **bus** service from Boston to Bourne,

The Cape Cod Canal

Between 1909 and 1914 a **canal** was dug across the westernmost portion of Cape Cod, effectively making the Cape an island. Initial work began in 1880, under the auspices of the Cape Cod Canal Company. In 1899 wealthy New York businessman Augustus Belmont took over the project; ten years later, state-of-the-art earthmoving equipment was introduced, and the canal was completed in 1914, though at the time it was too shallow and narrow to allow anything but one-way traffic. In 1928 the federal government purchased the canal, and enlarged it as a WPA project during the Great Depression. By 1940 the canal was the widest in the world. You don't have to be on the water to enjoy it, though; the views of the canal and its verdant shores from the Sagamore and Bourne bridges are some of the most dramatic on the East Coast. There is also a **bike trail** on either side of the waterway.

Woods Hole, Falmouth and Hyannis, while Plymouth & Brockton (one-way Boston to Hyannis $25, to Provincetown $35; ☎508/746-0378, ⓦwww.p-b.com) has a more complete set of Cape destinations. You can also take a **ferry** from Boston to Provincetown: Bay State Cruise Company (☎617/748-1428, ⓦwww.baystatecruisecompany.com) runs three boats daily in the summer from Boston's Commonwealth Pier (1hr 30min express round-trip $79, 3hr standard ferry round-trip $44), while Boston Harbor Cruises (☎617/227-4321, ⓦwww.bostonharborcruises.com) does two to three express services a day from Long Wharf to Provincetown (1hr 30min; $79 round-trip). There's also a Plymouth to Provincetown ferry (1hr 30min round-trip; $40; ☎508/747-2400 or 1-800/225-4000, ⓦwww.provincetownferry.com). Finally, a number of **airlines** fly direct to Cape Cod, most notably Cape Air (☎1-800/352-0714, ⓦwww.capeair.com), which heads to Hyannis and Provincetown from Boston several times a day, even in winter.

The main Cape Cod **visitors' centre**, situated at the junction of routes 6 and 132 in Centerville (Mon–Sat 10am–5pm, winter till 3pm; ☎508/362-3225), has information about all the towns on the Cape. You can also research the area and make reservations online before you go at the Cape Cod Chamber of Commerce's website, ⓦwww.capecodchamber.org.

Getting around

Once on the Cape, a **car** is the best way to get around. Rentals are available throughout: *Thrifty* has outposts in Orleans (☎508/255-2234), Hyannis (☎508/771-2057) and Sandwich (☎508/888-3333); *Enterprise* is in Hyannis (☎508/778-8293), Falmouth (☎508/540-7784) and Orleans (☎508/255-2997); and *Hertz* has an operation in Hyannis (☎508/778-1640). Alternatively, the Cape Cod Regional Transit Authority (☎1-800/352-7155, ⓦwww.capecodtransit.org) runs frequent public **buses** (generally 6.30am–7pm, although this varies according to bus route) along routes 28 and 132 connecting the Cape's outlying towns; simply flag them down on the side of the road (excepting Rte-6, on which they do not stop for safety reasons) and cough up $2. The Cape also has plentiful and scenic **bike** paths; you can rent at *Bike Zone* ($20/day; ☎508/775-3299), which has locations in Hyannis, East Falmouth and North Falmouth. A more touristy option, from Hyannis anyway, is the **Cape Cod Scenic Railroad** (late-May to Oct; $21; ☎508/771-3800, ⓦwww.capetrain.com), which runs twice a day from Main Street along a meandering two-hour circuit west through cranberry bogs to Sandwich and the Cape Cod Canal.

The south coast

Route 28, which hugs the Nantucket Sound coast of the Cape until it merges with routes 6 and 6A at Orleans, is certainly not the most attractive or scenic route on the Cape; much of it is lined with motels and commercial buildings, and it can get seriously clogged with traffic during the summer. Nonetheless, it runs through a number of important hubs along the south coast, notably **Falmouth** and **Hyannis**. At its end are two delightful reasons for hitting this path, the quiet town of **Chatham** and the even quieter **Monomoy National Wildlife Refuge**.

Falmouth and Woods Hole

FALMOUTH boasts more coastline than any other Cape Cod town and no fewer than fourteen harbours among its eight villages, at the centre of which is **Falmouth Village**, with its prim, picket-fence-encircled central green surrounded by Colonial, Federal and Greek Revival homes. Typical of New England, a

---

Cape Cod beaches

With over 300 miles of coastline, Cape Cod certainly doesn't lack **sand**. What it does lack is parking and facilities at its beachfront locations; what few have the full gamut of services (restrooms, lifeguards and snack bars) are, not surprisingly, usually busiest. The island's southern stretches, facing Nantucket Sound, tend to be calmer and warmer than its northern options, making this coast more family-oriented than its Atlantic side, where the water tends to be chillier and rougher, but also good for riding waves on boogie boards. **Parking** across the Cape is a bit of a crapshoot: some counties allow daily non-permit beach parking (usually between $15 and $20/day), whereas others limit beach parking to residents. Your best bet, if you're planning on hitting the beach a good deal during your stay, is to visit the local town hall and inquire about non-resident parking permits (which can range from $35 for three days to $55 a week). These town beaches are most often bay or pond, whereas the best ocean beaches are pay as you go – so don't rush to buy a pass until you have an idea of where you'd like to swim.

Falmouth
Old-Silver Beach Off Rte-28A in North Falmouth. Popular, calm beach with great sunsets; college kids and young families gather here, the latter drawn to its natural wading pool.

Surf Drive Beach Off Shore Street. Another family favourite; a shallow tidal pool between jetties is known as "the kiddie pool".

Hyannis and around
Craigville Beach Off Craigville Beach Road in Centerville, just west of Hyannis. Well-oiled and toned sun-worshippers flock to this broad expanse of sand nicknamed "Muscle Beach"; lifeguards and toilets on offer.

Kalmus Beach Off Gosnold Street in central Hyannis. A big windsurfing destination at the mouth of the busy harbour, with full facilities but an urban feel.

Sandwich
Sandy Neck Beach Off Sandy Neck Road, East Sandwich. Six-mile-long barrier beach loaded with low dunes favoured by off-roaders; the paths are shut down in summer to encourage the local bird population's hatching season.

Town Neck Beach Off Town Neck Road. Narrow and rocky beach 1.5 miles out of town with pretty views of passing ships and decent facilities. One fun way to get there is via the raised boardwalk on Jarves Street, which passes over marshlands before reaching the dunes.

number of these old sea captains' houses are now B&Bs, and are complemented by a touristy mixture of clothing shops, ice cream parlours and restaurants. The 1794 **Conant House**, 55–65 Palmer Ave (mid-June to mid-Oct Tues–Fri 10am–4pm, Sat 10am–1pm; $5; ℡508/548-4857, ⓦwww.falmouthhistoricalsociety.org), run by the Falmouth Historical Society, contains scrimshaw, rare glass and china and sailors' memorabilia. There's also a room dedicated to local girl **Katherine Lee Bates**, who composed the song **America the Beautiful**; she was born in 1859 down the road at 16 Main St. The Historical Society also maintains the **Julia Wood House**, next door to the Conant House (same hours and price), an early nineteenth-century doctor's home, one room of which is set up as a clinic, with a horrifying display of primitive dental utensils.

If you find you're needing a drink after your visit here, pop by the **Cape Cod Winery** at 681 Sandwich Rd (May to mid-Dec Sat & Sun 11am–4pm; July & Aug also Thurs & Fri 11am–4pm; $5 for tastings; ℡508/457-5592, ⓦwww .capecodwinery.org). Nestled amidst picturesque farmland (complete with rooster, ducks and chickens), the winery is kid-friendly and uses only local grapes in the

Wakeby Pond Ryder Conservation Area, John Ewer Road. The Cape's largest fresh-water pond has a life-guarded beach and full facilities.

Eastham
Coast Guard Beach Off Ocean View Drive. Pristine and picturesque Cape Cod National Seashore beach with views for miles, as well as lifeguards and restrooms; you can catch a shuttle bus from the Little Creek parking area. Frequent seal sightings.

Nauset Light Off Ocean View Drive. Scenic Atlantic-facing beach connected to Coast Guard Beach by shuttle bus and also part of the Cape Cod National Seashore; serviced by lifeguards and restrooms.

Orleans
Nauset Beach Off Rte-28, East Orleans. Arguably the Cape's biggest beach scene, this ten-mile-long barrier beach has terrific facilities (and regular sunset concerts), plus prime windsurfing and boogie-boarding conditions.

Wellfleet
Cahoon Hollow Beach Off Ocean View Drive. Good surfing and full facilities make this town-run beach popular with the thirty-something set. Don't miss the famous *Beachcomber* shack for delicious oysters.

Marconi Beach Off Marconi Beach Road. Dramatic cliff-framed beach best hit in the morning before the sun falls behind the bluffs. Good facilities.

White Crest Off Ocean View Drive. The main distinction between White Crest and neighbouring Cahoon is the clientele – here, it's a predominantly young college crowd.

Provincetown
Herring Cove Beach Off Rte-6. Easily reached by bike or through the dunes, and famous for sunset-watching, this beach is actually more crowded than those nearer town, though never unbearably so.

Long Point Beach Blissfully quiet beach at the end of a trail lined with scented wild roses and beach plums; you can get there on foot (it's a *long* walk on the jetty) or by frequent shuttle from MacMillan Wharf.

Province Lands Off Rte-6. Vast sweeping moors and bushy dunes are buffeted by crashing surf.

Race Point Beach Off Race Point Road. Abutting Province Lands, this wide swathe of white sand is backed by beautiful, tall dunes – the archetypal Cape Cod beach.

production of its plonk. Another area delight is the paved 10.7-mile **Shining Sea Bikeway**, which winds its way along a (blessedly flat) oceanside trail, taking in a glacial kettle hole, a salt marsh and a cranberry bog along the way (free parking available at the County Road lot, off Rte-151 in North Falmouth).

The salty drop of a town that is **WOODS HOLE** owes its name to the water passage, or "hole", between Penzance Point and Nonamesset Island, linking Vineyard Sound and Buzzards Bay. It's little more than a clump of casual restaurants clustered around the harbour, picture-perfect Nobska Point Lighthouse, on Nobska Road, and the **Woods Hole Oceanographic Institution**, 15 School St (May–Oct Mon–Sat 10am–4.30pm; Nov & Dec Tues–Fri 10am–4.30pm; rest of year by appointment; $2 donation; ☎508/289-2252, ⓦwww.whoi.edu). The latter houses an exhibit on the rediscovery of the *Titanic* in 1986, a project the institute spearheaded, and some neat submarine capsules that children will enjoy, but little else besides. During the summer the Institute offers **tours** once a day (reserve in advance) where you get to walk through some of their otherwise off-limits labs. Also worthwhile are the informative, hands-on cruises run from the harbour by **OceanQuest**: lobster and scallop traps are pulled up for inspection and those on board are encouraged to handle the sea-life (July–Aug Mon–Fri 10am, noon, 2pm & 4pm, more sporadically on summer weekends and in Sept; $22; ☎1-800-37-OCEAN, ⓦwww.oceanquest.org).

Back on land, much of the sea-life that lurks off the Cape's shores is kept behind glass at the Woods Hole Science Aquarium, at the corner of Albatross and Water streets (Tues–Sat 11am–4pm; free; ☎508/495-2001, ⓦwww.nefsc.noaa.gov), which maintains America's oldest **aquarium**. With a mission to preserve local marine life, its displays are mostly limited to the likes of cod, striped bass, lobster and other piscine creatures that are more appealing on a plate; the exception, the institute's pet seals, Bumper and LuSeal, give visitors a thrill at feeding time (daily 11am & 4pm).

Accommodation

Falmouth has some lovely **accommodation** options that make a good base for exploring the Cape and catching the **ferry** from Woods Hole to Martha's Vineyard.

Captain's Manor Inn 27 W Main St, Falmouth ☎508/388-7336, ⓦ.captainsmanorinn.com. Dating to 1849, this gorgeously restored sea captain's home is done up with Greek revival accents – intended to please the original owner's southern bride. Lots of pampering perks, like rain showerheads, snacks and a nightly turndown service; its innkeepers are tops. $215.

Inn on the Sound 313 Grand Avenue, Falmouth ☎508/457-9666, ⓦwww .innonthesound.com. A stunning location (45ft above the bay), mesmerizing views and a

blazing fireplace make this posh B&B a real treat; luxury linens and a well-stocked library mean you may not want to venture out at all. Rates fluctuate wildly according to season; $135–345.

Woods Hole Passage 186 Woods Hole Rd, Falmouth ☎508/548-9575, ⓦwww.woodshole passage.com. Brightly painted chambers in a refurbished red-shingled carriage house set on spacious grounds. This is the place to go to save some money in the area. Rooms $165–195 in summer.

Eating and drinking

The Clam Shack 227 Clinton Ave, Falmouth ☎508/540-7758. A local institution which serves up heaping plates of fried seafood (and obviously clams) on outside picnic tables and a smashing rooftop deck with prime waterfront views.

Fishmonger's Cafe 55 Water St, Woods Hole ☎508/540-5376. Laidback natural-foods eatery with a surprising number of vegetarian dishes in addition to eclectic seafood fare; try the fine fisherman's stew loaded with shrimp, scallops and mussels ($20).

Mary Ellen's Portuguese Bakery 829 Main St (behind Dairy Queen), Falmouth ☎508/540-9696. A worthwhile stop for Portuguese favourites at breakfast and lunch: omelettes with linguiça sausage, kale soup, grilled home fries and renowned coffee. Extremely casual; cash only.

Hyannis

HYANNIS is primarily a transportation and commercial hub – it's home to the Cape's largest airport, as well as the main ferry service to Nantucket – and while travelling through it may be necessary, it's not the Cape's most scenic destination. Much of the city has an urban feel, although there are some pleasant public beaches and quaint B&Bs for those who need to stay. Nevertheless, it still sparkles a bit from the glamour it earned when the **Kennedy compound** at Hyannisport placed it at the centre of world affairs.

If it's Kennedy-ana you've come to see, the best place to start is the **John F. Kennedy Hyannis Museum**, 397 Main St (mid-April to late May Mon–Sat 10am–4pm, Sun noon–4pm; late May to Oct Mon–Sat 9am–5pm, Sun noon–5pm; Nov & Dec Thurs–Sat 10am–4pm, Sun noon–4pm; $5; ☎508/790-3077), which displays the expected nostalgia, mainly in the form of old black-and-white photographs. It's not a comprehensive history, and instead focuses on Kennedy's relationship with Cape Cod. For a welcome non-presidential diversion, you might take a free tour of the **Cape Cod Potato Chip Factory**, at 100 Breed's Hill Rd near the Cape Cod Mall (Mon–Fri 9am–5pm; free; ☎1-888/881-2447, ⓦwww .capecodchips.com). The tasty chips, once a local phenomenon but now found almost everywhere, are made with natural ingredients hand-cooked in kettles; it's hard to resist the free samples, in any case. If you have little ones in tow, the swash-buckling **Pirate Adventures** cruise (mid-June to early Sept; $21; reservations required; ☎508/394-9100, ⓦwww.pirateadventurescapecod.com) is a must-do: don your eye-patch and head out to find sunken treasure; you'll get to launch water-spraying cannons at a rival ship.

Practicalities

The local Chamber of Commerce maintains an **information centre** at 397 Main St (mid-March to mid-May Thurs–Sat 10am–4pm, Sun noon–4pm; late May to Oct Mon–Sat 9am–5pm, Sun noon–5pm; ☎508/775-2201, ⓦwww.hyannis .com), not to be confused with the Cape Cod Visitor Center just up the road. If you have a boat to catch and need to **stay** in Hyannis, options include the family-oriented *Sea Beach Inn*, 388 Sea St (☎508/775-4612, ⓦcapecodtravel.com /seabeach; $90), with small, neat, affordable rooms, the *Sea Coast Inn*, 33 Ocean St (☎508/775-3828, ⓦwww.seacoastcapecod.com; $118), which offers clean and functional motel-style accommodation close to the ferry docks; helpful owners throw in free breakfast and internet use. There's also the *HI-Hyannis*, a beautiful new, gut-renovated **hostel** with 44 beds in a shingled house across the street from the ferry docks; free continental breakfast and wi-fi included (111 Ocean St; ☎508/775-7990, ⓦcapecodhisusa.org; $39 dorm bed).

Many of Hyannis's **restaurants** are on Main Street, which is unfortunately not all that near the hotels – and so, as public transport stops at 7pm, it's helpful to have a car. Be sure to indulge in the full *rodizio* at the well-loved 🍴*Brazilian Grill*, 680 Main St (☎508/771-0109), where mouth-watering meats are delivered straight from the skewer onto your plate. For more of a local flavour, the *Naked Oyster*, right by the JFK Museum at 410 Main St (☎508/778-6500), features an impressive raw bar and excellent (albeit pricey) seafood entrees in a mahogany-panelled dining room. Close to the Barnstable Airport, *Pain D'Avignon*, at 15 Hinckley Rd

(⊤508/771-9771), is the place to go for exquisite baked goods and café fare (dinner sees expensive French classics like steak frites; $26). Since 1934, *Four Seas*, by the Craigville Beach in Centerville at 360 S Main St (⊤508/775-1394), has been the place to go for enormously fantastic ice cream cones.

Chatham

Another worthwhile stop on the South Shore is genteel **CHATHAM**, a long 21 miles east on Route 28 from Hyannis. Here, the quiet and posh small-town atmosphere centres on **Chatham Village**, whose **Main Street** is home to a variety of upscale boutiques, provisions stores and some sophisticated restaurants and charming inns.

A few minutes' drive outside the village, the 1877 **Chatham Lighthouse** stands guard over a windswept bluff beyond which many a ship met its doom on the "Chatham Bars", a series of sandbars that served to protect the town from the worst of the Atlantic storms – until in January 1987, when a fierce Nor'easter broke through the barrier beach to form the **Chatham Break**, leaving Chatham exposed to the vagaries of the ocean. Right below the lighthouse is a nice beach, but with parking limited to half an hour you're better off biking there from town. A mile north on Route 28, the **Fish Pier** on Shore Road provides a spot to wait for the fleet to come in mid-afternoon.

Accommodation

Chatham is well endowed with tasteful **accommodation**, and the **B&Bs** here are a bit more upscale than those found elsewhere on the Cape. Despite the ample selection, reservations are strongly advised, even outside of high season.

The Captain's House Inn 369–377 Old Harbor Rd ⊤1-800/315-0728, ⓦwww .captainshouseinn.com. Easy elegance prevails at this sumptuously renovated 1839 Greek Revival whaling captain's home; most rooms have fireplaces, and prices include delicious breakfasts and afternoon tea with freshly baked scones. $260.

The Carriage House Inn 407 Old Harbor Rd ⊤508/945-4688, ⓦwww.thecarriagehouseinn .com. This year-round B&B with young, friendly owners provides six exquisite rooms in beach hues of yellow and blue, each with a jar of home-made cookies, flat-screen TVs and slightly lower prices than the surrounding inns. $239.

Monomoy National Wildlife Reserve

Stretching out to sea for nine miles south of Chatham, desolate **Monomoy National Wildlife Refuge** is a fragile barrier beach that was attached to the mainland until breached by a storm in 1958. A subsequent storm in 1978 divided the island in half, and today the islands are accessible only by boat – when weather conditions permit. The refuge spreads across 2750 acres of sand and dunes, tidal flats and marshes, with no roads, no electricity and, best of all, no human residents, though a small fishing community once existed here. Indeed, the only man-made buildings on the islands are the South Monomoy Lighthouse and lightkeeper's house.

It's a perfect stopover point along the North Atlantic Flyway for almost three hundred species of shorebirds and migratory **waterfowl**, including many varieties of gull and the endangered piping plovers. In addition, the islands are home to white-tailed deer, and harbour and grey seals are frequent visitors in summer. Several organizations conduct island **tours**, among them the Monomoy Island Ferry, a small boat run by Keith Lincoln ($30; ⊤508/237-0420, ⓦwww.monomoyislandferry.com). Make sure you drop in at the headquarters of the Wildlife Refuge, located on Morris Island, which also has a **visitors' centre** (⊤508/945-0594) offering leaflets on Monomoy. Morris Island is accessible from Morris Island Road, south of the Chatham Light.

Pleasant Bay Village Resort Motel 1191 Orleans Rd ☏ 508/945-1133, ⓦ www.pleasant bayvillage.com. Some of the more affordable digs in town, with spacious, clean motel rooms (suites available), pool and Jacuzzi,

a hot breakfast (for purchase) in the morning and stunningly beautiful gardens that are nestled inside six acres of woodlands. $185; weekly rates start at $1235 in peak season.

Eating

Not surprisingly, given its status as one of the more sophisticated destinations on Cape Cod, Chatham abounds in upmarket **restaurants**, as well as the more casual eateries typical in these parts. If you have kids in tow, don't miss the nostalgic goodies at Chatham Penny Candy (6 Seaview St) or the **fudge** at Chatham Candy Manor (484 Main St).

The Blue Coral 483 Main St ☏ 508/348-0485. Walk down a short flagstone pathway and transport yourself to the Caribbean at this under-the-stars restaurant and bar, long on palm fronds and frozen rum drinks. Lunch and dinner daily, with a seafood-oriented menu, and occasional live music at night.
Chatham Bars Inn 297 Shore Rd ☏ 508/945-0096. The Gatsby-esque hotel's formal dining room offers expensive New England cuisine with wonderful ocean views; also great for breakfast or drinks on the veranda.
Chatham Pier Fish Market 45 Barcliff Ave Ext. ☏ 508/945-3474. Order lobster rolls and inexpensive plates of fried seafood as you watch the seals swim up and the lobster boats unload.
Chatham Squire 487 Main St ☏ 508/945-0945. This informal and affordable spot has a raw bar, an eclectic menu that sometimes incorporates elements of Mexican and Asian cuisine, and often live acoustic bands at night. Kid-friendly.
Corner Store 1403 Old Queen Anne Rd ☏ 508/432-1077. Think you can't find good

Mexican food on the Cape? Think again. Located at the intersection of Rte-137 and Old Queen Anne Road, this counter-service gem offers a savoury smorgasbord of burrito options accompanied by fresh salsas and toppings. The only downsides are the minimal seating and limited hours (it closes at 6pm).
Hangar B Eatery 240 George Ryder Rd, at the airport ☏ 508/593-3655. Watch the planes coming and going at this superb breakfast and lunch airport eatery. Locally roasted Chatham coffee, house-made hash and brioche French toast are its hallmarks; lunch sees the likes of memorable fish tacos and grilled cheese and tomato soup. Open until 2pm; closed Tues.
Marion's Pie Shop 2022 Rte 28 ☏ 508/432-9439. Popular with locals and tourists alike for delicious sweet apple pies, savoury chicken pies and chewy breakfast cinnamon rolls. Note that "misbehaving children will be made into pies". A Chatham must-do.

The north coast

The meandering stretch of Rte-6A that parallels the Cape Cod Bay shoreline between Sandwich and Orleans is among the most scenic in New England, affording glimpses of the Cape Cod of popular imagination: salt marshes, crystal-clear ponds, ocean views and tiny villages. What began as a Native American pathway from Plymouth to Provincetown became the Cape's main road in the seventeenth and eighteenth centuries. There are hundreds of historic buildings along the 34-mile stretch, a large number of which have been turned into antiques shops or B&Bs. The towns that hold these are pleasant enough, though **Sandwich** and Brewster have the highest concentration of well-preserved historical homes. Even if you're travelling by car, it's worth it to temporarily ditch the wheels in favour of a bike to take the **Cape Cod Rail Trail**, a flat and popular bike path on the site of the former Old Colony Railroad track, running from Dennis, about fifteen miles past Sandwich, through Brewster to **Wellfleet**, a distance of twenty-four miles up the Cape.

Sandwich

Overlooked **SANDWICH** kicks off Route 6A with little of the commercialization common to so many Cape towns, thanks in part to its position so close to the mainland. The first permanent settlement on Cape Cod, Sandwich traces its roots to Pilgrim traders in the late 1620s who appreciated its proximity to the **Manomet Trading Post**, where they could barter goods and knowledge with the local Native Americans. The salt marshes in the area also provided an abundant supply of hay for their animals. Unsurprisingly, agriculture was Sandwich's main industry until the 1820s, when Bostonian Deming Jarves established a glass-making factory here. Though the dense woodlands supplied plenty of fuel for the furnaces, by the 1880s the Sandwich factory was no longer able to compete with the coal-fired glassworks of the Midwest.

A stroll around Sandwich's old **village centre** gives you a good taste of things to come along Route 6A: a little village green, white steepled church, a smattering of bed and breakfasts, antiques shops and a general store. Near Main and Water streets, the **Shawme Duck Pond** and adjacent **Dexter Grist Mill**, a replica of one built in 1654, make for a pleasant, peaceful stop, especially if you want to hear about (and maybe even see in progress) the milling process, they also, rather charmingly, grind their own organic cornmeal for sale (June to mid-Oct daily 10am–5pm; $3 tours, $3.50 cornmeal; ☎508/888-4910). Close to the shore, at 129 Main St, the **Sandwich Glass Museum** (Feb & March Wed–Sun 9.30am–4pm; April–Dec daily 9.30am–5pm; $5; ☎508/888-0251, ⓦwww.sandwich glassmuseum.org) contains fourteen galleries that house artefacts from the Boston & Sandwich Glass Company, which set up shop here in 1825. Besides thousands of functional and decorative pieces, the museum has a working glassblowing studio, with presentations on the hour.

Sandwich's attractions also include several miles of **beach** on Cape Cod Bay. The water here (like all the Cape's bayside beaches) is several degrees cooler than over on the Nantucket Sound side. It will cost you $10 to park at **Town Neck Beach**, accessed by a nifty raised boardwalk on Jarves St off Route 6A.

Practicalities

The place to **stay** in Sandwich is the ⚘ *Annabelle Bed & Breakfast*, 4 Grove St (☎508/833-1419, ⓦwww.annabellebedandbreakfast.com; rooms starting at $170 in summer), an elegant, cheerfully painted home modelled after Henry Wadsworth Longfellow's house in Cambridge, MA. Its horticulturalist owner takes great care in the surrounding garden, and its divine six rooms (two with fireplaces, and several with private decks) offer in-suite massage services and come with a much-lauded breakfast. The *Belfry Inne & Bistro*, 8 Jarves St (☎508/888-8550, ⓦwww.belfryinn.com; rooms from $189–295 in summer), comprises three restored period buildings, including a former Catholic church; this property's rooms in particular have an imaginative architectural style, some illuminated by original stained-glass windows.

The *Inne* also runs the *Painted Lady Café* and a dinner *Bistro* in what was once the church's nave. But really, the best places in Sandwich for **food** are the *Brown Jug*, at 155 Main St (☎508/888-4669), a wine, cheese and sandwich shop with antique plank floors and a patio, and *Beth's Special Teas Bakery and Café*, at 16 Jarves St (☎508/888-7716), offering a more comprehensive lunch menu than the *Jug* as well as fresh baked goods served until 6pm.

Eastham

Largely undiscovered **EASTHAM**, up Route 6 past Orleans as the Cape begins to curve toward Provincetown, is home to fewer than five thousand residents, most of whom are quite content to sit and watch the summer traffic pass by on its way north. Though the sum of Eastham's commercial facilities is little more than a small strip of shopping malls and petrol stations along Route 6, if you veer off the highway in either direction you will capture some authentic Cape flavour.

The first detour is the **Fort Hill** area, part of the Cape Cod National Seashore, with a scenic overlook for sweeping views of **Nauset Marsh**, a former bay that became a marsh when **Coast Guard Beach** was formed ($15 parking; free shuttle buses to the beach). North of here, at the corner of Ocean View Drive and Cable Road, is the red-and-white **Nauset Light**, originally located in Chatham, but installed here in 1923 and moved back 350ft a decade ago when it was in danger of crumbling into the sea. In 1838, this spot was home to no fewer than three brick lighthouses, known as the "Three Sisters", built 150ft apart. In 1892, serious erosion necessitated their replacement by three wooden towers; two were eventually moved away in 1918 and the third five years later. Having been acquired by the National Park service, they now stand in the woods well away from today's coastline.

On Eastham's bayside, **First Encounter Beach**, off Samoset Road, refers to the first meeting of Pilgrims and Native Americans in 1620. It was hardly a cordial rendezvous; with the *Mayflower* anchored in Provincetown, an exploration party led by Myles Standish came ashore only to meet a barrage of arrows. Things settled down after a few gunshots were returned, and since then the beach has been utterly tranquil. A plaque set back in the dunes describes the encounter in detail.

Practicalities

The place to **stay** in Eastham is the *Fort Hill Bed & Breakfast*, 75 Fort Hill Rd (℡508/240-2870, Ⓦwww.forthillbedandbreakfast.com; $245), where guests can choose to rest their head in either a smartly designed spacious suite or a silvery clapboard cottage with views of the sea. Nestled in the woods, the basic but adorable cottages of *Cottage Grove*, 1975 Rte-6 (℡508/255-0500, Ⓦwww .grovecape.com; $130), feature knotty pine walls, updated bathrooms, kitchenettes and plenty of quietude. There's also a **hostel**, *Mid-Cape American Youth Hostel*, right off the Cape Cod Rail Trail bike path at 75 Goody Hallet Drive (℡508/255-2785, Ⓦwww.hiusa.org; $30 non-members; closed mid-Sept to mid-May), in a collection of newly renovated woodsy cabins.

Cape Cod National Seashore

The protected **Cape Cod National Seashore**, which President Kennedy saved from development because of his fondness for it, extends along much of the Cape's Atlantic side, stretching forty miles from Chatham north to Provincetown. A programme of grass-planting helps to hold the whole place together: 3ft of the sands south of the National Seashore are washed away each year.

Displays and films at the **Salt Pond Visitor Center**, on Route 6 just north of Eastham (daily 9am–4.30pm, till 5pm in summer; ℡508/255-3421, Ⓦwww.nps.gov/caco), trace the geology and history of the Cape. A pretty road and hiking/cycling trail head east to the sands of **Coast Guard Beach** and **Nauset Light Beach**, both of which offer excellent swimming. You can also catch a free shuttle ride there from the visitors' centre in summer. Another fine beach is **Head of the Meadow**, halfway between Truro and Provincetown. In several areas parking is restricted to residents only, but you can often park by the road and strike off across the dunes to the shore.

Folks are obsessed with the onion rings at *Arnold's Lobster & Clam Bar*, 3580 Rte-6 (☎508/255-2575), a wildly popular seafood **restaurant**, beer garden and mini-golf venue, while *Sam's Deli*, 100 Brackett Rd (☎508/255-9340), is the place to go for bulging beach sandwiches. Just north on Rte-6, the fish market and seafood snack bar *Friendly Fisherman's* in North Eastham (☎508/255-6700) has great lobster rolls and fried clam strips, while in Orleans, the romantic and Mediterranean-inspired *Abba*, 89 Old Colony Way (☎508/255-8144), is one of the best restaurants in the region, with the likes of lobster in yellow curry sauce with butternut jasmine rice ($29).

Wellfleet

WELLFLEET, with a year-round population of just 2500, is, like Eastham eight miles to the south, one of the least developed towns on the Cape. Once the focus of a thriving oyster-fishing industry, today it is a favourite haunt of writers and artists who come to seek inspiration from the unsullied landscape and the heaving ocean. Despite the fact that a number of art galleries have surfaced – most of them along **Main** or **Commercial streets** – the town remains a remarkably unpretentious place, with many of the galleries themselves resembling fishing shacks and selling highly distinctive original work aimed at the serious collector. The Wellfleet Art Galleries Association produces a guide to the galleries which can be picked up at the **information booth** at the corner of Route 6 and LeCount Hollow Rd (☎508/349-2510).

The most scenic part of town is actually outside the centre, at the bluff-lined **Marconi Beach**, east off Route 6 in South Wellfleet, where Guglielmo Marconi issued the first transatlantic radio signal on January 18, 1903, and announced greetings from President Roosevelt to King Edward VII. Nothing remains of the tall radio towers built for this purpose, but there are some scale models beneath a gazebo-type structure overlooking the ocean. A short trail up the cliffside leads to a vantage point from which you can see horizontally across the entire Cape – just a mile wide at this point. Marconi is a good spot for a beach day, too: there are lifeguards, public restrooms and showers and parking ($15) that rarely fills to capacity.

Practicalities

If you want to **stay** the night in Wellfleet, try the two-room *Home Sweet Om*, 30 Captain Bellamy Rd (☎508/214-0113, ⓦwww.homesweetomcapecod.com; $250), a serene abode with bright, colourful rooms, lush gardens, a yoga studio and outstanding breakfasts. *Sweet Liberty B&B*, 220 Holbrook Ave (☎508/349-1751, ⓦwww.sweetlibertywellfleet.com; $150), has three simply furnished rooms in a beautiful two-hundred-year-old home walkable to downtown. For a more budget

---

Oyster shucking

No visit to Wellfleet would be complete without a taste of the town's famous oysters. In fact, the little molluscs are so abundant here that the French explorer Samuel de Champlain named the town "Port aux Huitres" (or oyster port) when he disembarked in 1606. The current name of Wellfleet, given by the English in 1763, also has an oyster heritage – it's a nod to England's own Wellfleet oyster beds. One of the best places to dive into a plate of the raw variety is the rowdy *Beachcomber*, on Cahoon Hollow Beach (☎508/349-6055), a fun beach shack with incredible waterfront views. You can also attend the Wellfleet **Oyster Weekend** (mid- to late Oct; ⓦwww.wellfleetoysterfest .org), complete with raw bars and shucking contests.

conscious option, there's a **hostel** further east in nearby Truro; the *HI-Truro*, on Rte-6 at 111 N. Pamet Rd (☎508/349-3889, ⓦwww.capecod.hiusa.org; $29–39; closed mid-Sept to mid-June), is housed in a sublime former Coast Guard Station right on the dunes, a mere five minutes' walk from tranquil Coast Guard Beach.

Tiny though Wellfleet is, there are a number of casual seafood **restaurants** worth checking out, such as *Moby Dick's*, at 3225 Route 6 across from Gull Pond Road (☎508/349-9795), which offers family seafood dining; *Mac's* (☎508/349-0404) has both a "glorified clam shack" and an upscale seafood eatery in two spots right on the Wellfleet Pier. For **nightlife**, the old-school 🎬 Wellfleet Drive-In Theatre, 51 Rte-6 (☎508/349-7176; ⓦwww.wellfleetdrivein.com), has outdoor movies and music in summer, replete with burgers and mini-golf; on weekends it doubles as a fun flea market. Wellfleet also hosts a renowned performing arts space – the **W.H.A.T Theater** – which stages contemporary productions in a state-of-the-art 220-seat theatre on Rte-6 (☎508/349-9428, ⓦwhat.org).

Provincetown

"Far from being out of the way, Provincetown is directly in the way of the navigator...
It is situated on one of the highways of commerce, and men from all parts of the
globe touch there in the course of a year".

from *Cape Cod* by Henry David Thoreau

The fishing burg of **PROVINCETOWN**, at the very tip of Cape Cod, is a gorgeous place, with silvery clapboard houses and gloriously unruly gardens lining the town's tiny, winding streets. Bohemians and artists have long flocked here for the sensational light and vast beaches. Over the past few decades, however, it has become known most famously as a **gay** resort destination, complete with frequent festivals and theme weekends. P-town, as this coastal community is often called, also has a drop of **Portuguese** culture, after a smallish population of fishermen began settling here in the mid-1800s. Throughout the summer, P-town's population swells into the tens of thousands, and there's often a carnival atmosphere in the bustling streets. This appealing hamlet should not be missed, especially as it's just a few hours' ferry ride from Boston.

Some history

The Pilgrims came ashore here and stayed for five weeks in 1620, signing the **Mayflower Compact**, before sailing across Cape Cod Bay to Plymouth. Provincetown was incorporated in 1727, and soon became a thriving fishing, salt-processing and whaling port; by 1880, the town was the richest per capita in Massachusetts. Fishing retains its importance here, but the town's destiny as one of the East Coast's leading **art colonies** was assured in 1899, when painter Charles W. Hawthorne founded the **Cape Cod School of Art**. By the early 1900s, many painters had begun to ply their trade in abandoned shacks by the sea, and by 1916 there were six art schools here. The natural beauty and laidback atmosphere also began to seduce rebellious young writers like Mary Heaton Vorse, who established the **Provincetown Players** theatre group in 1915. **Eugene O'Neill** joined the company in 1916, premiering his *Bound East for Cardiff* in a waterfront fish house done up as a theatre. **Tennessee Williams** was another frequent visitor, and more recently, **Michael Cunningham** wrote portions of *The Hours* here. Today, thanks in part to strict **zoning laws** designed to protect Provincetown's fragile environment, major development has been kept at bay, preserving the flavour of the old town.

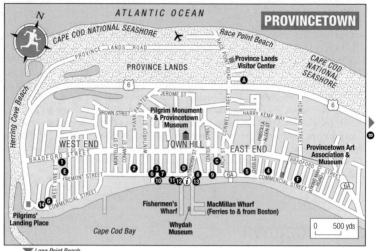

ACCOMMODATION		EATING		Portuguese Bakery	12
Carpe Diem Guesthouse	C	Bubala's by the Bay	6	Spiritus Pizza	3
Dune's Edge Campground	A	Café Edwige	8	Victor's	1
HI-Truro Hostel	B	Café Heaven	7	**BARS & CLUBS**	
Land's End Inn	G	Devon's	5	Atlantic House	11
Oxford Guesthouse	E	Karoo Kafe	9	Boatslip	2
Secret Garden Inn	D	Lobster Pot	13	The Pied	10
White Horse Inn	F	Mews Restaurant & Café	4	Red Inn	14

Arrival and information

Two companies make the ninety-minute trip across Massachusetts Bay from Boston to Provincetown: **Boston Harbor Cruises** departs from **Long Wharf** (mid-June to mid-Oct; $79 round-trip; ☎617/227-4321, ⓦwww.bostonharborcruises.com), while **Bay State Cruises** leaves from the **Commonwealth Pier** by Boston's World Trade Center (late May to early Oct; $79 round-trip; ☎617/748-1428, ⓦwww .boston-ptown.com). The latter has an excellent **excursion fare** for weekend day-tripping, too: $44 round-trip will get you to P-town and back with a three-hour window to tool around in – but keep in mind that these slower boats take three hours each way (late June to early Sept). There is also a Plymouth to Provincetown ferry (1hr 30min round-trip; $40; ☎1-800/225-4000, ⓦwww.provincetownferry.com).

Provincetown is at the end of **Route 6**, the Cape's main highway, and **buses** regularly trawl this stretch from Boston and all the major Cape towns; Bonanza Bus Lines (☎401/751-8800 or 1-888/751-8800, ⓦwww.bonanzabus.com) and Plymouth & Brockton buses (☎508/746-0378, ⓦwww.p-b.com) are the ones to call. Buses stop right in the middle of town near MacMillan Wharf. This is also where you'll find the **visitors' centre**, at 307 Commercial St (☎508/487-3424), full of all sorts of information.

Getting around

Provincetown is a very **walkable** place; **bicycles** can come in handy, though, especially if you want to venture a bit further afield. For rentals, try Arnold's at 329 Commercial St (☎508/487-0844), right in the centre of town, or Gale Force Bikes, 144 Bradford St Ext (☎508/487-4849), located close to the **bike trails** that meander through the Province Lands. Bikes at both places go for about $20 per day. Provincetown also claims the title of first **whale-watching** spot on the East Coast; the best company is the Dolphin Fleet (April–Oct; $39; ☎508/349-1900 or 1-800/826-9300, ⓦwww.whalewatch.com), with cruises leaving frequently from MacMillan Wharf.

If you want to take a **boat ride**, Flyer's Boat Rentals, 131A Commercial St (☎508/487-0898, ⓦwww.flyersrentals.com), provides a range of rental boats, from kayaks to powerboats. Alternatively, take their **shuttle** across Cape Cod Bay to Long Point Beach ($10 one-way, $15 round-trip).

Accommodation

Many of the most picturesque cottages in town are **guesthouses**, some with spectacular views over Cape Cod Bay. Prices are generally very reasonable until mid-June, and off-season you can find real bargains. Dune's Edge Campground, on Rte-6 just east of the central trafficlights (☎508/487-9815, ⓦwww.dunes-edge.com), charges $40 for use of one of its wooded sites.

Carpe Diem Guesthouse & Spa 12 Johnson St ☎1-800/487-0132, ⓦwww.carpediemguesthouse .com. Friendly, accommodating owners, beautifully-appointed rooms with a bit of an Eastern vibe, horseback riding, a spa and an afternoon wine and cheese hour at this lovely B&B on a quiet side street. $199.

HI-Truro Hostel 111 N. Pamet Rd, Truro ☎508/349-3889, ⓦwww.capecod.hiusa.org. Eleven miles east, in Truro, this hostel has the area's best bang for the buck: 42 dorm beds in a former coastguard station that's right on the beach. $29–39.

Land's End Inn 22 Commercial St ☎508/487-0706, ⓦwww.landsendinn.com. Imaginatively decorated rooms and suites done up in a detailed Art Nouveau style, many with sweeping ocean views, in a turreted house perched high upon a hill. Continental breakfast and daily wine-and-cheese hour included. A truly original and very special place. $315.

Oxford Guesthouse 8 Cottage St ☎508/487-9103, ⓦwww.oxfordguesthouse.com. Seven rooms and suites elegantly decorated in English "country style", with classical drapes and patterned wallpaper adding to the vintage ambience – you get continental breakfast, cookies in the afternoon and a civilized "wine hour" every evening. CDs, DVDs and wi-fi available. $189.

Secret Garden Inn 300A Commercial St ☎508/487-9027, ⓦwww.secretgardenptown .com. This 1830s captain's house is a relative bargain, with seven quaint rooms done up in country furnishings and, just outside, a beautiful garden and veranda. Continental breakfast included. $120.

White Horse Inn 500 Commercial St ☎508/487-1790. A whimsical, colourful, art-strewn space; some rooms have shared baths. There are also family-sized apartments with kitchens. Beach access, and a beatnik vibe. $70 for a single room with a shared bath, $185 for an apartment.

The Town and around

The town centre is essentially two three-mile-long streets, **Commercial** and **Bradford**, that follow the harbour and are connected by about forty tiny lanes of no more than two short blocks each. Though diluted by tourism, the beatnik spirit is still in evidence, most pronounced in regular Friday-night expositions in the many art galleries along Commercial Street. On summer evenings this narrow street fills with hordes of sightseers, locals and, amazingly, cars, even though they can do little more than crawl along. **Fisherman's Wharf**, and the more touristy **MacMillan Wharf**, busy with whale-watching boats, yachts and colourful old Portuguese fishing vessels, split the town in half. Macmillan Wharf also houses the **Whydah Museum**, 16 Macmillan Wharf (April–May & Sept–Oct daily 10am–5pm; June–Aug till 7pm; $10; ☎508/487-8899, ⓦwww.whydah.com), which displays some of the bounty from a famous pirate shipwreck off the coast of Wellfleet in 1717. The lifelong quest of native Cape Codder Barry Clifford to recover the treasure from the one-time slave ship *Whydah* – repository of loot from more than fifty ships when it sank – paid off royally with his discovery of the ship in the summer of 1984. Thousands of coins, gold bars, pieces of jewellery and weapons were retrieved, ranging from odds and ends like silver shoe buckles and flintlock pistols to some absolutely horrifying gadgetry for shackling slaves.

Two blocks north of the piers, atop aptly named Town Hill, is the 252ft granite tower of the **Pilgrim Monument and Provincetown Museum** (daily: April to late May & mid–Sept to Nov 9am–5pm; late May to mid–Sept 9am–7pm; $7; ☎508/487-1310, ⓦwww.pilgrim-monument.org), which commemorates the Pilgrims' landing and their signing of the Mayflower Compact. It's 116 steps to the observation deck; on a clear day, you can see all the way to Boston. Back on the main drag, the delightful **Provincetown Art Association and Museum**, 460 Commercial St (late May to September daily 11am–8pm, Fri till 10pm, Sat & Sun till 5pm; Oct–May Thurs–Sun noon–5pm; $7, free Fri after 5pm; ☎508/487-1750, ⓦwww.paam.org), rotates works from its two-thousand-strong collection, with equal prominence given to local and established artists. Friday night is best (and free), when artist openings frequently take place.

On the other side of the wharves is the quieter and slightly less cramped **West End**, where many of the weathered clapboard houses are cheerfully decorated with colourful blinds, white picket fences and wildflowers spilling out of every crevice. At Commercial Street's western end, the Pilgrim **landing place** is marked by a modest bronze plaque on a boulder. Nearby, just past the *Provincetown Inn*, is the **Breakwater Trail**, a mile-long **jetty** leading to Long Point Beach, a great place to watch the sun set.

A little way beyond the town's narrow strip of sand, a string of **undeveloped beaches** is marked only by dunes and a few shabby huts. The Province Lands **visitor centre**, in the middle of the dunes off Race Point Rd (late May to early Sept daily 9am–5pm; early Sept to late-Oct & April to late May daily 9am–4.30pm; ☎508/487-1256), has an observation deck from which you might spot a whale – or even, when the tide is right, the ruins of the **HMS Somerset**, a sunken British battleship from the Revolutionary War. Province Lands is also home to one of Cape Cod's best **bike paths**, roaming through the dunes without a building in sight.

Eating

Food options abound in Provincetown. Whenever possible, especially in the few restaurants where you can eat al fresco (mosquitoes can be a big problem), arrive early or call ahead to make a reservation; many restaurants are packed in season. Most eateries **close** in the winter, though some remain open on weekends.

Bubala's By the Bay 183 Commercial St ☎508/487-0773. A fun hangout right on the water, with a vast menu providing something for everyone; although it's really more about the ambience here, top picks are the fish and chips ($17) and the market-priced fresh shellfish.

Café Edwige 333 Commercial St ☎508/487-2008. Breakfast's the thing at this popular second-floor spot; try one of the omelettes of the day or get the famed fresh fruit pancakes. Creative bistro fare at dinnertime.

Café Heaven 199 Commercial St ☎508/487-9639. Breakfast nirvana – white walls bedecked with bright, contemporary paintings, eggs Benedict with home-made English muffins and fresh-squeezed juice; great salads, sandwiches and dinner options, too. Just like heaven, there's usually a wait to get in.

Devon's 401 1/2 Commercial St ☎508/487-4773. Cute fishing shack that's been converted into a fine-dining outpost with just 37 seats and an open kitchen - try to reserve a table by the window. The menu features French/

American fusion cuisine; pairing items like local sea scallops with truffle zabaglione.

Karoo Kafe 338 Commercial St ☎ 508/487-6630. Tasty, inexpensive South African fare. Order the Cape Malay stew (curry, coconut milk and veggies over rice; $14) at the counter and enjoy it amongst sunny, zebra-striped seating.

Lobster Pot 321 Commercial St ☎ 508/487-0842. Its landmark neon sign is like a beacon for those who come from far and wide for the ultra-fresh crustaceans. Affordable and family oriented.

Mews Restaurant & Café 429 Commercial St ☎ 508/487-1500. Since its opening in 1961, this unassuming spot has served everyone from Judy Garland to Marc Jacobs, and continues to garner rave reviews for its rotating fresh fusion cuisine (think pork vindaloo or almond-crusted cod; both $26) and extensive vodka bar (286 and counting).

Portuguese Bakery 299 Commercial St ☎ 508/487-1803. This old standby is the place to come for cheap baked goods, particularly the tasty fried *rabanada*, akin to portable French toast. Also great for a morning breakfast sandwich; ask for it on a Portuguese muffin.

Victor's 175 Bradford St Ext ☎ 508/487-1777. Small plates are the *mots du jour* at this New American dinner spot with menu delights like blood orange grilled shrimp ($12) and deconstructed tuna napoleon ($14). There's also a raw-bar happy hour ($1.25 oysters, shrimps and clams) Thurs–Sun 3–6pm.

Nightlife and entertainment

Provincetown loves to party. Each in-season weekend, boatloads of revellers seek out P-town's notoriously wild **nightlife**. Heavily geared towards a **gay** clientele, resulting in ubiquitous tea dances, drag shows and video bars, some establishments have terrific waterfront locations and terraces to match, making them ideal spots to sit out with a drink at sunset. After the clubs close, partygoers assemble around late-night slices at *Spiritus Pizza*, 190 Commercial St (☎ 508/487-2808) to figure out the next big thing.

Atlantic House 6 Masonic Place, behind Commercial St ☎ 508/487-3821. The "A-House" – a dark drinking hole that was a favourite of Tennessee Williams and Eugene O'Neill – is now a trendy gay dance club and bar; everyone ends up here around 12.30am.

Boatslip 161 Commercial St ☎ 508/487-1669. The daily tea dances (4pm) at this resort are legendary; you can either dance away on a long wooden deck overlooking the water, or cruise inside under a disco ball and flashing lights; afterwards, people usually head to *The Pied*.

The Pied 193 Commercial St ☎ 508/487-1527. Though largely a lesbian club (it's the oldest in the country), the outdoor deck and inside dance floor at this trendy waterfront space attract a good dose of men, too, for their longstanding After Tea T-Dance (daily 6.30–9pm).

Red Inn 15 Commercial St ☎ 508/487-7334. For a complete change of nightlife pace, head to the classy *Red Inn*, where you can swill your martini over wide plank hardwood floors in an historic house by the sea.

Nantucket

T he thirty-mile, two-hour sea crossing to **NANTUCKET** from Cape Cod may not be an ocean-going odyssey, but it does set the "Little Grey Lady" apart from her larger, shore-hugging sister, Martha. Just halfway out from Hyannis, neither mainland nor island is in sight, and you realize why the Native Americans dubbed it "Distant Land". Once you've landed, you can avert your eyes from the smart-money double-deck cruisers with names like *Pier Pressure* and *Loan Star* and let the place remind you that it hasn't always been a rich folks' playground. Indeed, despite the formidable prowess of its seamen, survival for settlers on the island's barren soil was always a struggle. The tiny, cobbled carriage-ways of **Nantucket Town** itself, once one of the largest cities in Massachusetts, were frozen in time by economic decline 150 years ago. Today, this area of delightful old restored houses – the town has more buildings on the National Register of Historic Places than Boston – is very much the island hub, while seven flat, easily cycled miles to the east the rose-covered cottages of **Siasconset** (always abbreviated to 'Sconset)

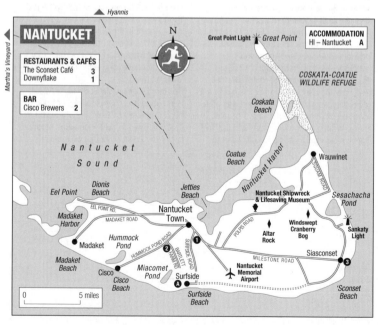

give another glimpse of days gone by. However appealing the island's man-made attractions are, it's Nantucket's gentle natural beauty that's the real draw, with heaths and moorlands, mile after mile of fabulous beaches and a network of bicycle paths that connect the many spots maintained by conservation trusts.

Arrival and information

Most likely you'll arrive in Nantucket by **ferry**. Both the Steamship Authority (T 508/447-8600, W www.islandferry.com) and Hy-Line (T 508/778-2600 or 1-800/492-8082, W www.hy-linecruises.com) run year-round passenger services to the island from Hyannis, but only the Steamship Authority's boats take cars. Both have fast ferries that charge $33–39 each way for passengers; the Steamship Authority's car ferry (mid-May to mid-Oct; $215 per vehicle) allows passengers only at $17. Island-hoppers can take Hy-Line's inter-island ferry ($84 round-trip), which runs daily from June to early September between Hyannis, Martha's Vineyard's Oak Bluffs and Nantucket. A much quicker way to get to the island is by **air**: Island Airlines (T 1-800/248-7779, W www.islandair.net) and Cape Air (T 508/771-6944, W www.flycapeair.com) run year-round daily services to and from Boston, New Bedford, Providence and Martha's Vineyard. The **airport** (T 508/325-5300, W www.nantucketairport.com) is about three miles southeast of Nantucket Town; flights average $150 round-trip.

Visitor information is available from the **Chamber of Commerce**, 48 Main St (Mon–Fri 9am–5pm; T 508/228-1700, W www.nantucketchamber.org), who can also assist you in finding a room on the island, or from the helpful **Nantucket Visitors' Information centre**, 25 Federal St (April–Dec daily 9am–5pm; rest of year Mon–Sat 9am–5pm; T 508/228-0925, W www.nantucket-ma.gov). The **Nantucket Historical Association**, 15 Broad St (Mon–Fri 9am–5pm; T 508/228-1894, W www.nha.org), which maintains twenty historical properties on the island, offers a $20 **combination ticket** for entrance to all its buildings including the Whaling Museum ($6 for only the historic sites).

Getting around

Once you've arrived, **getting around** should pose no problem. From the moment you get off the ferry you're surrounded by **bike** rental places and tour companies. Try Young's Bicycle Shop (T 508/228-1151, W www.youngsbicycleshop.com), conveniently located on Steamboat Wharf; it should cost $30 per day for a standard mountain bike. Driving a **car** makes little sense here, especially in peak season, when island arteries can easily get clogged, and it won't endear you to the locals. If you didn't bring one with you on the ferry, there is an expensive and limited on-island supply available from Young's Bicycle Shop, as well as at Windmill (T 508/228-1227, W www.nantucketautorental.com) and two spots by the airport, Nantucket Island Rent-A-Car (T 508/228-9989, W www.nantucketislandrentacar.com) and Hertz (T 508/228-9421, W www.hertz.com); the former rents a fleet of 4WD jeeps suitable for beach driving.

A better way to get around is by **bus**: five shuttle routes on the island are operated between May and September by the Nantucket Regional Transit Authority (daily 7.30am–11.30pm; T 508/228-7025, W www.shuttlenantucket.com), with fares starting at $1 (exact change) per journey for in-town travel; you can get unlimited travel for three days ($12), a week ($20), or a month ($50). Barrett's Tours (T 508/228-0174 or 1-800/773-0174; $25) runs ninety-minute narrated bus tours around the island, stopping in 'Sconset, the historic windmill, beaches and a

The whalers of Nantucket

Scores of anonymous Captains have sailed out of Nantucket, that were as great, and greater than your Cooke...for in their succorless empty-handedness, they, in the heathenish sharked waters, and by the beaches of unrecorded, javelin islands, battled with virgin wonders and terrors that Cooke with all his marines and muskets would not willingly have dared.

From *Moby Dick*, by Herman Melville

The whalers of Nantucket drew the attention of many with their skill and resultant domination of a notably treacherous trade. The early chronicler Crèvecoeur provided an extensive account of Nantucket as it was in 1782 in his *Letters from an American Farmer*. Although perturbed by the islanders' universal habit of taking a dose of opium every morning, he held them up as a model of diligence and good self-government. Whaling was a disciplined profession, unmarred by the stereotyped debauchery of sailors elsewhere, and to feed themselves and equip their ships the islanders kept up a shrewd and extensive trade with the mainland. The whalemen were not paid; instead each had a share (a "lay") of the final proceeds of the voyage. And what a voyage it was – the common occurrence when a harpooned whale would speed away, dragging a ship helter-skelter behind it for endless terrifying hours, was known as a "Nantucket Sleighride". You can read more about the whalers in Herman Melville's *Moby Dick*, a valediction of sorts since by the time it was published in 1851, Nantucket's fortunes had gone into an abrupt decline. As a magazine article of 1873 reported, "Let no traveler visit Nantucket with the expectation of witnessing the marks of a flourishing trade...of the great fleet of ships which dotted every sea, scarcely a vestige remains".

cranberry bog. You probably won't need the aid of **taxis** while here, but they are usually available at the airport or by the ferry terminal; A-1 (☎508/228-3330) and Chief's Cab (☎508/284-8497) are both reliable.

Accommodation

But for the youth hostel, **accommodation** on Nantucket can be expensive, although there is quite a range of options available; in Nantucket Town, you'll find everything from resorts with pools, health clubs and sophisticated restaurants to cosy inns and B&Bs, though it's not easy to find a room for under $175 in high season, and most doubles cost over $200. Further afield, you can rent private homes by the week – try ⓦ www.summerhome.com/Nantucket.htm for reliable rental listings posted by local residents. The following rates are all for the summer; you can expect deep discounts throughout the rest of the year.

Century House 10 Cliff Rd ☎508/228-0530, ⓦ www.centuryhouse.com. Elegant rooms with polished pine floors and country-house ambience in this 1833 late-Federal home. $175.

Cliff Lodge 9 Cliff Rd ☎508/228-9480, ⓦ www.clifflodgenantucket.com. Quiet B&B in a residential area with some low-priced singles in the off-season; owned by the same lovely proprietors as the *Martin House Inn*. In summer: $155 single, $195 double.

HI-Nantucket Surfside Beach ☎508/228-0433, ⓦ capecod.hiusa.org. Dorm beds in a former lifesaving station, a stone's throw from Surfside Beach, just over three miles south of Nantucket Town (it's right by a shuttle stop). Rates range $29–39 per night and include a continental breakfast and free internet access. Closed Oct to mid-May.

Martin House Inn 61 Centre St ☎508/228-0678, ⓦ www.martinhouseinn.com. Thirteen lovely rooms, some with working fireplaces, offer good value in this romantic 1803 seaman's house; close to shops and ferries. In summer: $125 single, $220 double.

The Nesbitt Inn 21 Broad St ℡ 508/228-0156. The central location, friendly innkeepers and affordable rooms, most with original furniture, compensate for the shared baths (three for twelve rooms) and occasional noisiness in this 1872 Victorian inn. Three apartments out back, and three rooms with private baths are also available. Singles from $125.

Sherburne Inn 10 Gay St ℡ 508/228-4425, ⓦ www.sherburneinn.com. Dating from 1835, this well-appointed B&B has elegant rooms, two parlours with fireplaces, wi-fi, a flower garden and patio and fresh-baked cookies in the afternoon. $250.

Ship's Inn 13 Fair St ℡ 508/228-0040, ⓦ www.shipsinnnantucket.com. Three-storey whaling captain's home dating from 1831, with eleven biggish rooms and an on-site restaurant. $275.

Union Street Inn 7 Union St ℡ 1-888/517-0707, ⓦ www.unioninn.com. Luxurious, well-loved B&B with all the trimmings: beautiful rooms with period wallpaper, cosy bathrobes, fancy soaps and fresh afternoon pastries. $345.

Veranda House 3 Step Lane ℡ 508/228-0695, ⓦ www.theverandahouse.com. The theme at this hotel is "retro chic", adding a refreshingly contemporary take on the island's traditional Victorian-style B&Bs; rooms are stylishly designed, most with harbour views, and come with free wi-fi and an epicure-style breakfast. $250.

Nantucket Town

Very much the centre of activity on the island, the cobbled walkways of **NANTUCKET TOWN** boast a delightful array of eighteenth- and nineteenth-century homes, most of them concentrated around **Main Street**. Before you hit there, though, you can get the salty feel of the half-dozen wharves around Nantucket's harbour when arriving on the ferry, which dock at **Steamboat Wharf** or lively **Straight Wharf**, just to the south, dating from 1723, and lined with souvenir shops and restaurants.

Steamboat Wharf leads directly to Broad Street, where the excellent **Whaling Museum**, 13 Broad St (late May to mid-Oct daily 10am–5pm; $17; $20 site pass includes Hadwen House, Oldest House, Quaker Meeting House and Old Mill; ℡ 508/228-1894, ⓦ www.nha.org), houses an outstanding collection of seafaring exotica in a former 1846 candle-making factory. Highlights include an exquisite scrimshaw collection carved by rough-and-tumble nineteenth-century sailors; there is also a luminous fresnel lens, formerly housed in the Sankaty Head Lighthouse. A gigantic sperm whale skeleton presides over the entrance; look for the rotted tooth on its jaw – officials believe it was a tooth infection that brought about the whale's demise. Before you leave, check out the phenomenal view over the town and harbour from the museum roof.

From the museum, it's a pleasant stroll along South Beach and Easton streets up to Brant Point and the 26ft **Brant Point Lighthouse**, guarding the entrance to the harbour. Completed in 1901 (the first version was erected in 1746), the whole site is a working coastguard station, but the grounds are open to the public.

Polpis Road

Polpis Road, an indirect and arcing track from Nantucket Town to 'Sconset, holds a number of natural attractions both on and off its main course, all easily accessed from the **bike path** that shadows the road. Your first stop should be the **Nantucket Shipwreck & Life Saving Museum**, off the northern side of the road at no. 158 (late May to mid-Oct daily 10am–4pm; $5; ℡ 508/228-1885, ⓦ www.eganmaritime.org), whose lifesaving motto was "you have to go out, but you don't have to come back"; the museum is filled with an evocative collection of early lifesaving surfboats, buoys, rescue equipment, photographs and artefacts from the *Andrea Doria*, which sunk off Nantucket forty years ago.

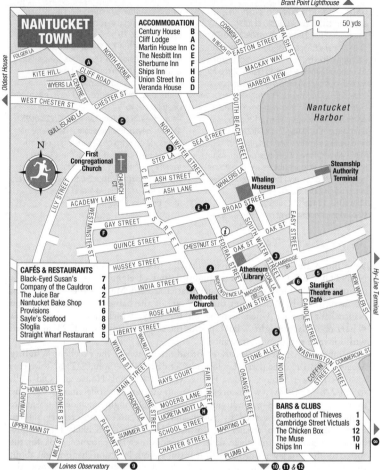

NANTUCKET TOWN

ACCOMMODATION
Century House	B
Cliff Lodge	A
Martin House Inn	C
The Nesbitt Inn	E
Sherburne Inn	F
Ships Inn	H
Union Street Inn	G
Veranda House	D

Nantucket Harbor

First Congregational Church

Whaling Museum

Steamship Authority Terminal

N

Atheneum Library

Methodist Church

Starlight Theatre and Café

CAFÉS & RESTAURANTS
Black-Eyed Susan's	7
Company of the Cauldron	4
The Juice Bar	2
Nantucket Bake Shop	11
Provisions	6
Sayle's Seafood	8
Sfoglia	9
Straight Wharf Restaurant	5

BARS & CLUBS
Brotherhood of Thieves	1
Cambridge Street Victuals	3
The Chicken Box	12
The Muse	10
Ships Inn	H

Loines Observatory ▼ ⑨   ▼ ⑩, ⑪ & ⑫

Further on, an unmarked track leads south to **Altar Rock**, the island's highest point, where you'll want to walk around for views of the surrounding bogs. One of these, the 200-acre **Windswept Cranberry Bog**, east on Polpis Road, is a feast of colour at most times of the year, especially so in mid-October, when the ripened berries, loosened from the plants by machines, float to the top of the water.

Siasconset, Great Point and Coatue

Seven flat miles east of Nantucket Town, the village of **SIASCONSET**, or 'Sconset as it's universally known, is filled with venerable cottages literally encrusted with salt and covered over with roses. Once solely a fishing village, it began to attract visitors eager to get away from the foul smells of Nantucket Town's whale-oil refineries, and in the late 1800s, enough writers and actors came from big cities to give 'Sconset artistic renown. There's not too much to see, other than the houses themselves along Broadway and Center streets – certainly picturesque enough – and the year-round population of 150 only supports a few commercial establishments, all close to one another in the centre of town.

A few miles north, the peppermint-striped **Sankaty Light**, an 1849 lighthouse, stands on a picturesque 90ft bluff, accented by unruly waves below. Further north still, **Coskata-Coatue-Great Point**, a five-mile-long, razor-thin slice of sand, takes in three separate wildlife refuges, and is accessible by four-wheel-drive (for which you'll need a special $125 permit purchased online at Ⓦwww .thetrustees.org, Ⓣ508/228-5646); it's free if you're on foot. You could also take one of the worthwhile tours offered by the Trustees of Reservations, leaving from the Wauwinet Gatehouse (2.5hrs; $40, reservations required; Ⓣ508/228-0006, Ⓦwww.thetrustees.org). In the Coskata section, the wider beaches are backed by salt marshes and some trees: with binoculars, you may catch sight of plovers, egrets, oystercatchers, terns and even osprey. The beach narrows again as you approach the **Great Point Light**, at the end of the spit, put up in 1986 after an earlier light was destroyed during a 1984 storm. This new lighthouse is solar-powered, and is said to be able to withstand 240mph winds and 20ft waves. Unsurprisingly, this is not the safest place to swim, even on a calm day. **Coatue**, the last leg of the journey, is the narrow stretch that separates Nantucket Harbor from the ocean; so narrow, in fact, that stormy seas frequently crash over it, turning Great Point into an island.

Nantucket beaches

With fifty miles of **beaches**, most of which are open to the public, Nantucket is more accessible than Martha's Vineyard for ocean enthusiasts. The island's southern and eastern flanks, where the water tends to have rougher surf, are ideal for surfers, while the more sheltered northern beaches are good for swimming. With extremely limited, albeit free, **parking**, it makes sense to walk or cycle to all but the most far-flung of the strands. You can rent **watersports equipment** (kayaks, windsurfers and sailboats, for $20–50) from Nantucket Community Sailing, on Jetties Beach (Ⓣ508/228-5358, Ⓦwww.nantucketsailing.org).

Nantucket Town
Brant Point Off Easton Street. Strong currents at the harbour entrance mean this beach is better equipped for tanning and watching the comings and goings of boats in the harbour, rather than swimming.

Children's Beach Off South Beach Street. Just minutes from Steamboat Wharf, this calm harbour beach is perfect for children, and has a full range of facilities.

Dionis Beach Eel Point Road. A quiet beach with high dunes and calm waters.

Jetties Beach Off Bathing Beach Road. Catch the shuttle bus that runs along North Water and South Beach streets in the centre of town, or leg it to this popular beach whose facilities include lifeguards, changing rooms and a snack bar.

East of Town
'Sconset Beach (Also known as Codfish Park). Off Polpis Road. Sandy beach with moderate surf and a full range of facilities. Just a short walk to several eating places.

South Shore
Cisco Beach Hummock Point Road. Long, sandy beach with heavy surf, lifeguards and restrooms; ideal for surfing.

Madaket Beach At the end of the Madaket Bike Path. Another long beach with strong surf and gorgeous sunsets over the water. Restrooms, lifeguards and a shuttle bus (leaves from Broad Street in Nantucket Town).

Surfside Beach Off Surfside Road. Wide sands attract a youthful crowd of surfers; there's a large car park, but you'd do better to take the shuttle bus from town.

Madaket

At the western tip of Nantucket, rural **MADAKET** is the small settlement located on the spot where Thomas Macy landed in 1659. There's little in the way of visitor attractions, but the area's peacefulness and natural beauty make up for that. Unspoiled **Eel Point**, a couple of miles north, sits on a spit of sand covered with all manner of wild plants and flowers, including wild roses and bayberries, which attract an array of birds, including graceful egrets. Free **maps** and **trail guides** can be downloaded from the Nantucket Conservation Foundation's website; they also have information in their office at 118 Cliff Rd (☎508/228-2884, Ⓦwww.nantucketconservation.com).

Eating

Nantucket abounds with first-rate dining **establishments**, but be prepared for the bill: prices are often comparable to those in Manhattan. As far as **drinking** goes, many of the restaurants have bars attached to them, though there are also a few pubby places to get boozed up. All of the establishments below, unless otherwise indicated, are in Nantucket Town.

Black Eyed Susan's 10 India St ☎508/325-0308. Beloved little brunch spot (also dinner Mon–Sat in summer) with inventive egg scrambles and cheery buttermilk pancakes. Worth the wait in line; cash only.

Company of the Cauldron 5 India St ☎508/228-4016. A romantic, vine-covered, candlelit haven with live harp music thrice weekly. Both seatings of a shifting prix fixe menu ($62) sell out quickly, so make reservations.

Downyflake 18 Sparks Ave ☎508/228-4533. The island's best diner, a bit out of the way on the edge of town but worth a visit for the reasonably priced plates of comfort food, and especially the fresh doughnuts (get them to go).

The Juice Bar 12 Broad St ☎508/228-5799. The best ice cream spot on the island. It's packed with patrons eager for hand-rolled waffle cones filled with inventive flavours like chocolate peanut butter cookie dough and classics like mint oreo.

Nantucket Bake Shop 79 Orange St ☎508/228-2797. A local landmark, the *Bake Shop* opens at 6.30am so that morning folks can get their hands on warm scones and fresh blueberry muffins; there are also tons of tasty cookies such as the "chocolate chunker".

Provisions 3 Harbor Square ☎508/228-3258. Great variety of bulging, gourmet sandwiches with names like the "Turkey Terrific" and the "Yacht Club" (smoked salmon, lemon caper cream cheese and cucumbers).

Sayle's Seafood 99 Washington St Extension ☎508/228-4599. Breezy, very casual seafood market where you can pick up fried cod, fish cakes and clam chowder, or choose your own lobster for them to steam up; take it to go or munch on the porch. There's also an all-encompassing "clambake" option ($36/person in-store, $65/person at your house).

The Sconset Café 8 Main St, Siasconset ☎508/257-4008. This endearing little institution is a flavourful oasis after the seven-mile bike ride out to 'Sconset. You'll find salads and sandwiches at lunch time, fresh muffins and baked goods throughout the day, and candlelit, New American fare at dinner, with rotating menu items like seared salmon with artichoke hearts ($30) and crab cakes remoulade ($14). Cash or cheque only.

Sfoglia 130 Lower Pleasant St ☎508/325-4500. Just outside of town, this rustic, romantic spot prepares seasonal Italian fare like *pappardelle alla Bolognese* ($14) with local mussels ($13) and chicken *al mattone* ($26). The setting is country-chic, with artfully mismatched tables and chairs and vases of fresh-cut flowers. Dinner only, reservations recommended.

Something Natural 50 Cliff Rd ☎508/228-0504. The place to go for sandwiches to take to the beach; fabulously fresh creations like avocado, cheddar and chutney on home-made bread ($8.75) are best washed down with Nantucket Nectar's "Matt Fee Tea" – named for the owner. No seating per se, but there are picnic tables and blankets on offer.

Straight Wharf Restaurant 6 Harbor Square ☎508/228-4499. Lovely New American spot with smoked bluefish pate and watermelon salad in an airy, art-strewn space overlooking the harbour. The bar shifts from seafood eatery to more of an *Animal House* vibe after dark; they also do a mean weekend brunch. Reservations recommended.

Nightlife and entertainment

For such a small island, Nantucket has a nice spectrum of **nightlife** offerings, ranging from martini bars and down-and-dirty local pubs to clambakes and impromptu beach get-togethers. One good spot to see a **movie** is the Starlight Theatre and Café, 1 N Union St (☎508/228-4435). Also in Nantucket Town, the Theatre Workshop of Nantucket puts on **plays** and musicals at the Methodist Church, 2 Center St (☎508/228-4305, ⓦwww.theatreworkshop.com); tickets rarely top $25. Additionally, the Nantucket Musical Arts Society stages **classical concerts** with renowned musicians on Tuesday evenings in July and August, in the First Congregational Church. Finally, head to the **Loines Observatory**, 59 Milk St (Mon, Wed & Fri 9–10.30pm weather permitting; $15, $10 kids; ☎508/228-9273, ⓦwww.mmo.org), where you can climb up to an aging telescope and peek into space, as well as admire a much newer 24-inch research telescope. Falling under the aegis of the Maria Mitchell Association (4 Vestal St; ☎508/228-9198, ⓦwww.mmo.org), the observatories are a homage to local girl Maria Mitchell, the first professional woman astronomer in the US.

Brotherhood of Thieves 23 Broad St ☎508/228-2551. This bar is a Nantucket institution and the place to go for live folk music, year-round; huddle in the dimly lit pub, or pose at the smarter bar upstairs.

Cambridge Street Victuals 12 Cambridge St ☎508/228-7109. A fun after-work type of bar with a deep blue interior, a good mix of folks and Guinness, Stella and microbrews on tap.

The Chicken Box 16 Dave St ☎508/228-9717. Literally a wooden box-like shack on the outskirts of town, every summer night, people of all stripes pack into "The Box" for great live shows and dive-y drinking environs. Shuffleboard and pool tables, too. Cash only, but there's an ATM inside.

Cisco Brewers 3 Bartlett Farm Rd ☎508/325-5929. More of a scenic outdoor bar than a tour-giving brewery, *Cisco's* relaxed, pastoral courtyard offers sample flights of home-made beer, wine and hard liquor to a contented crowd; patrons are encouraged to bring along food for their drinks. The only drawback is its location – it's 2.5 miles out of town. Take a cab (getting here by bike is a little hairy).

The Muse 44 Surfside Rd ☎508/228-6873. A mix of rock, reggae and just about anything else you can dance to, as well as a few pool tables, keep this venue popular.

Ship's Inn 13 Fair St ☎508/228-0040. Also doubling as a French fusion restaurant and B&B, the *Ship's Inn* houses a sophisticated bar in the basement of its 1831 whaling captain's home.

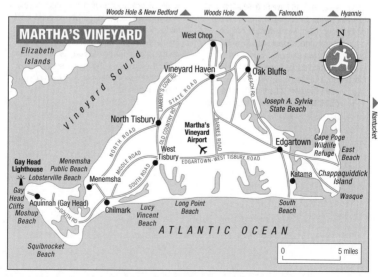
Martha's Vineyard

T he largest offshore island in New England, twenty-mile-long **Martha's Vineyard** offers enough fantastic beach fare, local history and standout clam shacks to win over even the surliest New Englander. It encompasses more physical variety (and has more of a laidback attitude) than Nantucket, with hills and pasturelands providing scenic counterpoints to the beaches and wild, windswept moors on the separate island of **Chappaquiddick**. Roads throughout the Vineyard are framed by knotty oak trees, which lend a romantic aura to an already pretty landscape. The most genteel town on the island is **Edgartown**, all prim and proper with its freshly painted, white-clapboard Colonial homes and manicured gardens. The other main town, **Vineyard Haven**, has a more commercial atmosphere, not surprising considering that it is one of the main places where the ferries call in. **Oak Bluffs**, in between the two, is more sizeable than Vineyard Haven (and the other docking point for ferries), and is known for its array of wooden gingerbread cottages and inviting eateries. Regardless of where you visit, watch out for the terminology: heading "Up-Island" takes you, improbably, southwest to the cliffs at **Aquinnah** (formerly known as Gay Head); conversely, "Down-Island" refers to the triumvirate of easterly towns mentioned above.

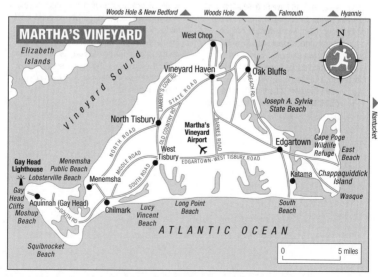

Ferries to Martha's Vineyard

The most frequent ferries – and the only ones that can take cars – run year-round from **Woods Hole** on Cape Cod. In summer, however, leaving from somewhere else can be more convenient; **Falmouth** and **Hyannis** have day-boats. In order to avoid weekend Cape Cod traffic, the ferries from **New Bedford** and **Quonset Point** in Rhode Island have become popular options; for New Yorkers, there is also a ferry that leaves from **Montauk**. In **winter**, ferries (from Woods Hole and Hyannis) run solely to Vineyard Haven.

Unless otherwise specified, the ferries listed below run several times daily in the peak mid-June to mid-September holiday periods. Most have fewer services from mid-May to mid-June and from mid-September to October. **Parking** at the ferries is usually $10 per day, and most charge extra for bikes (up to $6 per). **Prices** listed below are for a round-trip. Be sure to reserve ahead as rides do sell out.

From Cape Cod

Falmouth to Oak Bluffs (about 35min). Passengers ($18), bikes ($6 extra), or kayaks ($12 extra). The *Island Queen* (cash or travellers' cheques only; ☎508/548-4800, ⓦwww .islandqueen.com).

Falmouth to Edgartown (1hr). Passengers and bikes only. A small boat, so call ahead for reservations Fri–Sun. Falmouth Ferry Service ($50; $5 for bikes; ☎508/548-9400, ⓦwww.falmouthferry.com).

Woods Hole to both Vineyard Haven and Oak Bluffs (45min). Car ferry, year-round. Reservations required to bring a car on summer weekends and holidays – you can bring a car standby all other times, though the wait can be long. Steamship Authority ($135 high season or $85 low season per car, not including passengers, who must pay $7.50 each-way; ☎508/477-8600, ⓦwww.steamshipauthority.com).

Hyannis to Oak Bluffs (about 1hr 40min; fast ferry about 50min). Year-round. Passengers only. Hy-Line ($43, $69 fast ferry; ☎1-800/492-8082, ⓦwww.hy-linecruises.com).

From elsewhere in Massachusetts, Rhode Island and New York

New Bedford to Vineyard Haven or Oak Bluffs (1hr). Passengers only. A great way to avoid Cape traffic, particularly if you're coming from Rhode Island or New York. ($70; ☎1-866/683-3779, ⓦwww.nefastferry.com).

Quonset Point, Rhode Island, to Oak Bluffs (1.5hr). Passengers only. Good for those traveling from Connecticut or New York; Quonset is south of Providence and Warwick. Viking Ferry ($69; ☎401/295-4040, ⓦwww.vineyardfastferry.com).

From June through September, the Hy-Line ferry company also runs a **connecting service** which runs once daily between Oak Bluffs, Martha's Vineyard's and Nantucket (one departure daily; pedestrians only; $34 one-way; ☎1-800/492-8082).

Arrival and information

Most people come to Martha's Vineyard by **ferry**, arriving at either Oak Bluffs or Vineyard Haven, usually from Woods Hole on Cape Cod (see box above for schedules and fares). You can also **fly** via Cape Air (☎508/771-6944, ⓦwww.flycapeair.com) from Boston (from which there's an hourly shuttle in the summer), Hyannis, Nantucket or New Bedford. The Vineyard's **airport** (☎508/693-7022) is in Vineyard Haven. **Taxis** greet all arriving ferries and flights; all companies use the same fare sheets, and some share phone numbers. Try Martha's Vineyard Taxi (☎508/693-8660), All Island (☎508/693-2929) or AdamCab (☎508/627-4462).

Tourist **information** is available at the Chamber of Commerce in Vineyard Haven or at the post office in Edgartown, both of which stock the requisite pamphlets and island maps.

Getting around

Martha's Vineyard has an increasingly frequent and reliable **bus** system that connects the main towns from around 7am to 12.45am daily (☎508/639-9440, ⓦwww.vineyardtransit.com); tickets cost $1 per town, including the town of origin, or $7 per day. Getting a day pass and a map is the best way to get around without a car, but there are also three-hour narrated **tours** run by Martha's Vineyard Sightseeing ($29; ☎508/627-TOUR, ⓦwww.mvtour.com); the trolleys run from spring to fall from all ferry arrival points. Another option is to **bike**; in Vineyard Haven you can rent from Martha's Bike Rentals at 24 Union St, just a block from the ferry (☎1-800/559-0312, ⓦwww.marthasbikerentals.com); in Oak Bluffs from Anderson Bike Rentals on Circuit Avenue (☎508/693-9346); or in Edgartown from R.W. Cutler Bikes at 1 Main St (☎1-800/627-2763, ⓦwww.marthasvineyardbike.com). A basic mountain bike generally starts at $20 per day, no matter the company.

Bringing a **car** over on the ferry is an expensive option, and often impossible on summer weekends without reserving months in advance. If you just can't do without a car, you can rent one from Budget, in Vineyard Haven, Oak Bluffs, Edgartown or the airport (☎508/693-1911 or 1-800/527-0700, ⓦwww.budget.com), or Adventure Rentals/Thrifty in Vineyard Haven and at Islandhoppers in Oak Bluffs (☎508/693-1959 or 508/696-9147, ⓦwww.islandadventurerentalsmv.com).

Accommodation

There's a tremendous variety of **accommodation** on Martha's Vineyard, ranging from resort hotels with every conceivable creature comfort to old sea captains' homes oozing with charm and personality, as well as rental cottages, usually booked on a weekly basis. Keep in mind that whatever type of lodging you decide on, summer accommodation in Martha's Vineyard gets booked up very early, so reserve well in advance. The following rates are for the summer season, and off-season prices can vary dramatically, making fall and spring a good time to call for discounted rates. If on a budget, check out the Martha's Vineyard Family **Campground** in Edgartown, 569 Edgartown Rd ($50 for two; ☎508/693-3772, ⓦcampmv.com).

Attleboro House 11 Lake Ave, Oaks Bluff ☎508/693-4346, ⓦwww.rentalsmv.com/attleborohouse. This old-fashioned Victorian guesthouse is a good budget option – it may have shared bathrooms and sloping ceilings, but the rooms are cosy and have access to a harbour-view front porch. $110.

Crocker House Inn 12 Crocker Ave, Vineyard Haven ☎508/693-1151, ⓦwww.crockerhouseinn.com. Elegant and accommodating, the *Crocker House* features summery rooms in hues of white and blue, free wi-fi, good proximity to shops and lots of home-made goodies. $295.

Edgartown Inn 56 North Water St, Edgartown ☎508/627-4794, ⓦwww.edgartowninn.com. This eighteenth-century home is a quintessential New England inn with colourful, affordable rooms – many with shared baths

– that evoke another era. The Garden House and Barn out back have the least expensive rooms. $125.

HI-Martha's Vineyard 525 Edgartown–West Tisbury Rd ☎508/693-2665 or 1-888/901-2087, ⓦ.capecod.hiusa.org. Seventy-eight dorm beds in an appealing setting at the forest's edge and away from town. Easily accessed by both bike paths and the #6 bus route, with free wi-fi and a big kitchen on offer. Dorm beds $29–39. Closed mid-Nov to March.

Hob Knob 128 Main St, Edgartown ☎1-800/696-2723, ⓦwww.hobknob.com. The place for unabashed eco-luxury, with antique-laden rooms looking out over the town, and plenty of extras: flat-screen tvs, wi-fi, filling breakfasts, lavish afternoon teas and a spa. $400.

Menemsha Inn & Cottages and Beach Plum Inn North Rd, Menemsha ☎508/645-2521,

www.menemshainn.com and www.beachplum
inn.com. These adjacent properties are both
beautifully maintained and managed. Within
walking distance of the Menemsha beach,
they also include access to private town
beaches on the south shore. The *Beach
Plum Inn* is better for younger adults, while
the cottages at *Menemsha* are better for
families. Open May–Nov; book early. Rooms
from $215; cottages starting at $2200/week.

Nashua House Hotel 30 Kennebec Ave, Oak
Bluffs ☎508/693-0043, www.nashuahouse
.com. Small rooms, some with shared baths,
but this very central and friendly hotel is an
easy walk from the ferry. It can get loud at
night, but with rates starting from $129 in
high season it's one of the less expensive
choices on the island.

Oak Bluffs Inn 64 Circuit Ave, Oak Bluffs
☎1-800/955-6235, www.oakbluffsinn.com.
Guests rave about the soothing, smartly
designed rooms (many of which are
kid-friendly), the wraparound porch, the
fantastic innkeepers and the proximity to
ferries, beaches and restaurants. $225.

Pequot Hotel 19 Pequot Ave, Oak Bluffs
☎508/693-5087, www.pequothotel.com.
Friendly, mid-sized hotel in the gingerbread
cottage neighbourhood with rocking chairs
on the porch, wi-fi and TVs in every room
and a quick walk to town – rooms are a bit
small and showing their age, though. $225.

Victorian Inn 24 South Water St, Edgartown
☎508/627-4784, www.thevic.com. This
historic B&B, set in a vintage whaling
captain's home, features bright, stately
rooms, with a quiet location just off Main
Street that's accessible to restaurants,
shops and the harbour. $245.

Winnetu Inn & Resort South Beach, Edgartown
☎508/627-4747, www.winnetu.com. This
family-friendly resort hotel is just a short walk
from a private stretch of South Beach; very
well-appointed rooms, many with kitchenettes. In high season expect 2- to 3-night
minimum stays. $245.

The island

The Vineyard is basically divided into two sections, the far busier of which is
"**Down-Island**", which includes the ferry terminals of **Vineyard Haven** and **Oak
Bluffs** and smart **Edgartown**. The largely undeveloped western half of the island,
known as "**Up-Island**", comprises woods, agricultural land, ponds and nature
reserves, with a smattering of tiny villages thrown in, including **West Tisbury**,
Chilmark and **Aquinnah** (Gay Head).

Vineyard Haven

Most visitors by boat arrive at **VINEYARD HAVEN** (officially named **Tisbury**), at
the northern tip of the island. Founded by islanders from Edgartown disillusioned
with the iron-fist Puritan rule of the Mayhew family, Vineyard Haven supplanted
Edgartown as the island's main commercial centre in the mid-1800s, because ferries
preferred the shorter run to the mainland; today, the town retains a business-like
ambience, and the main draw for visitors is the selection of high-end antique,
clothes, jewellery and gift **shops**.

The **bus terminal**, visible as you get off the ferry, is also home to a small **visitors'
kiosk**, but for more detailed information and help in finding accommodation, walk
up Beach Road to the **Chamber of Commerce**, 24 Beach Rd (Mon–Fri 9am–5pm,
Sat 10am–4pm; ☎508/693-0085, www.mvy.com). Along the way you'll pass the
Black Dog Tavern, as famous for its souvenirs as for its comestibles (see p.260).

Oak Bluffs

OAK BLUFFS, just across Lagoon Pond from Vineyard Haven, is the newest
of the island's six towns. It was a quiet farming community until the Methodists
established their campground here in the 1850s. This section of Oak Bluffs, centred
on the circular **Trinity Park**, remains filled with the brightly coloured "carpenter
Gothic" or **gingerbread cottages** they built. During the summer, family-oriented
events, Sunday-morning church services and secular Saturday evening concerts are

still held in the **tabernacle** in the centre. The best-known event that takes place here is **Grand Illumination Night** (third Wed in Aug; free), when all the cottages put up Japanese lanterns. At one end of Wesleyan Grove, the sweet 1867 **Cottage Museum**, 1 Trinity Park (mid-June to Sept Mon–Sat 10am–4pm, Sun 1pm–4pm; $2 donation), offers a charming collection of photographs, old Bibles and other artefacts from the campground's history.

Near the waterfront, most of the current action focuses on **Circuit Avenue**, where the shops and bars attract a predominantly young crowd. The restored **Flying Horses Carousel**, at Circuit and Lake avenues (June to early Sept daily 10am–10pm, call for hours in other warm-weather months; $2 per ride; ☏508/693-9481), is the oldest operating carousel in the country; hand-carved in 1876, the 22 horses on parade here have bonafide horsehair manes.

Oak Bluffs also has a few beaches worth checking out, though the **town beach**, on Sea View Avenue, can get very noisy and crowded in season. Further south, the **Joseph A. Sylvia State Beach**, a sandy six-mile stretch of shore, is more appealing, and it parallels an undemanding bike path that leads all the way to Edgartown, with pleasant views to accompany you.

Edgartown

Six miles southeast of Oak Bluffs, **EDGARTOWN**, originally known as Great Harbor, is the oldest and swankiest settlement on the island, its elegant Colonial residences glistening white and surrounded by exquisitely maintained gardens. It doesn't end there: downtown brims with upmarket boutiques, smart restaurants and artsy galleries.

Once you've got your bearings at the seasonal **visitors' centre** on Church Street (late May to early Sept daily 8.30am–10pm) – basically just public restrooms, a bus stop and a place to pick up brochures – it's a short walk to the **Vineyard Museum**, at the corner of Cooke and School streets (mid-June to mid-Oct Tues–Sat 10am–5pm; rest of year Wed–Fri 1–4pm, Sat 10am–4pm; $7; ☏508/627-4441, ⓦwww.marthas vineyardhistory.org), a complex of buildings maintained by the Martha's Vineyard Historical Society. One of them, the 1845 **Captain Francis Pease House**, is full of native arrowheads and, best of all, an Oral History Center, which traces the history of the island through more than 250 recorded narratives of older locals.

A short walk along North Water Street leads past charming sea captains' homes to the white cast-iron **Edgartown Lighthouse** – it's a replacement of the 1828 original, destroyed in the hurricane of 1938. Take the bus (route #8) from the visitor's centre to **South Beach** in Katama, three miles south of town, for some of the island's best public access to the Atlantic Ocean.

Chappaquiddick

CHAPPAQUIDDICK (aka "Chappy") is a strikingly beautiful and sparsely populated little island, just yards away from Edgartown's shores. Unfortunately, its name will always be associated with scandal: Edward (Ted) Kennedy ruined his chances for the presidency in the summer of 1969 when 28-year-old Mary Jo Kopechne drowned in her car at **Dike Bridge**, under circumstances that conspiracy theorists still debate (locals, however, are quite tired of hearing about it). The island is an easy five-minute jaunt from Edgartown via the ferry ($4 per person, $12 for a car and one driver; ☏508/627-9427), which departs frequently from a ramp at the corner of Dock and Dagget streets. There are no stores, restaurants, or hotels on Chappy, just private residences and hundreds of acres of dunes, salt marshes, ponds and scrubland. The island is too large to walk comfortably, though easy to get around on a bike.

The Trustees of Reservations' small Japanese garden **Mytoi**, on Dike Road (daily dawn–dusk; free), is worth stopping by – it's unusual to see the typical rounded bridges and groomed trees in a pine forest. The Trustees are also the caretakers of **Wasque Point**, a windswept stretch of beach that is a continuation of South Beach in Edgartown, but much less crowded. On Chappy's far east side you'll find the five-hundred acre **Cape Poge Wildlife Refuge** (late May to mid-Oct; $3; ☎508/627-7689), an important habitat and migration stopover for thousands of birds. Half the state's scallops are harvested here, too. The best way to see it is to take various **natural history tours** run by the Trustees, involving walking and kayaking; most run May to October (1hr 30min–3hr; $15–30; ☎508/627-3599).

West Tisbury

In 1999, **WEST TISBURY** joined Chappaquiddick in the lore of the Kennedy curse, when **John Kennedy, Jr.'s** plane crashed in the water less than twenty miles from the landing field. Most of West Tisbury's history has been considerably more peaceful, and the village, the largest of the up-island communities, also has some of the best culture on the island.

The **Farmers' Market**, held at the 1859 **Old Agricultural Hall** on South Road every Saturday morning (and sometimes Wed mornings in the summer), attracts visitors from all over the island for its colourful displays of locally grown produce. Across the street from the old hall is the **Field Gallery**, 1050 State Rd (☎508/693-5595), locally famous for Tom Maley's larger-than-life sculptures of ladies dancing on the grass. Also on State Road next to the Old Ag Hall is **Alley's General Store** (☎508/693-0088), an island institution since 1858, selling everything from canned goods to mini *ouija* boards, and with a wide front porch where locals often meet for a chat. A short drive away, at 636 Old County Rd, is the picturesque **Granary Gallery** (daily dawn–dusk; free), featuring Ella Tulin's sculpture of a woman with a small torso and 7ft-high thighs sitting in front, and a variety of notable Vineyard and New England artists' work within.

West Tisbury has a bountiful supply of conservation areas, including the 216-acre **Cedar Tree Neck Wildlife Sanctuary** on Indian Hill Road (daily sunrise–sunset; free), in which bayberry bushes, swamp azaleas, tupelos and pygmy beech trees all grow. Three main trails lead to a pretty but stony beach and a bluff with views to Aquinnah (Gay Head) and the Elizabeth Islands. Meanwhile, the **Sepiessa Point Reservation**, on New Lane off West Tisbury Road (daily dawn–dusk; free), surrounds West Tisbury Pond with trails ideal for bird-watching.

Chilmark

Five miles west of Tisbury, unspoiled **CHILMARK**, with just over eight hundred year-round residents, is the land that time almost forgot, full of pastures separated by stone walls, dense woodlands and rugged roads. That's not to say that the twenty-first century hasn't arrived: **Beetlebung Corner**, where Middle, State, South and Menemsha Cross roads meet, and which is named for the wooden mallets (aka "beetles") and stoppers ("bungs") once made from the nearby tupelo trees, is the village's centre, heralded by the *Chilmark Store* (known for its standout pizza) and the unmissable *Chilmark Chocolates* (see p.260).

On South Road, the tranquil **Chilmark Cemetery** is the final resting place of writer Lillian Hellman and comedian John Belushi, who claimed that the island was the only place in the world where he could get a good night's sleep. Near the entrance, a boulder engraved with the comedian's name – a decoy to prevent fans from finding his actual unmarked grave – is often blessed with rather unceremonious "offerings", like beer cans and condoms. Nearby, a dirt track leads to **Lucy Vincent Beach**, named after the town's prim and proper librarian, who saw it as her mission to protect Chilmark residents from corruption by cutting out from her library books all pictures she deemed to be immoral. Rather ironically, the beach, which is open only to residents and their guests in the summer, today doubles as a **nudist** spot in its less-crowded areas. Off North Road, pick up a map at the trailhead of **Waskosim's Rock Reservation** for a fascinating three-mile hike through a variety of habitats including wetlands and black gum and oak woods.

In the northern part of Chilmark, another tiny island community, **Menemsha**, is a picturesque collection of grey-shingled fishing shacks with a man-made harbour used for location shots in the movie *Jaws*. The harbour also serves as an important commercial and sports-fishing port, much of the catch ending up at restaurants all over the island. Stroll past the fish markets of **Dutcher's Dock** for a real sense of the island's maritime heritage, or bring an early evening picnic to pebbly **Menemsha Public Beach** to enjoy the spectacular sunsets. The **Menemsha Hills Reservation**, off North Road a couple of miles toward West Tisbury, is also well worth a visit, its mile-long rocky shoreline and sand bluffs along Vineyard Sound peaking at **Prospect Hill**, the highest point on the Vineyard, with wonderful views of the Elizabeth Islands.

Martha's Vineyard beaches

The island's **beaches** vary from calm, shallow waters, predominantly on the northern and eastern sides, to long stretches of pounding surf on the southern side, where the water also tends to be a bit warmer. Unfortunately, many of the best beaches are private, or are only open in the summer to residents, but there are some notable exceptions. All of the beaches listed below have lifeguards in at least some areas during summer days.

Aquinnah (Gay Head)
Lobsterville Beach Lobsterville Road. Two miles of prime Vineyard Sound beach backed by dunes. Parking on Lobsterville Road is prohibited, so bike or get here by taking the ferry from Menemsha.

Moshup Beach (Gay Head Public Beach) State Road/Moshup Drive. Gorgeous setting at the foot of Gay Head Cliffs, best reached by bicycle, shuttle bus, or taxi. Parking costs $15 a day in season.

Chappaquiddick
Cape Poge Wildlife Refuge At the end of Dike Road. This sandy beach is less crowded than Wasque at the far east end of the island. $3 per person for non-members.

Wasque at the end of Wasque Road south of School Road. Wide-open South Shore beach. $3 per person and $3 per vehicle.

Chilmark
Lucy Vincent Beach Off South Road. Sandy beach with access to some of the island's clay cliffs (note that bathing in the clay puddles is restricted) through the end of September to residents and visitors with passes.

Menemsha Public Beach Next to Menemsha Harbor. The only Chilmark beach open to the public, with sparkling waters and a picturesque setting. It becomes *very* crowded around sunset, since it is one of the few places to see the sun go down over a beach on the East Coast.

Squibnocket Off State Road at the end of Squibnocket Road. This narrow, rocky beach is less attractive than the other Chilmark beaches, but the waves break

Aquinnah (Gay Head)

In 1997, the people of **AQUINNAH** voted to revert the town's name back to its original Wampanoag Indian name from its more familiar title – Gay Head – the culmination of a ten-year-plus court battle in which the Wampanoags won guardianship of 420 acres of land, to be held in perpetuity by the federal government and now known as the **Gay Head Native American Reservation**. Most people come to this part of the island (its westernmost point) to see the multicoloured-clay **Gay Head Cliffs**, whose brilliant hues are the result of millions of years of geological work. When the oceans were high, and the Vineyard underwater, small creatures died and left their shells behind to form the white layers. At other times, the area was a rainforest and vegetation compressed to form the darker colours. The weight of the glaciers thrust the many layers of stone up at an angle to create the cliffs, dubbed "Gay Head" by passing English sailors in the seventeenth century on account of their bright colours. The clay was once the main source of paint for the island's houses, but now its removal merits a fine; in any case, the cliffs are eroding so fast that it's not safe to approach them too closely.

A short path behind the *Aquinnah* restaurant leads the way from the parking lot to the **overlook**, which affords stunning views to the Elizabeth Islands and, on a clear day, as far as the entrance to Rhode Island's Narragansett Bay. The imposing red-brick **Gay Head Lighthouse** (mid-June to mid-Sept Fri–Sun evenings; $5),

further offshore, making it the best island spot for **surfing**. It's a town beach, which means it's off-limits during summer days, but anyone can show up after 5pm and in September – one of the best times to catch the waves.

Vineyard Haven

Lake Tashmoo Town Beach Herring Creek Road. Swim in the warm, brackish water of the lake, or in the cooler Vineyard Sound.

Owen Park Beach Off Main Street. A harbour beach close to the centre of town. Not much of a swimming hole, or a beach, but it's a walkable distance from downtown.

Oak Bluffs

Joseph A. Sylvia State Beach Along Beach Road between Oak Bluffs and Edgartown. A narrow two-mile strand of sandy beach with clear, gentle waters and plenty of roadside parking.

Oak Bluffs Town Beach Between the Steamship Authority Dock and the State Beach. Narrow sliver of beach on Vineyard Sound that gets very crowded in season.

Edgartown

Bend-in-the-Road Beach Beach Road. Really an extension of the Joseph A. Sylvia State Beach, with similar facilities and access.

Katama Beach (South Beach) End of Katama Road. Beautiful barrier beach backed by protected salt pond. Strong surf and currents – known for its "good waves and good bodies".

Lighthouse Beach Starbuck's Neck, off North Water Street. Close to town, this harbour beach can get a bit mucked with seaweed.

West Tisbury

Lambert's Cove Beach Lambert's Cove Road. One of the island's prettiest, but open only to residents during high season.

Long Point Wildlife Refuge Beach Off South Road. The perfect Vineyard beach: long and wide, with a freshwater pond just behind. Get there early for a parking space, on the south side of the street near the airport.

built in 1854 to replace a wooden structure that dated from 1799, is well situated for sunset views. Below the lighthouse, though not accessible from it, a **public beach** provides an equally impressive view of the cliffs from a different angle. To reach it, take the wooden boardwalk from the **Moshup Beach** parking lot to the shore, then walk round towards the lighthouse.

Eating

It's easy enough to find something to **eat** on Martha's Vineyard; the ports in particular have rows of places to tempt tourists who've just disembarked the ferries. Three of the island's six towns are **dry**, meaning you can only purchase alcohol in Oak Bluffs, Vineyard Haven and Edgartown. Note, though, that you can bring wine or beer purchased there to restaurants in the other towns.

ArtCliff Diner 39 Beach Rd, Vineyard Haven ☎508/693-1224. Perfect for a pre-ferry send-off breakfast, with the likes of almond-crusted French toast and chorizo, egg and pepperjack sandwiches. Get there early to avoid a crazy wait. Lunch is also available, and dinner is served until late from a tasty truck parked out front. Closed Wed.

Back Door Donuts 5 Post Office Sq (behind *Martha's Vineyard Gourmet Café and Bakery*), Oak Bluffs ☎508/693-3688. Local institution knocking out hot doughnuts in honey-dipped, Boston cream and cinnamon varieties; you'll see stars with their apple fritter, and we mean that in the best possible way. Daily 9pm–12.30am.

The Bite 29 Basin Rd, Menemsha ☎508/645-9239. Roadside/seaside nirvana. Fried clams, scallops and zucchini, served in paper bags from a tiny seaside shack. Good chowder, too. Cash only.

The Black Dog Bakery and Tavern 20 Beach St Ext, Vineyard Haven ☎508/693-9223. Though you'll see their T-shirts all over the island and the mainland (never a good sign), the original restaurant serves tasty – although inconsistent – fare. If you don't want to chance it, skip the full and "light" (less expensive) seafood dinners and instead go next door to stock up on the bakery's muffins and bagels for the return ferry ride.

Chilmark Chocolates 19 State Rd, Chilmark ☎508/645-3013. Lines form out the door for *Chilmark's* island-grown berries dipped in habit-forming organic chocolate. Closed Mon–Wed.

Détente 3 Winter St, Edgartown ☎508/627-8810. A good place for a romantic splurge, *Détente's* petite dining room, dark-wood panelling and well-paired New American mains (think roasted venison with thyme spaetzle, $32) make for some of the island's

most memorable meals. Reservations recommended.

Larsen's Fish Market 56 Basin Rd, Menemsha ☎508/645-2680. One of New England's best fishmongers, for about $15 you can pick out your very own lobster here and then eat it on low-key flats overlooking the harbour. Good steamers too.

Le Grenier 96 Main St, Vineyard Haven ☎508/693-4906. Don't mind the fussy ambience and weird murals; this fancy French spot has stood the test of time and still serves up some of the tastiest dinner fare on the island (steak au poivre for $39).

Humphrey's Bakery 455 State Rd, Tisbury ☎508/693-6518; 32 Winter St, Edgartown ☎508/627-7029; 1 Lake Ave, Oak Bluffs ☎508/696-6890. Home-made cookies, doughnuts and bulging sandwiches on fresh bread – great to bring to the beach. Locals claim, with some justification, that the turkey sandwiches ($6) are the best in the world.

Menemsha Galley 515 North Rd, Menemsha ☎508/645-9819. Great take-out spot with soft-serve ice cream and nostalgic delights like grilled-cheese sandwiches and lobster rolls ($11). Eat it on the picture-perfect deck, or picnic nearby on the beach. Cash only.

The Net Result 79 Beach Rd, Vineyard Haven ☎508/693-6071. Sells fish "so fresh" it will "make you blush". Along with its catch of the day, the *Net* offers rave-worthy prepared foods like sushi and heaping lobster rolls (a steal at $12).

Slice of Life 50 Circuit Ave, Oak Bluffs ☎508/693-3838. Great New American spot, particularly for lunch. Order the fried green tomato BLT and ogle the tourists from the sunny enclosed patio. The owners also run *The Sweet Life Café*, a standout at dinnertime and just down the block at 63 Circuit Ave (☎508/696-0200).

Drinking and nightlife

First-run **movies** can be seen at Capawock, an Art Deco theatre on Main Street in Vineyard Haven (☎ 508/627-6689), or in Edgartown at Entertainment Cinemas, 65 Main St (☎ 508/627-8008). For current **listings** information, check the *Vineyard Gazette* (🌐 www.mvgazette.com), good for cultural events, and the weekly *Martha's Vineyard Times* (🌐 www.mvtimes.com), better for nightlife listings.

David Ryan's 11 N Water St, Edgartown ☎ 508/627-4100. On summer nights, this restaurant transforms into a loud two-storey bar with a chi-chi Martini lounge upstairs and a raucous mojito-swilling crowd getting crazy downstairs.

Lola's Southern Seafood *Island Inn*, Beach Rd, Oak Bluffs ☎ 508/693-6093. Frequent live jazz and rock abounds at this island standby, really an upscale restaurant serving southern-fried cuisine.

The Newes from America 23 Kelley St, Edgartown ☎ 508/627-4397. Swill five hundred beers in this atmospheric pub (not necessarily all in the same night) and they'll name a stool after you; New England favourites like Harpoon, Smuttynose and Otter Creek are all here ($6). Decent and affordable pub grub, too.

Offshore Ale Company 30 Kennebec Ave, Oak Bluffs ☎ 508/693-2626. Friendly local brewpub with wooden booths, toss-on-the-floor peanut shells, and live shows almost nightly in season. If you're there in the evening, be sure to stop by *Back Door Donuts* across the street (see above) for a life-changing apple fritter.

Ritz Café 4 Circuit Ave, Oak Bluffs ☎ 508/693-9851. This cupboard-sized dive is anything but ritzy, but its live-music acts (nightly in summer; check online schedule for rest of year) and authentic Thai food make a nice escape from the dance scene.

Sand Bar & Grill 6 Circuit Ave, Oak Bluffs ☎ 508/693-7111. Come here in the afternoon for drinks and snacks at this restaurant where you can sink your feet directly into the sand. The sushi gets good reviews, but the rest of the menu is passable; here, it's more about the ambience. The *Sand Bar* really heats up at night, and if loud DJs are not your thing, you may want to jump ship at that point, matey.

Contexts

Contexts

History

B oston has been an important city since its colonial days. Numerous crucial and decisive events, especially related to America's struggle for independence, have taken place here; it's also been fertile ground for various intellectual, literary and religious movements throughout the years. What follows is a short overview of the city's development, with an emphasis on the key happenings and figures behind them; for a more in-depth look, check out some of the volumes listed in "Books", p.276.

Early exploration and founding

The first indications of explorers "discovering" the Boston area are the journal entries of Giovanni da Verrazano and Estevan Gomez, who – in 1524 and 1525, respectively – passed by Massachusetts Bay while travelling the coast of North America. The first permanent European settlement in the Boston area was undertaken by a group of 102 British colonists, around half of them Separatists – better known now as **Pilgrims** – chased out of England for having disassociated themselves entirely from the Anglican Church. They had tried to settle in Holland, but the Dutch wouldn't let them become citizens, so they boarded the Mayflower ship to try the forbidding, rugged coast of North America, where they landed in 1620 near Plymouth Bay – after a short stopover at the tip of Cape Cod – and founded Plimoth Plantation. Within the first decade, one of them, a disillusioned scholarly loner by the name of **William Blackstone**, began searching for land on which to make a new start; he found it on a peninsula at the mouth of the Charles River known as Shawmut by the local Indians. Blackstone thus became Boston's first white settler, living at the foot of modern-day Beacon Hill with a few hundred books and a Brahma bull.

In 1630, close to one thousand Puritans, led by **John Winthrop**, settled just across the river to create Charlestown, named after the king of England. Unlike the Pilgrims, the Puritans didn't necessarily plan to disconnect themselves completely from the Anglican Church, but merely hoped to purify themselves by avoiding what they considered to be its showy excesses. Blackstone eventually lured them to his side of the river with the promise of a better water supply, and then sold them the entire Shawmut Peninsula, keeping only six acres for himself. The Puritans subsequently renamed the area after the town in England from which many of their company hailed: **Boston**.

The colonial period

Early Bostonians enjoyed almost total political autonomy from England and created a remarkably democratic system of government, whose primary body was the town meeting, in which white male church members debated over and voted on all kind of matters. This liberal approach was counterbalanced, however, by religious intolerance: four Quakers and Baptists were hanged for their non-Puritan beliefs between 1649 and 1651.

Also, during these times Boston and neighbouring **Cambridge** were making great strides in culture and education: Boston Latin, the (not yet) nation's first secondary school, was established in 1635; **Harvard**, its first university, a year later; and the first printing press in America was set up in Cambridge in 1639, where the Bay Psalm Book, New England Primer and freeman's oath of loyalty to Massachusetts were among the first published works.

With the restoration of the British monarchy in 1660, the crown tried to exert more control over the increasingly prosperous and freethinking Massachusetts Bay Colony, appointing a series of governors, notably the despotic **Sir Edmund Andros**, who was chased from the colony by locals in 1689, only to be reinstalled by the monarchy the following year. Britain's relentless mercantilist policies, designed to increase the nation's monopolistic hold on the new colonies, resulted in a decrease in trade that both plunged Boston into a depression and fanned the anti-British resentment which would eventually reach a boiling point during the mid-1700s. The Molasses Act of 1733, for example, taxed all sugar purchased outside the British Empire, dealing a stiff economic blow to the colonies, who were dependent upon foreign sources for their sugar supply.

The American Revolution

At the outset of the 1760s, governor Francis Bernard informed the colonists that their success was a result of "their subjugation to Great Britain", before green-lighting the **Writs of Assistance**, which gave British soldiers the right to enter colonists' shops and homes to search for evidence of their avoiding duties. The colonists reacted with outrage at this violation of their civil liberties, and a young Boston lawyer named James Otis argued in front of a panel of judges headed by lieutenant governor Thomas Hutchinson to repeal the acts. After listening to his four-hour oration, many were convinced that revolution was justified, including future US president John Adams, who wrote of Otis's speech: "Then and there the child Liberty was born".

Nevertheless, in 1765 the British introduced the **Stamp Act**, which required stamps to be placed on all published material (the revenue on the stamps would go to the Imperial coffers), and the **Quartering Act**, which stipulated that colonists had to house British soldiers on demand. These acts galvanized the opposition to the English government, a resistance based in Boston, where a group of revolutionary firebrands headed by Samuel Adams and known as the "Sons of Liberty" teamed up with more level-headed folks like John Hancock and John Adams to organize protest marches and petition the king to repeal the offending legislation. Though Parliament repealed the Stamp Act, in 1766 it issued the **Declaratory Acts**, which asserted the Crown's right to bind the colonists by any legislation it saw fit, and, in 1767, the **Townshend Acts**, which prescribed more tariffs on imports to the North American colonies. This was followed by a troop increase in Boston; prior to this incident, there were between thirty and forty British soldiers for every colonist, whereas afterwards the ratio became a narrow one to one.

The tension erupted on March 5, 1770, when a group of British soldiers fired into a crowd of townspeople who'd been taunting them. The **Boston Massacre**, as it came to be known, was hardly a massacre – only five people were killed, and the accused soldiers were actually defended in court by John Adams and Josiah Quincy – but the occupying troops were forced to relocate to Castle Island, at the tip of South Boston.

The coming crisis was postponed for a few years following the Massacre, until December 16, 1773, when Samuel Adams led a mob from the Old South Meeting House to Boston Harbor as part of a protest against a British tax on imported tea. A segment of the crowd boarded the brig Beaver and two other ships and dumped the entirety of their tea cargo overboard in an act that's become known as the **Boston**

Tea Party; Parliament responded by closing the port of Boston and passing the so-called Coercive Acts, which deprived Massachusetts of any self-government. England also sent in more troops and restricted access across the Boston Neck, the only land entrance to Boston. Soon after, the colonies convened the first **Continental Congress** in Philadelphia, with the idea of creating an independent government.

Two months after the province of Massachusetts was declared to be in a state of rebellion by the British government, the "shot heard 'round the world" was fired at Lexington on April 19, 1775, when a group of American militiamen skirmished with a company of British regulars; they lost that fight, but defeated the Redcoats in a subsequent incident at Concord Bridge, and the **Revolutionary War** had begun. The British troops left in Boston were held under siege, and the city itself was largely evacuated by its citizens.

The first major engagement of the war was the **Battle of Bunker Hill**, in which the British stormed what was actually Breed's Hill, in Charlestown, on three separate occasions before finally dislodging American battlements. Despite the loss, the conflict, in which the outnumbered Americans suffered fewer casualties than the British, bolstered the patriots' spirits and confidence.

George Washington took over the Continental troops in a ceremony on Cambridge Common on July 2, 1775; however, his first major coup didn't even require bloodshed. On March 16, 1776, under cover of darkness, Washington ordered much of the troops' heavy artillery to be moved to the top of Dorchester Heights, in view of the Redcoats. The British awoke to see battlements sufficient to destroy their entire fleet of warships; on March 17, they evacuated the city, never to return.

This was largely the end of Boston's involvement in the war; the focus soon turned inland and southward. After the Americans won the Battle of Saratoga in 1778, the French joined the war as their allies; on October 19, 1781, Cornwallis surrendered to Washington at Yorktown. Two years later, the United States of America became an **independent nation** with 1783's Treaty of Paris.

Economic swings and the "Athens of America"

Boston quickly emerged from the damage wrought by British occupation. By 1790, the economy was already booming, primarily due to the maritime industry. An elite merchant – popularly known as the "cod millionaires" – developed and settled on the sunny south slope of Beacon Hill. These were the original **Boston Brahmins** – though that name would not be coined until seventy years later – infamous for their stuffed-shirt elitism and fiscal conservatism. Indeed, the trust fund was invented in Boston at this time as a way for families to protect their fortunes over the course of generations.

The outset of the nineteenth century was less auspicious. Severe restrictions on international trade, notably Jefferson's Embargo Act in 1807, plunged the port of Boston into recession. When the **War of 1812** began, pro-British Bostonian Federalists derided the conflict as "Mr. Madison's War" and, as such, met in Hartford in 1814 with party members from around New England to consider seceding from the Union – a measure that was wisely, though narrowly, rejected. America's victory in the war shamed Bostonians back into their patriotic ways, and they reacted to further trade restrictions by developing manufacturing industries; the city soon became prominent in textiles and shoe production.

This industrial revival and subsequent economic growth shook the region from its recession. By 1820, Boston's population had grown to 43,000 – more than double its total from the census of 1790. The city stood at the forefront of American intellectual and political life, as well, earning Boston the moniker "Athens of America".

One of these intellectual movements had its roots back in the late-eighteenth century, when a controversial sect of Christianity known as **Unitarianism** – premised on the rational study of the Bible, voluntary ethical behaviour and (in Boston only) a rejection of the idea of a Holy Trinity – became the city's dominant religion (and one still practiced at King's Chapel), led by Reverend Ellery Channing. His teachings were the basis for **transcendentalism**, a philosophy propounded in the writings of Ralph Waldo Emerson and rooted in the idea that there was an entity known as the "over-soul", to which man and nature existed in identical relation. Emerson's theory, emphasizing intuitive (a priori) knowledge – particularly in contemplation of nature – was put into practice by his fellow Harvard alumnus, Henry David Thoreau, who, in 1845, took to the woods just northwest of the city at Walden Pond in an attempt to "live deliberately".

Boston was also a centre of literary activity at this time: historical novels by Nathaniel Hawthorne, such as *The Scarlet Letter*, tweaked the sensibilities and mores of New England society, and poet Henry Wadsworth Longfellow gained international renown during his tenure at Harvard. For more on these developments throughout the nineteenth century, see p.46.

This intellectual flowering was complemented by a variety of social movements. Foremost among them was the **abolitionist movement**, spearheaded by the fiery William Lloyd Garrison, who, besides speechmaking, published the anti-slavery newspaper *The Liberator*. New England resident Harriet Beecher Stowe's seminal 1852 novel, *Uncle Tom's Cabin*, turned the sentiments of much of the nation against slavery. Other Bostonians who made key contributions to social issues were Horace Mann, who reformed public education; Dorothea Dix, an advocate of improved care for the mentally ill; Margaret Fuller, one of America's first feminists as well the editor of *The Dial*, a journal founded by Emerson; and William James, a Harvard professor who pioneered new methods in psychology, coining the phrase "stream of consciousness".

Social transformation and decline

The success of Boston's maritime and manufacturing industries attracted a great number of **immigrants**; the Irish, especially, poured in following Ireland's Potato Famine of the 1840s. By 1860, the city was marked by massive social divide, with overcrowded slums abutting beautiful mansions. The elite that had ruled for the first half of the century tried to ensure that the lower classes were kept in place: "No Irish Need Apply" notices accompanied job listings throughout Boston. Denied entry into "polite" society, the lower classes conspired to grab power in another way: the popular vote.

To the chagrin of Boston's WASP elite, Hugh O'Brien was elected mayor in 1885. His three-term stay in office was followed by that of John "Honey Fitz" Fitzgerald, and in the 1920s, the long reign of James Michael Curley began. Curley was to serve several terms as mayor, and one each as governor and congressional representative. These men enjoyed tremendous popularity among their supporters, despite the fact that their tenures were often characterized by rampant corruption: Curley was elected to his last term in office while serving time in a Federal prison for fraud. Still, while these mayors increased the visibility and political clout of otherwise disenfranchised ethnic groups, they did little to improve the lot of their constituents, which was steadily worsening – along with the city's economy.

Following the **Civil War**, competition with the railroads crippled the shipping industry, and with it, Boston's prosperous waterfront. Soon after, the manufacturing industry as well felt the impact of bigger, more efficient factories in the rest of the nation. The shoe and textile industries had largely disappeared by the 1920s; many companies had started to move south, where costs were much lower, and industrial production statewide fell by more than $1 billion during that decade. The **Great Depression** of the 1930s made a bad state of affairs even worse, as there were few natural resources the city provided that could keep it as an economic powerhouse.

On the heels of the depression, **World War II** turned Boston's moribund shipbuilding industry around almost overnight, but this economic upturn still wasn't enough to prevent a massive exodus from the urban centre.

From the 1950s to the 1980s

In the 1950s, a more long-lasting turnaround began under the mayoral leadership of **John Collins**, who undertook a massive plan to reshape the face of Boston. Many of the city's oldest neighbourhoods and landmarks were razed, though it's questionable whether these changes beautified the city. Still, the project created jobs and economic growth, while making the Downtown area more attractive to businesses and residents. By the end of the 1960s, a steady economic resurgence had begun. Peripheral areas of Boston, however, did not share in this prosperity. Collins' programme paid little attention to the poverty that afflicted outlying areas, particularly the city's southern districts, or to the city's growing racial tensions. The demographic redistribution that followed the "white flight" of the 1940s and 1950s made Boston one of the most racially segregated cities in America by the mid-1970s: Charlestown's population was almost entirely white, while Roxbury was almost entirely black.

Along with other cities nationwide, Boston was ordered by the US Supreme Court to implement **busing** – sending students from one neighbourhood to another and vice-versa in an attempt to achieve racial balance. More than two hundred area schools were involved, and not all reacted kindly: many Charlestown parents, for their part, staged hostile demonstrations and boycotted the public school system, which was especially embarrassing for Boston considering its history of racial tolerance. City officials finally scrapped their plan for desegregation after only a few years. The racial scars it left began to heal, thanks, in part, to the policies of Ray Flynn, Boston's mayor during the upbeat 1980s, helping to make the decade one of the city's healthiest in recent memory, both economically and socially.

The 1990s and into the twenty-first century

That resurgence spilled over into the 1990s, a decade that saw the job market explode and rents spiral upward in reaction to it. The increase in housing prices was further augmented by the 1996 state vote to abolish rent control in the city, a decision that pushed much of the lower-paid working class out to neighbourhoods like Roxbury, and kick-started a **condominium boom**, especially in the South End, which was radically transformed from a near slum into the trendy hotspot it is today.

Indeed, the city has encountered little strife in the last decade. The most notable, and notorious, hubbub occurred in 2002, when the archdiocese of the local Catholic church, the Church of the Holy Cross, found itself at the centre of a sex abuse scandal that prompted calls for an overhaul of the procedures concerning the handling of errant priests. While reforms remain undecided, the protesters who took up residency in front of the church doors during the heat of the scandal quietened down in short order, and the church quickly returned to business as usual – though with a tarnished reputation.

Of far greater impact on Bostonian life, Downtown's **Big Dig project** (see p.7) was, at over \$1.6 billion per mile, the most expensive highway construction project in US history. Though the project was officially completed in 2005 (fourteen years after the first jackhammer sounded in Charlestown), the prettification portion of the Big Dig, namely the landscaping of the 27 acres left in the wake of downtown's Central Artery, continued until 2009. In the meantime, the cleanup of Boston Harbor has had a great effect in reclaiming abandoned beaches and reinvigorating species of long disappeared fauna, many of which are making their homes on the Boston Harbor Islands, a group of idyllic offshore isles originally used as defence posts, but declared a national park in 1996 and subsequently opened to the public, accessible via regular ferries from Long Wharf.

The city's positive economic growth by the end of the twentieth century endowed a number of cultural institutions with funds to spruce up their digs; two of Boston's most intriguing libraries – the staid Boston Athenæum and the eccentric Mary Eddy Baker Library – reopened to the public in 2002, following substantial renovations. The most significant facelifts, however, are taking place at the Isabella Stewart Gardner Museum and the Museum of Fine Arts; at the latter, a recently inaugurated multimillion-dollar expansion project designed by renowned British architect Sir Norman Foster is slated for completion by the end of 2010. Much to local fans' relief, Fenway Park, the country's oldest ballpark and home of the beloved Sox appears to have missed the chopping block, as plans to build a newer, more spacious stadium have been momentarily put to rest.

Architecture and urban planning

T he land to which William Blackstone invited John Winthrop and his Puritans in 1630 bore almost no resemblance to the contemporary city of Boston. It was virtually an island, spanning a mere 785 acres, surrounded on all sides by murky swamps and connected to the mainland only by a narrow isthmus, "the Neck", that was almost entirely submerged at high tide. It was also very hilly: three peaks formed its geological backbone and gave it the name that Puritans used before they chose Boston – the Trimountain – echoed today in the name of Downtown's Tremont Street.

Colonial development

The first century and a half of Boston's existence saw a sleepy Puritan village slowly expand into one of the biggest shipping centres in the North American colonies. Narrow, crooked footpaths became busy commercial boulevards, though they retained their sinuous design, and the pastureland of **Boston Common** became the place for public gatherings. By the end of the eighteenth century, Boston was faced with the dilemma of how to accommodate its growing population and thriving industry on a tiny geographical centre; part of the answer was to create more land. This had been accomplished in Boston's early years almost accidentally, by means of a process known as wharving out. Owners of shoreside properties with wharves found that rocks and debris collected around the pilings, until eventually the wharves were on dry land, necessitating the building of more wharves further out to sea. In this way, Boston's shoreline moved slowly but inexorably outward.

Post-revolution development

Boston's first great building boom began in earnest following the American Revolution. **Harrison Gray Otis**'s company, the Mount Vernon Proprietors, razed two of Boston's three peaks to create tracts for new townhouses. The land from the tops of these hills was placed where Boston Common and the Charles River met to form a swamp, extending the shoreline out even farther to create what is now known as "the flat of the hill". Leftover land was used to fill some of the city's other coves and ponds, most significantly Mill Pond, near present-day North End. The completion of the Mount Vernon Proprietors' plans made the resulting area, Beacon Hill, the uncontested site for Boston's wealthy and elite to build their ideal home – as such, it holds the best examples of American architecture of the late-eighteenth and early nineteenth centuries, ranging in styles from Georgian to early Victorian.

This period also ushered in the first purely American architectural movement, the Federal style. Prime examples of its flat, dressed-down facades are prevalent in townhouses throughout Downtown and in Beacon Hill. **Charles Bulfinch** was its leading practitioner; his most famous work was the 1797 gold-domed Massachusetts State House looming over Boston Common, a prototype for state capitols to come. For more information on Bulfinch, see the box on p.79.

The expansion of the city

Boston continued to grow throughout the 1800s. Mayor Josiah Quincy oversaw the construction of a large marketplace, **Quincy Market**, behind the overcrowded Faneuil Hall building. These three oblong Greek Revival buildings pushed the Boston waterfront back several hundred yards, and the new surface area was used as the site for a symbol of Boston's maritime prosperity, the US Custom House. While Boston had codes prohibiting overly tall buildings, the Federal Government was not obligated to obey them, and the Custom House building, completed in 1847, rose a then-impressive sixteen storeys.

Meanwhile, the city was trying to create enough land to match the demand for housing, in part by transforming its swampy backwaters into useable property. Back Bay, for example, was originally just that: a marsh along the banks of the Charles. In 1814, however, Boston began to dam the Charles, filling the resulting area with debris. When the project was completed in 1883, Back Bay quickly became one of Boston's choicest addresses, drawing some prominent families from their dwellings on Beacon Hill. The layout followed a highly ordered French model of city planning: gridded streets, with those running perpendicular to the Charles arranged alphabetically. The district's main boulevard, Commonwealth Avenue, surrounded a strip of greenery that terminated to the east in the Public Garden, a lush park completed by George Meachum in 1859, with ponds, statuary, weeping willows and winding pathways that is the jewel of Back Bay, if not all Boston.

As if this weren't enough, Back Bay's Copley Square was also the site of numerous high-minded civic institutions built in the mid- and late-1800s, foremost among which were H.H. Richardson's Romanesque Trinity Church and the Public Library, a High Victorian creation of Charles McKim, of the noted firm McKim, Mead and White. But the most impressive accomplishment of the century was certainly Frederick Law Olmsted's **Emerald Necklace**, a system of parks that connected Boston Common, the Public Garden and the Commonwealth Avenue Mall to his own creations a bit further off, such as the Back Bay Fens, Arnold Arboretum and Franklin Park.

While Boston's civic expansion made life better for its upper classes, the middle and lower classes were crammed into the tiny Downtown area. The city's solution was to **annex** the surrounding districts, beginning with South Boston in 1807 and ending with Charlestown in 1873 – with the exception of Brookline, which remained a separate entity. Toward the end of the century, Boston's growing middle class moved to these surrounding areas, particularly the southern districts, which soon became known as the "streetcar suburbs". These areas, once the site of summer estates for the wealthy, were built over with "triple-deckers", clapboard rowhouses that hold a family on each floor.

Modernization and preservation

New construction waned with the economic decline of the early 1900s, reaching its lowest point during the Great Depression. The streetcar suburbs were hardest hit – the white middle class migrated to Boston's nearby towns in the 1940s and 1950s, and the southern districts became run-down, low-rent areas. **Urban renewal** began in the late 1950s, with the idea of creating a visibly modern city, and while it provided Boston with an economic shot in the arm, the drastic changes erased some of the city's most distinctive architectural features. The porn halls and dive bars of Scollay Square were demolished to make way for the dull grey bureaucracy complexes of Government Center, while the West End, once one of Boston's liveliest ethnic neighbourhoods, was flattened and covered over with high-rise office buildings. Worst of all, the new elevated John F. Fitzgerald Expressway (I-93) tore through Downtown, cutting off the North End and water-front from the rest of the city. (Thankfully this eyesore – courtesy of the Big Dig – is now underground.)

Following this period, the fury of displaced and disgruntled residents forced planners to create structures that either reused or integrated extant features of the city. The **John Hancock Tower**, designed by I.M. Pei and completed in 1975, originally outraged preservationists, as this Copley Square high-rise was being built right by some of the city's most treasured cultural landmarks; however, the tower managed a delicate balance – while it rises sixty storeys smack in the middle of Back Bay, its narrow wedge shape renders it quite unobtrusive, and its mirrored walls literally reflect its stately surroundings. Quincy Market was also redeveloped and, by 1978, what had been a decaying, nearly defunct series of fishmongering stalls was transformed into a thriving tourist attraction. Boston's showiest architectural newcomer, the **Institute of Contemporary Art,** opened its cantilevered digs in 2006 and brought with it a whole slew of condo developers and restaurateurs eager to expand on the newly repackaged Seaport District. Subsequent development has, for the most part, kept up this theme, preserving the city's four thousand acres – and most crucially its Downtown – as a virtual library of American architecture.

Literary Boston

America's literary centre has not always been New York; indeed, for much of the nineteenth century, Boston wore that mantle, and since then it has retained a somewhat bookish reputation despite no longer quite having the influence it once did on American publishing.

Puritanism and religious influence

John Winthrop and his fellow colonists who settled in the Boston area had a vision of a theocratic, utopian "City on a Hill". The Puritans were erudite and fairly well-off intellectuals, but religion always came first, even when writing: in fact, Winthrop himself penned *A Model of Christian Charity* while crossing the Atlantic. Religious sermons were the real literature of the seventeenth century – those and the now-forgotten explorations of **Reverend Cotton Mather** such as *Memorable Providences, Relating to Witchcraft and Possessions,* a look at the supernatural that helped foment the Salem Witch Trials.

During the eighteenth century, in the years leading up to the Revolutionary War, Bostonians began to pour their energy into a different kind of sermon – that of anti-British sentiment, such as rants in radical newspapers like the *Boston Gazette*. Post-revolution, the stifling atmosphere of Puritanism remained to some extent – the city's first theatre, for example, built in 1794, had to be billed as a "school of virtue" in order to remain open. But writers began to shake off Puritan restraints and explore their newfound freedom; in certain instances, they drew upon the repressiveness of the religion as a source of inspiration.

The transcendentalist movement

Ironically enough, Boston's deliverance from parochialism began in the countryside, specifically Concord, scene of the first battle of the Revolutionary War. The transcendentalist movement of the 1830s and 1840s, spearheaded by **Ralph Waldo Emerson**, was born of a passion for rural life, intellectual freedom and belief in intuitive knowledge and experience as a way to enhance the relationship between man, nature and the "over-soul". The free thinking the movement unleashed put local writers at the vanguard of American literary expression; articles by Emerson, Henry David Thoreau, Louisa May Alcott, Bronson Alcott (Louisa's father) and other members of the Concord coterie filled the pages of *The Dial*, the transcendentalist literary review, founded by Emerson around 1840 and edited by Margaret Fuller. Fuller, an early feminist, also wrote essays prodigiously; while Alcott penned the classic *Little Women*, and Thoreau authored his famous study in solitude, *Walden*. Meanwhile, a writer by the name of **Nathaniel Hawthorne**, known mainly for short stories like "Young Goodman Brown", published *The Scarlet Letter*, in 1850, a true schism with the past that examined the effects of the repressive Puritan lifestyle and legacy.

The abolitionist movement and literary salons

The **abolitionist movement** also helped push Boston into the literary limelight. Slavery had been outlawed in Massachusetts since 1783, and Boston attracted the likes of activist William Lloyd Garrison, who published his firebrand newspaper, *The Liberator*, in a small office Downtown beginning in 1831. Years later, in 1852, Harriet Beecher Stowe's slave narrative *Uncle Tom's Cabin* hit the printing press in Boston and sold more than 300,000 copies in its first year of publication. It, perhaps more than anything else, turned national public opinion against slavery, despite the fact that its writer was a New Englander with little first-hand knowledge of the South or the slave trade.

Another Bostonian involved with the abolitionist cause was John Greenleaf Whittier, who also happened to be among the founding members of Emerson's famed "Saturday Club", the name given to a series of informal literary gatherings that took place at the Omni *Parker House Hotel* beginning in 1855. Oliver Wendell Holmes and poet Henry Wadsworth Longfellow were among the moneyed regulars at these salons, which metamorphosed two years later into *The Atlantic Monthly*, from its inception a respected literary and political journal. One of its more accomplished editors, William Dean Howells, wrote *The Rise of Silas Lapham*, in 1878, a novel on the culture of commerce that set the stage for American Realism. Around the same time, more literary salons were being held at the Old Corner Bookstore, down the street from the Parker House, where leading publisher Ticknor & Fields had their headquarters. Regulars included not only the likes of Emerson and Longfellow, but visiting British authors like William Thackeray and Charles Dickens, who were not only published by the house as well, but also friends with its charismatic leader, Jamie T. Fields. Meanwhile, Longfellow was well on his way to becoming America's most popular poet, writing "*The Midnight Ride of Paul Revere*", among much other verse, while a professor at Harvard University.

The end of an era

In the last burst of Boston's literary high tide, sometime resident **Henry James** recorded the sedate lives of the moneyed – and miserable – elite in his books *Watch and Ward* (1871) and *The Bostonians* (1886). His renunciation of hedonism was well-suited to the stifling atmosphere of Brahmin Boston, where well-appointed homes were heavily curtained so as to avoid exposure to sunlight; however, his look at the emerging battle of the sexes was in fact fuelled by the liberty-loving principles of Emerson and colleagues in Concord thirty years before.

The fact that Boston's literary society was largely a members-only club contributed to its eventual undoing. **Edgar Allen Poe** slammed his hometown as "Frogpondium", in reference to the Saturday Club-style chumminess of its literati. Provincialism reared its head in the Watch & Ward Society, which as late as 1878 instigated boycotts of books and plays it deemed out of the bounds of common decency, spawning the phrase "Banned in Boston". To many observers, Howells's departure from *The Atlantic Monthly* in 1885 to write for *Harper's* in New York signalled the end of Boston's literary golden age.

Books

In the reviews below, publishers are listed in the format US/UK, unless the title is only available in one country, in which case the country has been specified. Highly recommended titles are signified by 🏃. Out-of-print titles are indicated by o/p.

History and biography

Cleveland Amory *The Proper Bostonians* (Parnassus Imprints US). First published in 1947, this surprisingly upbeat volume remains the definitive social history of Boston's old-money aristocracy.

Jack Beatty *The Rascal King: The Life and Times of James Michael Curley, 1874–1958* (Addison Wesley US o/p). A thick and thoroughly researched biography of the charismatic Boston mayor and Bay State governor; valuable too for its depiction of big-city politics in America.

David Hackett Fischer *Paul Revere's Ride* (University of Massachusetts Press/Oxford University Press). An exhaustive account of the patriot's legendary ride to Lexington, related as a historical narrative.

Esther Forbes *Johnny Tremain* (Houghton Mifflin US). Fictionalized tale about a cocky young silversmith who comes of age during the American Revolution. It's pretty much required reading for American schoolchildren; Bart Simpson thought it should be re-titled "Johnny Deformed".

Jonathan Harr *A Civil Action* (Vintage Books US). The story of eight families in the community of Woburn, just north of Boston, who took a major chemical company to court in 1981, after a spate of leukemia cases raised suspicion about the purity of the area's water supply; made into a movie starring John Travolta in 1998.

Sebastian Junger *The Perfect Storm* (HarperCollins US). A nail-biting account of the fate of the *Andrea Gail*, a six-man swordfishing boat from Gloucester caught in the worst storm in recorded history; later turned into a movie starring George Clooney in 2000.

Jonathan Kozol *Death at an Early Age: The Destruction of the Hearts and Minds of Negro Children in the Boston Public Schools* (Penguin US). Winner of the National Book Award, this is an intense portrait of prejudice and corruption in Boston's 1964 educational system.

🏃 **J. Anthony Lukas** *Common Ground: A Turbulent Decade in the Lives of Three American Families* (Vintage US). A Pulitzer Prize-winning account of three Boston families – one Irish-American, one black, one white middle-class – against the backdrop of the 1974 race riots sparked by court-ordered busing to desegregate public schools.

Michael Patrick MacDonald *All Souls: A Family Story from Southie* (Beacon Press US). A moving memoir of growing up in South Boston in the 1970s among the sometimes life-threatening racial, ethnic, class and political tensions of the time.

🏃 **Louis Menand** *Metaphysical Club* (Farrar, Strauss & Giroux US). Arguably the most engaging study of Boston heavyweights Oliver Wendell Holmes, William James, Charles Sanders Pierce and John Dewey ever written, this Pulitzer Prize-winning biography links the foursome through a short-lived 1872 Cambridge salon (the book's title), and extols the effect of their pragmatic idealism on American intellectual thought.

Mary Beth Norton *In the Devil's Snare: The Salem Witchcraft Crisis of 1692* (Knopf US). Analysis of the witchcraft accusations and executions in and around Salem in 1692; collecting newly available trial evidence, correspondence and papers, Norton argues that the crisis must be understood in the context of the horrors of the Second Indian War, which was being waged at the time in the area around Salem.

Mark Kurlansky *Cod* (Penguin). Does a fish merit this much obsessive attention? Perhaps only in New England, and Kurlansky makes a good case for viewing the cod as one of the more integral parts of the region's fabric.

Dan Shaughnessy *The Curse of the Bambino* (Penguin US). Shaughnessy, a Boston sportswriter, gives an entertaining look at the Red Sox's "curse" – no championships for 86 years – that began after they sold Babe Ruth to the Yankees. His *At Fenway: Dispatches from Red Sox Nation* (Crown Publishing US) is another memoir of a Red Sox fan.

Hiller B. Zobel *The Boston Massacre* (W.W. Norton US). A painstaking account of the circumstances that precipitated one of the most highly propagandized pre-Revolution events – the slaying of five Bostonians outside the Old State House.

Guidebooks

Charles Bahne *The Complete Guide to Boston's Freedom Trail* (Newtowne Publishing US). Unlike most souvenir guides of the Freedom Trail, which have lots of pictures but little substance, this one is chock full of engaging historical tidbits on the stories behind the sights.

John Harris *Historic Walks in Old Boston* (Globe Pequot US). In most cases, you'll be walking in the footsteps of long-gone luminaries, but Harris infuses his accounts with enough lively history to keep things moving along at an interesting clip.

Walt Kelley *What They Never Told You About Boston (Or What They Did*

Were Lies) (Down East Books US). Who would have guessed that in 1632, Puritans passed the world's first law against smoking in public? This slim book is full of such engaging Boston trivia.

Thomas H. O'Connor *Boston A to Z* (Harvard University Press US). This terrific, often irreverent, guide to the Hub will give you the low-down on local hotshots from John Adams to "Honey Fitz", institutions like the Holy Cross Cathedral and the L Street Bathhouse and local lore on everything from baked beans to the Steaming Kettle.

Architecture, urban planning and photography

Philip Bergen *Old Boston in Early Photographs 1850–1918* (Dover Publications US). Fascinating stuff, including a photographic record of Back Bay's transition from swampland to swanky residential neighbourhood.

Robert Campbell and Peter Vanderwarker *Cityscapes of Boston: An American City Through Time* (Houghton Mifflin US). An informative pictorial

tome with some excellent photos of old and new Boston.

Charles Haglund *Inventing The Charles River* (MIT Press US). The past, present and future of this artificially created river.

Jane Holtz Kay *Lost Boston* (Houghton Mifflin US). A photographic essay of long-gone architectural treasures.

Alex Krieger, David Cobb, Amy Turner and Norman B. Leventhal (eds) *Mapping Boston* (MIT Press US). Irresistible to any map-lover, this thoughtfully compiled book combines essays with all manner of historical maps to help trace Boston's conception and development.

Barbara Moore and Gail Weesner *Back Bay: A Living Portrait* (Centry Hill Press US). If you're dying to know what Back Bay's brownstones look – and looked – like inside, this book of hard-to-find photos is for you. They do a similar book on Beacon Hill.

Nancy Seasholes *Gaining Ground* (MIT Press US). A wonderful piece explaining just why Boston is 75 percent landfill. Marvel at how much was done in post-Puritan times to radically change the city's landscape.

Susan and Michael Southworth *AIA Guide to Boston* (Globe Pequot US). The definitive guide to Boston architecture, organized by neighbourhood. City landmarks and dozens of notable buildings are given exhaustive but readable coverage.

Walter Muir Whitehill *Boston: A Topographical History* (Harvard University Press US). How Boston went from a tiny seaport on the Shawmut Peninsula to the city it is today, with detailed descriptions of the city's many land-reclaiming projects.

Fiction and drama

Margaret Atwood *The Handmaid's Tale* (Anchor Books US). Cambridge's Ivy League setting inspired the mythical Republic of Gilead, the post-nuclear fallout backdrop for this harrowing tale about women whose lives' purpose is solely reproduction.

James Carroll *The City Below* (Houghton Mifflin US). Gripping historical novel of later-twentieth-century Boston, centred on two Irish brothers from Charlestown.

Michael Crichton *A Case of Need* (Signet US). Written long before Crichton conceived of "ER" or even *Jurassic Park*, this gripping whodunnit opens with a woman nearly bleeding to death on the operating table of a Boston hospital; she goes on to accuse her physician of attempted murder, and finds a trusty colleague trying to get at the truth of the affair.

Nick Flynn *Another Bullshit Night In Suck City: A Memoir* (W.W. Norton & Company US). Boldly headlined with one of literature's best titles (it's derived from a phrase used by Flynn's dad to describe nights on the street), this book is an elegiac depiction of the author's relationship with his homeless father, a sometime resident of Boston's *Pine Street Inn* shelter.

Nathaniel Hawthorne *The Scarlet Letter* (Signet Classic US). Puritan New England comes to life, in all its mirthless repressiveness, starring the adulterous Hester Prynne.

George V. Higgins *The Friends of Eddie Coyle* (MacMillan Publishing US). The godfather of crime novels, Higgins' masterful dialogue in this gritty tale of an underling caught between the Feds and the Irish-American mob still throws a punch after nearly forty years in print.

William Dean Howells *The Rise of Silas Lapham* (Viking Press US). This 1878 novel was the forerunner to American Realism. Howells's less-than-enthralling tale of a well-off Vermont businessman's failed entry into Boston's old-moneyed Brahmin caste gives a good early portrait of a uniquely American hero: the self-made man.

Henry James *The Bostonians* (Viking Press US). James's soporific satire traces the relationship of Olive Chancellor and Verena Tarrant, two fictional feminists in the 1870s.

Jhumpa Lahiri *Interpreter of Maladies* (Houghton Mifflin US). Pulitzer prize-winning collection of short stories, many set in Boston, run through with themes of marital discord, emotional isolation and the disconnection between first- and second-generation Indian-Americans. Lahiri's second book, *The Namesake*, was made into a film, starring Kal Penn, in 2007.

Dennis Lehane *Darkness Take My Hand* (Avon Books US). Perhaps the best in Lehane's Boston-set mystery series; two private investigators tackle a serial killer, the Boston Mafia and their Dorchester upbringing in this atmospheric thriller.

Michael Lowenthal *The Same Embrace* (Plume US). A young man comes out to his Jewish, Bostonian parents after his twin brother disowns him for his homosexuality; courageous and complex.

John Marquand *The Late George Apley* (Buccaneer Books US o/p). Winner of the 1937 Pulitzer Prize, this novel satirizes a New England gentry on the wane.

Carole Maso *Defiance* (Plume US). A Harvard professor sits on death row after having murdered a pair of her own star students, in this fragmentary, moving confessional.

🏃 **Robert McCloskey** *Make Way for Ducklings* (Viking Press US). Two duck parents search for a home in this beloved children's classic; along the way they fly over a number of Boston landmarks, hatch eight ducklings and compel a crew of police officers to direct traffic so that they can arrive safely home. The set of bronze mallard statues in the Public Garden is a tribute to this plucky bunch.

Arthur Miller *The Crucible* (Penguin US). This compelling play about the 1692 Salem witch trials is peppered with quotes from actual court transcripts and loaded with appropriate levels of hysteria and fervour.

Sue Miller *While I Was Gone* (Ballantine US). An emotional psycho-drama centred on a middle-aged woman who spends time under an assumed name in a Cambridge commune, while on the run from her husband.

Susan Minot *Folly* (Washington Square Press US). This obvious nod to Edith Wharton's *Age of Innocence* is set in 1917 Boston instead of New York and details the proclivities of the Brahmin era, in which women were expected to marry well, and the heartbreak that ensues from making the wrong choice.

🏃 **Edwin O'Connor** *The Last Hurrah* (Little, Brown US o/p). Fictionalized account of Boston mayor James Michael Curley, starring a 1950s corrupt politician; the book was so popular that the bar at the *Omni Parker House* hotel was named after it.

Ann Patchett *Run* (Harper US). Domestic drama centring on Doyle, a widower and former Boston mayor, who raises three sons (including two adopted African-American boys) and urges them to follow in his politicking footsteps. The novel deftly describes a number of Boston whereabouts; there's a particularly evocative excerpt set in the Harvard Museum of Natural History.

Sylvia Plath *The Bell Jar* (Harper Perennial USA). Angst-ridden, dark, cynical – everything a teenaged girl wants out of a book. The second half of this brilliant (if disturbing) autobiographical novel about Esther Greenwood's mental breakdown is set in the Boston suburbs, where she ends up institutionalized.

🏃 **George Santayana** *The Last Puritan* (MIT Press US). The philosopher's brilliant "memoir in the form of a novel", set around Boston, chronicles the short life and education

Boston on film

In the last ten years, Boston has become a star in its own right owing to blockbusters filmed on location here by big-name directors like Martin Scorsese and Clint Eastwood. If you'd like to "see Boston through Hollywood's eyes", check in with Boston Movie Tours (see p.28); its walking tours scout over thirty movie location sites.

Two Sisters from Boston
(Henry Koster, 1946)

Walk East on Beacon
(Alfred L. Werker, 1952)

The Actress (George Cukor, 1953)

The Last Hurrah (John Ford, 1958)

The Boston Strangler (Richard
Fleischer, 1968)

The Thomas Crown Affair (Norman
Jewison, 1968)

Love Story (Arthur Hiller, 1970)

Between the Lines (Joan Micklin
Silver, 1977)

Starting Over (Alan J. Pakula, 1979)

The Bostonians (James Ivory, 1984)

Tough Guys Don't Dance
(Norman Mailer, 1987)

Glory (Edward Zwick, 1989)

With Honors (Alex Keshishian, 1994)

Good Will Hunting (Gus Van Sant, 1997)

A Civil Action (Steve Zaillian, 1998)

Next Stop Wonderland
(Ben Anderson, 1998)

Legally Blonde (Robert Luketic, 2001)

Mona Lisa Smile (Mike Newell, 2003)

Mystic River (Clint Eastwood, 2003)

Spartan (David Mamet, 2004)

The Departed (Martin Scorsese, 2006)

Gone Baby Gone (Ben Affleck, 2007)

The Town (Ben Affleck, 2010)

---

of protagonist Oliver Alden coming to grips with Puritanism.

Erich Segal *Love Story* (Avon US). This sappy story about the love affair between Oliver Barrett IV, a successful Harvard student born with a silver spoon in his mouth, and Jenny Cavilleri, a Radcliffe music student who's had to struggle for everything, has the uncanny ability to captivate even the most jaded reader; made into a movie in 1970.

Jean Stafford *Boston Adventure* (Harcourt Brace US). Narrated by a poverty-stricken young girl who gets taken in by a wealthy elderly woman, this long – but rewarding – novel portrays upper-class Boston in all its magnificence and malevolence.

Henry David Thoreau *Cape Cod; Walden* (Penguin US). *Walden* is basically a transcript of Thoreau's attempt to put his transcendentalist philosophy into practice, by constructing a cabin

on the banks of Walden Pond, in Concord, Massachusetts, and living the simplest of lives based on self-reliance, individualism, spiritual enlightenment and material frugality. Nature also plays a part in *Cape Cod*, an account of the writer's walking trips published after his death.

David Foster Wallace *Infinite Jest* (Little, Brown US). Sprawling magnum opus concerning a video that eliminates all viewers' desire to do anything but watch the said video. Many of the book's best passages take place at Enfield, a fictional tennis academy set outside Boston; another plot line involves a Canadian terrorist separatist cell in Cambridge.

William F. Weld *Mackerel by Moonlight* (Pocket Books US). The former federal prosecutor and governor of Massachusetts turns his hand to writing, in this uneven – though not unworthy – political mystery.

Local accent and jargon

Boston has a language all its own, plus a truly unmistakable regional accent. One of Boston's most recognizable cultural idiosyncrasies is its strain of American English, distinguished by a tendency to drop one's "r"s, as on the T-shirts that exhort you to "Pahk the cah in Havvid Yahd" ("Park the car in Harvard Yard"). Enlightened readers take note – Harvard Yard is not a car park, and locals will be quick to school you if you utilize this oft-repeated expression in their presence.

Bostonian speech is also characterized by its use of "wicked" as an adverb, which residents sprinkle liberally into conversation (invoking it in other parts of the country is a great way to show off your Boston stripes): "Joo see the Sox game lahst night? Wicked wasome!" What follows is a glossary of sorts for proper terms, slang and jargon in and around Boston.

Terms and acronyms

Bang Make a turn. As in, "bang a left on Comm Ave".

BC Boston College.

Beantown Nickname for Boston – a reference to the local speciality, Boston baked beans – that no one uses any longer.

The Big Dig The project to put the elevated highway I-93 underground.

Brahmin An old-money Beacon Hill aristocrat.

BU Boston University.

Bubbler Water fountain, although this term is less and less in circulation.

The Cape Shorthand for Cape Cod.

The Central Artery The stretch of I-93 that runs underground through Downtown; before the Big Dig, it was an elevated expressway that separated the North End and the waterfront from the rest of the city.

The Chuck Nickname for Charlestown.

Colonial Style of Neoclassical architecture popular in the seventeenth and eighteenth centuries.

Comm Ave Commonwealth Avenue.

Dot Ave Dorchester Avenue.

Eastie East Boston.

Federal Hybrid of French and Roman architecture popular in the late-eighteenth and early nineteenth centuries.

Frappe Milkshake (meaning milk, ice cream and syrup) – the "e" is silent.

Georgian Architectural style popular during the late-colonial period; highly ornamental and rigidly symmetrical.

Greek Revival Style of architecture that mimicked that of classical Greece. Popular for banks and larger houses in the early nineteenth century.

Grinder A sandwich made of deli meats, cheese and condiments on a long roll or bun. Less used now as the more ubiquitous "sub" takes over.

Hamburg Ground beef sans bun. Add an "–er" at the end for the classic American sandwich.

Hub Like Beantown, a nickname for Boston not really used anymore.

Jimmies Ice-cream sprinkles.

JP Jamaica Plain.

Mass Ave Massachusetts Avenue.

MBTA (Massachusetts Bay Transportation Authority) The agency in charge of all public transit – buses, subways, commuter trains and ferries.

MGH Massachusetts General Hospital; also, "Mass General".

Packie Liquor store (many signs say "Package Store").

The People's Republic Another name for Cambridge, thanks to the liberal attitude of its residents.

The Pike The Massachusetts Turnpike (I-90); also, "Mass Pike".

Pissah Bostonian for "cool". Sometimes used with "wicked" ie "wicked pissah", meaning double good.

The Pit Sunken area next to Harvard Square where skaters hang out.

P-town Provincetown.

Scrod Somewhat of a distasteful generic name for cod or haddock. Almost always served breaded and sold cheap.

Southie South Boston.

The T Catch-all for Boston's subway system.

Three-decker Three-storey house, with each floor a separate apartment. Also called a "triple-decker".

Victorian Style of architecture from the mid- to late-1800s that is highly eclectic and ornamental.

Wicked The definitive word in the Bostonian patois, still used to intensify adjectives, as in "wicked good".

Small print and

Index

A Rough Guide to Rough Guides

Published in 1982, the first Rough Guide – to Greece – was a student scheme that became a publishing phenomenon. Mark Ellingham, a recent graduate in English from Bristol University, had been travelling in Greece the previous summer and couldn't find the right guidebook. With a small group of friends he wrote his own guide, combining a highly contemporary, journalistic style with a thoroughly practical approach to travellers' needs.

The immediate success of the book spawned a series that rapidly covered dozens of destinations. And, in addition to impecunious backpackers, Rough Guides soon acquired a much broader and older readership that relished the guides' wit and inquisitiveness as much as their enthusiastic, critical approach and value-for-money ethos.

These days, Rough Guides include recommendations from shoestring to luxury and cover more than 200 destinations around the globe, including almost every country in the Americas and Europe, more than half of Africa and most of Asia and Australasia. Our ever-growing team of authors and photographers is spread all over the world, particularly in Europe, the US and Australia.

In the early 1990s, Rough Guides branched out of travel, with the publication of Rough Guides to World Music, Classical Music and the Internet. All three have become benchmark titles in their fields, spearheading the publication of a wide range of books under the Rough Guide name.

Including the travel series, Rough Guides now number more than 350 titles, covering: phrasebooks, waterproof maps, music guides from Opera to Heavy Metal, reference works as diverse as Conspiracy Theories and Shakespeare, and popular culture books from iPods to Poker. Rough Guides also produce a series of more than 120 World Music CDs in partnership with World Music Network.

Visit www.roughguides.com to see our latest publications.

Rough Guide credits

Text editor: Keith Drew
Layout: Nikhil Agarwal
Cartography: Lokamata Sahu
Picture editor: Mark Thomas
Production: Louise Daly
Proofreader: Serena Stephenson
Cover design: Nicole Newman, Dan May and Chloë Roberts
Photographer: Susannah Sayler
Editorial: **London** Andy Turner, Edward Aves, Alice Park, Lucy White, Jo Kirby, James Smart, Natasha Foges, Róisín Cameron, James Rice, Emma Beatson, Emma Gibbs, Kathryn Lane, Monica Woods, Mani Ramaswamy, Harry Wilson, Lucy Cowie, Alison Roberts, Lara Kavanagh, Eleanor Aldridge, Ian Blenkinsop, Joe Staines, Matthew Milton, Tracy Hopkins; **Delhi** Madhavi Singh, Jalpreen Kaur Chhatwal, Jubbi Francis
Design & Pictures: **London** Scott Stickland, Dan May, Diana Jarvis, Mark Thomas, Nicole Newman, Sarah Cummins, Emily Taylor; **Delhi** Umesh Aggarwal, Ajay Verma, Jessica Subramanian, Ankur Guha, Pradeep Thapliyal, Sachin Tanwar, Anita Singh, Sachin Gupta

Production: Rebecca Short, Liz Cherry, Erika Pepe
Cartography: **London** Ed Wright, Katie Lloyd-Jones; **Delhi** Rajesh Chhibber, Ashutosh Bharti, Rajesh Mishra, Animesh Pathak, Jasbir Sandhu, Swati Handoo, Deshpal Dabas
Online: **London** Faye Hellon, Jeanette Angell, Fergus Day, Justine Bright, Clare Bryson, Aine Fearon, Adrian Low, Ezgi Celebi; **Delhi** Amit Verma, Rahul Kumar, Narender Kumar, Ravi Yadav, Debojit Borah, Rakesh Kumar, Ganesh Sharma, Shisir Basumatari
Marketing & Publicity: **London** Liz Statham, Jess Carter, Vivienne Watton, Anna Paynton, Rachel Sprackett, Laura Vipond; **New York** Katy Ball; **Delhi** Aman Arora
Digital Travel Publisher: Peter Buckley
Reference Director: Andrew Lockett
Operations Assistant: Becky Doyle
Operations Manager: Helen Atkinson
Publishing Director (Travel): Clare Currie
Commercial Manager: Gino Magnotta
Managing Director: John Duhigg

Publishing information

This sixth edition published March 2011 by
Rough Guides Ltd,
80 Strand, London WC2R 0RL
11, Community Centre, Panchsheel Park, New Delhi 110017, India

Distributed by the Penguin Group

Penguin Books Ltd,
80 Strand, London WC2R 0RL

Penguin Group (USA)
375 Hudson Street, NY 10014, USA

Penguin Group (Australia)
250 Camberwell Road, Camberwell, Victoria 3124, Australia

Penguin Group (NZ)
67 Apollo Drive, Mairangi Bay, Auckland 1310, New Zealand

Rough Guides is represented in Canada by Tourmaline Editions Inc. 662 King Street West, Suite 304, Toronto, Ontario M5V 1M7

Cover concept by Peter Dyer.

Typeset in Bembo and Helvetica to an original design by Henry Iles.

Printed in Singapore
© Rough Guides 2011
Maps © Rough Guides
No part of this book may be reproduced in any form without permission from the publisher except for the quotation of brief passages in reviews.
296pp includes index
A catalogue record for this book is available from the British Library
ISBN: 978-1-84836-588-9
The publishers and authors have done their best to ensure the accuracy and currency of all the information in **The Rough Guide to Boston**, however, they can accept no responsibility for any loss, injury, or inconvenience sustained by any traveller as a result of information or advice contained in the guide.

1   3   5   7   9   8   6   4   2

Help us update

We've gone to a lot of effort to ensure that the sixth edition of **The Rough Guide to Boston** is accurate and up-to-date. However, things change – places get "discovered", opening hours are notoriously fickle, restaurants and rooms raise prices or lower standards. If you feel we've got it wrong or left something out, we'd like to know, and if you can remember the address, the price, the hours, the phone number, so much the better.

Please send your comments with the subject line "**Rough Guide Boston Update**" to ⓔmail@uk.roughguides.com. We'll credit all contributions and send a copy of the next edition (or any other Rough Guide if you prefer) for the very best emails.

Find more travel information, connect with fellow travellers and book your trip on ⓦwww .roughguides.com

Acknowledgements

There were a lot of troopers who supported the evolution of this guidebook. First and foremost, I would like to thank the editor, Keith Drew, who tirelessly shaped text and, when deadlines loomed large, remained patient, insightful and kind. He also assured me that I don't look like a squirrel in my author photo. Mark Thomas deserves a shout for the great cover and guide photos, as well as Molly Hamill, for daily dispatches and for the use of her incredible apartment in Jamaica Plain, Paul "the Champ" Lenti, for sports tips, Katie Lloyd-Jones for map dexterity, and Tripp Cofield for "the Great Elm" and Bell's first phone call. Team Johnson/Zedek provided invaluable restaurant advice, home-cooked meals, last-minute edits and generosity when sharing their encyclopedic knowledge of the Boston area. All praise to my mama, for teaching me at a very young age the pleasures of a North End pastry addiction. And to the one who stood by me through all the ups and downs (one computer virus, two parking tickets, a minor fender bender, game night at Fenway Park, donut scouting adventures, blissful days at the Gardner museum, late-night read-aloud revisions and a Provincetown ferry ride from hell with 12-foot waves and barf bags), Michael McLaughlin, you know who you are.

ROUGH GUIDES

SMALL PRINT

Readers' letters

Thanks to all the readers who have taken the time to write in with comments and suggestions (and apologies if we've inadvertently omitted or misspelt anyone's name):

Adrian Bresler, Whytnee Bush, Phillippa Pitts, Bob Schwartz, Amy Waters.

Photo credits

All photos © Rough Guides except the following:

Introduction
Downtown at night © Steve Dunwell/Getty Images
Beacon Hill © Chuck Pefley/Getty Images
Old clock and flag © Neil Emmerson/Getty Images
Park Street church © Amanda Hall/Getty Images
Leonard P. Zakim Bunker Hill Bridge © Leonard P. Zakim/Getty Images
Fall in Christopher Columbus Park © Mike Perry/Alamy

Things not to miss
01 Boston Public Library © Nick Higham/Alamy
06 The USS Constitution © Ed Rhodes/Alamy
09 Boston Public Garden © Kim Karpeles
11 Boston Athænum © Visual Mining/Alamy
12 Fenway Park © Jerry Driendi/Getty Images
13 Provincetown © DK Images
16 Gallery space at the Museum of Fine Arts © The Museum of Fine Arts
17 Arnold Arboretum © Daniel Templeton/Alamy

19 Primates in the Museum of Natural History © Ross o'Donohue
20 Symphony Hall © DK Images

The Sporting Life colour section
Pitcher © Getty Images
The Boston Celtics © Ronald Martinez/Getty Images
Fenway Park sign © Getty Images
Charles Regatta © Visions of America/Alamy
Boston Marathon © Getty Images
Boston Public Garden © Stuart Pearce/Alamy
Charles River Esplanade © Michael Dwyer/Alamy

Yankee cooking (and drinking) colour section
Boston Cream Pie © Bon Appetit/Alamy
Chowder © Nina Gallant/Getty Images
Grilled oyster © Nina Gallant/Getty Images
Samuel Adams Beer © Corbis

Index

Map entries are in colour.

INDEX

G

H

I

J

K

L

V

W

Y

Z

So now we've told you about the things not to miss, the best places to stay, the top restaurants, the liveliest bars and the most spectacular sights, it only seems fair to tell you about the best travel insurance around

🏃 WorldNomads.com
keep travelling safely

Recommended by Rough Guides

Map symbols

maps are listed in the full index using coloured text

—— ···	State boundary		◉	Accommodation
═══	Expressway		♣	Baobab
══	Main road		☥	Church (regional maps)
══	Minor road		ⓘ	Information office
▓▓▓	Pedestrianized road		🏛	Monument
━●━	Railway		♥	Museum
– – –	Ferry route		♦	Point of interest
——	Waterway		⊠	Post office
‿	Bridge		▣	Restaurant
-----	Footpath		☉	Statue
ⵟ	Lighthouse		✡	Synagogue
✈	International airport		▬	Building
Ⓣ	T station		⊞	Church (town maps)
⊠	Gate		▒	Park
ⵟ	Gardens		⊞	Cemetery
⊞	Hospital		⬚	Beach

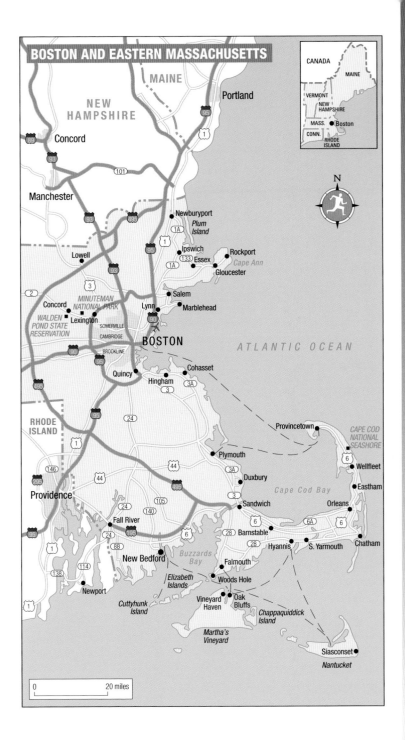

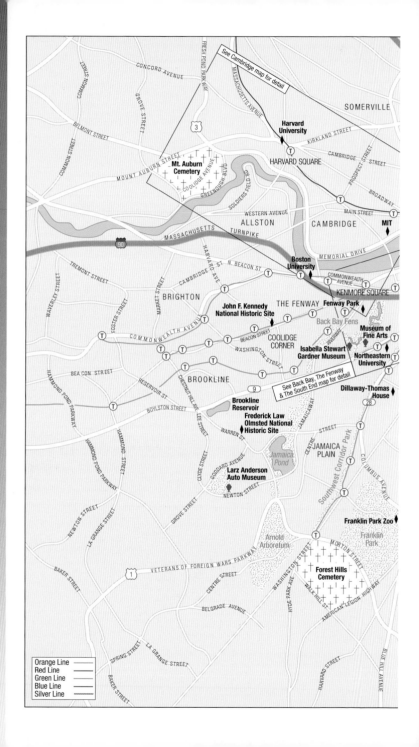

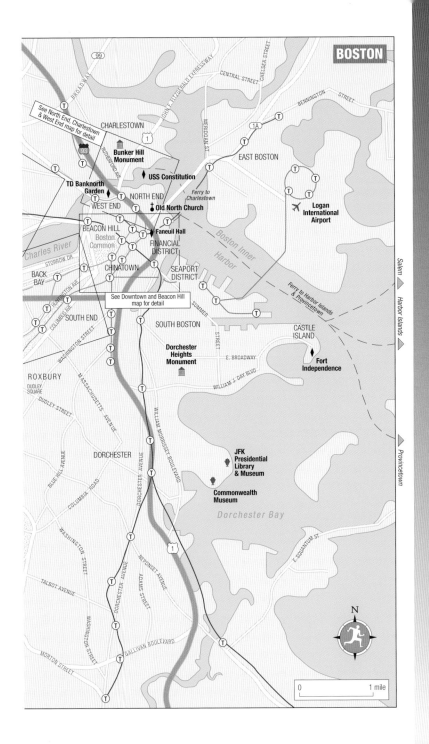

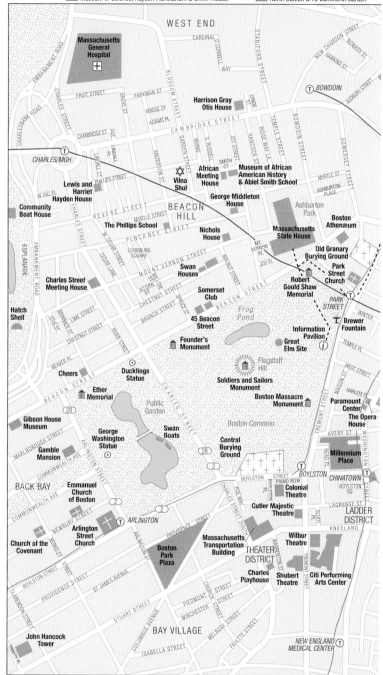

WEST END

Massachusetts
General
Hospital

CARDINAL

O'CONNELL

STANFORD STREET

WAY

NEW CHARDON STREET

BOWKER ST

EMBANKMENT ROAD

FRUIT STREET

PARKMAN ST

GROVE ST

BRIDGE ST

ADAMS PL.

BLOSSOM STREET

Harrison Gray
Otis House

LYNDE ST

LINDE ST

TEMPLE STREET

RIDGE WAY LA.

BOWDOIN STREET

BOWDOIN

SUDBURY STREET

CHARLESBANK ROAD

CHARLES STREET

CAMBRIDGEST AVE

CAMBRIDGE STREET

GARDEN STREET

IRVING

R. RUSSELL

SMITH
CT

JOY STREET

HANCOCK ST

SOMERSET STREET

CHARLES/MGH

LINDALL

PHILLIPS STREET

ANDERSON STREET

African
Meeting
House

Museum of African
American History
& Abiel Smith School

MYRTLE ST

ASHBURTON
PLACE

Lewis and
Harriet
Hayden House

W.HILL PL.

Vilna
Shul

George Middleton
House

Ashburton
Park

Boston
Athenæum

Community
Boat House

REVERE STREET

MYRTLE STREET

BEACON
HILL

The Phillips School

PINCKNEY STREET

Nichols
House

Massachusetts
State House

MT.
VERNON
PL

Old Granary
Burying Ground

ESPLANADE

EMBANKMENT ROAD

W.CEDAR STREET

CEDAR LANE

LOUISBURG
SQUARE

MOUNT VERNON STREET

WILLOW ST

WALNUT STREET

JOY PL.

Park
Street
Church

PARK
STREET

Charles Street
Meeting House

BRIMMER STREET

OTIS ST

ACORN
ST

CHESTNUT STREET

SPRUCE ST

Swan
Houses

Somerset
Club

BEACON STREET

Robert
Gould Shaw
Memorial

WINTER

Hatch
Shell

LIME STREET

CHESTNUT STREET

RIVER STREET

BRANCH STREET

45 Beacon
Street

Frog
Pond

Information
Pavilion

Brewer
Fountain

TEMPLE PL.

Founder's
Monument

Great
Elm Site

Cheers

BEACON STREET

Ducklings
Statue

Ether
Memorial

Public
Garden

Flagstaff
Hill

Soldiers and Sailors
Monument

WEST STREET

MASON STREET

HARLEM PL

Gibson House
Museum

BEAVER PL.

Boston Massacre
Monument

Paramount
Center

The Opera
House

MARLBOROUGH STREET

Gamble
Mansion

George
Washington
Statue

ARLINGTON STREET

Swan
Boats

Boston Common

Central
Burying
Ground

AVERY ST.

HEAD PL.

Millennium
Place

WASHINGTON STREET

COMMONWEALTH AVE.

BACK BAY

Emmanuel
Church
of Boston

CHARLES STREET

POE WAY

BOYLSTON STREET

BOYLSTON STREET

BOYLSTON

PIANO ROW

Colonial
Theatre

BOYLSTON

BOYLSTON
SQ

CHINATOWN

Church of the
Covenant

NEWBURY STREET

Arlington
Street
Church

ARLINGTON

PROVIDENCE STREET

CHARLES STREET SOUTH

Cutler Majestic
Theatre

LAGRANGE ST.

KNEELAND

LADDER
DISTRICT

ELLIOT

BERKELEY STREET

Boston
Park
Plaza

Massachusetts
Transportation
Building

THEATER
DISTRICT

Wilbur
Theatre

ELIOT ST

BOYLSTON STREET

PROVIDENCE STREET

ST. JAMES AVENUE

Charles
Playhouse

Shubert
Theatre

WARRENTON ST

TREMONT ST

Citi Performing
Arts Center

CLARENDON STREET

John Hancock
Tower

TRINITY PL.

STUART STREET

COLUMBUS AVENUE

ISABELLA STREET

PIEDMONT STREET

WINCHESTER STREET

CHURCH STREET

MELROSE STREET

FAYETTE STREET

BAY VILLAGE

NEW ENGLAND
MEDICAL CENTER

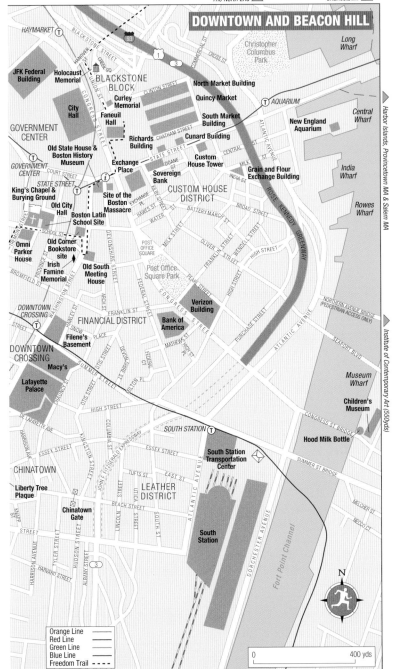

DOWNTOWN AND BEACON HILL

HAYMARKET Ⓣ

BLACKSTONE STREET

93

1

3

CROSS ST

COMMERCIAL ST

Christopher Columbus Park

Long Wharf

HANOVER ST

GREEN ST

CONGRESS STREET

HAYMARKET SQ

CLINTON STREET

JFK Federal Building

Holocaust Memorial

BLACKSTONE BLOCK

Curley Memorial

North Market Building

Quincy Market

Ⓣ AQUARIUM

Central Wharf

City Hall

Faneuil Hall

CHATHAM STREET

South Market Building

New England Aquarium

GOVERNMENT CENTER

Richards Building

Cunard Building

Custom House Tower

GOVERNMENT CENTER Ⓣ

COURT STREET

Old State House & Boston History Museum

STATE STREET

DOANE ST

Grain and Flour Exchange Building

India Wharf

Exchange Place

Sovereign Bank

MILK ST

INDIA ST

STATE STREET Ⓣ

EXCHANGE PL

CUSTOM HOUSE DISTRICT

ROSE KENNEDY GREENWAY

Rowes Wharf

King's Chapel & Burying Ground

Site of the Boston Massacre

KILBY ST

BATTERY MARCH ST

BROAD STREET

Old City Hall

Boston Latin School Site

HAWES ST

WATER ST

ATLANTIC AVENUE

SCHOOL ST

Omni Parker House

Old Corner Bookstore site

DEVONSHIRE STREET

MILK STREET

OLIVER STREET

WENDELL STREET

HIGH STREET

PROVINCE STREET

POST OFFICE SQUARE

BROMFIELD ST

Irish Famine Memorial

Old South Meeting House

ARCH ST

Post Office Square Park

FRANKLIN STREET

PEARL STREET

NORTHERN AVENUE BRIDGE (PEDESTRIAN ACCESS ONLY)

DOWNTOWN CROSSING

WASHINGTON ST

HAWLEY ST

FRANKLIN ST

FEDERAL STREET

CONGRESS STREET

Verizon Building

FINANCIAL DISTRICT

Bank of America

PURCHASE STREET

ATLANTIC AVENUE

SEAPORT BLVD

DOWNTOWN CROSSING Ⓣ

SNOW PLACE

Filene's Basement

OTIS STREET

DEVONSHIRE ST

FEDERAL CT

MATHEWS ST

HIGH ST

Macy's

SUMMER STREET

Museum Wharf

Lafayette Palace

HAUSER ST

OTIS STREET

FULTON PL

Children's Museum

DE LAFAYETTE AVE

HIGH STREET

CONGRESS ST BRIDGE

HARRISON AVE

COLUMBIA ST

KINGSTON STREET

SOUTH STATION Ⓣ

Hood Milk Bottle

SUMMER ST BRIDGE

ESSEX STREET

EDWARD FITZGERALD EXPRESSWAY

ESSEX STREET

South Station Transportation Center

CHINATOWN

TUFTS ST

EAST ST

ATLANTIC AVENUE

MELCHER ST

Liberty Tree Plaque

LEATHER DISTRICT

UTICA ST

BEACH STREET

NECCO CT

KNAPP STREET

Chinatown Gate

HUDSON STREET

NCONT

SOUTH ST

South Station

DORCHESTER AVENUE

Fort Point Channel

HARRISON AVENUE

TYLER STREET

HARVARD STREET

HUDSON STREET

ALBANY STREET

3

N

Orange Line	——
Red Line	——
Green Line	——
Blue Line	——
Freedom Trail	- - -

0   400 yds

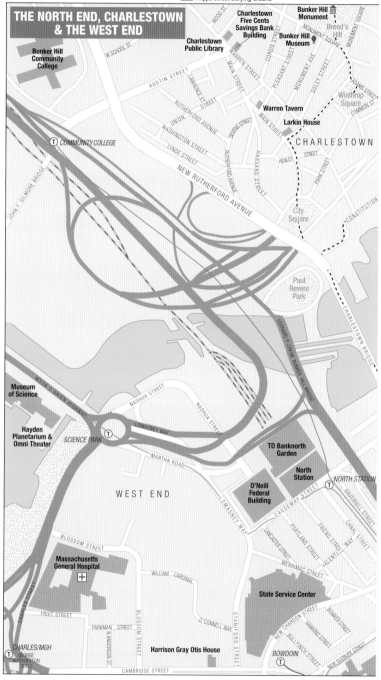

△ Phipps Street Burying Ground

THE NORTH END, CHARLESTOWN & THE WEST END

Bunker Hill Community College

Charlestown Public Library

Charlestown Five Cents Savings Bank Building

Bunker Hill Monument

Breed's Hill

Bunker Hill Museum

WOOD ST

W SCHOOL ST

AUSTIN STREET

LAWRENCE STREET

RUTHERFORD AVENUE

UNION STREET

WASHINGTON STREET

WARREN STREET

CORDIS STREET

PLEASANT STREET

MONUMENT AVE

SOLEY STREET

MAIN STREET

MONUMENT SQUARE

ADAMS STREET

Winthrop Square

COMMON ST

Warren Tavern

Larkin House

DEXIS STREET

MAIN STREET

HARVARD STREET

HENLEY STREET

CHARLESTOWN

PARK STREET

T COMMUNITY COLLEGE

LYNDE STREET

NEW RUTHERFORD AVENUE

RUTHERFORD AVENUE

City Square

CONSTITUTION

JOHN F. GILMORE BRIDGE

Paul Revere Park

CHARLESTOWN BRIDGE

Museum of Science

NASHUA STREET

NASHUA STREET

LEONARD P. ZAKIM BUNKER HILL BRIDGE

MSGR O BRIEN HIGHWAY

LOMASNEY WAY

Hayden Planetarium & Omni Theater

SCIENCE PARK

T

MARTHA ROAD

TD Banknorth Garden

North Station

NORTH STATION

T

HAVERHILL STREET

WEST END

O'Neill Federal Building

LOMASNEY WAY

CAUSEWAY STREET

CANAL STREET

LANCASTER STREET

PORTLAND STREET

FRIEND STREET

VALENTI WAY

BLOSSOM STREET

Massachusetts General Hospital
✚

WILLIAM CARDINAL

MERRIMAC STREET

State Service Center

CHARLES STREET

FRUIT STREET

PARKMAN STREET

N ANDERSON ST

BLOSSOM STREET

STANIFORD STREET

O'CONNELL WAY

NEW CHARDON STREET

BOWKER STREET

HAWKINS STREET

CHARLES/MGH

T

GEORGE WASHINGTON STATUE

Harrison Gray Otis House

BOWDOIN

T

BULLFINCH STREET

NEW SUDBURY STREET

CAMBRIDGE STREET

Legend
- Orange Line
- Green Line
- Blue Line
- Freedom Trail - - -

N

MBTA Ferry to Long Wharf & Downtown

Labels on map:

Ropewalk Building

Pier 9
Pier 8
Pier 7
Pier 6
Pier 5
Pier 4
Pier 3
Pier 2
Pier 1

Shipyard Park

USS Constitution Museum

Charlestown Navy Yard

Boston National Historical Park

USS Constitution (Old Ironsides)

USS Cassin Young

Bunker Hill Pavillion

Constitution Plaza

Mystic River

Boston Harbor

Constitution Wharf

North End Playground

US Coast Guard Station

Battery Wharf

Copp's Hill Terrace

Copp's Hill Burying Ground

Fire Boat Dock

Lincoln Wharf

Narrowest House

Old North Church

All Saints Way

Union Wharf Building

Union Wharf

NORTH END

Paul Revere Mall

Clough House

Donegal Square

Bova's Bakery

St Stephen's Church

St Leonard's Church

Polcari's Coffee

Sargents Wharf

Paul Revere House

Pierce/Hichborn House

North Square

Lewis Wharf Building

Lewis Wharf

Haymarket Square

HAYMARKET

Commercial Wharf

JFK Federal Building

Christopher Columbus Park

0   500 yds

Downtown

Street names:
PROSPECT STREET, TREMONT STREET, MT. VERNON STREET, CHESTNUT STREET, CHELSEA STREET, 3RD AVENUE, 5TH STREET, 6TH STREET, 8TH STREET, 9TH STREET, 1ST AVENUE, 2ND AVENUE, ROAD, KEANEY SQUARE, COMMERCIAL STREET, CHARTER STREET, HULL ST, SNOW HILL STREET, PRINCE STREET, FOSTER ST, HENCHMAN ST, GREENOUGH ST, BATTERY STREET, SALUTATION STREET, SALEM STREET, UNITY ST, TILESTON ST, HANOVER STREET, HARRIS ST, CLARK STREET, N BENNET ST, FLEET STREET, MIDWAY ST, NORTH STREET, LEWIS STREET, N WASHINGTON STREET, THATCHER STREET, LYNN STREET, ENDICOTT STREET, N MARGIN STREET, COOPER STREET, WIGET ST, STILLMAN ST, MORTON ST, SALEM STREET, PRINCE STREET, CROSS STREET, RICHMOND STREET, FULTON STREET, COMMERCIAL STREET, WHARF WEST, WHARF EAST, ATLANTIC AVENUE, NEW SUDBURY STREET, CONGRESS STREET, BLACKSTONE ROAD, HANOVER STREET

Cambridge ◢

BACK BAY, THE FENWAY & THE SOUTH END

Harvard Bridge

The Castle

STORROW DRIVE

Boston University

BACK STREET

COMMONWEALTH AVENUE

BAY STATE ROAD

2A

Allston-Brighton Agganis Arena ◢

CUMMINGTON STREET

GRANBY ST

BLANFORD ST

SHERBORN ST

MOUNTFORT ST

Morse Auditorium

DEERFIELD ST

Shelton Hall

Citgo Sign ◆

BEACON STREET

KENMORE

Myles Standish Hall

CHARLESGATE WEST

CHARLESGATE EAST

MASSACHUSETTS AVENUE

Brookline ◢

YAWKEY

KENMORE SQUARE

NEWBURY STREET

KENMORE

Oliver Ames Mansion

OAKLAND AVENUE

BURLINGTON ST

BROOKLINE AVENUE

LANSDOWNE ST

IPSWICH STREET

Stable Shops

FULLERTON ST

Fenway Park

VAN NESS STREET

IPSWICH STREET

CHARLESGATE EAST

BOYLSTON STREET

Berklee College of Music

CAMBRIA

KILMARNOCK STREET

YAWKEY WAY

BOYLSTON STREET

Victory Gardens

BOYLSTON STREET

Back Bay Fens

HAVILAND ST

HEMENWAY STREET

NORWAY STREET

MASSACHUSETTS AVE

ST GERMAIN

CLEARWAY ST

PETERBOROUGH STREET

THE FENWAY

QUEENSBERRY ST

THE FENWAY

AGASSIZ ROAD

WESTLAND AVE

Mapparium

PARK DRIVE

Kelleher Rose Gardens

SYMPHONY ROAD

Christian Science Mother Church

Back Bay Fens

HEMENWAY ST

GAINSBOROUGH

Horticultural Hall

STREET

Muddy River

THE FENWAY

FORSYTH WAY

ST STEPHEN

OPERA

Symphony Hall

SYMPHONY

THE FENWAY

PALACE RD

Isabella Stewart Gardner Museum

Museum of Fine Arts

HUNTINGTON AVENUE

FORSYTH WAY

Jordan Hall

WATSON ST

EVANS WAY

FENWAY

MUSEUM ROAD

LOUIS PRANG ST

9

MUSEUM

GREENLEAF ST

HUNTINGTON AVENUE

NORTHEASTERN

CAMDEN STREET

DILWORTH ST

VANCOUVER ST

PARKER STREET

Northeastern University

WARD STREET

TAVERN ROAD

LEON STREET

FORSYTH STREET

MCGREEVEY WAY

PARKER STREET

RUGGLES STREET

ST CYPRIAN'S PLACE

Southwest Corridor Park

COLUMBUS AVENUE

DAVENPORT ST

BURKE ST

COVENTRY ST

BENTON ST

HAMMOND ST

KENDALL ST

LENOX ST

PRENTISS ST

RUGGLES

MINDORO STREET

HAMMETT ST

GRINNELL ST

CHANDO ST

SEARS FIELD

TREMONT STREET

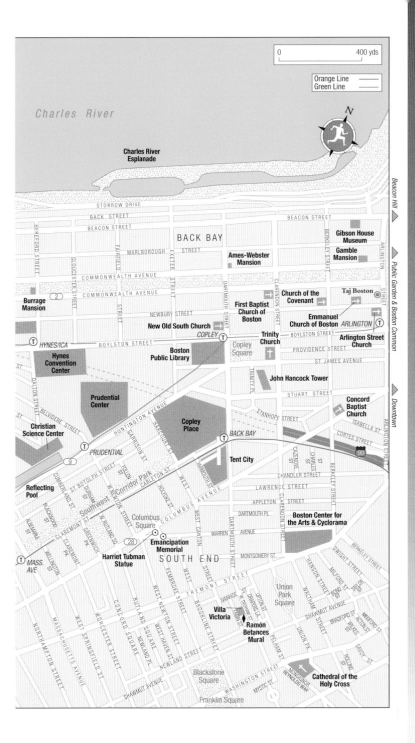

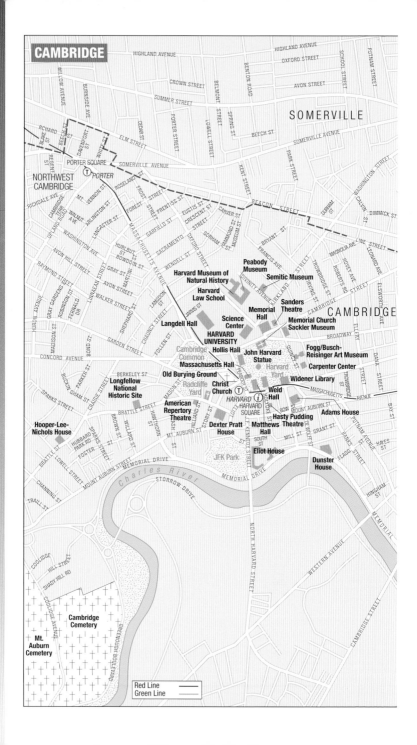

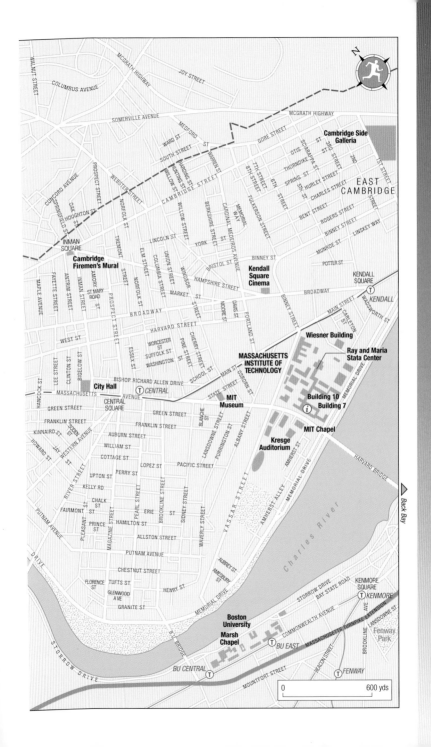

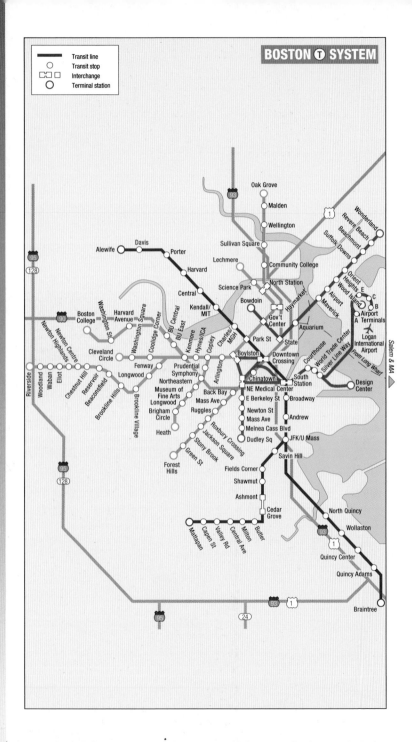